G000124899

A Legacy of Leadership

Commemorating the Centennial of the
National Governors Association

Governors at the White House, May 13–15, 1908

A Legacy of Leadership

Governors and American History

EDITED BY
CLAYTON MCCLURE BROOKS

PENN

University of Pennsylvania Press

Philadelphia

Published by
University of Pennsylvania Press
Philadelphia, Pennsylvania 19104-4112

The views expressed here are those of the authors and do not necessarily represent those
of the National Governors Association or the Woodrow Wilson Presidential Library.

Printed in the United States of America on acid-free paper
10   9   8   7   6   5   4   3   2   1

Library of Congress Cataloging-in-Publication Data
A legacy of leadership : governors and American history / edited by Clayton McClure
Brooks.
      p   cm.
   Includes bibliographical references and index.
   ISBN 978–0-8122–4094–8 (hardcover : alk. paper)
   1. Governors—United States—History—20th century.   2. United States—Politics and
government—20th century.   3. Women governors—United States.   4. Decentralization
in government—United States—History—20th century.   I. Brooks, Clayton McClure.
   JK2447.L45   2008
   973.9092'2—dc22   2008000035

Frontispiece: Governors at the White House, May 13–15, 1908. Invited by President (and
former governor) Theodore Roosevelt to discuss conservation issues, governors assembled
for this group photograph outside the White House. Roosevelt is seated near the middle
of the first row. The president and governors are joined by cabinet members, Supreme
Court justices, and other dignitaries, including Andrew Carnegie and William Jennings
Bryan (seated fourth and fifth from left in first row). Reprinted with permission of the
National Governors Association.

Contents

Foreword

In May 1908, President Theodore Roosevelt convened the nation's governors at the White House to discuss conserving the country's resources. Both the president and vice president attended, as did cabinet members, Supreme Court justices and thirty-nine state and territorial governors. They were joined by a cadre of guests known for their innovative thinking and influential actions, including populist William Jennings Bryan and industrialist Andrew Carnegie.

The meeting achieved its goal, yielding a policy declaration concerning conservation, but it also was notable for another idea—the creation of a national organization for governors. As Louisiana Governor Newton Blanchard noted, "Personally, I have long thought that, if the governors of the states could themselves from time to time get together, exchanging ideas and views touching the governmental and other affairs of their states, much good would come out of it." The idea found favor among his colleagues, and in 1910 the governors met twice: in Washington, D.C., and later in Kentucky. At the Kentucky meeting, New Jersey Governor-elect Woodrow Wilson proposed the formation of a national association for governors and, in 1912, the organization was constituted.

A century after the 1908 meeting, the governors convene today as the National Governors Association, representing all fifty-five governors of the states, territories, and commonwealths. The bipartisan association assists governors on domestic policy and state management issues and provides a forum for governors to speak with a unified voice to the president and Congress.

The 2008 meeting in Philadelphia marks the centennial for the organization, and this book and a companion volume have been published as part of that commemoration. The purpose of this book is to shed greater light on the important role governors have played during critical periods of the past hundred years. The book is not merely a comprehensive treatment of visionary governors; it is a work of historical interpretation. We live, to a great extent, in a country that governors helped create. It is interesting to note that seventeen state governors in our nation's history have become president—seven of them over the course of the National Governors Association's hundred-year history. Perhaps more significantly, four out of the past five presidents were former governors, a testament to the importance citizens ascribe to the states' highest office.

Early in the planning of this book, the National Governors Association partnered with the Woodrow Wilson Presidential Library because of both the library's unique scholarly approach to the life and contributions of one of our most admired governors and Wilson's role in the development of the National Governors Association. We are fortunate that some of the finest scholars in the nation wrote individual chapters, and we owe them a huge debt of gratitude for shining a light on these important events. We also thank Clayton Brooks for managing both the quality and the swift schedule of this book.

Raymond C. Scheppach   Eric J. Vettel
Executive Director   Executive Director
National Governors Association Woodrow Wilson Presidential Library

Introduction

Governing the Twentieth Century

Building a History of the Modern Governorship

CLAYTON McCLURE BROOKS

In May 1908, Governor Joseph W. Folk of Missouri stood before an unprecedented assembly of governors at the White House. While every man there carefully guarded the sovereignty of his state, these governors believed that the interests of their states as well as the nation as a whole necessitated greater communication and cooperation. Standing before his peers, Folk declared that the meeting had transpired by the providence of history, a country no longer hampered by sectional strife and poor transportation. "We [meet] here now as one large family," Folk mused, "In looking at the map on the wall before us I have been impressed by the fact that the States in this Union are, after all, closely connected in blood and in interest. . . . What concerns one is the concern of all; the achievements of one are the glory of all."[1] With these words, in this place, and at this gathering, a national governors' conference was born. This act of organization marked the beginning of the modern governorship with its expanded perspectives and broader horizons. To tell this story so central to American democracy, *A Legacy of Leadership* builds a new synthesis to better understand this transformative era in gubernatorial history.

That first historic meeting grew out of the concerns of a former governor of New York, President Theodore Roosevelt, about the slow progress of conservation policy within the United States. Hoping to ignite the interest of governors and increase awareness of environmental concerns, Roosevelt invited all state and territorial governors to the White House as well as members of Congress, the Supreme Court, the cabinet, and myriad special guests. Drawing from his own experience, Roosevelt believed state executives were the key to furthering conservation policy across the country. Media proclaimed the event, held May 13–15, 1908, to be one of the most august gatherings in American history. Leaders across the nation—legislators, justices, and experts—all converged on the White House. Recorded verbatim for posterity, the conference consisted primarily of lengthy speeches evaluating environmental studies and policy. However, the impressive numbers of governors in attendance proved the main source of interest. Thirty-four state governors arrived, in addition to governors from the Alaska, Arizona, Hawaii, and New Mexico territories, the District of Columbia commissioner, and the governor of Puerto Rico.[2]

Contemporaries praised the event as significant for being the first inclusive mass meeting of state governors. In the past, governors had met occasionally in small groups to discuss regional interests, yet operated largely within their individual states, more concerned with protecting state interests than cooperating across state lines. In the early years of the twentieth century, state isolationist policies became increasingly impractical. Modern dilemmas such as dealing with cars and roadways, accelerated industrialization and urbanization, the nationalization of a consumer culture, and conservation forced state executives to pursue interstate cooperation as the country became more connected. As sectional strife abated, people across the country—Virginians, Californians, Nebraskans, and so on—began to identify themselves foremost as Americans. Recognizing this trend, Elihu Root, Roosevelt's secretary of state, mused, "[As] the population of our states increases; as the relations between the People of each State and other States grow more frequent, more complicated, more important, more intricate, what every State does becomes more important to the People of every other State."[3] James Garfield, secretary of the interior, reiterated this sentiment: "We act as a People together, not divided. The State lines mean much; but the State lines have been overlapped by the work of the men and women of this country."[4] New technological and cultural demands required modern governors to become well versed in national and international policy.

When the conference concluded on May 15, Theodore Roosevelt declared the venture a success, believing the groundwork had been laid for conservation awareness. Some governors took these ideas to heart, while others probably dismissed what they heard before leaving the White House. But the legacy of the conference was precedent, not policy. Speaking on behalf of many of his colleagues, Governor Newton C. Blanchard of Louisiana reflected, "Personally, I have long thought that, if the Governors of the States could themselves from time to time get together, exchanging ideas and views touching the government and other affairs of their States, much good would come of it."[5] Blanchard proposed forming a new organization of governors. Although no official action was taken at the time, with the exceptions of 1909 and 1917, United States governors have met every year since.

A Legacy of Leadership jump-starts the process of creating a new synthesis of gubernatorial history over the past one hundred years—an effort missing from current historiography. Excellent biographies have been written about individual governors (by scholars like T. Harry Williams, Dan Carter, and Lou Cannon), and great studies have been published about the office of governor (by scholars like Thad Beyle and Joseph Schlesinger). Building on that foundation, this book combines a political science perspective with a historical one. It places governors in contrast with and in comparison to one another, as well as within the context of their times.

One of the greatest difficulties in building this narrative is the overwhelming number of individuals to encompass. Since 1908, more than one thousand men and women have served as elected or acting governors in the United States and its territories. Rather than surveying all governors and resorting to impossibly broad generalities, this book takes an eclectic approach, looking at six selected governors for detail along with studies addressing governors as a collective group within a set period of time. Each perspective tells a different part of the story. Woodrow Wilson, Huey Long, Thomas Dewey, George Wallace, Ronald Reagan, and Ann Richards were not equally successful (although several are considered among the top governors in American history). But their experiences illustrate issues unique to the eras in which they served, from Wilson's struggles to legislate Progressive ideals to Ann Richards's inspiration of a new generation of feminists. These five men and one woman were selected to highlight different issues and historical dilemmas. Their stories are presented not as insular biographies, but as opportunities for detailed and intimate discussions of unique concerns facing governors at specific points in American history. Personality plays a significant role in the success, failure, and scope of governorships, from what type of governor they wish to be to how they interpret the responsibilities of their office, and if they are able to convince the legislature to follow their lead. Individuals shape governorships. Agenda, will, power, and personality all go far in determining how a governor is remembered by history. In contrast to this biographical detail, three essays considering governors as a group tie together broad concerns, such as the fluctuations in the federal-state balance, facing all governors. These policy issues either unite governors and invite cooperation or tear them apart.

Central to creating this new synthesis, compiled from biographies and case studies, is the question of how the office of governor has evolved over the past one hundred years and how these changes have defined the modern governorship. When the twentieth century began, state executives had the luxury of concerning themselves primarily with affairs contained within their state borders. By 2000, that reality was long defunct. The emergence of the United States as a world superpower, unprecedented technological advances in communication, booming mass consumerism, international economic competition, and global terrorism, among other factors, revolutionized and refocused the scope of state government. Governors can no longer effectively manage state interests without a close involvement and clear understanding of national policy and foreign affairs. Modernity demands a broader perspective, greater communication, and more efficient organization. Although federalism remains alive and well, state and national governmental responsibilities are no longer neatly divided. Now, cooperation as well as competition among all levels of government (state, national, and local) have become necessary in administering the programs of an activist government and addressing the diverse needs of citizens—from health, education, welfare, and homeland security to highway construction and maintenance. In this new world, governors must not only appeal as stump speakers but also act as effective professional administrators, innovators, businessmen, representatives, advocates, and, when needed, reassuring leaders to guide their states in times of tragedy.

A Legacy of Leadership recounts the history of governors over the past one hundred years, beginning with the founding of the National Governors Association (NGA) in 1908 marking the emergence of the modern governorship. More than a celebration of NGA's centennial, and sponsored also by the Woodrow Wilson Presidential Library, this work provokes new debate about the power of governors, the limits of the office, and how these men and women have truly democratized the American political system. Structured chronologically, this book presents nine essays written by some of the nation's leading journalists and scholars. Each contributor either analyzes an individual governor or studies key topics from a particular decade. Together, the volume builds a narrative for understanding gubernatorial history—how the office has evolved, how the challenges of modernity necessitated a new era of communication among state governors, and how NGA responded to these needs and aided in the transformation of the gubernatorial office.

Following the path of most gubernatorial careers, Chapter 1 begins with the process and, at times, ordeal of campaigning and learning to govern. John Milton Cooper, Jr., explores the struggles Woodrow Wilson encountered as an idealistic Progressive campaigning against party bosses while simultaneously being promoted by a political machine. Wilson, a novice to politics, defined his political identity as governor of New Jersey by fighting to fulfill his campaign promises while maintaining his integrity. The chapter illuminates governors' struggles with their legislatures to accomplish set agendas as well as the unique challenges Progressive governors faced in the early twentieth century as they attempted to redefine government's responsibility and relationship to its citizens.

Turning south to Louisiana and heading into the late 1920s, Chapter 2 opens with the 1928 election of Huey Long as governor. Richard D. White, Jr., turns from the idealistic Wilson to Long, a governor also deeply concerned about his legacy but considerably less bothered by political corruption. Perhaps more than any other governor in the twentieth century, Long understood the potential power of state government and exploited the loopholes of democracy to rule Louisiana as an uncrowned king. Although genuinely caring for the "little people" of his state, Long thrived on the power of the office—a drive to rule that perhaps could have led him to the White House if he had not been stopped by an assassin's bullet. Whereas Chapter 1 focuses on idealism, Chapter 2 explores the excesses of the gubernatorial office in the hands of a demagogue.

Heading north to New York, Chapter 3 enters into a new era of gubernatorial history in which performance became more important than popularity. In Thomas Dewey, the public found both. Richard Norton Smith highlights Dewey's careful attention to administration and great pride in efficiency during his three terms as governor of New York. Far from a Long-style demagogue, Dewey redefined the gubernatorial office, adjusting to a country in flux following two world wars, the Great Depression, and a New Deal that revolutionized government. Dewey was a modern governor—a governor for a modern United States. Though powerful in his own right, he cared deeply about bringing accountability to government and preparing New York to meet the evolving needs of its citizenry, as with the building of the New York State Thruway. Smith's analysis not only sheds new light on the remarkable career of Thomas Dewey, but also focuses on the demands governors confronted across the country as they adapted to the post–World War II world.

Cruising into the 1950s, Dan McNichol explores the topic of road building and how governors worked, quite literally, to connect America. Focusing primarily on Eisenhower's "Grand Plan" of building a national interstate system, and the work of governors to make that dream come to pass, McNichol also looks back at the first efforts of governors, like Thomas Dewey, to build turnpikes and U.S. Routes. The problems governors encountered and their resolve as well as reluctance in cooperating with other governors to connect roads and regularize signs and road numbers offers a new dimension to the expanding gubernatorial role.

McNichol presents governors as both individual road builders and as a collective group trying to negotiate evolving responsibilities and come to terms (sometimes awkwardly) with the national component of their office. Governors in the 1950s found it necessary to represent their citizens in national concerns, or face being excluded from modern advancements. As McNichol illustrates, NGA aided governors in this transformation.

Chapter 5 enters the turbulent and bloody 1960s as the struggle over civil rights forced governors across the nation to take a stand on the politics of race. Jeff Frederick presents the infamous George Wallace, governor of Alabama, as a dominant factor in southern (as well as national) politics, questioning how one dynamic man had such widespread influence—to some an example to emulate and to others a pariah to rail against. Loved by some, abhorred by others, Wallace was one of the best known governors of the twentieth century. Frederick reflects on how Wallace purposely chose a racist stance to further his political career, believing race baiting was the best way to get elected in the Deep South. Wallace articulated the civil rights movement, particularly in the 1960s, to be an issue of states' rights rather than morality and an affront to his powers as governor. He became infamous for dramatic gestures like standing before the door of the University of Alabama to defy (however briefly) military-enforced integration. Across the United States, many governors felt differently, leading to fierce debate at NGA's annual meetings in the early 1960s. Frederick depicts Wallace not as a representative governor but as a catalyst and center point for understanding the crux of gubernatorial politics in the 1960s.

The following chapter leaves the South for the West and California, believed by many to be the land of opportunity. Lou Cannon begins in the late 1960s and brings this story into the 1970s, recounting the tale of Ronald Reagan, an actor-turned-governor who eventually became president. Since the 1976 election of Jimmy Carter, four out of the last five presidents have served as governors. In this vein, Cannon considers the influence of gubernatorial experience as a training ground for the presidency. He explains how Reagan, a political novice, learned the ropes of politics by working with his legislature and negotiating with his political adversaries. Reagan eventually mastered the hands-on duties required of the governor of California, from overseeing the creation of a budget and tax increase to sitting down with Democratic leadership and hammering out a welfare compromise. Reagan's experience in many ways reflects that of Woodrow Wilson, a political outsider working to define his style of leadership. Cannon's essay offers insight into the making of a political giant as well as the changing scope of the gubernatorial office in the 1970s.

Chapter 7 returns to a broader collective lens with a topic of paramount interest to all governors—federalism and the transformation of the federal-state relationship in the twentieth century. Richard P. Nathan traces the evolution of the devolution movement from the early 1970s through the George W. Bush administration. He evaluates how changes in the federalism bargain have concrete consequences for state government, particularly as innovative "laboratories of democracy." Nathan's essay encapsulates the ever-present issue of federal-state balance central to this gubernatorial history, and how trends have led, over time, to the growth of state government.

Following the politics of devolution, Chapter 8 refocuses on a state—Texas—examining the issue of gender and office. Jan Reid recounts the experiences of Ann Richards taking on the "good old boy network" of her state. Reid places Richards within the context of the growing number of women elected governor in recent decades. Through Richards's story and that of a handful of other female governors, Reid reveals how women, across party lines, have established themselves as strong candidates for office. As a result of these pioneering women, female candidates, at least in state politics, are now commonplace rather than political rarities.

The final essay ties together the themes of the previous chapters through an overview of the evolution of the gubernatorial office over the past one hundred years. Thad Beyle elaborates on and quantifies how the governorship has expanded, from the relative powers of governors to who becomes governor and the skyrocketing cost of campaigns. He recounts the history of the National Governors Association as one of a number of state organizations seeking a greater voice in Washington, D.C., in order to respond effectively to the national and international dimensions of the modern governorship and state government. Beyle also tells of NGA's role in supporting and training governors to adapt to the ever-increasing responsibilities of their office.

Between chapters are textual snapshots of the twentieth century, highlighting the issues at the forefront of each decade that governors confronted, as well as providing examples of how state chief executives across the country responded to those challenges.

More than one thousand governors, elected and acting, served in the twentieth century. Some are forgotten, but others will be remembered forever. These individuals have shaped the governorship from state to state, and decade to decade. They have made the gubernatorial office into the essence of American democracy—a melting pot of personalities, religious beliefs, political ideologies, and regional interests. Although white men still constitute the majority of governors, diversity is growing, particularly in terms of gender, but also, although more slowly, in race and ethnicity. Thus, governors represent a more democratic cross-section of society than those elected to the U.S. presidency. In composition and action they reflect the values and histories of the states they serve.

A Legacy of Leadership begins to build a synthesis of the history of the modern governorship, addressing both how governors guided their states through the vicissitudes of time and how those events have altered the scope and responsibilities of the gubernatorial office. Governors must be the doers of politics who attend to the needs of their citizens. These demands force governors into action rather than abstract discussions of political theory and heated partisanship. Speaking before the 1989 annual meeting of the National Governors Association, Dan Rather, then of CBS News, neatly summed up this reality: "I know that you folks, you Governors, have one of the hardest jobs in America; and I think you do have the toughest job in American politics." In contrast to members of Congress, governors live in constant contact with the citizens they serve and whose lives their policies affect. "Unlike your merry pranksters in Washington," Rather continued, "you cannot hide behind that well-insulated wall, that institutionalized thing we call the Congress. There's only you, the top man or woman, up there alone, facing the voters in the front line with your back to the wall."[6] By governing the twentieth century through national triumphs and tragedies, war and peace, depression and prosperity, stability and revolution, governors, the more than one thousand men and women who have served over the past century, have shaped the meaning of democracy and the course of American history.

Governing the 1910s

Reflecting the optimism of the Progressive Era, governors in the 1910s were excited about the opportunity for greater interstate cooperation. Reuniting in 1910, they began to lay the framework for their association. Charles Evans Hughes (1907–1910), then governor of New York and later secretary of state and chief justice of the Supreme Court, predicted, "The future prosperity of the country must largely depend upon the efficiency of State governments," an efficiency possible because of "an increasing intimacy of relations and facility of communication" among states. Hughes proudly proclaimed, "The ancient jealousies that have divided us are now forgotten. The sentiment of national unity has overcome divisive prejudices."[1] Governor Adam Pothier of Rhode Island (1909–1915, 1925–1928), an advocate of executive power who wrested control of the budget from his legislature, believed that the potential of governors working together was limitless. "We come together here as an organization," Pothier reflected, "imperfect as yet perhaps, but with a nucleus around which will be formed a substantial, lasting and powerful agency for the promotion of uniformity in state laws, the protection of State rights . . . the facilitating and expansion of inter-State rights, and the facilitating and expansion of inter-State relations."[2] Pothier and Hughes were perhaps overly exuberant in their pronouncements of unity, but they captured the spirit of the new organization. Governors embraced the idea of meeting annually and quickly staked their independence by moving their Governors' Conference meetings out of Washington, D.C., to alternating locations across the country from Richmond to Boston, and even as far west as Salt Lake City.

Governors in the 1910s eagerly tested the boundaries of their new association and learned to work together. Annual gatherings became opportunities for these men to meet one another, share experiences, learn how their individual interests fit into the larger national picture, and often air grievances. They enthusiastically discussed a wide range of topics from traffic laws and public utilities to workers' compensation. Some governors, like Augustus Willson of Kentucky (1907–1911), a prominent supporter of temperance legislation, used the meetings to express fears about expanding federal powers and, in particular, the proposed Sixteenth Amendment to institute a national income tax. He urged everyone to stand together and not "enable Congress to destroy the power of the State."[3] Governors were concerned with the invasive actions of the federal government and of other states. Leaders of western states, for example, argued that eastern states—whose exhaustion of their own natural resources had gone unregulated—now unfairly looked to the federal government to regulate the rich resources of the West. Governors also clashed over the interstate implications of specific laws. Tasker Oddie (1911–1915), governor when Nevada granted women the right to vote, called for more uniformity between state laws. A supporter of liberal divorce laws, Oddie argued that because women were no longer "chattel" and "since wife slavery has gone out of fashion," that "the demand has come for a new adjustment of privileges," but neighboring governor James Hawley of Idaho (1911–1913), a Roman Catholic, sternly disagreed.[4] He denounced liberal divorce laws and rejected any attempts to impose those laws on unwilling states. "No state," Hawley declared, "should permit its courts to become the agency for washing the dirty linen of another commonwealth."[5]

Governors began to mold their new organization into an effective forum for addressing twentieth-century problems, particularly those resulting from accelerated urbanization and industrialization. Labor unrest led to strikes nationwide throughout the 1910s. Treacherous working conditions plagued the labor force and resulted in events such as the horrific Triangle Shirtwaist Factory fire in New York in 1911 that brutally cut short the lives of 146 garment workers. The Great Migration, witnessing more than half a million African Americans leaving the South looking to escape Jim Crow laws and seek better jobs, compounded these problems by heightening economic competition and fueling racial tensions. Trouble also brewed internationally as most of Europe became embroiled in combat. By 1917, the United States abandoned its isolationist policy and entered World War I. But the end of the war the following year brought little peace at home. Lynchings and nationwide race riots greeted returning African American soldiers daring to hope for the democracy at home that they had fought for abroad. The same year, a deadly influenza epidemic took millions of lives worldwide, including more than half a million Americans.

These challenges and tragedies encouraged many governors to advocate Progressive ideals that redefined government's responsibilities to its citizens. These leaders promoted numerous reforms from the recall, referendum, and secret ballot to labor and anti-trust laws. Innovative initiatives were tested first at the state level. Prohibition activists and women suffragists went state by state, building momentum for national campaigns. A governor, Robert M. La Follette of Wisconsin (1901–1906), was the famed leader of Progressivism. Although La Follette had entered the U.S. Senate in 1906, governors across the nation in the 1910s were still influenced by his example and some followed in his footsteps. In California, Governor Hiram Johnson (1911–1917) became nationally renowned for fighting corrupted railroad companies.

Another prominent Progressive who gained national fame was Woodrow Wilson of New Jersey (1911–1913). As governor, Wilson fought his state's entrenched Democratic Party machine and expanded gubernatorial power vis-à-vis the state legislature. His success propelled him into the national spotlight and to two terms as president, during which he led the nation through World War I. A dedicated proponent of activist governorships, Wilson foresaw great potential in the new association of governors. Attending the November 1910 Governors' Conference meeting as governor-elect, Wilson prophesied, "If these conferences become fixed annual events . . . as an habitual means of working towards common ends of counsel and co-operation, this council will at least become an institution. . . . If it grows into a dignified and permanent institution, it will be because we have found it necessary to supply some vital means of co-operation." "A wise co-cooperation," Wilson concluded, was not only "desirable . . . but imperative in the common interest."[6]

Chapter One
Challenges of a New Century
Woodrow Wilson and the Progressive Era

JOHN MILTON COOPER, JR.

The early years of the twentieth century before World War I were a glorious time for America's governors. The challenges of the industrial revolution, particularly the rise of big business and its ties to political machines, were slow to be addressed by government at the national level, particularly after conservative forces won a decisive electoral victory in 1896 under President William McKinley and his pro-business wing of the Republican Party. McKinley's successor, Theodore Roosevelt, would be a different kind of Republican, and he would gradually begin to push a reform agenda in Washington. In the meantime, dynamic governors and state-level political movements forged ahead with new measures to regulate business and make government more responsive and accountable to the public. The pioneer in these new politics was an insurgent Republican, Robert M. La Follette, a short, dramatic man who earned the nicknames "Fighting Bob" and "Wisconsin's Little Giant." Starting in 1901, La Follette battled bosses, polarized state politics around himself and his following, and pushed through a program of railroad regulation and direct primaries for party nominations. His movement called itself "progressive" and thereby brandished a label that reformers elsewhere proudly adopted. These Wisconsin "progressives" made their state the center of national attention as a "laboratory of democracy."

During the decade following La Follette's debut, others went down the trail that he blazed. Republican insurgents in Iowa, led by Governor Albert Cummins, and in New York, led by Governor Charles Evans Hughes, likewise clashed with their party's entrenched leaders and enacted laws to regulate business. Democratic governors Joseph Folk in Missouri and Hoke Smith in Georgia accomplished similar feats, while in Oregon a bipartisan reform movement without a gubernatorial leader pushed through such dramatic political reforms as the initiative, referendum, and recall. In all of this ferment, however, no one displayed as much boldness and pushed as far as La Follette, and as this decade wore on the "progressive" tide appeared to be ebbing at the state level, even in Wisconsin. That fallback was deceptive. In the 1910 elections, a fresh wave of "progressivism" broke over many states, with a new batch of reform governors emerging, most notably in Wisconsin again and in California. Yet the most impressive of these progressive triumphs came in an unlikely place—boss-ridden, politically somnolent New Jersey—and the boldest and most effective of the new reform governors was a long-jawed, bespectacled fifty-four-year-old political neophyte named Woodrow Wilson, who was a former professor of political science and president of Princeton University.

Woodrow Wilson's success seemed even odder because in his long, distinguished career as an academic political scientist, he had seldom studied state politics and had rarely written about the office of governor. Likewise, except for speaking in the mid-1890s at one meeting for a municipal reform movement in Baltimore and another for a Democratic candidate for governor in New Jersey, he had never involved himself in local or state politics. In 1910, Wilson had lived in New Jersey for twenty years, but he had seen little of his adopted state. Speaking engagements as president of Princeton sometimes took him to Jersey City, Morristown, or Newark, but he visited few other places in the state, and he had never set foot inside the capitol in nearby Trenton. It might seem odd, then, even ironic, that Wilson first entered active politics by running for and winning the governorship of New Jersey in 1910. In fact, this turned out to be an ideal way for him to begin his political career. All the circumstances seemed to conspire to propel him on a meteoric rise in both state and national politics. He became a political star practically overnight and a hot prospect for his party's presidential nomination almost as soon as the ballots were counted in New Jersey in November 1910.

Irony abounded especially in the way that Wilson got the Democratic nomination for governor. This freshly minted progressive and future reformer at the state and national levels owed his start in politics to conservatives, machines, and bosses. The magazine editor and conservative Democrat George Harvey got the ball rolling. Harvey owned a seaside home in New Jersey, which gave him good connections in like-minded Democratic circles there, as well as at the national level. For several years, Harvey had been working to interest the main leader of the New Jersey Democrats in Wilson. This was James Smith of Newark, a wealthy one-time United States senator. Widely known as "Sugar Jim" because of his earlier senatorial services to the sugar refining industry, Smith fit the popular image of the political boss. He was a big, smooth-faced Irish

American with expensive tastes and a hearty manner. Politics was a family business with him; his son-in-law, James Nugent, was the boss of Newark's Democratic machine and his second-in-command in the state party. No two figures roused greater enmity among New Jersey's fledgling progressive Democrats, who were spearheaded by Mayor Otto Wittpenn of Jersey City, Wilson's friend and Princeton classmate Edwin Stevens of Hoboken, and Joseph P. Tumulty, a young Irish American state assemblyman, also from Jersey City. Yet it was Smith and, to a lesser extent, Nugent who made Wilson the Democrats' choice for governor.[1]

The Princeton president and the party bosses engaged in a lengthy and elaborate mating dance. In 1907, at Harvey's behest, Smith had swung votes in the legislature to Wilson for the U.S. Senate seat. But with the Republicans firmly in control of both houses, that was no more than a gesture. More recently, Democratic organizers had invited Wilson to speak at a gathering in Plainfield, where he had delivered a strong progressive message. People had occasionally written to urge him to run for governor, and he had batted the idea around with his wife, Ellen. Matters finally began to come to a head early in 1910. It was starting to look like a good political year for Democrats at both the state and national levels. In Washington, the Republicans were teetering on the brink of civil war as progressives led by La Follette, who was now a senator from Wisconsin, openly rebelled against William Howard Taft's administration over the recently passed Payne-Aldrich tariff and other issues. In Trenton, the Republicans were similarly suffering from internal strain, as local progressives also challenged that party's conservative bosses. In these circumstances, New Jersey's Democratic bosses liked the idea of having an attractive, respectable new face at the top of their ticket to enhance the party's prospects.

Again, George Harvey, whose horn-rimmed glasses and slicked-down hair made him look like an owl, put Wilson's name in play with Smith. In January 1910, the editor and the boss met twice for dinner at Delmonico's restaurant in New York. Afterward Harvey assured Wilson, "The nomination for governor shall be tendered to you on a silver platter, without your turning a hand to obtain it"; to which Wilson reportedly replied, "If the nomination should come to me in that way I should regard it as my duty to give the matter very serious consideration." Writing to Ellen from Bermuda the next month, Wilson joked that he might write an article for Harvey's magazine: "I shall call it, I think, 'Hide and Seek Politics.' Is that not a pretty good account of myself?" Rumors about Wilson's possible nomination began to circulate in the spring, and he talked about the idea with some of his supporters on the Princeton board of trustees.[2]

Curiously, however, the road to Wilson's gubernatorial nomination really began in Chicago. Smith was there in June 1910 at a luncheon with the city's Democratic boss, Roger Sullivan. At the luncheon, another Irish American, a successful banker and manufacturer named Edward Hurley, talked the Princeton president up to the New Jerseyan. The instigator behind this encounter was John Maynard Harlan, a Chicago lawyer, Princeton graduate, and friend of the trustee and Wilson's classmate Cyrus McCormick. Hurley and Harlan continued to act as intermediaries, and their efforts, together with Harvey's, bore fruit at a meeting between Wilson and party leaders in New York in the middle of July. He evidently impressed the bosses, although issues related to prohibition caused some problems. According to later accounts, Wilson said that he favored local option on liquor sales, which did not please Smith. The Princeton president struck some of the party men as unfamiliar with state issues, but he reportedly assured them that he would not try to interfere with the Democratic organization. Three days after that meeting, Wilson issued a public statement in which he asserted that if "it is the wish and hope of a decided majority of the thoughtful Democrats of the State that I should consent to accept the party's nomination for the great office of Governor, I should deem it my duty, as well as an honor and a privilege, to do so." In other words—to use a phrase soon to be made famous by Theodore Roosevelt, the man who would become Wilson's greatest political rival—his hat was in the ring.[3]

Wilson was not yet home free for the nomination. Smith's son-in-law Nugent wanted a different candidate: the party's nominee in the last gubernatorial election, Frank Katzenbach, another Princeton graduate, who came from a wealthy family and was mayor of Trenton. "Of course," Nugent reportedly told a newspaper editor, referring to his father-in-law, "I will do whatever the Big Fellow wants." In August, Wilson drafted a set of suggestions for the New Jersey Democrats' platform, expressing progressive ideas. He also made some public pronouncements to cover divergent political bases. In a letter to the editor of a labor publication, Wilson insisted, "I have always been the warm friend of organized labor," and he thought unions were necessary in order "to secure justice from organized Capital." Conversely, in a speech to the American Bar Association he praised the corporation "as indispensable to modern business enterprise," saying, "I am not jealous of its size or might."[4]

Coming out in the open as an aspiring politician gave Wilson mixed feelings. "I feel very queer adventuring upon the sea of politics," he told a Princeton friend, "and my voyage may be brief; but after what I have been preaching to my classes all these years about the duty of educated men to accept every legitimate opportunity for political service, I did not see what else I could do." Katzenbach's candidacy bothered him, especially because Mercer County, where both of them lived, backed Wilson's rival. Wilson also chafed under an injunction from the bosses not to talk to reporters, although he acknowledged that it allowed him to duck the liquor question. "I hate timidity," he told Harvey, "but I do not wish to make a blunder, and feel myself inexperienced." In these circumstances, he confided to Mary Peck, his friend and frequent correspondent, that he felt oddly disengaged: "It interests and amuses me but does not seem to touch me."[5]

Wilson did not have to put up with enforced silence for long. The Democratic state convention opened in Trenton on September 14. Smith arrived, accompanied by Harvey, and ensconced himself in Room 100 of the Trenton House, the place where party bosses customarily resided. From there, he and Nugent worked through the night to round up the votes needed to nominate Wilson. "It was the busiest night of Jim Smith's political life," one observer later recalled. The party's progressives were furious at having a political unknown shoved down their throats by the bosses, but Wilson was duly nominated. Harvey telephoned him with the news and suggested that he come and speak to the convention. In fact, Wilson had already prepared an acceptance speech, and a few minutes after five o'clock in the afternoon on September 15, 1910, he strode into the auditorium where the delegates were meeting. Many of the progressives sat in sullen silence while machine supporters and Princeton students shouted and cheered. Few of those present knew what to expect from their new nominee for governor, and few had ever seen or heard him. "God, look at that jaw!" one man reportedly exclaimed.[6]

What Wilson said impressed the delegates even more than his appearance. "As you know," he began, "I did not seek this nomination." Therefore, if he was elected governor, there would be "absolutely no pledge of any kind to prevent [him] from serving the people of the State with singleness of purpose." On the major issues, Wilson declared, "I take the three great questions before us to be reorganization and economy in [government] administration, the equalization of taxation and the control of corporations." Other important issues included employers' liability for workplace injuries, corrupt practices in elections, and conservation of natural resources. Wilson sounded a conservative note when he asserted, "We shall not act either justly or wisely if we attack established interests as public enemies." But he also called for establishment of a public service commission to regulate rates for utilities and transportation, to be modeled on "the admirable commission so long in successful operation in Wisconsin." In closing, Wilson proclaimed, "We are witnessing a renaissance of public spirit, a re-awakening of sober public opinion, a revival of the power of the people, the beginning of an age of thoughtful reconstruction that makes our thought hark back to the great age in which Democracy was set up in America. With the new age we shall show a new spirit."[7]

At that point, Wilson offered to stop, noting that the delegates must be tired after so many hours of work. Cries arose from the floor: "Go on!" "You're all right." He then repeated his promise to serve only the people and his demand for a public service commission. He declared that the state needed to control corporations and asked the delegates, "Will you control them?" Wilson again called for reconstruction "by thoughtful processes" of economic and political life: "This reconstruction will be bigger than anything in American history." Appealing to the "ideal" of America "as an haven of equal justice," he observed that the white and red stripes of the flag stood for "parchment and blood . . . parchment on which was written the rights of man, and blood spilled to make these rights real. Let us devote the Democratic party to the recovery of these rights."[8]

The speech was a triumph. The bosses' progressive foe Joseph Tumulty later recalled that many delegates stood with tears running down their cheeks and left the auditorium filled with crusading zeal. One progressive yelled, "I am sixty-five years old, and still a damn fool!" In the many tales that he would later tell about Wilson, Joe Tumulty would show a penchant for sentimental exaggeration, but this time his recollection was on the mark. Four days after the convention, Dan Fellows Platt, Wilson's former student at Princeton and an active Democrat, reported to Wilson that after the speech Tumulty "threw his arms about me & said 'Dan—this is one of the happiest days of my life—the Wisconsin R. R. law! —the best in the country—if Wilson stands for legislation of that caliber, Jim Smith will find that he has a "lemon."'" Tumulty, who instantly became one of Wilson's most ardent backers, went on to be his right-hand man as governor and president. It was the beginning of a beautiful political friendship.[9]

Wilson's speech and the progressives' response evidently did not bother the party bosses, who assumed they could control their hand-picked nominee. Four days after the convention, a group of them visited him at Prospect, the Princeton president's official residence. Standing on the portico and gazing at the tree-lined campus, Smith asked James Kerney, the editor of the *Trenton Evening Times*, "Jim, can you imagine anyone being damn fool enough to give this up for the heartaches of politics?" Inside, as Wilson's daughter Nell later recalled, the politicians seemed ill at ease in the president's book-lined study. "Do you read *all* these books, Professor?" Smith reportedly asked. "Not every day," Wilson answered. His jocularity broke the ice, and, he told Nell, "they treated me like a school boy once they got over the professorial atmosphere." The politicians spent three hours instructing their pupil about campaign plans, and Kerney recalled that he impressed them with his familiarity with local affairs and people. "We were charmed by the reception he had given us," Kerney wrote later. "When he unbent he could be the most urbane and delightful of companions."[10]

At the same time, Wilson was making no secret of his progressive views. In newspaper interviews right after the convention he hotly denied "that I am the Wall Street candidate for Governor of New Jersey," and he blamed the high cost of living on "the Republican party, with its Payne-Aldrich tariff and its trust connections." Writing to a progressive New York newspaper editor, he protested against the notion that "I was out of sympathy with the point of view of the plain people, that I put conventional property rights above human rights." He also stated, "I am not a preponderant state rights man." At opening ceremonies for the campaign on September 28, Wilson lauded the Democrats as both the party of "the great body of the plain people" and a "conservative party," but he added, "I do not mean a party which tries to hold men back, because nothing is so conservative as progress." In the two other speeches he gave in September, Wilson again stressed the need for a strong public service commission, and he endorsed a constitutional amendment to require popular election of senators.[11]

By that time he was in the thick of the campaign. Some observers later recalled that Wilson seemed a bit stiff and formal in his first speeches, more like a professor than a politician. That may have been the case, since Wilson was still a rookie on the stump. He certainly had a lot to learn about modern political campaigns, especially how much they cost. Wilson originally thought that he could pay, as he told one of his Princeton trustee supporters, "every cent of my own personal expenses in this campaign out of my own pocket." He was still president of Princeton and drawing his salary, and after the election he planned to earn $500 from speaking fees to cover those expenses. Wilson evidently thought about only the cost of his own travels around the state. Overall financing of the campaign he left to his conservative sponsor Harvey and the "Big Boss," Jim Smith, who later claimed to have personally contributed $50,000 to the party. In all, according to one historian's estimate, the Democratic managers spent $119,000 during the campaign—which was big money in those days. Wilson's conservative and machine-based sponsors still had their uses.[12]

The nominee quickly became a pungent, hard-hitting stump speaker. He stressed partisanship and national issues from the outset. "I am a Democrat by conviction because I am persuaded that it is the party through which the salvation of the country must come," he asserted in a newspaper interview early in October. "The Republican party has been guilty of forming an unholy alliance with the vast moneyed interests of the country." At the same time he declared in a speech in Long Branch, "Between a real Democrat and a really progressive [Republican] insurgent there is very little difference. What has been happening to these insurgents is that they have been catching the Democratic infection."[13]

Wilson did not neglect state issues. At the outset of the campaign his Republican opponent presented him with a golden opportunity to play to his greatest strengths. Dominant since the mid-1890s, the New Jersey Republicans had experienced a much stronger progressive insurgency than the Democrats. Four years earlier, there had been a party revolt by "New Idea" Republicans, whose moral and intellectual leader was an irascible transplanted Maine Yankee named George L. Record. Those insurgents had attacked their party's alliances with big business and pushed for the kind of reform in taxation that Wilson advocated in 1910. The New Idea men had gone down to defeat before the forces of the conservative machine, but Record and his followers remained a force to be reckoned with. In 1910 the Republicans bowed in their direction by picking a moderate progressive as their gubernatorial nominee. He was Vivian M. Lewis, a good-looking and respected lawyer who was the state commissioner of banking and insurance. Lewis opened his campaign by likewise calling for a powerful public service commission and by endorsing a favorite progressive idea, the direct primary to pick party nominees. Lewis also announced his "firm purpose of observing the constitutional limitations placed upon the authority of the Governor's position." Lewis affirmed that he would never use the governorship "to coerce the Legislature in subordinating its judgment to my own." Those words would help ensure his defeat at Wilson's hands.[14]

A friendly newspaper editor alerted the Democratic nominee to the political opening by noting that the Republican nominee's pledge not to use the powers of the governor's office would ensure that his party's machine would remain in control. Wilson seized upon the issue and announced in one speech, "I cannot be that kind of a constitutional Governor. . . . If you elect me, you will elect a Governor, who in the opinion of Mr. Lewis, will be an unconstitutional Governor." Warming to the attack, Wilson announced in another speech that he came "of a Scotch-Irish stock that cannot help fighting to save its life," and he appealed to the "constitution of Americanism underlying the constitution of New Jersey and the constitution of the United States," which required leaders to express the will of the people: "That is the whole spirit of our government; that is the spirit of the constitution of America."[15]

When he could make speeches like that, which drew upon his deepest thoughts about political leadership and democratic government, Wilson was having the time of his life. "I am in the midst of the hardest and

most interesting job I ever undertook," he told a former Princeton colleague later in October. As he crisscrossed New Jersey by train and automobile—going places he had never gone before and giving two or three
speeches a day—Wilson had other opportunities to translate ideas from
his academic study of politics into campaign discourse. In Atlantic City,
he remarked, "We are very much mistaken when we suppose that government is an intellectual matter. What we are ruled by is our passions."
The real task was to use such "splendid, handsome passions" as love,
honor, and patriotism to restrain and block such base passions as hatred,
cupidity, and envy. In Flemington, he defended party government. "I
am just as anxious [as you are]," he argued, "to break up the power—
the secret power—of the political machine. But I am not here to break
up parties." Parties were indispensable instruments for addressing complicated issues and channeling popular opinion and desires into concrete, constructive action. In Newton, he argued that "the economically
strong classes" could take care of themselves but government was
needed "to protect the unprotected classes, the classes that cannot look
out for themselves." Law was really "intended for the poor man and
when properly administered, is first of all and chiefly the poor man's
friend."[16]

Yet, gratifying as such opportunities to express his ideas were, Wilson
had an election to win. He needed to overcome two liabilities. The first
was his party label. Though weakened by factional strife, the Republicans were still by far the stronger party in New Jersey, and Wilson had to
persuade many of them to vote for him. The second, more glaring liability was his sponsorship by Smith and the bosses. George Record in
particular was harping on the way Wilson had gotten his party's nomination. The Republican insurgent challenged the Democratic candidate to
debate him on state issues. Wilson accepted on condition that the
Republicans would endorse Record as their spokesman. Predictably, the
Republican leaders balked, and Wilson declined to debate but added
that he would publicly answer any written questions that Record put to
him. "I jumped at the proposal," Record later told Wilson's biographer
Ray Stannard Baker, "for I thought it would be easy enough to smoke
him out." On October 17 Record sent Wilson a sharply worded letter
that posed nineteen questions about subjects that ranged from the powers of a public service commission to primaries to popular election of
senators to corrupt election practices to workmen's compensation. The
letter contained a denunciation of machines and asked, "Do you admit
that such a system exists as I have described it? If so, how do you propose
to abolish it?" Record also asked whether Wilson would overthrow the
Democratic bosses and demand that candidates for the legislature
pledge themselves to progressive reforms.[17]

This letter presented Wilson with a golden opportunity to show his greatest talents as a campaigner—boldness and articulateness. A week later, in a carefully crafted letter of his own, Wilson quoted Record's questions back in their entirety, followed by his answers. To most of them, particularly the ones about state reforms, he simply said, "Yes." To some, such as the direct primary, he said that he favored even stronger measures than Record proposed. Only to the last question, about requiring candidates to favor progressive measures, did he answer no, stating that it was up to voters to assess candidates. The questions about the boss system afforded Wilson a chance to affirm that he admitted its existence and proposed to abolish it by passing new laws, by electing "men who will refuse to submit to it and bend all their energies to break it up, and by pitiless publicity." That last phrase would later become one of his favorite slogans. As to whether he would fight the Democratic bosses, Wilson shot back, "Certainly!" He claimed to be already reorganizing his own party, and he avowed, "I should deem myself forever disgraced should I in even the slightest degree cooperate in any such system or any such transaction as you describe in your characterization of the 'boss' system."[18]

Record knew at once that he had met his match. "That letter will elect Wilson governor," he was quoted as saying at the time. Years later, Record added to Ray Stannard Baker, "If he had been a small man, such a set of questions would have finished him off, but he had the boldness and courage and he could rise to a great emergency." This letter became the sensation of the campaign. Progressives and conservatives alike hailed it, and according to one report, the editor of the state's largest newspaper, the *Newark Evening News*, "thought it was the greatest political document he had ever read. . . . There is no longer any lukewarmness in the News office." The editor's reaction jibed with other reports that previously skeptical reformers were now flocking to Wilson.[19]

The splash Wilson made with that letter allowed him to finish the campaign with a flourish. Record, who was not completely won over, later complained to Baker that Wilson "never said another word in the campaign about the specific reforms. He went back to generalities." That was true, but Wilson's "generalities" in the last two weeks of his race for governor were strongly, unequivocally progressive. At Rutherford he declared, "I understand a progressive is a man who wishes certain reforms of our economic policy, together with certain radical reforms of our political methods, because you can't get the policy without the methods." At Perth Amboy he asked, "Do you want big business benevolently to take care of you, or do you want to take care of yourselves? Are you wards or are you men?" In his closing speech of the campaign at

Newark, Wilson sounded like Theodore Roosevelt when he affirmed, "We have begun a fight that it maybe will take many generations to complete—the fight against special privilege, but you know that men are not put into this world to go with the path of ease; they are put into this world to go the path of pain and struggle. . . . We have given our lives to the enterprise, and that is richer and the moral is greater."[20]

The only discordant note in the final weeks of the campaign came out of Princeton. On October 20 as a result of long-standing tensions during his tenure as president, Wilson's opponents on the board of trustees forced him to resign. He had planned to step down anyway, but he and his supporters had hoped he could wait until after the election. "Yesterday's business, as it affected, you, almost broke my heart," his friend and supporter Cleveland Dodge wrote him. "I don't blame you for being mad—you are not half as mad as I am." For his part, Wilson told another friend that he was glad the campaign "absolutely dominated my thoughts. Otherwise I believe I should have broken down under the mortification of what I discovered last week to be the real feelings of the Pyne [opposition] party toward me." On the campaign trail the day of the trustees' action, Wilson joked in a speech, "I feel like the man in England whom I asked which party he belonged to, [and he] replied, 'I can't tell you exactly, I am between sizes.' I feel as if I am between sizes in occupation." Wilson refused to accept any further salary from Princeton, although he and his family did continue to live at Prospect, the president's home, until the following January.[21]

Wilson did not have to wait "between sizes" for long. On November 6, 1910, the voters of New Jersey elected him governor by a wide margin. Wilson polled 233,682 votes to Lewis's 184,626, a margin of 54 percent to 43 percent. Only one previous gubernatorial candidate in New Jersey had gotten a bigger majority—a Republican who rode Roosevelt's coattails in 1904. Wilson carried fifteen counties to Lewis's six, all of which were Republican strongholds, and he came close to winning two of those. Wilson ran ahead of other Democratic candidates, but the party also did well. The Democrats picked up four congressional seats and swept the state assembly, gaining forty-one of the sixty seats. They did not win control of the state senate, but their margin in the assembly gave them enough votes to choose a U.S. senator when the legislature met in January. As the returns came in on November 8, a crowd that included many students gathered in Princeton and marched to Prospect. Visibly moved, Wilson thanked the throng, but for once he was at a loss for words: "I think I have said all I know in my speeches in the campaign." In a prepared statement for the press he pledged "to be the servant of all classes and of all interests, in an effort to promote the common welfare."[22]

At the outset of their terms newly elected officials usually enjoy what observers of politics call a "honeymoon." Much as Wilson would have liked a honeymoon as governor, especially because he wanted time to think and plan, he did not get his wish. The spoiler was Sugar Jim Smith. Ever since the "Big Fellow" first sponsored Wilson as his choice for governor, rumors had persisted about his wanting an attractive candidate to help gain enough seats in the legislature for him to go back to the U.S. Senate. When the two men met a week after the election, the boss evidently did not raise the question of his candidacy, but he later claimed that the governor-elect had dismissed the state's non-binding senatorial primary as a "farce" and called the man who won it a "disgrace." This was James M. ("Farmer Jim") Martine, a perennial aspirant for office and one of New Jersey's few supporters of the William Jennings Bryan wing of the Democratic Party.[23]

Within days, however, Wilson changed his mind about the senate seat. Though professing high regard for Smith personally, Wilson declared to George Harvey that "his election would be intolerable to the very people who elected me and gave us a majority in the legislature. . . . It was no Democratic victory. It was a victory of the 'progressives' of both parties, who are determined to live no longer under either of the political organizations that have controlled the two parties of the State." That fact ruled Smith out for the senate seat and meant that "ridiculous though it undoubtedly is,—I think we shall have to stand by Mr. Martine." Wilson urged Harvey to get Smith to bow out. He reminded the editor that the situation was fraught with opportunity and peril, and he raised the specter of a Roosevelt revival—the prospect that frightened conservative Democrats most. "It is a national as well as a State question," Wilson warned. "If the independent Republicans who in this State voted for me are not to be attracted to us they will assuredly turn again, in desperation, to Mr. Roosevelt, and the chance of a generation will be lost to the Democracy; the chance to draw all the liberal elements of the country to it, through new leaders, the chance that Mr. Roosevelt missed in his folly, and to constitute the ruling party of the country for the next generation."[24]

Wilson started to line up support. Joe Tumulty took him to meet with several legislators and with the local Jersey City boss, who said he owed Smith his personal support but would not feel "hurt" if others opposed him. On December 6, Wilson made one last effort to avert a clash by traveling to Newark to see Smith at his home. "You have a chance to be the biggest man in the state by not running for the Senate," Wilson reportedly told him and added that he, Wilson, could not ignore the results of the primary. Smith refused to step aside and asked if Wilson would be satisfied simply to announce his opposition and then leave the choice to the legislature. "No," Wilson answered. "I shall actively oppose you with every honorable means in my power." He warned that he would go public with his opposition if Smith did not reconsider within the next two days. When that deadline passed, the governor-elect issued a statement to the press noting that the voters in the primary had chosen Martine: "For me, that vote is conclusive. I think it should be for every member of the Legislature."[25]

Wilson braced for a fight. He predicted "hard sledding," and to a Princeton friend he called Smith a "tough customer." During the rest of December he met with legislators at Prospect and in New York. "Things go as usual with me," he told his friend Mrs. Peck, "it is Smith, Smith, Smith all the days through." He and Smith gave conflicting statements to the press about whether Smith had earlier offered not to run and what was at stake. "The issue is plain," Wilson avowed. "If Mr. Smith is sent back to the United States Senate, the Democratic party and the State itself is [sic] once more delivered into the hands of the very influences from which it had struggled to set itself free." Early in January he decided to appoint Tumulty, whom he called "one of the ablest of the young Democratic politicians of the State," to be his secretary as governor "in order that I may have a guide at my elbow in matters of which I know nothing." With Tumulty's guidance he continued to lobby legislators before and after his inauguration as governor on January 17, 1911.[26]

Wilson also resorted to a favorite tactic that he brought from his Princeton presidency: he spoke directly to constituents. On January 5, he addressed a big rally in Jersey City, where he charged that Smith represented "a system of political control . . . an alliance—a systematic, but covert alliance—between business and politics." Wilson likened his move toward breaking up that alliance by opposing Smith to "cut[ting] off a wart." Eleven days later, on the eve of his inauguration, he addressed a public meeting in Smith's hometown, Newark, where he dismissed the boss's candidacy as "a colossal blunder in political judgment." Smith was supposed to be "an astute politician," but an astute politician would have recognized that times had changed.[27]

Wilson read the situation right. The big boss turned out to be a paper tiger. After the legislature convened, Smith journeyed once more to Trenton and ensconced himself in the same hotel room where he had previously labored to secure Wilson's nomination for governor. This time he had no magic to work. At the party caucus, nine Democrats from the state senate and twenty-four from the assembly supported Martine; only fourteen backed Smith. Because the New Jersey constitution required a majority of the members of both houses voting together to choose a senator, the caucus canvass left Martine only eight votes short of the forty-one needed to elect him. By the time of the first ballot in the joint session of the legislature on January 24, switches gave Martine forty votes, just one short of victory, and Smith threw in the towel, releasing his supporters. The next day the joint session elected Martine with forty-seven votes, which included all but four of the Democrats. Wilson greeted the outcome with mixed feelings. "My victory last week was overwhelmingly complete," he told a friend. "The whole country is marvelling at it, and I am getting more credit than I deserve. I pittied [*sic*] Smith at the end. It was so plain that he had few real friends—that he held men by fear and power and the benefits he could bestow. . . . It is a piteous game, in which, it would seem, one takes one's life in one's hands,—and for me it has only begun!"[28]

The Smith affair may have spoiled Wilson's political honeymoon, but it gave him as big a boost as governor as Record's letter had given him as a candidate. As he and several observers commented, this fight burnished his credentials as a progressive not only in New Jersey but throughout the country. Most newspapers of any size covered these doings. The nation's leading Democratic journal, the *New York World*, anointed this new governor as a special hero because the same fight was going on in New York, where the leader of Tammany Hall was also trying to grab a senate seat for himself. "New York needs a Woodrow Wilson," proclaimed the *World*. Curiously, Wilson's conservative patrons did not take offense at his fight with Smith. A prominent conservative Democrat, the Kentucky newspaper editor Henry Watterson, told Harvey, "The Martine incident may after all serve a purpose with certain elements needful at the critical moment. Smith is a fool—an old fool—and deserves what he got." Wilson himself welcomed the publicity because it dispelled notions that he was an impractical academic who would be putty in the hands of the bosses or a tool of Wall Street. But one aspect of this attention bothered him: "Thought of the presidency annoys me in a way. I do not *want* to be President. There is too little play in it, too little time for one's friends, too much distasteful publicity and fuss and frills." As in his earlier disclaimers, the gentleman did protest too much. The eyes of the nation were on Wilson, and he was never going to be just another governor.[29]

The fight with Smith likewise helped Wilson in New Jersey. This struggle gave him a chance to know and master his party's men in the legislature and thereby get his legislative program off to a fast start. Despite Wilson's complaints about the time that this affair took, he did not let it distract him too much from planning what he wanted to do once he took office. Soon after the election Wilson gave some foretastes of his intentions. "Pitiless publicity is the sovereign cure for the ills of government, which can be applied easily and effectively by the men whom the people intrust temporarily with executive duties," he asserted in a newspaper interview. As governor-elect at the Governors' Conference meeting held in the fall of 1910, Wilson described his new office with the same paraphrase of what he had said about the presidency in *Constitutional Government*: "There is no one in any legislature, who represents the whole commonwealth—no one connected with legislation who does, except the Governor," he declared. The governor had a duty, therefore, to appeal to the people over the heads of the legislators: "There is no executive usurpation in . . . that." At the end of December, Wilson gave the presidential address to the American Political Science Association. In this farewell to the academic study of politics, he urged the student to be "more like a human being and a man of action" and the man of action to "approach his conclusions more like a student."[30]

Family affairs and practical matters similarly required attention. Most of this work fell to Ellen Wilson, particularly the family's move out of Prospect. For the first time in more than twenty years the Wilsons did not have a home of their own. New Jersey did not provide a governor's mansion, although there was a summer residence at Sea Girt on the Atlantic coast, where the Wilsons spent the warmer months of 1911 and 1912. In the meantime, Ellen put most of their possessions in storage, and she and her husband and daughters moved into a suite of rooms in the Princeton Inn; the following fall they rented a house in Princeton at 25 Cleveland Lane. It was from the rooms at the inn and this house that Wilson commuted six miles to the governor's office in the capitol at Trenton.[31]

Running that office also required attention to practical matters. This was where Tumulty proved to be a godsend. He held the title of "secretary," but he really functioned as the governor's chief administrative and legislative assistant and liaison to the press. Thirty-year-old Joseph Patrick Tumulty was a trim, neat man of medium height with a smooth, round face that made him look like a young priest. He seemed to fit the popular stereotype "lace curtain Irish," but he did not. His Irish-born father was a Union veteran who had been wounded in the Wilderness campaign and later struggled to establish himself as the owner of a corner grocery store. His mother, also Irish-born, could not read or write, but she had pushed her children to go to Catholic schools. Joe, the seventh of nine who survived, was a graduate of St. Peter's College in Jersey City. His opposition to the political machine did not prevent him from knowing and savoring all sides of public life. Tumulty loved the game of politics and reveled in trading gossip and inside information with reporters and politicians. His gregariousness and attention to small things made him a perfect complement to Wilson, who still liked to spend time by himself pondering political questions in their larger dimensions. The two men quickly developed a smooth working relationship, one that was warm and informal. Wilson did not call his secretary "Joe." When others were present he called him "Tumulty," but when they were alone he often addressed him as "my dear boy." Tumulty, in turn, called his boss "Governor."[32]

From his own study of the issues and the campaign encounter with Record, Wilson had a good idea of what he wanted on his legislative agenda. Nevertheless, he met privately with Record, and the day before his inauguration he presided over a conclave at a New York hotel that included, besides Record, several legislators, newspaper editors and publishers, and veteran reformers. The group agreed that election reform, public utility regulation, and employers' liability laws should be top priorities. In schoolmaster fashion, Wilson assigned Record the task of drafting new primary and corrupt election practices laws. One of the legislators at the meeting leaked news of the deliberations to Smith. The boss's forces, in turn, denounced Wilson for secret dealings and perfidy to the party by ceding power over legislation to Record and other progressive Republicans. Wilson shot back with a statement to the press that Record was "one of the best informed men in the State with regard to the details of the reforms proposed" and that the conference "was nonpartisan in purpose and meant in the public interest." The new governor was getting his own dose of "pitiless publicity."[33]

On January 17, Wilson set the tone for his governorship with a hard-hitting inaugural address. "The air has in recent months cleared amazingly about us," he declared, "and thousands, hundreds of thousands have lifted their eyes to look about them, to see things that they never saw before." Offering a bit of reassurance to conservatives, he observed that corporations were not "unholy inventions of rascally rich men," but he also affirmed that "wise regulation, wise adjustment," was nothing less than "an imperative obligation." Turning to specifics, Wilson spelled out the agenda agreed upon the day before. Employers' liability came first "because it is the adjustment for which justice cries loudest." He likewise called for stronger corporate regulation, a new public service commission, tax reform, and conservation of natural resources. Beyond these lay "something that goes to the root of the whole matter. . . . How are you going to get genuine representatives, who will serve your real interests, and not their own or the interests . . . of the few and not of the many?" That could come only through "the direct primary, the direct choice of representatives by the people." Unusually for him and contrary to prevailing oratorical practice, Wilson closed the speech not with a stirring peroration but with further specific measures, including consideration of initiative, referendum, and recall legislation, corrupt practice and campaign finance reform, and investigation of how cold storage rates affected food prices.[34]

He then moved into the governor's office in the state capitol and went to work. The change from academic life had already come as a wrench, especially the constant demands for meetings, but he adjusted quickly. "He seemed to be perfectly at home from the start and the duties seemed easy and pleasant to him," one of his stenographers, Ida Taylor, later told Ray Stannard Baker, Wilson's biographer. "He was an indefatigable worker and spent long hours at his desk." Wilson attended to correspondence first thing when he arrived in the morning. He would dictate to one of the staff, sometimes from shorthand notes that he had made. He once reportedly tried using a dictating machine, but he was amused at how unnatural he thought his voice sounded. Wilson also did much of his own typing. After attending to correspondence, the governor spent much of the rest of the day with appointments. He maintained an open-door policy, never turning away a caller, at least until after he was elected president. By his fourth week in office, Wilson could tell that "when I am at them the things I deal with day by day do not pall upon me at all. I take them, on the contrary, with zest and unflagging interest."[35]

He exaggerated. One aspect of the governorship evidently did not interest Wilson—patronage. He resented the waste of time and energy in dealing with rival claimants for jobs, and he left patronage largely to Tumulty. Wilson did make some first-rate appointments. These included Record, who was named to the Board of Assessors; Samuel Kalish, the first Jew to become a justice of the New Jersey Supreme Court, and Winthrop Daniels, Wilson's former faculty colleague from Princeton, who would be appointed to the Public Utility Commission. In contrast, he genuinely enjoyed personal interaction with legislators and other politicians. In one-on-one encounters he demonstrated the persuasive powers that he had exercised as president of Princeton. In group settings he bared his playful side. At an outing with state senators in Atlantic City in April 1911, Wilson revealed, as he later recalled, "that my long, solemn face was not a real index to my countenance, that I was something different from the ascetic schoolmaster." After a fried chicken supper, the governor and the senators joined in singing and dancing, and he led them in the cake walk. "Such are the processes of high politics!" he joked. "This is what it costs to be a leader."[36]

Such frolicking also served a serious purpose. It helped Wilson do the part of his new job that he cared about most—legislative leadership. As soon as the senatorial election was settled, the governor started pushing the legislature to enact the measures he had enumerated in his inaugural address. The primary became the storm center of this legislative offensive. Record drafted a far-reaching measure that required primaries for all elected officials and delegates to the parties' national conventions; it also required that legislators vote for the person who won their party's primary for U.S. senator and restricted state conventions to drafting platforms. Wilson enlisted a Democratic assemblyman and former student of his from Princeton, Elmer Geran, to introduce the measure. Smith-Nugent Democrats charged once more that Wilson was turning their party over to that insidious radical Record.[37]

The governor responded with an inside and an outside strategy. Throughout February 1911, Wilson met repeatedly with legislators, listened to their comments and criticisms, and eventually agreed to accept some amendments to what everyone was calling the "Geran bill." Meanwhile, he went around the state speaking in favor of his reform program. Besides the primary, he touted other measures such as the proposed public utility commission for being modeled on the Wisconsin agency "introduced by that very able and energetic man, Mr. La Follette." Wilson also drew upon his earlier ideas about the nature of politics to ask, "If your tree is dying, is it revolution to restore the purity of its sap and to purify the soil that will sustain it? Is this a process of disturbance? No! It is a process of life; it is a process of renewal; it is a process of redemption." The speaking engagements tired him, but Wilson enjoyed himself; "It is an absorbing, and on the whole fascinating, occupation."[38]

The showdown came in March. "Things are getting intense and interesting again," Wilson observed, adding, "My spirits rise as the crisis approaches." He stepped up his speaking schedule. "Now the object of the Geran bill is to restore government to the people," he asserted in a speech at Hoboken; "and the Geran bill is going to be adopted. . . . I am going to stand for this thing through thick and thin." Back in Trenton he made another bold move. "Why not invite me to the caucus?" Wilson reportedly said to the Democratic leader in the state assembly. "It is unprecedented, I know. Perhaps it's even unconstitutional; but then I'm an unconstitutional governor." On March 6, when he attended the assembly Democratic caucus, one member challenged the constitutionality of his presence. "Since you appeal to the constitution," Wilson reportedly replied, "I think I can satisfy you." He pulled a copy of the New Jersey constitution out of his pocket and read the clause that authorized the governor to communicate with the legislature and recommend "such measures as he may deem expedient." Wilson then spent two hours explaining features of the public utility commission, corrupt practices, and employers' liability measures, as well as the Geran bill. The assemblymen easily reached agreement to support the first three measures, but they wanted more time to consider the Geran bill.[39]

A week later, on March 13, Wilson again went before the caucus. During the three-hour meeting the governor spoke for more than an hour to plead for the Geran bill: "I beg you to remember, in this which promises to be an historic conference in the annals of the party of the state, you are settling the question of the power or impotence, the distinction or the ignominy of the party to which the people with a singular generosity have offered control of their affairs." One legislator recalled soon afterward, "I have never known anything like that speech. Such beautiful Saxon English, such suppressed emotion, such direct appeal. . . . It was like listening to music. And the whole thing was merely an appeal to the better side of our natures."[40]

The speech did not win over everyone. According to a newspaper report, a machine Democrat challenged Wilson by observing that all those present owed their places to political organizations. The governor responded that he knew what the assemblyman was referring to. He acknowledged that he owed his own nomination to the party organization, but he "owed his election to the people only, and he would refuse to acknowledge any obligation that transcends his obligation to the people who elected him." That answer and others Wilson gave evidently impressed the legislators even more than his speech. "Where did this schoolmaster learn so much about politics," one of them reportedly asked, "not only legislation, but practical politics?" When Wilson responded to the legislators, according to one description, "he acted like a small boy playing his favorite game; he certainly enjoyed the proceeding to the full." The governor must have enjoyed the outcome even more. The assembly Democrats voted to support the Geran bill, 27 to 11.[41]

Wilson was winning, but he was not home free. Smith's son-in-law Nugent was working the hall of the capitol against the primary. Between the Democratic holdouts and the Republicans, there were enough votes in the assembly to defeat the Geran bill. But Nugent underestimated Wilson. On March 20, the governor invited the Newark boss to his office and asked Nugent, in his capacity as Democratic state chairman, to support the bill. When Nugent refused, Wilson claimed that he had the votes lined up to pass it. "I do not know by what means you got them," Nugent replied. "What do you mean?" Wilson asked. "The talk is that you got them by patronage," Nugent responded. Wilson stood up and waved Nugent out: "Good afternoon, Mr. Nugent." Nugent made a crack that Wilson was no gentleman, and Wilson repeated, "Good afternoon, Mr. Nugent." In a public statement, the governor recounted the incident and commented, "I invited him here and he insulted me." Privately, he told a friend, "It was a most unpleasant incident which I did not enjoy; but apparently it did a lot of good. . . . I feel debased to the level of the men whom I feel obliged to snub. But it all comes in the day's work." The incident may have left a bad taste in Wilson's mouth because there was some truth in Nugent's charge. Tumulty evidently had been using patronage to line up support for the Geran bill, as he had done earlier in the fight over the senate seat. He had acted with the governor's implicit approval, if not his detailed knowledge.[42]

Besides patronage and favorable publicity, Wilson had one other card to play. Wittingly or not, he had done a shrewd thing by enlisting Record to write the primary law. Record now persuaded two progressive-leaning Republican assemblymen to announce that they would vote for the Geran bill. That move broke the back of the opposition. The bill passed the assembly on March 21 by a vote of 34 to 25. Thirty-one Democrats and three Republicans voted in favor, while ten Democrats and fifteen Republicans voted against. Ironically, the bill had an easier time in the Republican-controlled senate. Both Democrats and Republicans in that chamber were less dependent on their party's machines and were not inclined to be obstructionist. Revised somewhat but not weakened, the Geran bill passed the senate unanimously on April 13. After assembly concurrence, also unanimous, the revised bill went to the governor for his signature on April 20. "This is certainly a grand consummation," the governor observed as he signed the bill into law.[43]

Victory in the fight over the primary law smoothed the way for passage of the rest of Wilson's program. Record drafted a corrupt practices bill based upon the Oregon law that many regarded as model progressive legislation in this area, just as the Wisconsin law was viewed in public utilities regulation. Record had to bargain with Republican leaders in the state senate over the legislation, but a strong bill emerged and passed easily in both chambers. Utility regulation likewise had an easy time, and the act that emerged went beyond even the Wisconsin law. One provision allowed the new Public Utility Commission to determine the physical valuation of a company's property as the basis for setting rates. This scheme ranked among the farthest-reaching regulatory proposals of the time and was an idea that La Follette and other progressives were pushing at the federal level. The only place where Wilson had to give way a bit was on employers' liability. State senator Walter Edge introduced a bill that established the principle but made compliance voluntary so that, its sponsors argued, it would not be overturned by the courts. The governor disliked the Edge bill because he thought it lacked force. After the senate passed this measure, however, and the assembly deadlocked over other bills, Wilson decided to accept the Edge bill as half a loaf worth having. These measures, together with the primary law, constituted what were known as the "governor's bills" and enacted the program that he had advanced during the campaign and in his inaugural address.[44]

Impressive as they were, those four laws did not exhaust the accomplishments of the 1911 legislative session. A number of reformers and civic associations wanted to allow municipalities to adopt the new city commission form of government, which enjoyed wide popularity in progressive circles. After some initial hesitation Wilson threw his weight behind municipal reform legislation that included local initiative, referendum, and recall provisions, as well as the city commission. The bosses put up a fight against this measure, and some Democrats in the assembly went over to their side. Wilson and the reformers decided to compromise and got a reasonably strong law in the end. Fittingly for a man with his professional background, the governor supported educational reform. The legislature enacted a set of laws that created a new state Board of Education with authority to conduct inspections and enforce standards, regulated districts' borrowing authority, and required special classes for students with handicaps. At the governor's urging, the legislature also enacted new food storage and inspection laws, strengthened oversight of factory working conditions, and limited labor by women and children.[45]

Wilson's only defeat occurred when he asked the legislature to ratify an amendment to the U.S. Constitution passed by Congress in 1909 to permit the levying of income taxes. "If this power be granted, the general government may adapt its whole system of taxation to the actual economic life of the country much more favorably than it is now adapted," Wilson maintained. "It may make it more just and may adapt it more nicely to the interests of the people at large." Unlike the election of a U.S. senator, ratification of an amendment to the Constitution required separate approval by both chambers. The assembly promptly complied with the governor's request, but the Republican-controlled Senate refused to go along. Almost two years would pass before New Jersey would ratify the income tax amendment. By then, Wilson had been elected president and carried enough Democrats on his coattails to control both houses of the legislature.[46]

Despite that defeat, Wilson had racked up an impressive record as a legislative leader and as a progressive. "I got absolutely everything I strove for,—and more besides," he exulted privately when the legislature adjourned late in April. He called this "as complete a victory as has ever been won, I venture to say, in the history of the country. I wrote the platform, I had the measures formulated in my mind, I kept the pressure of opinion constantly on the legislature, and the programme was carried to the last detail." Pride did not blind Wilson to the secrets of his success. He correctly credited the spirit of the times for much of what he been able to do: "I came to the office in the fullness of time, when opinion was ripe on all these matters, when both parties were committed to these reforms."[47]Indeed, "progressivism" was a rapidly rising tide in American politics, and Wilson was not the only governor to push through this kind of reform program. The year 1911 marked a particularly dramatic juncture in this march of political and economic reform. In Wisconsin, La Follette's forces recaptured control of the governorship and legislature and were filling out an ambitious reform agenda that resembled Wilson's. In California, a band of Republican progressives led by their newly elected governor, Hiram Johnson, were pushing through a comparable program, although one that would stress direct popular measures such as initiative and recall far more than Wilson did. The accomplishments of this academic-turned-governor were part of a bigger picture, and many of these reform leaders in other places were men with whom he would cross paths and swords in coming years.

Still, Wilson unquestionably earned most of his success on his own. Given New Jersey's history as a boss-ridden, conservative-leaning state, it would have been easy for him to fall far short of such sweeping accomplishments. A vivid illustration of what could have happened lay just across the Hudson River. In New York, the Democrats had likewise ridden the reform wave in 1910 to win the governorship and control of the legislature for the first time since the mid-1890s. Yet despite the Empire State's previous experience with dynamic governors such as Roosevelt and Hughes and its moderately reformist record, the situation there deteriorated into a hopeless wrangle between progressive Democrats and Tammany Hall. The progressives did succeed in keeping the Tammany boss from becoming a senator, but the machine blocked most reform legislation. The *New York World* had been prophetically right when it said that its state needed a Woodrow Wilson.

What the former president of Princeton brought to his governor's office was a potent mix of personal and intellectual gifts. As he noted, he planned things in advance and then kept the legislators at their jobs and focused on the task at hand. This required foresight, force, and perseverance—traits that Wilson would soon show again as a legislative leader in Washington. He also put into practice the ideas that he had developed earlier about how to be such a leader. Wilson acted like a prime minister. By meeting so often with legislators, he acted as if he were one of them. By joining his party's caucus, he became its leader. In effect, the proposals that he had advanced years before in his writings about giving cabinet members seats in Congress were finding practical application. All this worked well, and it offered the first demonstration of how readily Woodrow Wilson could translate the study of politics into the practice of politics.

Wilson's smashing success in New Jersey in 1911 launched his political career in the best possible way. His legislative accomplishments as governor won him his spurs in the hottest political arena of the time. The eyes of the nation were upon him. Even before the limelight he attracted in the fight over the senate seat, notions about higher office had been in the air for him. Now, even before the end of the legislative session, a presidential boomlet started. The professor-turned-politician and college president-turned-governor was on his way to the White House.

Governing the 1920s and 1930s

In the 1920s and 1930s, governors embraced interstate cooperation and became confident this practice would empower governors and states. They began to enjoy the expanded scope of their office while warily noting similar expansion in the national government. In these years, governors led the nation through prosperity and pitfalls. They drew on the strength of the Governors' Conference to voice their concerns and affect national events. In the midst of this sea change, governors became even more convinced of the benefits of cooperation, assured of their association, and willing to consider new national and international perspectives. They overcame their hesitancy to confront the federal government on points of conflict and began to take formal positions, such as a 1926 resolution urging congressional legislation to promote U.S. agriculture in the world market. A new innovation of "governors only" sessions, resulting from an effort to contain grandstanding on the issue of prohibition, shut out the media and other guests to ensure more candor and less political pandering to constituents back home.

While staking the boundaries of expanded governorships in the 1920s, these leaders confronted a decade of opportunity; full of drama, both heroic and tragic. The ratification of the Nineteenth Amendment brought women into the national electorate and also into the gubernatorial office. In 1924, two women, Nellie Tayloe Ross of Wyoming (1925–1927) and Miriam "Ma" Ferguson of Texas (1925–1927, 1933–1935), were elected governor. At the 1925 governors' meeting, Ross (officially the first female governor) thanked her male colleagues for their "generous attitude toward feminine invasion of a realm that tradition has recognized as exclusively the preserve of men."[1] Many Americans, however, were not so welcoming of change. Tired of war, the nation tried to retreat once more into isolationism, feeding a violent dislike of immigrants and a promotion of 100 percent Americanism based on the argument that only white Protestants were truly American. Millions of whites nationwide flocked to the newly rejuvenated Ku Klux Klan, which fueled not only racial fears but also xenophobic and religious prejudices. In 1925, the Scopes trial in Dayton, Tennessee, became a national sensation as traditional creationists battled the modern theories of evolution. Compounding these fears that change was corrupting the nation, scandal rocked the White House when the Harding administration gained the reputation as one of the most dishonest in history with shady dealings like those concerning the Teapot Dome oil reserves. Harding's death in 1923 brought Calvin Coolidge, a former governor of Massachusetts (1919–1921), to the presidency. In the midst of this unrest and distrust, the Jazz Age also offered prosperity and even wealth for some. Cultural creativity in music and literature flourished as the Harlem Renaissance focused attention on gifted African American artists and authors, such as Langston Hughes and Zora Neale Hurston. This refocused cultural energy extended outside of Harlem. Americans considered Ernest Hemingway, although he was then living in Paris, a national treasure. And F. Scott Fitzgerald gained widespread fame for his 1926 publication of *The Great Gatsby*, epitomizing the lavish yet desolate mood of the decade. Looking for heroes, the country turned to individuals like Charles Lindbergh and Babe Ruth, who many believed defined what it meant to be American.

In these years of stark contrast, governors focused their annual meetings on addressing the problems that lay beneath the era of seeming prosperity. Learning from one another, these men and women worked to cover a broad range of issues that all seemed of paramount importance—agriculture, the reorganization of state government, industrial relations, crime and penal reform, and taxation, among others. The KKK was one common, recurring concern, even to some segregationist white southern governors. Ma Ferguson secured the passage of anti-Klan legislation prohibiting wearing masks in public, although courts later overturned the legislation. Governor Harry F. Byrd, Sr., of Virginia (1926–1930), still building his political machine that would last for more than thirty years, made lynching a state crime. Governors also dealt with the issue of political corruption illustrated so clearly by the Harding administration. At the 1927 meeting, Governor Gifford Pinchot of Pennsylvania (1923–1927, 1931–1935) expounded on the evils of campaign fraud, declaring, "If a nation cannot rule itself, I cannot see that it makes much difference whether it is ruled by a foreign tyrant with arms or by a domestic tyrant with stolen votes."[2]

One relatively new gubernatorial concern was a growing need for road construction as cars became cheaper and more readily available. Governors debated speed limits, the comity of state driving laws, and the connection of interstate routes. Highway safety became a national concern and, in 1924, governors shared ideas for appropriate legal sanctions for drunk drivers. Funding new roads was a major issue leading governors to question both the sources and control of taxation. Governor George Shafer of North Dakota (1929–1933), like many of his colleagues, believed that the gas tax, first enacted by Oregon, was the answer to "the great demand for rapid improvement of the highway systems," but he vehemently opposed any federal claims to "that one form of taxation that has proven so successful and so popular."[3] Governors across the nation caught the fever of road building. Even Governor Theodore G. Bilbo of Mississippi (1916–1920, 1928–1932), a man who was not progressive, enthusiastically supported the idea of an advanced state highway system.

Despite their excitement about new projects and technology, governors were aware of signs of underlying economic unease. In tune with the increasing hardship of some of their citizens, governors routinely discussed the problems of agriculture and the need to help rural areas. By the mid-1920s, the South was already in the midst of a serious economic decline, resulting from overproduction and plummeting cotton prices. During their 1928 meeting in New Orleans, a group of governors shared their fears about the unstable economy and postulated about whether government intervention might be necessary. The situation took a turn for the worse on Black Tuesday, October 29, 1929. The economy collapsed and Americans entered the Great Depression.

Many governors took more activist roles as state executives and drew upon the resources of their organization when confronted by widespread unemployment and the pressing immediate needs of their citizens. In contrast, President Herbert Hoover continued to espouse his policy of smaller government and lower taxes, believing scaling back to be the best solution. He relayed this message at the 1932 Governors' Conference meeting in Richmond, Virginia, by announcing that the federal government was doing its share of belt-tightening and directing state and local governments to do the same. Some governors followed the president's lead, but others tried to innovate to relieve the situation at home. Some hesitated in taking decisive action that could reshape governmental tradition, while others felt the situation was too dire to wait. At times, it was not lack of political will that stymied gubernatorial action, but simply lack of money. Meanwhile, the situation for the vast number of Americans worsened when the unemployment rate reached as high as 25 percent in 1932.

People across the nation suffered hardship in the 1930s. Individuals dealt with the Depression as best they could but many found few options to help their families. Some became migrants, such as the "Okies" who left the Dust Bowl of Oklahoma for dreams of a better life in golden California. Their experiences, encapsulated by John Steinbeck in his novel *Grapes of Wrath* (1939), symbolized the struggles of average Americans working to survive in the midst of a national crisis. Others blamed the government for their misfortunes. In 1932, a group of World War I veterans, calling themselves the Bonus Army, marched on Washington to demand early payment of the cash bonuses they were promised. Congress refused to concede and a violent encounter with the U.S. Army left two veterans dead. The situation further damaged the nation's morale and Americans' trust in President Hoover. Emergency tent towns, or "Hoovervilles," became the legacy of a president hesitant to call for a more activist government. In 1932, the concern expressed by North Dakota Governor George Shafer in the 1920s was realized when, for the first time, a federal tax was imposed on gasoline. Governors were concerned about this as well as the potential implications of increased federal assistance on states' rights but, regardless, the situation was dire and states needed federal aid.

Relief began when a governor, trained in the necessity of providing directly for his constituents, moved into the White House. Franklin Delano Roosevelt won the presidential election of 1932 in a landslide by offering renewed hope to the American people. But his New Deal was not entirely new; rather it drew inspiration from innovative state programs. Roosevelt had articulated these ideas during his years as governor of New York (1929–1932) and used the annual governors' meetings to learn from colleagues who both pioneered and opposed these theories. At the 1930 gathering in Salt Lake City, Governor Roosevelt discussed his support of old-age insurance. The following year he argued, "More and more, those who are the victims of dislocations and defects of our social and economic life are beginning to ask respectfully but insistently of us who are in positions of public responsibility why Government cannot and should not act to protect its citizens from disaster."[4] He was not alone in believing that a more activist government, on both the state and federal levels, was the answer to the widespread suffering. But later as president, Roosevelt became frustrated with the reluctance of some governors to act. He fought against inertia by using the radio, a newly popular medium, to speak directly to Americans. This practice angered a number of politicians who believed that the national government was overstepping its bounds. Critics of the president's New Deal included Alfred E. Smith (1919–1920, 1923–1928), Roosevelt's gubernatorial predecessor in New York. Yet, assessments of the administration were mixed. Other prominent governors, like Alfred Landon of Kansas (1933–1937), were enthusiastic supporters of the president and his New Deal.

Loved and hated, Roosevelt's controversial policies redefined federal-state relations and challenged the traditional practice of state and local government administering direct aid to citizens. Some governors readily accepted that drastic times demanded drastic measures. John Winant of New Hampshire (1925–1927, 1931–1935), who later ran the Social Security Board, became the first governor to cooperate with the National Planning Board and meet the New Deal's Civilian Conservation Corps' enrollment numbers. At the 1932 governors' meeting, Winant explained his support of federal aid: "It is not necessary to reject the assumption that self-interest is one of the primary motivating forces in our social order to recognize that a selfish individualism has been allowed to override the collective interest of the people and that it is still a destructive force in the effort to rehabilitate the normal life of the Nation."[5] Some criticized the Roosevelt administration but, in the urgency of the 1930s, most governors accepted if not appreciated the larger national government and increased federal aid to states. With the advent of the New Deal, governors began to rethink the federalism balance. In 1937, Olin Johnston of South Carolina (1935–1939, 1943–1945) presented a scenario to his fellow governors in which the federal government could be relied on for education assistance without wresting control of schools from state and local government. "There is no reason," Johnston argued, "why a national department of education could not be organized to assist education in the several states without in any way conflicting with the sacred rights of states." But Johnston also cautioned that the states "would not tolerate any unequivocal and arbitrary standardization of the principles of practices in the operation of schools." Perhaps presciently, he went on to say that if such an attempt at standardization occurred, an authority would be created "like no other bureau we have ever seen. It would probably be under a cabinet officer—a man chosen by the President of the United States."[6]

The Great Depression and New Deal altered irrevocably the federalism bargain in the United States. These years cemented a new era in the modern governorship in which governors had no choice but to reach across state lines and speak out on national politics. Interstate cooperation was now a necessity, and the Governors' Conference gave these leaders a forum to articulate their concerns regarding federal-state relations. At their 1935 meeting, governors debated a resolution seeking greater state control over the administration of relief programs. And in 1937, they discussed conflicting federal and state tax sources and the increasing scope of federal authority. This era of association, however, did not hamper or lessen individual state innovation. Not solely reliant on federal aid, governors across the nation tested different approaches for dealing with the new demands on state resources. Henry Horner of Illinois (1933–1940), for example, decided to institute a permanent state sales tax to increase revenue. But few had the influence, popularity, and notoriety of Huey Long (1928–1932). Long convinced the masses of Louisiana that he was their savior who could solve their economic woes. Yet his legacy is not one of salvation, but of the pitfalls of absolute power.

Chapter Two

Huey Long and the Great Depression

Rise of a Populist Demagogue

RICHARD D. WHITE, JR.

From 1928 until his violent death in 1935, Huey Long did more good for the people of Louisiana than any politician before or since. In the midst of the Great Depression, he built nine thousand miles of new roads, erected more than a hundred bridges over swamps and rivers, and pulled his state from the horse-and-buggy days into the age of modern transportation. By giving free textbooks to students he allowed thousands of poor children to attend school, and his adult night classes taught 175,000 illiterate Louisianans to read, including many poor blacks. He doubled the number of beds in the state's charity hospitals. He raised the state university to national stature in size and scholarship. He lessened the burden on poor farmers by giving a homestead property tax exemption and allowed thousands of them to vote when he abolished the poll tax. To legions of ill-housed, ill-fed, and ill-clothed Louisianans, Long incarnated the savior of the common man and the liberator of the downtrodden.[1] The country people "worshiped the ground he walked on," a newspaperman observed. "He was part of their religion."[2]

Paradoxically, Huey Long also did more harm to the state of Louisiana than any politician before or since. As governor and later U.S. senator, he seized near-absolute control and by the end of his tempestuous reign dominated almost every aspect of government. He conquered the state legislature and ordered it to slavishly pass hundreds of bills that increased his power, destroyed his enemies, and stretched the very limits of constitutionalism. He packed the courts with his loyalists to ensure that his increasing power went unchecked. He used political whim to hire thousands of state government workers, from cabinet secretaries to laborers shoveling gravel onto highways, while thousands of local school-teachers, sheriff deputies, and courthouse clerks fell under his political boot. His lust for power led him to ruthlessly destroy his enemies' political careers, ruin their businesses, raise their taxes, and fire their relatives from government jobs.[3] He orchestrated elections, padded voting lists, and directed the counting of ballots. He assaulted freedom of the press by proposing a gag law that prohibited newspapers from criticizing him. He deployed the state militia as his personal police force and declared martial law in cities that refused to submit to his mastery. He packed the membership of government boards, courts, and parish councils with his own majority, gerrymandered political divisions to remove enemies from office, stripped opposing public officials of their power to hire and fire people and to make and spend money, and, without warning, revised the dates for elections and length of time in office to oust his enemies and open the door for his loyalists. When his cronies broke the law, he pardoned them.[4]

Today it is difficult to understand how one man could do both so much good and so much harm for so many people in such a short amount of time. How did Huey Long capture such absolute control over a modern, democratic state? Like other states, Louisiana possessed all of the checks and balances necessary to prohibit a political dictatorship from being created. So, why did the legislature not stop his rise to dictatorship? Why did the courts allow his unconstitutional efforts to go unchecked? Most important, why did the people of Louisiana surrender almost unlimited power to one man, their governor, and, in the end, allow him to trample democracy?

Huey Long's complete control over Louisiana was unsurpassed and unprecedented. Many factors contributed to his rise to dictatorship. First, of course, was Long himself. He possessed unflagging energy, razor-sharp political savvy, and absolute brilliance. "Listen, there are smarter guys than I am," Long once admitted, "but *not* in Louisiana."[5] At the time he made the boast, many Louisianans agreed with his oversized opinion of himself, that he was the fastest-thinking, fastest-talking politician in the state and, if not the smartest, indeed the most shrewd and powerful. He also had an unquenchable thirst for power, allowing no one to stand in his way and ruthlessly crushing any opposition.[6] Long had help from a horde of bootlicking followers who did his bidding without question. Some he coerced, some feared him, some were freebooters, plunderbunds, and sycophants who joined him because they saw an opportunity for lucre. A few of his loyalists followed him because they agreed with his populist ideology and saw him as an energetic realist who sincerely tried to help the people of Louisiana. All of them, nevertheless, obeyed his orders unquestioningly.

Louisiana's unique history contributed to Long's rise. The distinctly American political system that developed in other states never gained a solid foothold in Louisiana, where large-scale white illiteracy, poverty, and African American disenfranchisement had deterred true democracy from thriving. Unlike states that began as British colonies with some representative government, democracy bypassed early Louisiana.[7] Under the French and Spanish, Louisiana had no representative assembly and its royal governors were all the more powerful.[8] Although Long's heavy-handed methods may have been more ruthless and increasingly demagogic, he nevertheless dominated the state much as the plantation aristocrats and New Orleans ward healers had done for generations.[9] Indeed, in 1935 the majority of people in the state were happy to be dictated to by Long and saw him as a much-preferred alternative to the Bourbon oligarchy of the past.[10]

The Great Depression also contributed to Long's rise to dictatorship. The grinding poverty of the time that afflicted most Louisianans created a fertile environment for his populist message. An impoverished people wanted change and he offered lots of it. He kept attacking the rich. "The billionaires are becoming bigger billionaires, the millionaires are becoming bigger millionaires, the poor are becoming poorer, and the middle class is disappearing," he roared in a speech.[11]

Long could have never risen to power without the support of the majority of people in his state. The poorer folk worried little about his roughshod political tactics and followed him blindly. The country people brushed aside the critics who claimed he was a dictator and firmly believed, with some good reason, that he was still the only politician who cared about their lot. Thousands of small dirt farmers and one-horse merchants saw only the free schoolbooks for their children, enjoyed driving along the new concrete highways, and listened raptly to his promises of a better life. They supported him staunchly, almost blindly, not worrying that he built a ruthless political machine or that he allowed corruption in state government or even that he pocketed some money himself.

Early Years and Education

Huey Long was born on August 30, 1893, in Winn Parish, Louisiana, in a region where a dark and relentless poverty sapped the lives of the straight-laced Baptists who struggled to survive there. Despite his later claims that he was raised in poverty, Long grew up in a middle-class family that lived more comfortably than his poor neighbors. As a child, he was headstrong, was impossible to discipline, and always demanded to be in charge. With a hot temper that fit his rust-colored hair, he could rage quickly into a tantrum. He quarreled often with his brothers and sisters, who were all smart and competitive. Of the four Long brothers and five sisters, three of the boys became attorneys, the fourth a dentist and later congressman, and the girls earned degrees in education from Louisiana Normal College in Natchitoches, one becoming a professor.[12]

Long received an early education in Louisiana's freewheeling politics. He grew up in a household in which the family argued politics each night at their large and noisy dinner table. When he turned seven, his father finished a distant third in a state senate race and ten years later finished sixth in a race for the parish's five aldermen.[13] As a boy, Huey often walked into Winnfield, where he listened to populist rabble rousers standing on the courthouse steps and sounding off at a political system that disenfranchised the poor population.

Huey had little patience for school. In 1910, just before his seventeenth birthday, his high school expelled him for his rebellious attitude. Never graduating, he took a job as a traveling salesman selling Cottolene, a lard substitute made from cottonseed oil, at nineteen dollars a week. He traveled across the South, hawking his product and distributing pie plates and cookbooks and holding baking contests in cities and towns. He next sold cured meats, lard, and canned goods, and later, fruits and vegetables. By late summer of 1912, he was selling for the Faultless Starch Company. Still not twenty, he rose quickly to regional sales manager, responsible for a four-state area and several salesmen, including his younger brother Earl.[14]

Long enjoyed traveling the dusty back roads of the South and sharing seedy hotels and boardinghouses with other salesmen. By this time, he was a smooth-tongued hawker who charmed housewives and country storekeepers. The skills he honed as a salesman were not much different from those he would soon use as a successful politician. He tailored his language to his customers, sensed when he had their attention, and if he did not, he would use his wit and charm to win them over. He met thousands of people as he traveled throughout Louisiana, staying overnight with farmers and establishing friendships, and with his extraordinarily keen memory, never forgetting them. Years later, during campaign speeches in the remote regions of the state, Long would point to a former customer in the crowd and cajole him for losing his hair or gaining a few pounds.

In 1913, Long moved to New Orleans, where he registered at Tulane's law school. After a year, he felt he had learned enough law, and besides, he was broke. By then he had completed only two law courses, corporation law and federal practice, failed two courses, and did not show up for the final exam in four others. His lackluster academic record, however, did not reflect his overall energy, for he cared less about formal academic grades than learning the practical applications of the law.

The impatient Long petitioned the chief justice of the Louisiana Supreme Court to take the bar exam early. Yielding to the irrepressible law student, the justice allowed an unusual special exam, which Long passed easily. Even before he finished his law studies, Long began plotting a political future that would not begin for another three years, when he was elected state railroad commissioner in 1918. He had earlier confided that he first planned to win a minor state office, then become governor of Louisiana, then United States senator, and finally president. "It almost gave you the cold chills to hear him tell about it," his wife remembered years later. "He was measuring it all."[15]

Campaigning for Governor

Huey Long first ran for governor of Louisiana in 1924, just after his thirtieth birthday. He finished a close third in the Democratic primary, carried all northern parishes except three, and received majorities in twenty-one of the state's sixty-four parishes. His 12,000 votes in New Orleans, however, were not enough.[16] With the New Orleans vote excluded, he would have won. After losing in 1924, Long never stopped campaigning and vowed to win four years later.

Long waged an unorthodox campaign in 1928, shunning the support of the Delta planters, wealthy businessmen, and New Orleans political bosses who traditionally met in secret to pick the next Democratic candidate for governor. Louisiana was a one-party state and the only election that made any difference was the primary. Even primary elections were of little consequence, however, as the powerful politicos decided the results beforehand and controlled the voting by methods both fair and foul. Candidates waged dull and meaningless gubernatorial campaigns. They made few promises and when elected, carried out fewer. They visited only the larger cities and token parish seats and ignored the rural and impoverished regions of the state.

Long spent little time in large courthouse towns and parish seats and focused instead on the scattered people of the hills and hollows. In the past, candidates for governor pursued local political bosses, who controlled the voters in their parishes, but Long did the opposite. "In every parish there is a boss, usually the sheriff," he told a friend. "[The boss] has forty percent of the votes, forty percent are opposed to him, and twenty percent are in-betweens. I'm going into every parish and cuss out the boss. That gives me forty percent of the votes to begin with and I will hoss trade them out of the in-betweens. . . . I always hit the big man first."[17]

While Louisianan politicians typically refrained from attacking their opponents, Long never hesitated in viciously smearing his rivals. He delivered his attacks by unconventional methods, becoming the first politician in Louisiana to broadcast his speeches over the radio, and on the road he employed two new sound trucks with huge loudspeakers attached to their roofs. One of the sound trucks always stayed ahead of him, arriving in the next town an hour early with music blaring and drumming up a crowd. Long knew that soapbox speaking was still important in rural Louisiana, where few people read newspapers and political rallies provided rare entertainment.

Knowing the powerful appeal of economics, Long pledged to lift his people out of financial misery. Unlike typical southern demagogues such as Governor Theodore Bilbo of Mississippi and Senator Tom Watson of Georgia, he did not resort to racism to strengthen his hold on newly franchised white sharecroppers, although he made little effort to promote racial equality or integration. Blacks were still without the right to vote, because the all-white Democratic primary denied them suffrage in Louisiana. Long, however, recognized that his uplifting economic message of taking from the rich and giving to the poor was much more appealing to Louisianans than bombastic racial diatribes, and besides, he was wise enough to know that someday in the not-too-distant future, the black population would become a potent voting force.[18]

Tramping the state, Long delivered more than 600 speeches, traveled 15,000 miles, and addressed 300,000 people.[19] In his speeches, he made a "wagonload of promises," such as vowing to remove the tolls from the state's bridges, make the state penitentiary self-supporting, place union representatives on state boards, and increase workers' compensation benefits. He promised to allow unlimited hunting and fishing year round and to abolish the State Conservation Commission, that "coon chasin' possum watchin' brigade. . . . I'll cut the tail off the Conservation Commission right up behind the ears," he vowed.[20] He tailored his speeches to the local audiences. In Alexandria and Shreveport, he promised to open the nearby Red River to navigation and bring shipping and commerce to the region. In Pineville, a small town near Alexandria, he had his father sit on the stage while he spoke, hoping to present more of a family image. In Baton Rouge, he promised to support the state university located there. When he spoke in New Orleans, he promised free bridges to connect the city with traffic arteries along the Gulf Coast and to replace the city's expensive synthetic gas supply with cheaper natural gas.[21]

Most important, Long always endeared himself to the people. "How many of you wear silk socks?" he asked a crowd of poor farmers. No one raised a hand. "How many of you wear cotton socks?" he then asked. As hands shot up, Long bent over and hitched up his pants leg to show that he too wore cotton socks. But he went a step further and asked, "How many of you have holes in your socks?" When a few farmers raised their hands, he pulled off one of his shoes to show his big toe sticking through a large hole in his sock. For the rest of their lives, whenever the farmers in that crowd rose early in the morning and pulled on their socks, they chuckled and thought of Long and his big toe. They also would give him their total loyalty, their votes in overwhelming numbers, and have no problem with giving him complete mastery over their state.[22]

Long understood the will of the people and knew that their approval was the wellspring of his power. Money, allies, and patronage were critical, but useless if he did not first possess popular sanction. To keep the people firmly in his grasp, he knew that they had to look upon him as one of their own and not as some distant and overbearing politician. He bragged of growing up barefoot and impoverished, never admitting that in reality his family lived quite comfortably when compared to their poorer Winn Parish neighbors. To Long, the truth was immaterial, such as when he suggested to one audience that he was Protestant and to another that he was Catholic. What mattered was that he identified with the masses and they identified right back.[23] He spoke colloquially and concocted homespun images that they understood, like his big toe sticking through the hole in his sock, because once he captivated and charmed them, their unfading loyalty followed.

His more powerful opponents, the Bourbon planters and New Orleans Ring, had never before faced anyone of his energy, intelligence, and lust for power. Yet, they were unable to put aside their own petty differences and build an organized effort to crush him. Before they realized it, it was Long doing the crushing. On January 17, 1928, his unorthodox campaigning and sheer energy paid off when he decisively won the Democratic primary for governor. Overall, he carried forty-seven parishes and six of the eight congressional districts, although he performed weakly in the cities and failed to win New Orleans, Shreveport, and the state capital of Baton Rouge. In some French parishes, however, he racked up surprising majorities of 60 to 70 percent. When the statewide votes were tallied, Long polled 126,842 votes to about 80,000 votes for each of his two opponents. For the first time, a Protestant politician had successfully invaded predominantly Catholic south Louisiana.

First Years in Office

As soon as he was inaugurated in May 1928, Governor Huey Long's first order of business was to take firm control of the state government bureaucracy and "kick the rascals out."[24] He dismantled agencies over which he had immediate authority, firing old appointees and selecting his own men for the jobs. With their thousands of workers, the Highway Commission, the State Board of Health, the Hospital Board, and the Orleans Parish Levee Board were his prime targets. Before the first week ended, he fired seventy-three New Orleans Dock Board employees and cashiered eighty out of one hundred Highway Commission speed cops.[25] Soon, he removed from office every major and minor employee whose job he controlled; by the time he finished, he commanded thousands of workers across the state and began amassing a powerful arsenal of spoils patronage and political support.

In little time, Long used his political skullduggery to go through the list of government employees, replacing dozens of officeholders of questionable loyalty with his own supporters. None of his enemies were too weak and no political job too unimportant to receive attention. A drawbridge tender in Plaquemines Parish lost his job when the governor, passing through the area, discovered the man was a friend of a wealthy state senator who opposed Long.[26] Long also settled old political grudges. He detested the president of the Board of Health, Dr. Oscar Dowling, who served under five previous governors. Dowling's term of office did not expire until 1932, but Long was determined to remove him. He forced the legislature to pass a bill cutting Dowling's term short and, a week later, fired Dowling and appointed his own replacement.[27] Long dealt similarly with the powerful New Orleans Levee Board, which maintained the dikes protecting the city from the Mississippi River and had one of the largest employment rolls in the state. He pressured the legislature to dissolve the old board and create a new five-member body. Four of the new appointees were Long supporters and the vast Levee Board patronage fell into his grasp.[28]

Long's crude methods shocked his opponents. Used to passive governors who seldom interfered with legislative prerogatives, his foes quickly realized that he ignored or rewrote the rules to force the legislature to carry out his political agenda. "I'd rather violate every one of the damned conventions and see my bills passed," he admitted, "than sit back in my office, all nice and proper, and watch 'em die."[29] With no hesitation, he dashed unexpectedly out of his office and up the sweeping spiral staircase to the capitol's second floor, bursting into the legislative chambers and brazenly accosting senators and representatives at their desks, ordering them to vote for his pet bills or against those of his opponents. Abandoning protocol and any separation of powers, he stomped through committee rooms and scattered committees with a nod of his head or the crooking of a finger. He entered the Senate and House and bullied the legislators with frowns, stinging jokes, and foul-mouthed threats. Many of the legislators loudly protested Long's meddling but he ignored them. After he barged unannounced into a committee hearing one night, one irritated senator threw a copy of the Louisiana Constitution at Long's head. "Maybe you've heard of this book," shouted the senator. The governor picked it up, looked at the title, flipped it aside and shot back, "I'm the constitution just now."[30]

Long quickly introduced several bills aimed to increase his control, including an act creating the Bureau of Criminal Identification. The BCI was independent of all sheriffs, police, and constables and possessed the unprecedented power to make arrests anywhere in the state without warrants for all violations of the law. He personally framed the act, which called for the governor to chair the BCI's board of managers and select its members. Secretive and powerful, the BCI provided Long with a hefty political weapon and signaled an ominous first step toward the creation of a police state.[31]

Nor was Long averse to nepotism. He appointed his brother Earl as inheritance tax collector earning $15,000 a year.[32] Within months of taking office, Long placed at least twenty-three of his relatives on the state payroll, including a sister on the faculty of a state college, two brothers-in-law in his new Bureau of Criminal Identification and Shreveport's charity hospital, plus an uncle and eighteen cousins in other state jobs. One of his cousins replaced the president of the state college in Natchitoches.[33]

Surviving Impeachment

Long soon depleted the state treasury with his modern highway system, new bridges, new schools, free textbooks, charity hospitals, a new governor's mansion, a new state capitol, and thousands of extra state workers to swell the patronage ranks. In one year, he spent $79 million, just $2 million less than a previous governor had spent in four years, and pushed the state debt from $11 million to over $100 million. He financed many of his expensive building projects by selling bonds, which forced the state deeper in debt. The deficit stimulated the economy and created jobs during the Depression, but Louisiana's credit rating eventually fell so low that state-issued bonds no longer could be sold. Long was bankrupting the state.[34]

Floating devalued state bonds produced little revenue, so Long looked for a new source of cash. He targeted Louisiana's most lucrative and powerful industry, the oil business, and especially Standard Oil, the operator of the world's largest refinery in Baton Rouge and the biggest employer in the state. Since his days as railroad commissioner he had held a personal grudge against Standard Oil and saw the opportunity not only to increase revenues but also to attack an old enemy.

Long called a six-day special session of the legislature in March 1929 and, with no warning, proposed a radically new processing tax on refined oil. Unlike the severance tax that imposed a levy on crude oil extracted at the wellhead, an oil-processing tax would impose a five-cent-per-barrel levy on finished petroleum.[35] He calculated that the new tax would yield nearly $2 million per year.[36] Long had lit the fuse of a political bombshell. Every legislator from oil-producing parishes knew that voting for a processing tax meant suicide in their next election. Businessmen feared that Long might expand occupational taxes in the future to include all types of business, not just oil.

Long's enemies felt he had gone too far with the oil-processing tax and that he was now vulnerable to impeachment. Chaos erupted in the legislature, where Long's friends and enemies waged a raucous fistfight. Overnight, anti-Long legislators drafted nineteen complaints, ranging from the frivolous and absurd to serious and felonious. The most serious impeachment charge originated from a former bodyguard who accused Long of planning to murder a political enemy. However, even Long's most bitter opponents admitted there was little likelihood of the bodyguard's charges being true. Long earlier had fired the bodyguard, a slow-moving and dull-witted former prizefighter, and vengeance was the likely motive.[37] Most legislators believed that although Long was a tyrant, he was incapable of murder, and later the House dropped the murder charge as well as frivolous complaints that accused Long of carrying a concealed weapon, violently abusing citizens visiting him on public business, gross misconduct in public places, repeatedly appearing on the floor of the House of Representatives, fondling a New Orleans nightclub stripper, and uttering "blasphemous and sacrilegious expressions by comparing himself to the Savior."[38]

Other charges, much more substantiated, provided solid grounds for impeachment by the House and, if convicted by the Senate, Long's removal from office. These more serious accusations alleged that he illegally influenced the judiciary, offered bribes to legislators, used the militia unlawfully to pillage private property, and improperly spent state money. Long's opponents later tacked on a twentieth, catchall charge that accused the governor of "incompetency, corruption and gross misconduct."[39]

The House impeachment proceedings raged for a month as both the Longites and anti-Longites traded insults, accusations, and punches. The House eventually passed seven of the original charges, including attempts to blackmail a newspaper publisher and bribe legislators; not accounting for state money he had spent on a new automobile; using mansion funds for personal purposes and the purchase of a private law library; and permitting a construction company to build defective culverts. On the final day of the proceedings, the House passed, 55 to 29, a last, catchall charge accusing Long of forcing appointees to sign undated resignations, insulting citizens, discharging a college president, appointing a corrupt parole officer, and demonstrating that he was incompetent and temperamentally unfit for his office.[40] Once passed by the House, the charges then went to the Senate for trial.

Louisianans expected the Senate impeachment trial to be as raucous as the House proceedings, but the Senate trial proved anticlimactic. Soon after convening, a pro-Long senator rose and announced that fifteen senators—one more than needed to kill the two-thirds vote for conviction—had signed a document saying they would vote to acquit Long, no matter what testimony followed and no matter what evidence was presented.[41] Long had outwitted his opponents again. He had known that his only chance of survival was in the Senate, and he knew exactly how many votes he needed and which senators he could coerce to support him. He understood the makeup of every legislative district in the state, how many votes were cast and who got them, and the political strengths and weaknesses of every senator. While the House proceedings dominated the headlines, Long used promises, threats, bribes, liquor, women, and any other stimulant he could devise to secure the votes of the fifteen senators, and with their signatures in hand, he survived his closest call with political extinction. Quietly, the senators realized there was nothing more they could do, adjourned *sine die*, and abruptly ended the impeachment proceedings.

After barely escaping impeachment, Long immediately began punishing his enemies and rewarding his friends. He was a changed man, more vengeful and ruthless. He became more grim and cynical, more secretive, and confided only to a small, tight group of trusted friends. "He didn't put his cards on the table as he used to," his sister remembered.[42]

Election to the U.S. Senate

Louisiana's daily newspapers constantly attacked Huey Long and most of them outwardly called for his impeachment. In March 1930, Long retaliated by founding his own newspaper, the *Louisiana Progress*. He financed the paper by requiring every state worker to take out a subscription and had it delivered to doorsteps by state trooper cruisers and highway department trucks. The *Progress* was a pugnacious tabloid, full of political rancor and outrageous propaganda and used by Long as a weapon to attack his opponents. The front page of the first issue displayed a large cartoon of Long handing free schoolbooks to children.

On July 16, 1930, a banner headline in the *Progress* announced that Long was running for the U.S. Senate. His opponent was incumbent Senator Joseph E. Ransdell, a seventy-two-year-old, slow-witted attorney from East Carroll Parish. Tall and thin, Ransdell was an archaic relic of past politics who had been in Washington for thirty-two years, serving as a congressman since 1899 and senator since 1912. He had never faced an opponent as energetic and aggressive as Long. The summer campaign deteriorated into one of the nastiest that Louisiana had ever seen, including the kidnapping of two of Long's opponents, who were held on a remote island until after the election. On September 9, 1930, Long won the Democratic primary, trouncing Ransdell, 149,640 to 111,451. Long carried fifty-three of the sixty-four parishes and won by a landslide in the rural regions, where 60 percent of Louisianans lived. The race was riddled with corruption. In the pro-Long bastion of St. Bernard Parish, which had only 2,454 registered voters, Long amassed a preposterous 3,979 votes while Ransdell received only nine.

From March 1931 until May 1932, Long served both as governor and U.S. senator. His attendance record in the Senate was abysmal, as he was constantly taking the train back to Baton Rouge to keep a tight rein on the legislature and shore up his power. Even when his term expired, he never gave up his control over Louisiana and continued as de facto governor.

Once in the Senate, his wild antics, uncouth manners, and long-winded filibusters made him the most entertaining show in Washington. He led a controversial crusade to limit the incomes of millionaires and redistribute their wealth to the poor. He proposed that Congress give a thirty-dollar pension to all needy persons over sixty, limit work hours to thirty hours a week, and give a free college education to deserving students.

In August 1932, Long traveled to Arkansas to campaign for the reelection of U.S. Senator Hattie Caraway, a demure widow who political experts said had no hope of winning. Long felt sorry for Hattie, and also saw the opportunity to build support for himself outside of Louisiana. In eight days, he covered more than 2,000 miles and delivered two tons of circulars spouting Caraway's platform and his own plan to share the nation's wealth. Long gave thirty-nine speeches to more than 200,000 Arkansans.[43] His efforts paid off, and for the first time in U.S. history, a woman was elected to a full term in the Senate. Caraway won sixty-one of seventy-five counties, and outdistanced her nearest opponent by more than two to one. Hattie Caraway returned to the U.S. Senate, where she served until 1945.

By 1935, the increasingly popular Long had organized his followers into the Share Our Wealth Society with eight million members nationwide.[44] Although economists discarded his notion to redistribute wealth as rash and impractical, a vast and growing number of poor Americans believed his plan was a workable answer to the Depression.[45] With his radical proposals and rude demeanor, Long became Franklin Roosevelt's archenemy and the most vocal critic of the New Deal. In 1935, Long announced he was running for president.

Absolute Power

By the mid-1930s, democratic rule held little sway in Louisiana. Huey Long now tightly controlled the executive, legislative, and judicial branches of government. Although he no longer retained any state office, he possessed vast political power and reigned supreme over the state capitol. He treated his hand-picked governor as little more than his personal errand boy who carried out his orders without question, even moving out of his office while Long was in town.

Long's rule over the legislature was absolute. Servile legislators rubber stamped his bills in record numbers, in record time, and disregarded the repressiveness and immorality of the laws he forced them to enact.[46] By the early 1930s he had defeated most of his legislative foes at the polls, and the handful of anti-Longs who remained were powerless.

From August 1934 through September 1935, Long called seven special sessions of the Louisiana legislature in which his representatives blindly passed 463 bills, most of them unread and undebated, creating the most repressive legislation in American political history.[47] He still needed new sources of revenue to pay for his increasing patronage. Ignoring the economic and political consequences, he ordered new taxes to be levied.[48] When Long took office in 1928, Louisiana was a state with few taxes, mainly a local property tax, inheritance tax, occupational license tax, and a severance tax on oil and minerals. By the end of his rule, some forty-five separate taxes reaped $38 million in state revenues, a 75 percent increase since 1927.[49] According to one of Long's workers, his theory on taxation was to "cover everything in sight . . . and to throw out a network of taxes with low rates to cover everything."[50] In May 1932, Long ordered a constitutional amendment that levied the state's first income tax. Even the income tax would not generate enough revenue, however, and Long ordered another amendment that increased sales taxes on cigarettes, gasoline, soft drinks, dairy products, chain stores, and business franchises. He also drafted a tax on insurance premiums collected in the state, a tax on electric power companies, and a franchise tax on all corporations. Poverty and backwardness in Louisiana increased as Long's seemingly endless taxation policies worsened the maldistribution of wealth. Conditions for the common people grew worse, not better, during the latter years of his reign.[51]

After his election to the U.S. Senate, Long did little to foster the economic liberation of the people of Louisiana.[52] Sizable accomplishments took place in the first few years of his reign, but real advancements like more roads and hospitals did not continue. True reform faltered as he abandoned his progressive crusade and devoted all of his energy to building, increasing, perpetuating, and centralizing his already enormous political power. Although deep in his heart he probably maintained sympathy for the "wool hat boys," Long's spending on public improvements dropped drastically after 1931 when his road-building program neared completion.[53] While his speech making in the U.S. Senate and on national radio called for sharing the nation's wealth, he put little of that philosophy into action in Louisiana, where, ironically, he could have ordered economic reforms with a nod of his head.

Sadly, Louisiana, in fact, possessed the resources needed to lift itself out of poverty and become one of the richest, instead of poorest, states in the nation. Beginning during Long's reign, oil companies and wildcatters discovered oil in forty-two of the state's sixty-four parishes. Yet Long and a few of his closest associates leased valuable petroleum rights to dummy corporations, which then subleased the property to legitimate oil companies. Sometimes land was leased for as little as a few cents an acre, then subleased for thousands of dollars, plus royalties that continued as long as the wells pumped oil. Royalties from oil leases could have filled the state's coffers but instead fattened the pockets of a few political insiders. The squandering of the state's natural riches by Long and those who followed him remains a disgraceful episode of Louisiana history.[54]

To increase his voting strength, Long forced through an amendment that repealed the poll tax and enfranchised 300,000 poor whites who had never voted. Long knew that when poorer white voters went to the polls, he had them firmly in his grasp. He also wrested complete control of the state election machinery, including the appointment of commissioners, the power to disqualify voters, and the privilege of padding voting lists wherever he deemed necessary. He now directed the counting of ballots and took from the courts any power to adjudicate election disputes or to oversee registrars.[55] During this period, he tightly managed elections in New Orleans. He sent twelve companies of the Louisiana National Guard into the city, where his troopers busted through the doors of the Registrar of Voters office and commandeered the voting lists.

By 1935, Long controlled almost every district judge, and of the few that he did not control, he ordered the state supreme court, now stacked with his loyalists, to overrule decisions he did not like. When he could not have recalcitrant judges or district attorneys voted out of office, he gerrymandered their districts and eliminated their judgeships. His attorney general, just as submissive as his puppet governor, provided legal justification for what Long already decided he was going to do, including overriding the action of any district attorney in the state.[56] After abolishing the state bar association and creating one of his own, he could make and break lawyers. "If a lawyer takes a case too obnoxious to Long," an attorney declared, "he will be walking the street in a week."[57]

Long tightly controlled government commissions, departments, agencies, the state treasury, state universities, and public hospitals. Long hired and fired 24,000 state, city, and parish government workers. These employees, from clerk to constable, depended completely upon Long for their paycheck and in return gave him their vote and a portion of their salary.[58] He directed law enforcement throughout the state, including scores of state troopers, city policemen, parish sheriffs and their deputies, an undisclosed number of his secretive State Bureau of Criminal Identification operatives, and three thousand National Guardsmen who served as his private janissary, carrying out wanton martial law and warrantless civil action. Long took from the sheriffs the power to name more than five deputies, and from district attorneys the right to name more than three assistants. He required all police and firemen to obtain commissions from the state. All of the pieces of a police state were now in place.

Among the dozens of bills Long rammed through the legislature, one stripped local school boards of the power to hire, fire, and pay teachers. Another bill created a state budget committee, consisting of the governor, superintendent of education, and state treasurer, which held absolute authority over the jobs of every teacher, school bus driver, and school janitor in the state.[59] At the first meeting, the budget committee fired dozens of teachers from anti-Long parishes, including twenty from Baton Rouge.[60] Other than giving children free schoolbooks, Long did little to improve the state's woeful level of education and paid scant attention to elementary and secondary schools. In 1933, the U.S. Bureau of Education ranked Louisiana forty-fourth in general education and forty-seventh in attendance. Although Long's administration taught nearly 200,000 illiterates to read, Louisiana remained next to last in the literacy level of its citizens. Teachers' salaries declined every year he was in power. In 1932, white elementary teachers were paid $622 a year, and black teachers only $219.[61] While he piled funds upon Louisiana State University, he ignored the other state colleges and politicized higher education, even to the point of ensuring that only the children of his followers received scholarships. Academic freedom existed at his caprice and he crushed any university student or professor who disagreed with him.

Long held an economic stranglehold over many Louisiana businesses. His public service commissioners, state tax commissioners, bank examiners, homestead agents, and property assessors dictated financial salvation or ruin. His bureaucrats prescribed licenses, permits, property assessments, and other commercial transactions not by necessity but often by political loyalty. They taxed misbehaving corporations into extinction and heaped contracts and largess upon the businesses of their friends.[62] Bank examiners stifled the credit of opponents' businesses, and state dock inspectors banned fruit, vegetables, and other cargo belonging to anti-Long shippers from being stored on state-owned wharfs.[63]

The Legacy of Huey Long

Huey Long never got the chance to run for president against Franklin Roosevelt. On September 8, 1935, Long was in Baton Rouge overseeing another session of the legislature. As Long walked through the capitol corridor a young doctor, Carl Weiss, stepped in front of him and gunshots rang out. Some eyewitnesses said Weiss shot Long in the chest, while others contend Long was hit by a ricochet from his bodyguards as they riddled Weiss's lifeless body with bullets. Long died two days later.

While Louisiana is no longer split between the Longites and anti-Longs, vestiges of Long's domination remain. Many Louisianans still respond to the populist rhetoric first popularized by Long, later perpetuated by his colorful brother Earl, who served three terms as governor, and continued into recent years by the charismatic but corruptive Governor Edwin Edwards. Compared with other states, Louisiana's governor possesses much of the unparalleled informal power amassed by Long, including substantial political patronage. The state legislature still bows to most of the governor's wishes. Since Long's reign, the governor has traditionally appointed the speaker of the house, the president of the senate, and other important committee chairmanships, even when a different party controlled the legislature. Louisiana politics are still among the most turbulent in the nation and, although the fisticuffs of Long's time are a bygone distraction, corruption continues to occur not too infrequently.

In the end, Huey Long's reign of power resembled a Shakespearean tragedy. He began with aspirations of populist greatness and, according to one critic, "the heights were there for him to climb, but he deliberately turned away, in willful ambitious pride, and sought to build a lower kingdom of his own."[64] Addicted to power, he sadly wasted his enormous talent and the opportunity to be a great democrat. A more foreboding tragedy was that Long not only destroyed many of his enemies, but he came close to destroying republican rule. According to novelist Robert Penn Warren, Long exploited one of the great flaws of democracy, for, ironically, democracy itself allowed an ambitious and remorseless leader like Long to exploit the weaknesses and fears of the people and, ultimately, to employ democratic means to achieve undemocratic ends.[65] Even a Louisiana State University faculty member fell for Long's political legerdemain. "There are many things Long has done that I don't approve of," the professor confided. "But on the whole he has done a great deal of good. And if I had to choose between him without democracy and getting back the old crowd, without the good he has done, I should choose Long. After all, democracy isn't any good if it doesn't work. Do you really think freedom is so important?"[66]

Governing the 1940s

In the 1940s, national emergency and the expanded activism of state and federal governments convinced governors that they had not only a right to become involved in national concerns, but a responsibility. Although Roosevelt's policies had gone far toward relieving the suffering of Americans, many governors were frustrated about the consequences of the New Deal—the erosion of state autonomy with an unprecedented expansion of the federal government. At the 1940 Governors' Conference meeting, Governor Herbert O'Conor of Maryland (1939–1947) announced that he would "like to see the Federal departments withdraw gradually from the field of direct administration, and supply to the States . . . advisory and supervisory service, along with financial participation."[1] O'Conor supported a more activist government overseeing the creation of Maryland's Department of Welfare and a state medical care program during his term as governor but, like many of his colleagues, opposed the federal government dictating policy to states. O'Conor was not alone; many governors reacted to the changing federalism balance by speaking out more forcibly on national issues. As a collective through the Governors' Conference, they issued resolutions directed at the president and Congress in which they sought, among other things, better coordination of state and federal taxes and the return of state employment service authority that the federal government assumed during the war.

America's entry into World War II and the profound effect that participation had on the nation's social and economic infrastructure accelerated the centralization of power in Washington and compounded the dilemma that governors faced with respect to their dependence on—and need to compete with—the federal government. Accordingly, their focus during the 1940s was on two primary, overriding issues: protecting the home front, during both World War II and the ensuing Cold War, and an uneasiness that the national government was slowly usurping state power.

In the early 1940s, war dominated all other issues. Their concerns about the federal government notwithstanding, governors enthusiastically aided the president and Congress with war preparation and mobilization. Although World War II began earlier when Nazi forces invaded Poland in 1939, the war did not become a center point in American lives until the attack on Pearl Harbor on December 7, 1941. To governors, this ambush on American soil drove home the need for individual states to protect their home front. In response, state executives became actively involved in civilian defense, war production, food rationing, price control, and the compulsory draft. Several western governors also dealt with the internment of Japanese Americans in holding camps. While some governors, like Earl Warren of California (1943–1953), supported this practice (a position he later reversed), others, including Ralph Carr of Colorado (1939–1943), became vocal opponents of the policy. Carr fought to help Japanese Americans retain their rights of citizenship and became personally involved with aiding the inmates of the Amache internment camp in Colorado—actions that ultimately ruined his political career.

This was not the first time U.S. governors had prepared for war. Just twenty years earlier, governors had faced a similar situation. Many governors in office during the 1940s had even fought in World War I (to name a few, Herbert O'Conor of Maryland, Dwight Green of Illinois, Roy Turner of Oklahoma, and Joseph Bracken Lee of Utah). But mobilization for World War II was unprecedented in terms of industrial war production. Numerous factories shifted to making airplanes and other implements of war and a new infrastructure of military installations burgeoned across the country. Regardless of their location or political beliefs, governors across the nation became active in ensuring that each state did its part in producing needed materials. They aided in the mobilization of the nation as a whole while also preparing and protecting their states' citizens. Even before Pearl Harbor, forty-six states had already created councils of defense. As part of the July 1941 meeting in Boston, the governors invited Mayor Fiorello LaGuardia of New York City, Roosevelt's director of civilian defense, to answer pressing questions, including whether states needed to issue citizens gas masks and if state guards could provide adequate protection. And throughout the war, governors used their annual meetings to share their home-front concerns and discuss policy implementation. The value of their contributions was reflected in the frequent presence of high-level military officials—generals Dwight D. Eisenhower and George C. Marshall among them—at the gubernatorial gatherings.

In 1945, the war finally ended, first with Germany's surrender and then Japan's surrender following the atomic bombing of Hiroshima and Nagasaki. The new president, Harry Truman, dealt with the aftermath through the Marshall Plan (providing extensive financial aid to Europe) and the Truman Doctrine (declaring the responsibility of the United States to promote freedom and to aid free peoples' rejection of subjugation by oppressive governments). Despite the peace accords, international relations remained tense as America's ally—the Soviet Union—gradually became its enemy. In these postwar years, Americans grew increasingly concerned about communism, an apprehension that helped usher in the Cold War. Many even worried that secretive communist forces from within the United States were working to overthrow the American way of life. This fear heightened when communists successfully took control of China in 1949.

Apart from these fears of communist subversion, governors also faced more local and immediate problems—the needs of returning veterans and a lagging educational system. Different states handled these issues in different ways. For example, South Dakota led by George T. Mickelson (1947–1951) distributed bonuses to veterans, while Thomas E. Dewey of New York (1943–1954) rejected the idea as economically impractical. Numerous veterans, through the 1944 G.I. Bill, entered colleges and other institutions of higher learning, placing new strains on states resources. Several states, including Illinois led by Governor Dwight Green (1941–1949), created programs aimed at training and helping to reemploy returning soldiers.

Governors were concerned as well about the long-term effects of wartime mobilization, particularly with increased urbanization, recent technological advances, and a massive wartime industrial infrastructure that was no longer needed. In the final days of the war in May 1944, California's Earl Warren shared his worries with his colleagues about the need to effectively reconvert wartime plants and find new uses for those built out of wartime necessity. Warren, future chief justice of the Supreme Court, explained, "The problems of reconversion are greatly intensified by the fact that under this war pressure we have developed new techniques, new machines, new materials." These innovations in efficiency "decreasing the manpower requirements per unit of production" meant that fewer workers were needed. Understanding this, Warren feared a return to a depression and widespread unemployment, concluding that "to allow these plants to shut down would be calamitous to the workers, their communities, and the states in which the plants are located."[2] Roy Turner of Oklahoma (1947–1951) had similar worries. Turner, the owner of a large cattle ranch, realized that the increasing "the mechanization of American farms is leading to larger acreages—and a reduction in the number of our small farmers." He predicted that unless small farmers were aided by the government and given the means to compete, governors "must face the problem of absorbing a large portion of our farm population into urban industries—and into additional services."[3] Others, including Governor Green of Illinois, saw the rosier side of technology, imagining a day when "our domestic airlines will experience . . . rapid growth and expansion. . . . With continued progress in aerodynamics and the development of all-weather flying, it is quite probable that the airlines soon will handle most of our transcontinental travel."[4] Governors both welcomed innovation and feared its consequences.

With the war over and facing a brave new world, governors debated both the newly expanded role of the state and state governors and their fears that the balance of federalism had shifted too far in favor of the national government. They focused on the separation of taxes between the federal government and the states, concerned their traditional sources of revenue were being usurped. Many governors, if not most, accepted federal aid as a necessity of post–World War II and New Deal America. Adlai Stevenson of Illinois (1949–1953) argued, "The industrial age has created problems of health, housing, education, transportation, and employment which inexorably flow over state boundaries. . . . I believe there is a way for all of the levels of government to pull together in a harmonious manner. . . . I suggest that we recognize the need for cooperation rather than hostility or capitulation between levels of government."[5] The Illinois governor believed the solution was to make government more efficient, remove duplication, and allow states more control over administration. Others, like J. Bracken Lee of Utah (1949–1957), a man known for his firm opposition to the federal income tax and any internationalization of American interests, feared the day when national interests would prevail. Addressing his colleagues in 1949, Lee warned "about the time when you won't even be Governor of your state—the Governor will be in Washington. . . . I think that a good majority of the Governors would be glad to give up [grants-in-aid] if they could get the taxing power back that the federal government has now."[6]

In this decade of war and peace, fear and hope, governors remained tireless advocates of their states and regional interests. But, increasingly, they claimed a larger stake in national issues as well. The experiences of these years further expanded the parameters of the modern governorship. Larger state governments with increased responsibilities meant that organized, professional administrations were more important than ever before. In the words of Thomas Dewey, three-term governor of New York, "The governors of the states are heard with new force and influence. . . . It stands for a revival of powers close to the people . . . the people want to bring responsibilities and obligations closer to home."[7] To meet this challenge, Dewey styled himself as a new governor for a modern era, valuing efficiency in administration over cronyism and patronage. His success made him popular. His legacy makes him central to the history of twentieth-century governors.

Chapter Three

The Gangbuster as Governor

Thomas E. Dewey and the Republican New Deal

RICHARD NORTON SMITH

New Yorkers like their governors strong, stylish, and, like themselves, a little bigger than life. After all, what is an Empire State without an emperor? It was Alexander Hamilton, that quintessential New Yorker, whose theories celebrating an energetic executive first found expression in *The Federalist Papers*, and then in shaping the American presidency to which so many New York governors have aspired. Ironically, Hamilton and his nation-making brethren may have drawn inspiration from New York's (seeming) governor for life, George Clinton. The son of Irish immigrants, Clinton opposed Hamilton's federal system as arbitrary and aristocratic, yet over time Clinton himself came to embody a state government more powerful than any other spawned by the American Revolution.

To the vast majority of George III's former subjects, centralized power was to be feared as an encroachment on individual liberty. Rotation in office supplied a check on dictators. Consequently, most governors in the new nation were chosen annually, or every other year, by an electorate of state legislators to whom they were expected to show proper deference. In New York, by contrast, the chief magistrate enjoyed the legitimacy of popular election, for a term of three years (a figure that fluctuated in the nineteenth and early twentieth centuries). Moreover, while few states permitted their governor to succeed himself, New York left it to the voters to decide if he served one term or a dozen. George Clinton won election seven times, six of them consecutively.[1]

Though required to share veto and appointive powers with Councils of Appointment and Revision, on both of which he sat, in all other respects Clinton exercised the boldly assertive leadership that would make New York a hothouse of innovation. Here breaking with tradition *was* a tradition, as demonstrated in a parade of visionary undertakings stretching from De Witt Clinton's Erie Canal ("Clinton's Folly") to Nelson Rockefeller's triumphalist South Mall ("Rocky's Stonehenge"). Swelled by immigrant waves from an ossified Europe, polyglot New York became itself a virtual nation, and its governorship an audition stage for the only job in America that made greater demands.

Martin Van Buren was the first of four American presidents who cut their administrative teeth in Albany. None was more colorful or contentious than Theodore Roosevelt. As a callow state assemblyman from a silk stocking district in Manhattan, TR denounced Jay Gould as "the arch thief of Wall Street" and Gould's journalistic mouthpiece, the *New York World*, as "a local stock-jobbing sheet of limited circulation and versatile mendacity." This gift for verbal combat, second only to his genius for self-dramatization, served Roosevelt well during his single term as governor. To the dismay of party regulars, TR made common cause with reformers horrified by filth-soaked tenements in neighborhoods that rivaled the worst slums of Calcutta. Having secured a revised building code, Governor Roosevelt turned the spotlight of publicity on urban sweatshops and civil service abuses. In demanding that street railways and gas, electric light, and telephone franchises pay their fair share of taxes, he helped charter a new course for a party traditionally in thrall to big business.[2]

At heart a pragmatic conservative, an American disciple of Benjamin Disraeli's property-holding One Nation, TR pursued reform in order to forestall revolution. So did his Republican successors in Albany, especially Charles Evans Hughes. A prosecutor of formidable intellect and chilly rectitude—Roosevelt famously labeled him the Bearded Icicle—Hughes initially gained notice for exposing unsavory links between insurance companies and politicians on the take. Elected governor in 1906, Hughes pioneered in consumer protection, establishing public service commissions to set transportation and utility rates. To rebalance the scales of political influence, the governor secured a ban on corporate contributions to parties. The state's first workmen's compensation law was but one of more than fifty labor-related pieces of legislation enacted during his two terms.

As a justice of the U.S. Supreme Court, Hughes evaded the great GOP schism of 1912 that pitted an increasingly radical Theodore Roosevelt against his handpicked White House successor, William Howard Taft. In Owosso, Michigan, ten-year-old Tom Dewey cheered himself hoarse for TR and his Bull Moose insurgency. Millions of nominal Republicans echoed his sentiments, more than enough to consign Taft to a humiliating third-place showing in November behind Woodrow Wilson and Roosevelt. His defeat was not total; in the vacuum created by TR's walkout, conservatives loyal to Taft seized control of the Republican organization.

In New York the Old Guard took orders from utilities, like the formidable Niagara-Hudson (later Niagara-Mohawk) holding company. Backstopping the power interests were downstate grandees, dubbed "the Barons" by author Robert Caro, who flaunted their Wall Street–generated wealth in seaside mansions from Oyster Bay to Montauk Point.

The Republican rupture opened the door for a new generation of Democratic reformers to appeal to the millions who lived in coldwater flats and rarely, if ever, heard the sound of waves slapping against a shore. Their plight was brutally dramatized on a horrific Saturday afternoon in March 1911, when 146 employees of the Triangle Shirtwaist Company, most of them teenage girls, were incinerated or driven to leap ten stories to their deaths after a tossed cigarette ignited cloth fragments and other litter in their high-rise sweatshop. Locked doors led to indescribable scenes of horror—and irrefutable demands for action.

As Democratic leader in the State Assembly, Al Smith raised the standard of living of working-class and immigrant New Yorkers. As a four-term governor, first elected in 1918, Smith made good on his promises by coupling a ferocious commitment to social justice with an equal passion for managerial efficiency. As noted by Joel Schwartz in *The Empire State: A History of New York*, Smith doubled the size and scope of state government, which he paid for through New York's first personal income and inheritance taxes. Overhauling a woefully haphazard administrative structure, the governor consolidated 187 agencies into eighteen departments, established an executive budget, and laid the groundwork for a four-year gubernatorial term.[3]

But Smith also created a State Board of Housing; modernized an archaic prison system, dramatically increased state aid to education, and insisted on paying women teachers the same as their male counterparts. Employing the new medium of radio to go over the heads of recalcitrant legislators, a raspy-voiced Smith insisted that hydroelectricity generated by the St. Lawrence and other rivers belonged to the people. A roused electorate voted nearly half a billion dollars in bonding authority with which to build hospitals, eliminate dangerous railroad crossings, and add hundreds of thousands of acres in new state parks and forests.

When his quarrelsome parks commissioner, Robert Moses, picked a fight with the Barons who opposed his plans to open Long Island to urban motorists and beachcombers, Governor Smith agreed to meet with the outraged men of property. Moreover, he was careful not to tip his hat; not, at least, until Horace Havermeyer, the so-called Sultan of Sugar, decried any project attracting "rabble from the city." Smith's face froze in disbelief. "Rabble?" he said to Havermeyer. "That's *me* you're talking about." Then and there Smith signed the paperwork authorizing a park in the Sultan's backyard.[4]

His gubernatorial successors, Franklin Roosevelt and Herbert Lehman, expanded the role of state government in aiding victims of economic storms. Though Republicans in the state legislature balked at FDR's request for social insurance against the vicissitudes of old age, they reluctantly agreed to limit the work week for women and children, and to establish a State Power Authority. When, less than a year into his term, Wall Street collapsed, sending shockwaves throughout the nation's economy, Roosevelt responded with the try-anything-once pragmatism that would characterize his presidency. He opened National Guard armories to the homeless, and set up the Temporary Emergency Relief Administration to make Albany the employer of last resort for 160,000 jobless New Yorkers. His willingness to provide direct assistance contrasted sharply with the refusal of the Hoover administration to countenance relief payments lest individual and national character be eroded by the dole.

After Roosevelt crushed Hoover in the 1932 presidential race, his place in Albany was taken by Lieutenant Governor Herbert Lehman. The state's first Jewish governor, scion of a great New York City banking family, Lehman's transparent integrity outweighed his less-than-riveting campaign style. Putting the state squarely on the side of organized labor against a discredited business community, Lehman and his party rode the wave of New Deal sentiment in 1934 to obtain, for the first time in a generation, majorities in both houses of the state legislature. This opened the floodgates to a torrent of social welfare and depression-fighting initiatives. Lehman gained approval for a minimum wage law, old age pensions, and a greatly expanded public housing program. Using a mix of state and federal funds, his administration leveled slums, laid down the Taconic Parkway, and constructed hundreds of bridges, sewer lines, and other infrastructure projects. A single New Deal agency, the Works Progress Administration (WPA), employed 17 percent of all New Yorkers on the state relief rolls. In New York City alone, the WPA undertook 1,700 projects.[5]

Having swung so far to the left, it was only a matter of time before the pendulum reversed course. By 1938 an economic recession had dulled the luster of FDR's once dazzling command. Overreaching attempts to remake the U.S. Supreme Court, and to expel dissenting lawmakers from his own party, demonstrated the limits of Roosevelt's usually faultless political judgment. Even in New York the New Deal was showing its age. After six years in office, Lehman hoped to hand off the baton to a Democratic successor. Yet no one else, it appeared, could prevent a

Republican comeback that fall, or the loss of the governorship to the unlikeliest of popular heroes.

As a newly minted graduate of Columbia Law School in the 1920s, Tom Dewey was once asked what he wanted out of life. "To start a great law firm," he answered, "and make a helluva lot of money." Both objectives would be realized, but only after a quarter-century detour through the treacherous terrain of state government and national politics. Born in 1902, Dewey had migrated to New York from small-town Michigan during the adventuresome years after World War I, when Manhattan was the acme of sophistication, cultural experimentation, and political sin (the latter attributable to Tammany Hall and its venal Beau Brummel of a mayor, James J. Walker). The newcomer originally hoped to excel, not in the courtroom but on the opera stage. A sore-throated recital changed his mind. Concluding, with typically unsparing logic, that a musical career would put him at the mercy of forces (like germs) beyond even his control, Dewey refocused his attention on the law.[6]

The baritone-turned-barrister was fired from his first New York law firm for defying the ancient adage that first-year lawyers, like children, were supposed to be seen and not heard. His next employers were more impressed by Dewey's exhaustive approach to library research. As a protégé of George Medalie, the U.S. attorney for the Southern District of New York, Dewey displayed an aggressiveness that was to be his hallmark. For him there was no such thing as overpreparation. To convict bootlegger Waxey Gordon, for example, Dewey and his staff sifted more than 200,000 bank deposit slips. For thirty-three months U.S. Treasury agents and lawyers worked two shifts a day seeking evidentiary needles in an apparently bottomless paper haystack.

But that was only the beginning. Perusing what had been gathered, Dewey stared off into space, lips pursed in a quizzical smile. Then, like a wild animal anticipating his dinner, he would pounce, and, according to one Treasury agent, methodically tear a briefcase full of evidence to shreds "with about a million questions, give or take ten." Piling certainty upon proof, the assistant U.S. attorney continued the process even after a defendant signaled a willingness to plead guilty. "We want to be ready if he changes his mind," he told exasperated gumshoes.[7]

Detractors attributed Dewey's bulldog manner to a swaggering sense of infallibility. This underestimated his shyness and sensitivity over his boyish appearance, which he offset by dressing in chesterfields and sober homburgs. Late in life, in a rare moment of introspection, he acknowledged, "Everything came too early for me." Dewey was all of thirty-three when a runaway grand jury, disgusted by the alliance between Tammany Hall and mobster Dutch Schultz, insisted that Governor Lehman name him special prosecutor to clean up racketeering and its criminal surtax on everything from artichokes to funeral parlors. This practice added as much as 20 percent to the cost of living for New Yorkers already struggling to make ends meet in the shriveled economy of the 1930s.[8]

A true meritocrat, as governor, Dewey was fond of saying that no one should be in public life who couldn't earn more on a private payroll. As New York's putative gangbuster, he sought similarly dedicated young lawyers willing to work around the clock for salaries ranging from $1,500 to $4,000 a year. Ultimately, nineteen men and one woman met his exacting standards. Ranging in age from twenty-five to forty, seven were Phi Beta Kappas, a third products of Harvard Law School. A disproportionate number were Jewish, at a time when most old-line law firms stuck to their Protestant rosters. Over the next two years the Dewey team brought seventy-three racketeering cases, and won seventy-two convictions. His fearless prosecution of underworld kingpins like Dutch Schultz and Lucky Luciano made Dewey a media phenomenon—and potential president—while he was still in his mid-thirties.

In November 1937, he overcame a four-to-one Democratic advantage in voter registration to become Manhattan district attorney. Soon Hollywood was cranking out a movie a week inspired by his crime-fighting exploits. *Mr. District Attorney* drew millions of radio listeners. Women in Harlem warned recalcitrant children to be good or Mr. Dewey would get them—just as he had nabbed racketeers and loan sharks. One young girl argued with her father over suing the Almighty following a long spell of rain. You can't sue God and win, she was told. "I can if Dewey is my lawyer," she replied.[9]

For all his success, Dewey remained a most unconventional politician, a latter-day Charles Evans Hughes, recalled by one campaign staffer as "cold—cold as a February icicle." His was the charisma of competence, abetted by a basso profundo radio presence and the celebrity stemming from being at the center of Manhattan's longest running melodrama. Acutely self-conscious about his height ("Someday I'm going to catch the guy who said I wore elevator shoes in a dark alley," he vowed), Dewey refused to don silly hats or kiss babies for photographers. A prominent gap in his front teeth went unfixed because Frances Dewey liked her husband's appearance as it was.[10]

The same held true for the trademark mustache adorning Dewey's upper lip. Admirers professed comparisons to Clark Gable; critics were reminded of Charlie Chaplin or, worse, Hitler. Likened to a swear word in an otherwise unexpressive sentence, the mustache complimented a pair of luminous, unrelenting eyes that bored through politicians as they had once unnerved defense witnesses. "The only piercing brown eyes

I've ever seen," huffed one courtroom opponent. A former staffer in the District Attorney's office put it differently: "Those eyes tell you this guy doesn't crap around."[11]

Indeed. Within months of being elected District Attorney, Dewey was glancing covetously at the fortress-like state capitol in Albany, in the 1930s no less than in Teddy Roosevelt's day an incubator of presidents. It was no accident that in his first run for governor, he should hearken back to "the great progressive days of Theodore Roosevelt and Charles Evans Hughes." Adapt or perish: that was his message to New York Republicans, shut out of the executive mansion for sixteen years. "It is the job of a majority party," Dewey told cheering GOP delegates in Saratoga Springs in September 1938, "to build, not to tear down, to go forward, not to obstruct. It is not the function of a political party to die fighting for obsolete slogans." In this Dewey merely recognized the political revolution launched by Al Smith and carried to full flower nationally by FDR.[12]

In his fall campaign against Lehman, goaded into running by his rival's harsh attacks on mere bookkeepers and political racketeers, Dewey put his prosecutorial reputation to work for him. Like Ronald Reagan thirty years later, the District Attorney used real-life stories to personalize the abstract failings of government. Ineptitude among those charged with administering unemployment insurance, for example, became a matter of urgency when seen through the eyes of an upstate woman forced to wait nine months after losing her machinist's job, only to learn that her benefits claim, too, had been lost. One evening, exercising his flair for radio dramatics, Dewey invited listeners to join him in visiting a tiny fourth-floor walk-up in Harlem, and meeting the unfortunate couple who paid twenty-five dollars a month "for the privilege of breathing their neighbor's cooking instead of fresh air."[13]

By taking the fight to Lehman, Dewey attracted national attention. By slashing to 64,000 the heavily favored incumbent's 1936 victory margin of 700,000, the gangbuster established himself as a serious presidential prospect for 1940. Convulsed by Hitler's European blitzkrieg, Republicans turned instead to a charismatic former utilities lawyer named Wendell Willkie. Dewey at thirty-eight could afford to bide his time. Two years later he barely broke a sweat in winning the governorship on his second try. Decrying "the deep ruts of comfortable routine," Dewey promised to rid Albany of its cobwebs and corruption. In Harlem he endorsed legislative reapportionment—a position that won him no friends among upstate Republicans—because the state senate was without a black face, "and we propose to get one." With help from a revitalized GOP organization, led by a transplanted Nebraskan named Herbert

Brownell, he rolled to a 647,000-vote landslide over the state's colorless attorney general John J. Bennett.[14]

November 3, 1942, was a meatless Tuesday. Vying for attention with the midterm elections was the latest war news from North Africa, where Bernard Montgomery was thrashing the once invincible Afrika Corps of Erwin Rommel at El Alamein. That night jubilant Republicans assembled at Manhattan's Hotel Roosevelt (named for Theodore, not Franklin) to celebrate the end of their twenty-year exile from power. In between lusty renditions of "We'll Heil! Heil! Right in der Fuhrer's Face," the happy crowd chanted "Dewey for president."

True to its breast-beating motto—"Excelsior"—New York State in 1943 lapped the field, its 13 million residents constituting one-tenth of the nation's population, and generating considerably more of its economic and cultural activity. The nexus of American finance, manufacturing, communications, fashion, and entertainment, New York City harbored more Italians than Rome, more Irish than Dublin, and more Jews than anywhere else on the planet. The challenges of governing so diverse a realm ensured that a national audience would be watching. In that sense, little had changed since the Civil War. Of the twenty-one elections between 1868 and 1948, only one—the McKinley-Bryan slugfest of 1896—was without a New Yorker on either the Republican or Democratic ticket. Fourteen times during the eventful period, America's coming of age, a current or former governor of New York led his party's campaign for the White House. In 1944, uniquely, in the race between Roosevelt and Dewey, the electorate faced a choice between two residents of the state's Dutchess County.

For all that, the prospect of inhabiting 1600 Pennsylvania Avenue scarcely compensated for life in Albany's tomblike executive mansion. To Theodore Roosevelt the turreted brick residence was "painfully suggestive of that kind of elegance which one sees in a swell Chicago hotel or in the boardroom of some big railway." Tom Dewey agreed, describing the oxblood red hallways that greeted his young family at the start of 1943 as an invitation to suicide. Pugnaciously blue collar, Dewey deadpanned to a friend that their new home was "not the sprightliest of cities." For Frances Dewey the transition from cosmopolitan New York was harder still. One winter afternoon, gazing out a window at a frozen tableau of swirling flakes, the first lady of New York murmured, "How I love it here when it snows." Asked why, she replied sweetly, "Because it covers up Albany."[15]

Aesthetic shortcomings notwithstanding, for a dozen years starting in 1943 the capital of New York was a hub of political and intellectual ferment as Dewey set out to prove "that government can have both a head and a heart, that it can be both progressive and solvent, that it can serve people without becoming their master." He wasted no time in modernizing the rococo governor's office or injecting fresh blood into a creaking bureaucracy. Form 76–1 was abolished as soon as Dewey learned that it took twenty-nine state employees to order seventy cents' worth of glue. Also eliminated, despite howls of protest from dairy farmers, was the Milk Publicity Board, a $300,000-a-year nest of patronage jobs. His most pressing task, said Lehman's successor, "is to get $50,000-a-year men to take $12,000-a-year salaries."[16]

By most accounts he succeeded admirably. Tipped off to scandalous Dickensian conditions at Creedmoor, a mental health facility in Queens, Dewey sacked the state's commissioner of mental hygiene. He replaced him with Dr. Frederick McCurdy, director of the Vanderbilt Clinic and professor of hospital administration at Columbia University. Henceforth the warehousing of patients yielded to curative treatment.

Dewey took eight months and rejected a corporal's guard of contenders, before settling on a commissioner of conservation. To oversee public works, the governor tracked his preferred candidate to Iran, before nabbing him at a Miami airport en route to South America. Assured that politics would be kept out of the job, Charles Sells finally said yes. Pleasantly surprised, Dewey couldn't help asking what had changed Sells's mind. "You did," said the distinguished engineer. "You finally convinced me that this job is more important than yours."[17]

Not everyone appreciated his methods. Around Albany, it was said, one needed a Dun and Bradstreet rating to get a job in the Dewey administration. This was only a slight exaggeration. Fond of quoting Jefferson's admonition that "the whole art of government consists of being honest," the governor decreed that no state job paying $2,500 a year or more could be filled until its leading applicant was fully vetted by the state police. He had no intention of being sandbagged by Republican operatives ravenous for patronage after twenty years of table scraps. Yet even as Dewey protected the professional politicians from themselves, he was party building in the broadest sense. Through his appointments, his successful economic management, and his sometimes ruthless approach to framing the policy debate, Dewey was able to capitalize the New York GOP for a generation of dominance.

At the same time, he was nothing if not realistic. Although his cabinet boasted non-political professionals, more traditional standards sufficed in bolstering the Republican organization where it was weak or nonexistent. At its apex, just below the governor, stood the "Buffalo Mahatma," state party chairman Edwin F. Jaeckle. Having converted his native city from a Democratic to a Republican citadel, Jaeckle forged a sometimes uneasy partnership with the governor whose offer to make him secretary of state Jaeckle instantly rejected. "I want to be a leader of the party and co-operate with you," he told Dewey, "but I don't want to have any commitments. . . . You and I are going to have a lot of conferences and talks. . . . If I'm not on your payroll you're going to give more consideration to what I've got to say."[18]

Less independent was J. Russell Sprague, who held sway over fast-growing Nassau County. A newly created state judicial district provided Sprague with a pair of supreme court judgeships and $100,000 worth of patronage jobs to dangle before the faithful. In lieu of Jaeckle, Manhattan Republican leader Tom Curran became secretary of state; his deputies included party leaders from Wyoming and Montgomery Counties. The victory-starved Albany machinery was liberally greased, with state jobs for its chairman, vice chairman, secretary, and ward leaders. For commissioner of motor vehicles, Dewey turned to the GOP boss of Utica County. As the state party waxed in strength and cohesion, little escaped the governor's notice. The inventor of the $100-a-plate dinner, Dewey selected each year's speaker, and did not hesitate to punish those out of favor by seating them behind a dining room pillar.

In his second floor capitol office the governor sat behind a desk as orderly as his mind, its surface unbroken save for a brown Morocco folder, a thermos jug of cold water, miniatures of an elephant or two, and four pencils, each sharpened to precisely the same length. Callers were whisked through the office at fifteen-minute intervals, with a simple lunch taken at the desk Dewey himself designed with four sliding shelves, the better to facilitate informal skull sessions. On being confronted with a new idea, he habitually put two favorite questions before advisers: "Is it right?" he demanded. "Will it work?" Coming from anyone else, these might have been spineless platitudes. What gave them weight was Dewey's willingness to scrape by on his $25,000-a-year salary, foregoing the wealth that could have been his in private law practice— that, and his adamant belief that good government was good politics. The governor never forgot how the birth of his second son had driven him to the brink of bankruptcy. Thus, he called to "humanize" the tax code by increasing medical deductions.

Dispensing with an inaugural parade or ball as a nod to wartime austerity, Dewey spent his first term grappling with questions of military production and civilian privation. By 1943 Dr. New Deal had long since been retired in favor of Dr. Win the War. Unfortunately Roosevelt's Washington too often indulged a taste for improvised chaos, duplication of effort, and bureaucratic dictation. The War Production Board, for instance, had seen fit to allocate exactly one manure spreader to the 2,100 farms of Albany County. Dewey resolved to do better. He established the Emergency Food Council, chaired by the dean of Cornell's

School of Agriculture. Each member was assigned a different facet of the problem—such as labor, transportation, and machinery—and authorized to act for the state of New York. One scout found 10,000 tons of oyster shells in Norfolk, Virginia, to be ground up and fed to hens to protect against too-soft shelled eggs. The state bought 26 million bushels of Canadian barley, and then taught chickens to eat the unfamiliar feed. More than a thousand sawmills were canvassed; those not manufacturing ammunition containers were asked to make apple boxes instead.

Before 1943 ended, 111,000 volunteers responded to their governor's appeal for help in harvesting crops. State workers agreed to work longer hours, in return for which Dewey raised the wages of the lowest paid among them by one-third. New York boasted the nation's best record of time lost to strikes, in part because its governor established a State School of Labor and Industrial Relations at Cornell, and added 400,000 workers to the ranks of those covered by minimum wage laws. A Department of Commerce was unveiled to boost New York's share of war contracts from twenty-eighth to second place among the states. New York became the first state to open its own office in Washington to lobby aggressively for federal largesse and guide entrepreneurs through a maze of wartime regulations. So far advanced was its postwar planning that New York after V-J Day managed to convert all but ten of 113 federally built war plants to peacetime uses.

Planning for the future was a Dewey fetish. To refute conservatives who accused him of aping the New Deal in a hopeless bidding war and liberals who dismissed his "Modern Republicanism" as the insincerest form of flattery, Dewey could point to his Postwar Reconstruction Fund. During his first six years in office, aided by wartime restraints on new construction, he amassed $623 million in black ink, while simultaneously reducing income tax rates by 50 percent and business taxes by half as much. Resisting legislative demands to raid the cookie jar—the state Democratic chairman called the surplus "unnatural"—the governor framed the fund in humanistic terms. Far from "mere bookkeeping entries" in an official ledger, "It is the problem of feeble-minded children sleeping on mattresses spread on the floors of dayrooms; of blind children going to school in fire traps; of prisons where the inmates sleep with bars between them and a bathroom; of highways that take a weekly toll of sudden death."[19]

In the end, the Postwar Reconstruction Fund made possible 14,000 new beds in the state's mental health system, along with public housing for 30,000 families, reforestation of 34 million trees, and a model veterans program. What it *wouldn't* fund was a $360 bonus for returning veterans. "I hate debt," snapped the governor, who took his economic theories straight from Adam Smith. On moving to Albany he had discov-

ered, to his horror, that residents of the Bronx would be paying for a
long-disused plank road called Central Avenue until the year 2147.
Thereafter it seemed as if everything went up in his state budget, except
the amount allocated to debt service. A generation that wanted benefits
must be willing to pay for them. This meant legislative and voter
approval of short-term bonds to underwrite the bonus. Anything else
savored of "the pickpocket scheme of government."[20]

Observers couldn't decide whether Lehman's successor was a conservative innovator or a pay-as-you-go liberal. Alerted by his experts that a
state health insurance program would cost $400 million a year, Dewey
blanched. Then he proposed a $14 million public health campaign,
including a crusade to wipe out tuberculosis by 1966. In much the same
way he endorsed the idea of a state university with a minimum of state
control, cobbling together existing schools, institutes, junior colleges—
even three converted military bases—and building a network of new,
two-year community colleges. The state would split construction costs
with host localities. Modest though it might be, the plan provoked fierce
opposition from private educators. What ultimately convinced Dewey to
go forward was a ten-page memo by assistant gubernatorial counsel
George Shapiro, documenting the rank discrimination visited on blacks
and Jews, particularly in private medical and dental schools.

A generation later it would fall to the free-spending Nelson Rockefeller to convert Dewey's decentralized system into the world's largest institution of higher learning. "I like you, Nelson," Dewey wryly informed
his successor. "I just don't know whether I can afford you."[21]

Dewey's notion of meritocratic teamwork, equaled only by his disdain
for the "crawling locusts of special interests," left scant room for the
shabby peerage that was the New York legislature. The governor made
lawmakers reform their comfortable ways of payroll padding by requiring legislative workers to justify in writing at regular intervals what they
had done to earn their salaries. Rural members of his party shook their
fists when Dewey imposed a reapportionment plan friendlier to Queens
apartment dwellers and the bedroom communities of Long Island than
to underpopulated, overrepresented GOP bastions upstate. Here, too,
he innovated to reduce risks, make change his ally, and stake out the
political center.

Every Sunday evening during the legislative session, the governor and
his closest advisers met Republican leaders over dinner and drinks at the
executive mansion. Afterward the group adjourned to the study, where
Dewey lit a cigarette and unfurled a pile of three-by-five-inch cards on
which he had taken notes throughout the previous week.

"Well," he began, "what do you want to talk about tonight?"[22]

The discussions thus commenced were freewheeling. Nothing emerged from these war councils unless agreed to unanimously, and nothing so endorsed failed to be enacted by the legislature, where an omnipotent rules committee (its presiding officer doubled as assembly speaker) routinely bottled up draft bills objectionable to Dewey or his agents. Feeling his oats, the governor invented the "pre-veto"; another child of the Sunday evening bull sessions, this enabled Dewey to side-track, without so much as a public hearing, proposals not to his liking.

In March 1944 Dewey moved to strip control of New York City schools from the teachers lobby that dominated the city's board of supervisors—and which he privately likened to Hitler's storm troopers—to a single professional superintendent. Education lobbyists shrieked dictatorship. Few who knew Albany were willing to bet against them. The governor was another matter. On the eve of the vote Dewey summoned lawmakers to his office for some gentle persuasion. County and local organization leaders took a more direct line, threatening rebels with the loss of jobs, their own included.

Confronted with so unpalatable a choice, the people's representatives figured they could always resort to the ancient, if not altogether honor-able, practice of absenting themselves from the capitol when the roll was called. They hadn't reckoned with their governor's resourcefulness. First assembly speaker Ozzie Heck ordered the sergeant at arms to round up missing legislators. Then he had the Assembly doors closed and the vote taken. One Buffalo member was discovered cowering beneath his desk. Wrenched to his feet, holding two fingers over his nose, he emitted a high-pitched "aye." In the aftermath of his 77-to-61 victory, Dewey could be overhead referring to "my legislature."

Some assemblymen quit in protest. Others were denied renomination by the governor's formidable machine. The leftish New York daily *P.M.* lambasted "the Little Brain at Albany." Voters, in contrast, were in no mood to complain about an executive so suspicious of malfeasance that he rejected anonymous campaign contributions and insisted on investi-gating the motives of large contributors unknown to him personally. "There's only one thing wrong with that fellow in there," said Al Smith after visiting Dewey in his newly streamlined capitol office. "He's a Republican."[23]

Fresh off his defeat at Roosevelt's hands in the 1944 presidential con-test, Dewey tacked to the left. He called for state development of the international rapids of the St. Lawrence River, and a rent control pro-gram that became steadily more stringent as real estate interests over-played their hand. Dwarfing both proposals in significance was the Ives-Quinn Bill, making racial or religious discrimination in the workplace a misdemeanor subject to a $500 fine or a jail term of up to a year. Dewey's failure to embrace an earlier antidiscrimination package, introduced in the closing days of the 1944 legislative session and faulted by the governor's legal counsel for shoddy draftsmanship, had drawn criticism from Dr. Alvin Johnson, president of the New School for Social Research.

It was Johnson who had chaired the commission that wrote the original bill. When the governor appointed his own advisory group to take up the issue, Johnson reluctantly agreed to stay on. In time he came to admire Dewey as "a liberal without blinkers." It didn't hurt that the governor appointed Bertha J. Diggs, a black woman from Buffalo, to be his secretary of labor. Among traditionalists, meanwhile, the Ives-Quinn Bill touched off a hurricane of protest. The state Chamber of Commerce predicted race riots. Robert Moses inveighed against officially mandated "quotas." If Dewey prevailed, Jewish families would be compelled to hire Nazi butlers, it was claimed, and theater producers forced to cast a black actress in the title role of *Gentlemen Prefer Blondes.* On the final roll call, the bill passed, but thirty-two upstate Republican assemblymen stood against the bill hailed by Congressman Adam Clayton Powell as the biggest advance for black Americans since the Fourteenth and Fifteenth Amendments.

With a minimum of dramatics, a five-member commission established conciliation councils in the state's larger cities, struck discriminatory clauses from job application forms and want ads, and investigated nearly five hundred complaints during its first year alone. "Colored only" sections disappeared from passenger trains. New York Telephone hired its first black switchboard operators. Within two years the number of black women employed in clerical and sales jobs quadrupled.[24]

Before leaving office Dewey saw to the outlawing of discrimination in education, public assistance housing, and accommodations. Justifiably proud of this record, in addressing a black Baptist convention in the fall of 1945, Dewey blasted the Daughters of the American Revolution for banning a young African American singer, Marian Anderson, from the stage of Constitution Hall in Washington. After complimenting the soulful choir he'd just heard perform, he said he wished he could take it on national tour, especially to DAR halls. "A great many people might discover that the American Revolution was fought for the democratic principle that all men are created equal."[25]

Reelected by a near-record margin in 1946, in more conventional times his record of political and administrative success would have earned Dewey the White House. For years students of the 1948 campaign have blamed his "don't rock the boat" strategy on overconfidence, the natural stance of one lampooned by partisans loyal to Ohio senator Robert Taft as "that snooty little governor of New York." The truth is more complicated. America in the late 1940s was a New Deal nation, enjoying record prosperity, less terrified of the Russians than of a return to the desperate hardship of the previous decade. Harry Truman's campaign-timed call for a special session of the Eightieth Congress made Republicans on Capitol Hill the issue in that fall's contest; their contemptuous dismissal of the White House agenda only reinforced voter doubts about the GOP's acceptance of the Rooseveltian welfare state.

An unhelpful Congress wasn't the only thing weighing on Dewey's mind. For the last month of the campaign the governor's antennae had picked up slippage, his gut feeling confirmed by films of lethargic whistle-stop crowds that he viewed prior to his final swing around the circle. With less than ten days to go until election day, Dewey's *Victory Special* witnessed a heated discussion, with the candidate giving vigorous expression to his desire to take off the gloves. Rhetorically it had hardly been a fair fight. Truman, desperate to galvanize his Democratic base, assailed Republicans as "bloodsuckers with offices on Wall Street," and mortal enemies of agriculture, guilty of "sticking a pitchfork in every farmer's back." In the home stretch the president ratcheted up the name calling, at one point likening Dewey himself to a fascist tool.[26]

Fed up with such tactics, Dewey produced a speech text that would, at last, give Truman a taste of his own medicine. Then he made a fatal misjudgment, directing his staff to poll the entire Republican national committee. Almost to a man, the professional politicians told him to stay on the high road. So did Frances Dewey. Reminding him of a prosecutorial rant delivered four years earlier in Oklahoma City ("the worst speech I ever made," the candidate himself conceded), Mrs. Dewey threatened to stay up all night if that is what it took to avoid a repetition. Rationalizing that he couldn't go against his entire party, Dewey at length yielded.[27]

Only after his unexpected defeat did he betray resentment. Vacationing at a western dude ranch, he squatted down to toss pennies with his teenage sons. Frances, ever conscious of her husband's dignity, urged him to get up. What if some photographer were to take his picture in so unflattering a stance? "Maybe if I had done this during the campaign," said Dewey, "I would have won."[28]

An elder statesman at forty-six, Dewey returned to Albany to find legislative conservatives in open revolt. At issue was a proposed sickness and disability program grafted onto existing unemployment insurance. Dewey insisted that the scheme, costing a mere thirty cents a week and jointly funded by contributions from workers as well as employers, would go far in warding off "the evils of socialized medicine." He got his way, but not before he was forced to accept steep budget cuts and repeal of a proposed gasoline tax increase. Never had the prospect of life after Albany looked so enticing.[29]

In the spring of 1950, the governor traveled to Princeton University for a series of lectures in which he publicly ruminated over the challenge he had privately addressed to Winston Churchill. "Somehow the conservative forces must relearn how to establish close relationships among all the classes of people," Dewey wrote the involuntarily retired prime minister, before mentioning his own "very limited success" in New York. Republicans, he told his Princeton audience, could never become the nation's governing party on a platform of "back-to-Methuselah." Then he posed a series of questions to distinguish genuine liberalism from the counterfeit variety advocated by "modern collectivists" who promised the lotus without toil.[30]

Did welfare measures build up individual independence and responsibility, he asked, or did they foster subservience? Did federal intervention widen or narrow the bounds of personal liberty? Did government attempt what a free people can and ought to do for themselves?

"I don't know what I'm still doing here," Dewey told a friend a few weeks after his sweeping reelection in November 1950. Although bloodied in internal party skirmishes, and embarrassed by the involvement of Russ Sprague and other Republicans in a racetrack scandal, much of Dewey's legacy would be cemented in his third and most difficult term. Some of it quite literally—thanks to the New York State Thruway, a high-speed, four-lane highway, without stop signs or traffic lights, that cut nine hours off the driving time between New York City and Buffalo, 486 miles away. Desiring hospital beds over roadbeds, the governor's opponents spoke scornfully of "Dewey's Folly." Its builder preferred to concentrate instead on the vast areas of the Empire State opened to economic development by his "Erie Canal for the Atomic Age."[31]

Paradoxically, Dewey's greatest victory came in a presidential campaign he influenced from the wings. Dwight Eisenhower's 1952 nomination was largely the work of New York's governor and his political circle. At a tumultuous Chicago convention, Dewey was characteristically forceful in stamping out signs of rebellion among his ninety-six-member delegation. In a tense caucus he invited each member of the group to rise and identify himself, before revealing the precise number of state jobs under his control. The parade concluded, Dewey regained the floor. Calmly he announced that any delegate who failed to vote his way on a rules amendment crucial to Eisenhower's cause could expect to find himself empty-handed. In the event, ninety-two New Yorkers lined up behind their governor; four supported Taft.

Among the Dewey men who helped staff the Eisenhower White House were press secretary Jim Hagerty, attorney general Herbert Brownell, secretary of the Air Force Harold Talbott, and appointments secretary Tom Stephens. John Foster Dulles, Dewey's Henry Kissinger, helped define the decade as Eisenhower's secretary of state. Ike tapped engineer Bertram Tollamy, chief builder of the New York Thruway, to oversee construction of the Interstate Highway System. And it was on Dewey's recommendation that the White House, early in 1954, enlisted Boston attorney Joseph Welch to defend the Army against Wisconsin senator Joseph McCarthy in nationally televised hearings. As for McCarthy's counsel Roy Cohn, Dewey pronounced him "the most unscrupulous man I ever met."[32]

That fall Dewey watched as his chosen successor, Senator Irving Ives, lost the governorship to W. Averell Harriman in the closest race in New York history. At last free to return to his first love, the law, Dewey wasted little time in reminiscing about the past, parts of which remained sensitive nonetheless. The senior partner skipped the firm's raucous Christmas party after the year his arrival prompted the band to play "Hail to the Chief." When he died on March 16, 1971, press accounts dwelled on the Man Who Might Have Been. Instant analysts, unaware of his invitation to a White House party that evening celebrating the engagement of Tricia Nixon, overlooked Dewey's final legatee, Richard Nixon, whom he had successfully promoted as Ike's running mate in 1952, and with whom he had maintained close relations ever since.

Nearly forty years later, Dewey's accomplishments loom larger than his disappointments. To be sure, he never became president. But he helped revitalize federalism, emphasizing state responsibilities over state's rights. He transformed the face of New York, making it a laboratory in which social activism and fiscal restraint complemented each other. The original compassionate conservative, in two presidential campaigns Dewey convinced his party to discard its isolationist foreign policy and to promote as much economic security as it held consistent with individual freedom. His gubernatorial heirs include such creative administrators as John Engler, Tommy Thompson, Pete Wilson, and Tom Ridge, not to mention another celebrity-turned-officeholder, similarly uncomfortable with ideological labels, Arnold Schwarzenegger.

Forget what might have been; the reality of Tom Dewey was impressive enough.

Governing the 1950s

In the 1950s, governors and the nation as a whole found themselves in a changed world. The United States was now a leading world power and the Cold War was heating up, forcing Americans and their leaders to rethink their own government and institutions. In reaction to this international uncertainty and a new war in Korea, many Americans in the 1950s sought a life of domestic tranquility and cultural unity. Increased population mobility from south to north and east to west had begun to meld regional cultures, creating, among other things, a musical genre called rock-and-roll that appealed to a new generation of young people. At the same time, Americans attempted to re-center their lives locally with a return to so-called traditional family values. They found comfort in the seeming domestic bliss of a quaint new home in the suburbs stocked with modern consumer goods and complete with a shiny new television. Middle-class whites fled en mass to these suburbs created in part through the illegal practice of "red-lining" (not lending to minority homebuyers) in such areas. But the ideal embodied in the television character of June Cleaver was beyond the reach of many Americans, including many minorities abandoned in increasingly economically depressed inner cities. Still others were unwilling to conform to the conservative expectations of the 1950s and joined the beatnik subculture. Nonetheless, despite those unwilling or unable to conform, the dream of domesticity was tangible and its implications, particularly guilt from not obtaining the ideal, shaped a generation of Americans. This strong desire to re-isolate, however, could not shut out the global or even domestic problems facing America, not for citizens or their elected leaders. Despite a cultivated image of a return to tranquility, a number of serious concerns lay beneath the surface.

A new era of nationalism and globalization had dawned, forcing modern governors to rethink their responsibilities. By mid-century, mass consumerism, advanced technology in communications, and an altered federal system required state governors to take a more national perspective. With the threat of the Cold War and widespread fears that enemies would attack American soil with atomic weapons, governors found it necessary to start voicing their opinions on international issues as well. The Governors' Conference, now an established organization nearing its fiftieth anniversary, aided state executives in this transition. Global concerns became frequent topics of conversation at annual meetings. In response, members of the association's executive committee toured the Soviet Union in 1959 to report their observations to their colleagues at the meeting held that year in San Juan, Puerto Rico.

Like many Americans, governors worried whether the United States lagged behind other world powers. Speaking at the 1959 meeting, Cecil Underwood of West Virginia (1957–1961, 1997–2001), a member of the gubernatorial delegation to the Soviet Union, reflected, "Many people in this country have supposed, since the advent of Sputnik I, that we should junk our educational system and trade it in for something like the Soviets'." Underwood, who had a long career in politics with a second term as governor forty years after his first term, rejected this view. "I do not accept this thesis," he insisted, "Our responsibility is not to destroy our own system, but to improve it whenever we can." He believed it was governors' responsibility to better education consistent with "our American free way."[1] G. Mennen Williams (1949–1961), who improved teachers' salaries and school facilities in Michigan, argued, "[with] 6 per cent of the world's population and 7 per cent of its resources . . . [Americans] have managed to amass 50 per cent of the material wealth of all the world." This prosperity, Williams argued, was a result of the country's great educational system founded on the belief "from our founding fathers on down that education was not something which was reserved for the elite, but which was something for all of our people."[2] Education, these governors believed, was the key to America staying competitive globally. Many of these leaders, like Edmund Muskie of Maine (1955–1959), increased funding to public schools during their tenures as governors.

Along with concerns of foreign competition and education, governors faced widespread domestic unrest bubbling beneath the 1950s seeming tranquility. Across the nation, the Communist witch-hunt led by Senator Joseph McCarthy uncovered little but distrust, hysteria, and the fragility of citizens' civil rights. In the South, African Americans heightened their protests of the injustices of Jim Crow laws. At the same time, many southern governors denounced the Supreme Court's 1954 decision in *Brown v. Board of Education*, which declared segregated schools to be unconstitutional. Then in Montgomery, Alabama, on December 1, 1955, Rosa Parks, a prominent member of the local National Association for the Advancement of Colored People (NAACP), refused to give up her bus seat to a white passenger. Her arrest sparked the Montgomery Bus Boycott, the first large-scale organized action of the civil rights movement as well as the emergence of Martin Luther King, Jr., as a leader. The sometimes-violent battle over segregation often pitted the interests of southern governors against those of the national government. The first physical federal-state confrontation came in the fall of 1957 when President Dwight D. Eisenhower challenged Governor Orval Faubus of Arkansas (1955–1967) by sending the U.S. military to force the integration of Central High School in Little Rock.

Although most clashes were not as dramatic, federal-state relations during the 1950s remained a source of tension for many governors across the nation. Clear lines of governmental division were increasingly hard to determine and separation of powers no longer neatly categorized. States accepted federal assistance, but resented the strings attached. In 1951, Val Peterson of Nebraska (1947–1953) summarized this sentiment. "There can be no quarrel," Peterson explained, "with increased power in the central government to the extent that the nature of modern life . . . requires it to be strong. We must admit that some progress must be ascribed to the grants-in-aid program. However . . . states lost much of their sovereignty . . . when they took the first dollar of federal aid."[3] Peterson, who later served as the nation's ambassador to Denmark and Finland, captured the feelings of many of his colleagues. The reworked intergovernmental arrangement was a necessary by-product of modernity, but it was still a bitter pill to swallow.

One policy example of how this altered federalism shaped the modern governorship is road building, an issue of utmost importance to governors in the 1950s. In the first half of the twentieth century, Americans became obsessed with cars and took to the roads in unprecedented numbers. Cars were a symbol of American freedom and creativity as well as a source of prosperity. G. Mennen Williams, governor of Michigan, home of the automotive industry, bragged about his state's prized asset, "It has been estimated that $1.00 in every $7.00 in our [national] business is the automobile industry. . . . I don't think anyone here is going to contend that the automobile industry hasn't had ingenuity, hasn't had the brains and hasn't had the energy to do a tremendous job."[4] With the emergence of a nation of drivers, more and better roads were needed. Initially, states addressed this dilemma with minimal federal support by improving the U.S. Routes system and, when able, building turnpikes and parkways. Several 1950s governors had extensive experience managing their states' highway systems even before taking office. Luther Hodges (1954–1961) was on North Carolina's State Highway Commission in the early 1930s, nearly twenty years before his gubernatorial term. Orval Faubus served on the Arkansas State Highway Commission in the late 1940s and then was promoted to director of highways.

But by the mid–1950s, the demand for roads and the anticipated need for road maintenance became more than most states could handle under current conditions. Convinced by the determined President Eisenhower, governors agreed to a partnership with the federal government in a national interstate initiative that was an unprecedented modern engineering feat, literally and figuratively connecting the United States as never before. This story of road building is one of governors adapting to changing times and accepting expanded gubernatorial and federal roles in the post–World War II world.

Chapter Four

Connecting the United States

Governors and the Building of the Interstate System

Dan McNichol

The Dwight D. Eisenhower National System of Interstate and Defense Highways has become an asphalt and concrete monument to greatness in government. A half-century after work on the project began it stands as a primary example of the powerful partnership between states and the federal government. The Interstate System, built by a state and federal coalition, has physically united the nation, modernized the economy, and strengthened national security. When he took office in 1953, President Dwight D. Eisenhower knew that in order to succeed this largest of federal programs needed the backing of every governor in the United States. Logically, he introduced the idea of his "Grand Plan" to his fellow chief executives who were attending the Governors' Conference of 1954. These governors became the ones most responsible for the program's success. Governors unleashed their state's resources, carrying the Interstate System through its crucial stage—the first few years of construction. In supporting the commander-in-chief's concept of one enormous superhighway system, governors handed members of Congress a mandate to do the same. Finally, it was these governors who got the program off the ground by raising funds, launching the work, and ensuring that the undertaking would prevail.

Winning the support of every governor proved challenging—even for the most victorious general in American history. During the 1950s, there were 166 governors. After Eisenhower's election to the Oval Office in 1952, there was only one president. The numbers were not in Eisenhower's favor.[1] Hosting a group of governors for lunch at the White House, Eisenhower broke bread in the first few hours of his first term. The topic of road building was raised. The consensus among the governors at the table: the federal government should get out, and keep out, of the road-building business. These governors believed that states should be the sole collectors of vehicle and gas taxes for road construction. Building highways was a state affair. A federally controlled road-building program was considered an affront to state sovereignty. Regardless, lobbying the newly sworn-in thirty-fourth president of the United States to abandon the building of a massive highway network was not a concern. In 1953, there was no grand plan to build the largest superhighway system in the world—at least not one the governors knew about. Yet today, fifty years later, the Eisenhower Interstate System stands as the largest engineering and construction project in the world. Not the Pyramids of Egypt, the Great Wall of China, nor the Suez or Panama Canals rank in scope or scale to this most remarkable undertaking.

The partnership between state governors and the federal government that built the Interstate System may be more impressive than the product of its asphalt, concrete, and steel. State governors working with the president and Congress put together the Interstate System to serve the nation while binding the states and their major cites to one another. Remarkably, it was a voluntary arrangement among the states. The multigovernmental effort stands as one of the ultimate examples of cooperation and trust between the states and the federal government. The roots of the joint venture date back to 1806 with the approval of the building of the National Road, the first federally funded road to cross several state borders. Even though the National Road was George Washington's vision and a legislative success of Thomas Jefferson, a debate about the role of the federal government funding internal improvements such as roadways and waterways quickly led to arguments concerning the power and independence of the states versus the implementation of federal projects.

In 1914, more than a hundred years later, the states and federal government committed themselves to road building and each other with the formation of the American Association of State Highway Officials (AASHO). A tool of governors, this state-based organization was made up of professional engineers working as commissioners of highways while supporting and promoting governors' agendas. AASHO became one of the most influential political groups in Washington, committed to advancing serious discussion and legislative agendas supporting state interests in transcontinental highways and local byways. AASHO was the key organization for state highway officials when dealing with the Office of Public Roads, which later became the Bureau of Public Roads and today's Federal Highway Administration. In 1956, building on forty years of collaboration, the state and federal partnership in AASHO was tested when their relationship was extended and complicated by the building of the National System of Interstate and Defense Highways, also known as the Interstate System.

During the fifty years of planning, construction, and maintenance of the Interstate System, any one of the governors could have quit the program by removing the red, white, and blue Interstate System shields along their sections of the superhighway. Instead, the state and federal partnership grew stronger. Five decades later, the partnership between the governors and their federal brethren known as the Federal-Aid Highway Program remains as the strongest state and federal partnership in the history of the United States.

States Uniting States

At the dawn of the twentieth century, the mass production of motor vehicles made the idea of building highways a popular movement. However, not one interstate highway existed. The only way for a traveler to cross the continent was to struggle over poorly marked trails of mud and frail wooden bridges, haphazardly linking one trail to another—if you were lucky enough to find your way. Standard highway signs and continuous numbered routes across state borders did not exist. Road maps were a novelty. In the 1920s, most of the paved rural roads in the country were in the Northeast or West along the coastlines. The only transcontinental routes were named trails like the National Old Trails Road, or the Lincoln Highway. Trail markers were almost nonexistent. If signs could be found, they were randomly placed and varied in size, shape, and color. Confusing and frustrating to motorists, the trails were laid out haphazardly. Supporters of trail associations often misdirected drivers to a town connected with their association instead of providing motorists the most direct route.

In 1922, in part to counter this problem, the governors of six northeastern states agreed to work out a regional system of numbered highways to replace the traditional but random trail signs and their confusing system of color-coded bands painted on telephone poles, trees, rocks, and the sides of barns. The numbering scheme was supposed to continue on through New York State. Yet, drivers found out the hard way that New York state highway officials decided not to cooperate, leaving the "regional" interstate system at a dead-end at the Hudson River.[2]

Nationally, governors and their highway officials were overwhelmed with demands for improvements. Motorists complained bitterly about getting lost while driving into the hinterlands. As a result, the states, through AASHO, agreed with the federal government to bring an end to the chaotic mazes of overlapping named trails. Wiping out names, the coalition began replacing them with numbers—creating an organized grid of numbered interstate routes. Through these efforts, the U.S. Routes system was born.

Road-Raging Governor

Showing the fragility of the partnership between the states, one angry governor, in late 1925, attempted to hold hostage the entire plan for numbering America's new U.S. Routes system. The plan involved assigning routes ending in a zero to be transcontinental highways running east and west, with the lowest-numbered ones running parallel to the Canadian border and highest-numbered even routes running parallel to the Mexican border. Governor William Fields of Kentucky rejected the national numbering plan because he wanted a major transcontinental highway, one of the ones ending in a zero, to pass through Kentucky. Roads ending in zero were assured to be longer routes carrying higher volumes of traffic and bringing with it tourists and commerce. U.S. Route 60 was originally designated to begin in Newport News, Virginia, and run through Kentucky, ensuring Kentucky a healthy amount of interstate traffic and business from the eastern states. Instead, Route 60 was reassigned as a route between Chicago and Los Angeles. Increasing Governor Fields's outrage was knowing that committee members creating the numbering system were highway officials from the very states that were trying to reroute U.S. Route 60 away from Kentucky. Governor Fields along with his congressional delegation wanted nothing to do with a shorter and inferior U.S. Route 62 being forced onto his state. Rightfully, Governor Fields believed his state had been blatantly bypassed by six new east-west interstates to the north and three main interstates to the south—every one of them ending with a zero. Fields and others felt that a group of western states wanting a highway between Los Angeles and Chicago were hijacking Kentucky's U.S. Route 60. Following through on the threat to hold out, Kentucky was the lone dissenter. Governor Fields and members of Kentucky's congressional delegation took their complaint to Washington, D.C. Meeting with the head of the Bureau of Public Roads, Chief Thomas MacDonald, the group hoped for an open-and-shut case. Despite his considerable power in federal government, MacDonald could do nothing. This matter was between the states.

All involved realized that the entire system of nationalizing America's highways was dependent on each state's agreement and cooperation. In April 1926, five months after the hostilities began, state highway officials from Oklahoma and Missouri meeting on routine business matters noticed that one desirable number in particular—66—had not been used for a highway route anywhere in the country. John Page, a chief engineer from Oklahoma, pointed out to attendees that U.S. Route 66 was available for the Chicago–Los Angeles interstate highway, which could potentially resolve the numbering crisis. Kentucky, for its part, agreed that U.S. Route 60 could end in Springfield, Missouri, and not continue through to the West Coast as long as the interstate highway through Kentucky was named U.S. Route 60. The Los Angeles-to-Chicago highway boosters said they could, in turn, live with U.S. Route 66. Agreement reached, these state officials dispatched a telegram to the Bureau of Public Roads in Washington, D.C.: "REGARDING CHICAGO LOS ANGELES ROAD IF CALIFORNIA ARIZONA NEW MEXICO AND ILLINOIS WILL ACCEPT SIXTY SIX INSTEAD OF SIXTY WE ARE INCLINED TO AGREE TO THIS CHANGE WE PREFER SIXTY SIX TO SIXTY TWO. AVERY PIEPMEIER."[3] In patriotic form, the final plan for America's first interstate system, the U.S. Routes, was adopted by the states voluntarily through AASHO and made public on Armistice Day (now Veterans' Day), November 11, 1926.

Finally in complete agreement, the governors and state and federal highway officials stepped back and admired their creation: a 96,626-mile system of interstate highways connecting the most desired routes between centers of populations. For the first time in history, drivers could follow a numbered highway across the country—even if some of the highway was a simple road of mud and dust.

Turnpikes, Tolls, and Tailfins

Although they were the most modern roads in the country, the nation's primary interstate highways, the U.S. Routes, soon became dangerous and congested. U.S. Route 66, known as Bloody 66, hosted high-speed neophytes. Like other U.S. Routes, Route 66 was known for its dangerous curves, deadly intersections, and narrow lanes. Head-on collisions were common in what were called suicide lanes—a no-man's-land between lanes of opposing traffic. The carnage in these suicide lanes was horrific. It was no better at railroad crossings. Ten percent of highway fatalities occurred where trains crossed highways at grade level. Without bridges separating trains, traveling along highways would remain that much more dangerous. Death, congestion, and financial losses on America's roadways demanded that governors in every state take action and begin improving their highways. The clearest path to reaching their objective was to divide and multiply.[4]

By 1937, states had built 1,200 miles of divided highways, as well as numerous showcase parkways. Parkways in and around major cities integrated roads into the beauty of their surroundings. These were more parks than roadways with smoother pavements, decorative bridges, and elaborate landscaping. The city of Los Angeles laid claim to the Arroyo

Seco Parkway, and New York City bragged of its Henry Hudson Parkway. The state of Connecticut showcased its Merritt Parkway, while the Bureau of Public Roads boasted its Mount Vernon Parkway in Virginia.[5] Parkways, really just extensions of parks, were more about Sunday drives than expediting commerce.

Governor George Howard Earle of Pennsylvania (1935–1939) led an effort to combine the beauty of a parkway with the efficiency of a four-lane highway. Governor during the darkest days of the Great Depression, Earle and the Pennsylvania legislature supported a far-reaching concept—a superhighway designed for vehicles traveling long distances at high speeds. The governor's vision became the Pennsylvania Turnpike and helped create jobs during the Great Depression. Only the second Democratic governor in Pennsylvania since the Civil War, Earle changed course from his Republican predecessors and incorporated federal-like programs into Pennsylvania's governmental services. As a tribute to President Roosevelt's successful New Deal job creation programs, many people called Earle's projects "Little New Deal" initiatives. President Roosevelt, clearly supporting his protégé's efforts, garnered federal funds to financially back the Pennsylvania Turnpike Authority.[6] Earle's turnpike was to be a scenic superhighway that passed through bucolic Pennsylvania Dutch farmlands and the Allegheny Mountains. However, its primary intent was to assist industry and move commerce. With World War II looming, President Roosevelt and Governor Earle's eventual plan to connect the steel plants of Pittsburgh with the Naval Yard in Philadelphia became a priority. The nation's first ever superhighway foreshadowed the future of modern interstate highways.

On October 27, 1938, work began at Mr. and Mrs. Eberly's farm near Shippensburg, Pennsylvania, and did not stop for two years. The turnpike opened to traffic on October 1, 1940. In their cars on the turnpike's first day of operation, Americans traveled faster, farther, and more safely than ever before. The turnpike's 160 miles of limited-access highway avoided contact with 939 local roads and 12 railroad right-of-ways along its path. Prior to its opening, the first vehicles to test the new superhighway were U.S. Army vehicles testing their engines at high speeds.

Pennsylvania's turnpike was an imitation of Germany's Autobahn. As a result, speed and safety were a part of its design. A wider, flatter road with longer sweeping curves than two-lane U.S. Routes, the Pennsylvania Turnpike improved a driver's visibility and therefore increased the chances of spotting dangers further down the road. The new superhighway's limited access design eliminated byway and railway crossings from the turnpike, allowing traffic to flow at unprecedented speeds while reducing congestion and collisions. Guardrails and graceful banked curves kept most vehicles on the road. Not since 1917, when the first centerline was painted down the middle of a road between Marquette and Ishpeming, Michigan, had highway safety been taken so seriously.[7] Ten-foot-wide grass medians built to protect motorists from head-on collisions were included in its revolutionary design. The median, a new innovation, was an important safety feature because speed limits were not enforced on the Pennsylvania Turnpike. Unintentionally, the median attracted picnickers who spread blankets and ate their lunch while admiring the futuristic roadway and its high-speed traffic.[8]

Pennsylvania was unique. Most governors did not have the backing or the traffic volume needed for building expensive turnpikes. Funding shortfalls, right-of-way issues, and lack of political power kept many governors from taking on these large public projects. As a result, most governors focused their limited resources and energy on piecemeal improvements along the existing U.S. Routes. Often it was the best they could do. A few governors, however, with strong political bases and supportive legislatures followed Governor Earle's example. Choosing not to wait for a federal initiative, these state governors began raising capital and building the dreamy superhighways Americans demanded and the private sector backed. Voters wanted roads and many were willing to buy bonds to support the construction. "Self-liquidating" state toll roads appeared to be the future.

Road-Building Ground Work

In 1928, Governor Alfred E. Smith of New York vacated his seat to run for the presidency, leaving Franklin Roosevelt to succeed him as governor and jumpstarting one of America's greatest political careers. With the stock market crash in 1929 and the ensuing Great Depression hitting New York as hard as any state, Roosevelt began implementing social programs in New York that would later become models for his national New Deal reform programs. Road-building projects were among his favorite job creation initiatives as governor and president. Roosevelt had a long-standing interest in roads. Before becoming New York's governor, Roosevelt served as chairman of the Taconic River Commission. Immersing himself in work he loved, Roosevelt was intimately involved with planning and designing the Taconic Parkway's bridge facades and even its picnic tables.[9]

Later, in 1937, then-President Roosevelt scratched six lines across a map of the United States—three running north and south and three running east and west. Calling Thomas MacDonald, the head of the federal Bureau of Public Roads, to the White House, the president handed him the map and asked MacDonald to look into the concept of transcontinental highways and report back to him. Thus, President Roosevelt began to explore the viability of the federal government building a national interstate system. World War II, however, subsequently consumed the president's agenda, and road building was put on hold.[10]

By 1944, however, the war was waning and Americans were winning. Again, President Roosevelt's attention turned toward planning a way to combat a possible postwar depression. Returning to his six-year-old idea, the president remained convinced that building a national system of interstate highways was the ideal job creation program. During the Great Depression, road building had been one of the Roosevelt administration's primary tools for making work for needy Americans. Thus, Roosevelt's administration saw road building as a good way to avoid the bullet of a postwar depression. Confiscating land for new interstate highways was going to be a challenge for the nation's governors, but central to starting any interstate highway construction. Debates dating back to America's first interstate highway, the National Road, resurfaced. Could the federal government use eminent domain to acquire land or would the states need to do that? The answer was both yes and no. A few states had constitutions preventing land takings by any government—state or federal. Legislation at the state level would have to be changed if a massive postwar highway-building program was to get off to a quick start. By raising the land-taking debate, Roosevelt and the nation's governors began the groundwork for clearing the right-of-way for the bigger highways that the nation would soon be demanding.

Americans went from wartime to boom-time without a postwar depression. The G.I. Bill gave returning soldiers cash for those seeking college degrees, homes in the suburbs, and automobiles to park in their driveways. The spending buoyed the economy. "After the War there was a traffic jam," explained Bud Gunderson, who grew up pumping gas at his father's filling station before World War II. As a returning veteran himself, Bud had a patriotic notion about travel: "One of the things every G.I. had fought for in World War II was to protect his rights as an American. And one of those rights was to be able to get in his car, turn the key and go anywhere he wanted to. There are no boundaries here; highways are not closed in the dark, or at state borders. As long as he had money for a car, he could go anywhere he wanted." And go they did. Topping off their gas tanks, veterans began visiting war buddies, moving to the suburbs, and taking family vacations.[11] Simultaneously, civilian noncombatants had saved disposable income that they had been unable to dispense. The rationing of food and fuel during the war had curtailed their consumerism. With peace came the propensity to spend, propelling the nation into prosperity. Rations were lifted and Americans went on a historic shopping spree.

Americans were ready to travel, but their roads were not ready to be traveled. Pre-war paving projects had been put on the back burner as Americans mobilized. Compounding the neglect, the biggest automobile manufacturers had stopped making cars and, instead, turned production to tanks, trucks, and warplanes. Government rationed gasoline and discouraged, at times forbade, unnecessary travel. The war's end changed these practices. Gas was plentiful, manufacturers produced new cars, and Americans began traveling again.

Reflecting on this era in his book *Truman*, historian David McCullough observed:

Profits were up. Farmers were prospering. American prosperity overall was greater than at any time in the nation's history. The net working capital of American corporations hit a new high of nearly $64 billion. For the steel, oil, and automobile industries, it was a banner year. Unemployment was below 4 percent. Nearly everyone who wanted a job had one, and although inflation continued, people were earning more actual buying power than ever before and all this following the record year just past, 1947, which, reported *Fortune* magazine, had been "the greatest productive record in the peacetime history of this or any other nation."[12]

Despite the good news, there was trouble. G.I.s bought homes and sat in classrooms, instead of operating equipment and building roads. The thirst for housing and record-strong housing starts overheated the materials and labor market. Steel, cement, lumber, and labor were needed but hard to find. Construction equipment was short in supply and high in demand. During the postwar 1940s, governors experienced two negatives: more demand for building roads to ever-expanding suburbs with fewer dollars and even fewer resources.

Regardless of the challenges facing their state governments, Americans wanted and expected roads to be built. Without a strong, well-funded federal program in place, governors had to go it alone. They struggled to resolve and fund the dilemma of highway shortages. Yet, building new superhighways or even simple two-lane roads would have to wait in most states as repairing and rebuilding roads torn apart during the largest mobilization in the nation's history took precedence. During the mobilization of supplying Europe with an "arsenal for democracy," East Coast governors saw their roads torn up by trucks making shipments between factories, forts, and ports. Western governors had also witnessed their previously well-built highways ripped apart by heavy vehicles. Maintenance had been deferred while supplying war efforts in Asia. To compound the problem and stress on the roads, manufacturing jobs during the war pulled people from small towns in the midwestern and southern states to northeastern and western states. After the war, thousands of factory employees became permanent citizens seeking the American Dream. Buying homes and suburbanizing cities became a national phenomenon. Governors of growth states experienced the greatest strains on their rundown and overburdened road systems.

Into the 1950s, governors across the nation faced road-building problems. Southern governors felt the stress on their roads as their states became the new location of choice for many textile manufacturers relocating from the Northeast to take advantage of the South's expansive and relatively inexpensive labor pool. In order to entice this growth and development, southern governors needed to turn old tobacco roads into modern highways to ease the shipment of goods and commute of factory workers. In the Northeast, governors focused on relieving congestion and strengthening antique bridges. Out West, governors wanted to replace old wagon trails and dirt roads with paved highways, but lots of land with miles of expensive roads to be financed by smaller populations was a grave concern. These governors resisted spending state funds on highways that would be used mainly by people passing through their state. They preferred spending state road funds on country roads their constituents used regularly. Uniting the governors, across regions, was their agreement that the federal government should stop collecting a federal gas tax from their voters' pockets. They strongly believed that only states were entitled to those funds. As governors saw it, the collected gas taxes would serve taxpayers better if controlled by state officials. Individually responsible but united in their intent, the nation's governors recognized the need to begin building the first superhighways that would modernize America.

Governors Going It Alone

Seven years after the construction of the Pennsylvania Turnpike, Horace Hildreth of Maine became the first governor to open a new turnpike after World War II. Shaking off the hardship of a nation at war, Maine dug into its soil and made highway history. Just two years after construction began, the road opened to traffic on a cold winter day, December 13, 1947. Governor Hildreth bragged not only that his Maine Turnpike was the second such superhighway in the nation, but that it was the first highway in the world made with a black travel surface. The state chose asphalt over concrete for both its efficiency and its cost savings. Those who thought concrete was the only material for an Autobahn-like road were suspicious. Highway engineers from around the world came to see Maine's asphalt superhighway for themselves and left impressed by what they witnessed: a sleek, smooth, and resilient superhighway that quickly paid for itself thanks to eager customers in the form of toll payers.

Immediately following the war, Governor Hildreth and the Maine legislature raised nearly $20 million in bonds sold to private-sector institutional investors in what was called a "revenue bonding" program and, thus, avoided the use of state assets as collateral. More quickly than expected, Maine retired its debt. In 1954, the state built on the success of its original forty-five miles of asphalt turnpike, and the Maine Turnpike Authority began construction of a sixty-six-mile extension, more than doubling the turnpike's original size. In a new era of streamlining goods and services in the public sector, the Maine Turnpike became a model of efficiency. Built for maximum use, the road served more people at a lower cost.

Causing a chain reaction, the success of Maine's turnpike inspired—even forced—its neighboring state New Hampshire to follow its example. Traffic moved so quickly down Maine's sleek new turnpike that it overwhelmed New Hampshire's older sections of U.S. Route 1. The construction of the fourteen-mile-long New Hampshire Turnpike began immediately after Maine's toll road began operation. Opening in 1950, the state designated the New Hampshire Turnpike the "Blue Star Memorial Highway" in honor of soldiers lost during World War II. Like Maine's turnpike, New Hampshire's was an instant, self-liquidating success. In response, Massachusetts, to the south, hurried its work on a toll road connecting to the New Hampshire Turnpike.

Similarly, the New Jersey Turnpike, called the Miracle Turnpike by some of the engineers who built it, furthered the practice of project streamlining. Unique in its method of borrowing $230 million on a borrow-as-needed basis, the super-wide, six-lane superhighway with its super-fast seventy-five-mile-an-hour design speed was completed in a record-breaking twenty-four months. If the Korean War had not caused a shortage of men and material, the turnpike authority could have seen its 240 bridges and 118 miles of road built even faster.[13] "The turnpike has the distinction of having been financed, designed, and built faster than any comparable project ever has been," explained the *New York Times.* On January 20, 1952, the newspaper enlightened readers about the significance and features of the new turnpike in their midst, reporting that the completion of the last nine-mile section brought an escape route to the city's "western doorstep." For the first time in history, citizens of the most populated city in America, New York, could drive out of their metropolis and state by hopping onto an interstate superhighway. The George Washington Bridge, the Lincoln Tunnel, and the Holland Tunnel offered direct access to the turnpike from Manhattan.[14] "The tortuous trip on the parallel road, U.S. No. 1 through Jersey City, Newark and Elizabeth, is only an unpleasant memory for persons willing to pay an average of 1 and a half cents a mile for express highway travel over the 118 miles of turnpike," *Road International* magazine proclaimed in the spring of 1952. The New Jersey Turnpike cut driving time between the Delaware and Hudson rivers from six to two hours. New Jersey lived up to its nickname, "The Corridor State."[15]

State governors tried to keep up with the demands for new roads but the task was overwhelming. Meanwhile, President Truman's administration, occupied with rebuilding war-torn Europe under the Marshall Plan and waging a war in Korea, was incapable of leading a serious effort to build a federal interstate highway system. Without federal support or assistance, governors did their best to build superhighways on their own, but they also recognized the need for interstate cooperation.

By the mid-1950s, governors of neighboring states worked together and coordinated where and how their turnpikes would meet. Soon after building the nation's first modern turnpike, Pennsylvania made plans with neighboring Ohio to link to that state's future turnpike. In turn, Ohio planned to connect with Indiana's and Illinois's toll roads. The New York Thruway eventually connected with the Massachusetts and Connecticut turnpikes to the east and the New Jersey Turnpike to the south. The West Virginia Turnpike became part of Virginia's and North Carolina's turnpikes. Yet, coordinating this linking of state turnpikes was arduous. Building a system of transcontinental highways at the state level proved inefficient and soon became overwhelming.

Cruising into the 1950s

The 1950s were heady times in the United States. Taking position at the head of the world order appeared the nation's destiny. Americans, totaling 5 percent of the world's population, controlled 95 percent of its wealth. Consuming conspicuously, the average U.S. citizen ate 50 percent more than their European counterpart. Controlling nearly 60 percent of the world's manufacturing might, the nation owned 80 percent of all electrical goods and busily forged 66 percent of the world's steel. When it came to world power, the United States produced 40 percent of the globe's electricity and refined 60 percent of its oil. A staggering 99.93 percent of new automobiles sold in the United States were also made within its borders. General Motors had more financial clout than many nations.[16] During the 1950s, Americans were fascinated with automation. Push-button technology and aerodynamic design signaled the modernization of everything from washing machines to airplanes. Automotive design, however, was the truest sign of the times. Reflecting the nation's self-image—powerful and bold—cars came equipped with big seats, lots of chrome, and rocket fins on their tails. Powerful engines proved a man's might and heralded the nation's supremacy. Cruising faster, riding lower, Americans were in search of highways that could accommodate their need for speed.

Coordinating by Centralizing

President Eisenhower, after situating himself in his new office on January 21, 1953, wrote in his diary, "My first day at President's Desk. Plenty of worries and difficult problems. But such has been my portion for a long time—the result is that this just seems (today) like a continuation of all I've been doing since July '41—even before that!"[17] Along with a war in Korea and the threat of a nuclear holocaust, President Eisenhower inherited an interstate system where 75 percent of its highways were incapable of handling the traffic they were carrying. The diplomatic and domestic crises were related. Mobilizing during a conventional war or evacuating a city after a nuclear strike were acts to be carried out on the nation's highways. As a general and a president, Eisenhower believed preparing the nation for war, a disaster, or just a better life required a system of not just improving old U.S. Routes but building new superhighways.

The U.S. Routes had been paved, but had little other improvements. Built to the standards of the 1920s and 1930s, they were narrow, curved, and filled with dangerous intersections. In short, these routes were outdated for the interstate traffic of the 1950s. Nearly 20 percent of all interstate highways were "critically deficient." The U.S. Routes were bogged down with 800 percent more traffic than they were built to handle. With exception of a few hundred miles of state-run turnpikes, America's interstate highways were in shambles.[18]

President Eisenhower knew the value of a good road. He cursed bad ones and praised good ones while making a career out of understanding how to put them to use. In 1919, he drove across the nation as part of the U.S. Army's first motorized transcontinental expedition. Witnessing the horrid condition of the country's roads, he saw how they left a gaping hole in the nation's defense network. In 1922, as an executive officer in the Panama Canal Zone, he charted and supervised the construction of jungle roads to protect the new canal from enemy attack. The roads were laid down in such trying conditions that they often disappeared under mudslides and tropical forest brush from one season to another—passable only by mule.[19] As the supreme commander in Europe, he led the largest land battle America had ever fought over the road. The Battle of the Bulge involved moving soldiers, firepower, and supplies over simple dirt roads at speeds faster than the world had ever seen. Moving his fighting forces over Adolf Hitler's Autobahn convinced Eisenhower that superhighways were the future. In his memoirs published in 1967, he concluded, "The old convoy started me thinking about good, two lane highways, but Germany had made me see the wisdom of broader ribbons across the land."[20] His popularity as a liberator

propelled him to the presidency of the United States, where road building became his favorite domestic agenda. As if conducting a military
operation, President Eisenhower began executing plans to achieve his
goals even before others knew what he was doing.

Within weeks of taking office, the president fired Thomas MacDonald, chief of the Bureau of Public Roads. Despite more than thirty years
of service, MacDonald was told to clear out his desk and be gone the
following day. The legendary road builder, now in his seventies, broke
the news to Ms. Fuller, his longtime secretary, saying, "I have just been
fired so we might as well get married." Weeks later the couple departed
for Texas by train.[21] Speaking with the press prior to his departure, Mac-
Donald sent a clear message to the public: much remained to be done
when it came to the U.S. Routes. The outgoing chief praised the legislation that created a solid state and federal partnership that worked
because of its checks and balances. Proudly, MacDonald claimed that he
"recognized the sovereignty of the states and the authority retained by
the states to initiate [highway] projects" and that "the same mechanism
of checks and balances has been maintained evenly so that the states and
the federal government both have to agree before they can accomplish
a positive program."[22] President Eisenhower strongly disagreed with
MacDonald's old-school view that the best way to promote interstate
travel was to make piecemeal improvements to the existing U.S. Routes.
MacDonald had dominated the Bureau of Public Roads for more than
three decades and consolidated near complete control of federal highway programs, exerting much influence over state highway departments.
Removing him gave Eisenhower clear channels to communicate his
vision and build a new highway system from scratch.

The Road Mess Business

To the disgust of many state governors, Eisenhower planned to expand
the federal role in road building. As conservative as his politics were, he
believed a centralized body, not forty-eight separate state governments,
should build a new interstate highway system under one giant governmental program. Eisenhower knew Italy, France, and Germany had built
the finest highway systems in the world from the top down and so would
the United States. The genius of Eisenhower's concept was in its simplic-
ity: build a new 40,000-mile superhighway system on a new right-of-way.
Trying to improve the antiquated U.S. Routes would be too costly and
disruptive because they ran through crowded city and town centers.
Using his State of the Union addresses over the next three years, the
president rallied support from the public.

Alluding to a "Grand Plan," President Eisenhower suggested during his State of the Union address on January 7, 1954, that a comprehensive system of interstate highways would make "a stronger America" while protecting "the vital interests of every citizen." Foreshadowing his centralized philosophy in road building, the president explained that in order to build a "safe and adequate highway system, the Federal Government is continuing its central role in the Federal Aid Highway Program. So that maximum progress can be made to overcome present inadequacies of the interstate highway system we must continue the Federal gasoline tax at two cents per gallon."[23]

The president intended to roll out his "Grand Plan" at the 1954 annual meeting of the Governors' Conference, held July 11–14 at Lake George, New York. He chose this venue because he considered these state executives to be his most important audience. Sadly, the president's sister-in-law passed away, causing him to cancel his appearance at the conference in order to attend the funeral. Nonetheless, Eisenhower, determined to present his idea at the conference, had his prepared remarks given to his vice president, Richard Nixon, to make on his behalf. Eisenhower believed that the time had come for delivering the parameters of his plan. Meanwhile, the governors' pleas for getting the federal government out of the road-building business were growing louder. Many governors felt the same as Allan Shivers of Texas. While hosting a gathering of governors in his state to discuss road building, Governor Shivers proclaimed, "As a stronghold of States' rights and of the belief in man's inalienable right to be left alone, Texas is the appropriate place for this meeting." Supporting a proposal for a tax-turnback, Shivers called for the federal government to return the gas tax revenue streams to the states, declaring, "Get the Federal Government out of the road mess business."[24]

Standing before a room filled with the nation's governors, Vice President Nixon revealed Eisenhower's "Grand Plan"—a new $50 billion highway system to be finished in ten years and pay for itself. The vice president reminded the governors in attendance of Eisenhower's trip in 1919 with the U.S. Army convoy. Using the president's prepared remarks, Nixon explained, "Our highway net is inadequate locally and obsolete as a national system."[25] Ticking off the penalties, Nixon again quoted Eisenhower, saying that "comparable to the casualties of a bloody war," 40,000 people a year were killed on the highways.[26] Civil suits clogged the courts and economic losses were in the billions of dollars because of highway inefficiencies, detours, and traffic jams. Nixon delivered the most gripping argument, that the roads were filled with "appalling inadequacies to meet the demands of catastrophe or defense, should an atomic war come."[27] "Where is the United States going and by what road?" questioned the vice president.[28] In asking, "by what road?" the message was clear: the governors of the nation needed to decide together what the next step was toward building the bigger, wider highways Americans were demanding.

Road building was one of the most urgent issues confronting governors in 1954. The concerns of an expanding federal government encroaching on what they believed should be state road-building programs weighed heavily on these state executives. Nixon proceeded with caution, sticking to Eisenhower's prepared remarks. He concluded, "I would like to read to you the last sentence from the President's notes, exactly as it appears in them, because it is an exhortation to the members of this Conference, 'I hope that you will study the matter, and recommend to me the cooperative action you think the Federal Government and the 48 states should take to meet these requirements, so that I can submit positive proposals to the next session of the Congress.' "[29] Eisenhower's appeal was straightforward—figure out what you want and let's build it together! The commander-in-chief asked his fellow chief executives to work as a team. The governors were stunned.[30]

Governors Speaking Out

By requesting the governors' recommendations for finding a solution, President Eisenhower also placed the onus of delivering improvements to the national transportation system on their shoulders. Building coalitions while keeping them united and effective was one of the retired general's greatest strengths. Eisenhower believed that in order to get Congress to follow, the nation's governors were going to have to take the lead. The "Grand Plan" had to be their project in order to succeed. Eisenhower asked the governors as a collective to reverse and abandon their positions regarding federal aid and road building. Only the past year, in 1953, the Governors' Conference had resolved to support freezing the amount of federal funds provided to the states. Going even further, the governors also had agreed that the federal government should cease and desist in the collection of gas taxes. Some of the governors from wealthier states with successful turnpike operations (like Pennsylvania and New Jersey) believed that the states could go it alone and survive, and would even perform better without federal assistance.[31]

Regardless of Republican or Democratic affiliations, the nation's governors knew that for Eisenhower's plan to succeed the construction of a new interstate highway system must be bipartisan. It was the governors' responsibility to be constructive leaders. Pressures to avoid engaging in destructive politics were acute, and their membership in the bipartisan Governors' Conference provided a precedent. Moreover, participating in the largest construction project the nation had ever known had the potential to bring individual governors desired notoriety.

The media primed the public for a showdown as well. Richard Weingroff, an expert on the Federal Aid Highway Program, has noted: "Washington's most prestigious newspaper of the day, *The Evening Star,* commented in an editorial: 'As numerous Governors have been quick to indicate, The President's "grand plan" for a vast program of highway improvement and expansion is more than a little bit controversial in terms of how the States are to figure in it. But what is not controversial about it is that some such program—regardless of conflicting views as to methods of financing and directing it—is imperative for the future well-being of the Nation.' "[32] All agreed that improved highways were necessary, but debate raged over funding and which level of government should take the lead.

Through Nixon, the president asked the state governors to work with the federal government and each other on an expensive, expansive interstate project. When Nixon addressed the Governors' Conference, he stressed the need for a "cooperative alliance between the federal government and the states," and assured the group that "local government will be the manager . . . of its own area" when it came to the questions of finances and road building.[33] Nixon concluded, "The body over which I preside in the United States Capitol calls itself the most exclusive club in the world. It is the United States Senate. I would say that this body can claim to be even more exclusive. There are only forty-eight of you. There are ninety-six in the United States Senate."[34] He made this point to remind the states how instrumental they were in making the president's dream a reality and also to reassure the governors that they had a voice and a choice in all aspects of the project.

On the morning of July 13, following Nixon's speech, governors launched into explosive debates about the challenges ahead if they were to take on the project. Foremost on their minds was the problem of financing a $50 billion project. Tolls, taxes, and tariffs were topics of great disagreement. Governor Lawrence W. Wetherby of Kentucky, a member of the Governors' Conference's executive committee, summarized, "We all realize the need. Therefore, the big problem is to determine how to meet the need. Several methods have been suggested, and several have been adopted by various states, including a toll road program, a third-level taxation approach, and an increase in gasoline tax, an increase in license or vehicle taxes."[35] Thomas E. Dewey, the governor of New York and the host of the meeting, pointed out, "I believe that both the trucking industry and the pleasure cars should pay their full and fair share, and that probably the toll systems . . . would bring us sooner to this immensely desired end of a national network of highways on which it will be safe to drive and on which the delivery of goods and raw materials of this country can be made at far less cost."[36] Governor Dewey understood the power of a turnpike. The Empire State was in the midst of building the largest toll road in the world—the New York Thruway. For Dewey, advocating tolls as a way to pay for the "Grand Plan" was natural—for other governors it was not.

Governors of less-populated states believed that toll roads would not work. Western governors, for example, knew this solution would mean building many more miles of road with far fewer drivers paying tolls. Traffic was not frequent enough for these roads to be profitable. Even some states with larger populations that were already building toll roads wondered if tolls were the best way to finance road building, or if tolls would only discourage drivers from using the very roads they were trying to finance.

Looking for revenue sources, other governors believed that the trucking industry should carry a heavy portion of the future financial burden. Trucking companies were clearly going to benefit from a superhighway system. In addition, their frequent and heavy loads broke down driving surfaces, causing high rates of wear and tear. However, collecting funds from the trucking industry posed challenges. In the 1950s, a truck driver carrying goods across state lines faced a multitude of tariff-collecting methods for use of a state's interstate highways. States such as New York built weigh stations to tax trucks as they traveled through the state. Some states imposed licensing fees and others relied on gas taxes. Ohio used the honor system, requesting that truckers make a report and pay a tax to the state at the end of every three months, based on the distance traveled and the number of axles.[37]

Many governors opposed the federal gas tax of two cents per gallon, claiming that it was not tied directly to funding highways. They believed that each individual state would benefit more from collecting its own gasoline tax. With a federal road-building program, many governors feared they would lose even more important revenue. As Governor Thomas B. Stanley of Virginia pointed out, "Virginia's full return on the federal tax of two cents per gallon would be $20 million per year. Last year we received $10,800,000 from the federal government for our highways. This year it is estimated that, with the increase, we will receive $16 million, which still leaves us at 80 percent of what we put in."[38] Governors of the more-populated turnpike states with their own sources of financing shared Governor Stanley's opinion. Getting back less than what they contributed, these governors were skeptical of a national program.

The states with smaller populations had other concerns. Governor Sigurd Anderson of South Dakota, reminding the conference that his state was 77,000 square miles but had only 657,000 residents, called out to his colleagues, "You governors of the states with millions and millions of people must consider those of us in the West and North who have few people and lots of area have problems that are mighty important, for that reason we hope you won't overlook those of us who have a lot of Indian reservations, lots of Indians who do not pay any tax on their lands. We have a more difficult problem than those of you who have these millions who can be tapped so easily, because we don't have so many."[39] Reinforcing Governor Anderson's stand, Governor Charles H. Russell of Nevada reminded the conference, "Nevada has 110,000 square miles and only 180,000 people in the area. Eighty-five percent of the land in Nevada is owned by the federal government."[40] This left his state with even fewer taxable citizens than his western neighbors. Finding an equitable solution proved difficult—seemingly insurmountable to some.

The governors in 1954 were hesitant for good reason. Committing to a flawed federal plan might in fact harm their states' efforts to build a stronger highway system. Worse, it might cost them a reelection. Governor Dewey of New York, citing the challenges of freeze-thaw cycles triggered by severe winter weather in the northern states, suggested that new interstate highways be built "so deep and so strong in the future that we won't face the continuing problem of deterioration which we now face with the old highways."[41] However, other governors believed building thick roads in the Northeast that were more expensive than ones in the Southeast and West might be unfair. Striking a balance between the miles needed in the Western states with the depth and quality of roads needed in the Northeast proved difficult to negotiate.

Shifting gears and voicing the concerns of governors struggling to balance the impact of congestion and the needs of their large cities with the exodus to the suburbs, Governor Goodwin Knight of California used the 1954 Governors' Conference to question what large cities needed in terms of superhighways and mass transit. Knight explained, "We have rapid transit authorities working on the ideas of subways, monorails and other kinds of rapid transit but we just don't know what to do with these masses of people. We can't afford a subway because Los Angeles, as you know from your experiences in WWII, when you saw all the signs in various parts of the world, is sixty miles wide and thirty miles long so a subway won't work there. A subway won't work in San Francisco because of the terrain and because of the threat of natural difficulties. Consequently, we just don't know what to do. We just don't know what to [do] with the people after we get them."[42]

Governor John Fine of Pennsylvania boasted that his state could go it alone—no federal assistance was needed. "In Pennsylvania we have 41,000 miles of state highways, all of which are improved, I believe, with one or two exceptions. We have spent—or will have spent—$537 million of state funds in the four years of my administration. We have more improved state highway mileage in Pennsylvania than all of the New England states, New York, New Jersey, Maryland, and Delaware, combined. In addition thereto, we have the great Pennsylvania Turnpike system, which pioneered all turnpike systems in America, 327 miles are already completed and in use; thirty-three miles more will take our present system (and that under construction) to the New Jersey border. We have 110 miles more of turnpikes under construction, which will be a link toward the New York State Thruway. We want to continue to build our roads, unimpeded by any federal system, because we have had a highway program in our state for some time. Our program will take us to twelve years hence."[43] Despite his confidence, Governor Fine admitted that there was a need for a national program. He concluded, "I do not believe we ought to let this opportunity pass, because it is an invitation to us to meet with someone and draft a program."[44]

Like Governor Fine, Governor G. Mennen Williams of Michigan also came from a state with a successful road-building program. He simply stated, "In our state I have made a recommendation to go ahead and build tomorrow's roads today, because if we don't build tomorrow's roads today, then by the time tomorrow comes around, we'll be driving on yesterday's road, and killing each other with great frequency."[45] In this idea, Williams encapsulated the crux of the president's "Grand Plan."

Governors' regional and local concerns had to be blended into the equation for the plan to receive unanimous support. The question remained, could California's dilemma with congestion and South Dakota's predicament of covering its expanses of unpopulated area somehow be addressed by one great civil undertaking? Even the boastful governor of Pennsylvania knew action was needed to help the states lacking in wealth and road-building accomplishment. At the Governors' Conference meeting, these men debated ways that every state in the Union could work together to answer President Eisenhower's challenge. The highway dilemma dominated the 1954 session.

Oregon, known for its effective tax collection policy and road-building programs, had become, in 1919, the first state to impose a state gas tax—an initiative that was instantly popular and copied by other states struggling with paying for roads that were in high demand. More than thirty years later in the 1950s, Governor Paul L. Patterson of Oregon realized how important it was for all state governors to unify. He proposed presenting the "Grand Plan" to Congress, arguing that he believed, "that we in Oregon should be willing to abandon or change or alter our approach, in order to get along with the other forty-seven states, and I think we have the right to ask the other states to do the same."[46] The consensus builder continued, "Our problem is to arrive at that last step as to how we can administer that law between ourselves, treating our people and your people equitably for the use of highways. It is something we should get at, and get at early."[47] Concluding, Governor Patterson laid out his own grand plan, "Now, going to what was said last night [Nixon's speech] it would seem to me that if we will take this problem of what we are talking about today and set up the machinery for trying to solve it between ourselves, and then stand together and work it out and go to our '55 legislature with that program," it will succeed.[48] Patterson summarized what Eisenhower already knew and the governors were quickly admitting—together they would prevail, divided they would fail.

The 1954 Governors' Conference kicked off Eisenhower's dream of a national interstate system. It proved a successful meeting for the road-building president. The governors also gained ground, because now they were allied with a popular president who handed them a central role in the national road-building agenda. Eisenhower's strategy gave governors the means and justification to accept federal aid while remaining state advocates. Eisenhower wanted governors to shape their own state-federal interstate initiative. Richard Weingroff explains, "The president [did not ask] the governors to conceive a program that he would adopt. He [asked] the governors to conceive a program that they would adopt."[49] To expedite this process, Eisenhower formed the Clay Commission to work with governors in designing a mutually acceptable plan and alleviate governors' concern that the new highway system would force states to contribute a matching share of funding and necessitate raising taxes. The governors moved to create a special committee of the Governors' Conference to study the issue and work with the Clay Commission. In turn, the group recommended that the 84th Congress pass legislation for building the president's "Grand Plan."

An Urgent Necessity

The tone of the 1955 conference was strikingly different from that of previous years. The governors were now in near-unanimous agreement with the concept of a giant, federal road-building plan. The special committee appointed in 1954 had kept the governors informed about the progress of the interstate highway proposal. Governor after governor echoed the sentiment that the interstates must be built. Governor Walter J. Kohler of Wisconsin, who headed the special highway committee, was the first to address the 1955 Governors' Conference. Since the previous meeting, the 84th Congress had failed to act on the highway legislation. Governor Kohler called the inaction "a tragic failure."[50] He went on to say, "The vital importance of the highway system to the national commerce and more particularly, to the national defense, make[s] an expanded highway program urgent and necessary."[51] In the year that had passed, the need for highways had become even more acute. Congestion and carnage grew on American highways. Constituents demanded action. Governors were now firmly convinced and in complete agreement that Eisenhower's plan was a necessity. In the words of Governor Kohler, "The interest of the American people in better highways, their desire to use them and their willingness to pay for them is evidenced by the experience on virtually every new highway constructed throughout the nation in recent years."[52]

The governors unanimously asked Congress to reach a decision as soon as possible. In 1954, their biggest concern had been financing the project. In 1955, the need to determine how to pay for the interstates was overshadowed by how soon the roads could be built. Hinting at the urgency in his own state, Governor Raymond Gary of Oklahoma reflected, "I am willing to take it either way—as a pay as you go or on a deficit financing basis. I believe the people are willing to take it either way. They want a modern system of interstate highways."[53] Going further, he blamed federal legislators for failing to deliver an agenda: "The people are very disappointed because Congress did not enact a stepped-up modernization and road-building program."[54]

Each governor put individual concerns aside and took up the common cause of a new interstate highway system. Disagreements over financing became secondary. Governor Joseph Blaine Johnson of Vermont articulated the consensus: "I think what we need is action, and the sooner, the better."[55] Joining him was Governor Theodore R. McKeldin of Maryland: "The value of good roads built within the borders of one state is reduced to a minimum if the major highways fail to meet their counterparts in adjoining states."[56] Governor Orval E. Faubus of Arkansas chimed in, saying, "A modern highway system for the nation will be worth what it costs under either plan, so I am not going to quibble about the method."[57] Governor Robert B. Meyner of New Jersey also picked up the sentiment, agreeing, "I think we realize the need is there and I think we should now concentrate on a mechanism by which we can have our voices heard and get a program worked out."[58]

In 1955, the responsibility of a federal highway program, for the most part, rested with Congress. Any former reservations governors had were overshadowed by the genuine need for roads. The president's position was well known. Governor Walter Kohler of Wisconsin may have best summarized the sentiments of the governors by declaring the need for a federal highway system to be "urgent and necessary."[59] Kohler believed,

"The federal highway program is of such importance and such urgency that no delay can be tolerated and I believe the President would be fully justified in calling a special session of congress to deal with it."[60] Eisenhower, eager to get his favorite domestic program under way, was sickened by the inaction. That year, Congress again failed to pass legislation for a national system of interstate highways. Yet, President Eisenhower refused a special session. Looking back, Eisenhower reflected, "The special session might [have been] necessary—but calling it [would have been] at the cost of the sanity of one man named Eisenhower. There was no sense in spending money to call them back when I knew in advance that the result would be zero."[61]

The 1956 Federal Aid Highway Act

In 1956, special interest groups followed the lead of the nation's governors and threw their support behind the president. Tire, automobile, truck, and petroleum manufacturers fell in line, along with construction and travel associations. Finally, Congressional Republicans and Democrats came to terms. Taking nothing for granted, the entire lot became a united coalition and gave the public what they had long been waiting for—the Federal Aid Highway Act of 1956. The bill's fiscal strength came from the Federal Highway Trust Fund, a concept brought to fruition by Louisiana Congressman Hale Boggs. Boggs's trust fund was designed so the federal government would collect money from user taxes like gasoline, then, in turn, use the money to pay states back 90 percent of the cost of constructing the Interstate System. Congress rejected the Clay Commission's original financing plan, but did adopt the recommended 10 percent state share, so governors would not be forced to raise taxes.[62] The House passed the Federal Aid Highway Act of 1956 with a vote of 388 to 19—an overwhelming 95 percent approval. The Senate did not even bother counting votes. Receiving the bill from the House, the Senate passed the landmark act with a voice vote.

Spontaneous Combustion—Instantaneous Construction

Emphasizing his administration's support for getting his "Grand Plan" under way, President Eisenhower invited his new federal highway administrator to the White House for a high-profile swearing-in ceremony. The president personally chose John Volpe, a building contractor and future governor of Massachusetts, to launch the construction of the Interstate System. With the president holding the Bible, Volpe took the oath of office. Never before nor since has the nation's highest-ranking highway administrator had the honor of an Oval Office induction.

Eisenhower was noticeably pleased to be getting his favorite domestic program underway. Building the Interstate System, however, proved bigger than any one person associated with the project. Once work began no one could claim to be in charge: presidents, governors, and leaders of industry became participants in and spectators to the biggest show on earth.

It was a year of spontaneous combustion and instantaneous construction. Immediately after the passing and signing of the Federal Aid Highway Act of 1956, planners, engineers, contractors, and highway officials began gearing up for a job that would span entire careers. Most Americans marveled—and some were angry—as more than 1,600,000 acres of land were set aside for the modern miracle. The states needed to purchase about forty acres of land for every mile of superhighway they were building—in total, twice the landmass of Rhode Island. To build all 41,000 miles required moving enough earth to cover the state of Connecticut knee-deep in dirt. The sand, gravel, and stone going into the Interstate System was enough to build a concrete wall nine feet thick and fifty feet high around the globe. Remarkably, the building of the Interstate System was scheduled for completion by October 1, 1972.

The turnpikes, built earlier by governors, were instructive precedents. Fulfilling their constituents' needs and wants these roads also served the nation during the 1950s. As physical examples of what the Interstate System required in engineering, construction, and maintenance, the turnpikes set high standards. States with turnpikes in operation generously shared this information, which proved invaluable contributions to the national effort—years of time, mountains of materials, and millions of dollars were saved by *not* reinventing the superhighway. The example of state innovation led the way. The Interstate System also meant that states no longer had to risk speculation on the success of a toll road. The project's 90 percent federal funding meant that states could build the highways they most needed without concerns of profitability. State governments no longer had to bend to the demands of private-sector financial lenders. Their partnership with the federal government empowered states.

In a tribute to its success, the Interstate System influenced the world beyond America's borders by setting global standards. The concepts behind the Interstate System's design have been freely exported around the world. The earth over, drivers travel in similar twelve-foot travel lanes with standardized signage, gradients, and curvatures. Even the partnering model has been imitated. China, building its own 50,000-mile superhighway system, followed the United States' federal and state program. Its twenty-one provincial governments interface with Beijing's central government in a similar and successful program that is halfway to completion. People now move from one end of China to another more freely than ever before.

Today, globalization has brought new challenges to every state's economy. The Interstate System, however, continues to be one of the most critical components in remaining competitive with the economic powers abroad. Unable to compete with lower wages, efficiency within United States industries' shipping and receiving operations is critical to the future success of the nation as a whole as well as individual states. Nearly every product shipped today passes along the Interstate System, reducing costs, improving profitability, and conserving fuel. Comprising only 2 percent of the nation's total road mileage, the Interstate System handles nearly 25 percent of its traffic.

Speaking on behalf of governors, Congress, and the executive branch, President Eisenhower reflected in his memoirs, "More than any single action by the government . . . this one would change the face of America. . . . Its impact on the American economy—the jobs it would produce in manufacturing and construction, the rural areas it would open up—was beyond calculation."[63] By the end of the 1950s, Eisenhower's "Grand Plan" was fast becoming a reality. Governors of every state in the nation, all 166 who served in the decade, oversaw the building of the *roads of tomorrow* that the people of today have come to trust.

Woodrow Wilson in 1912: Governor of New Jersey and President-elect Wilson visits his birthplace in Staunton, Virginia, on his fifty-sixth birthday, December 28, 1912. He is joined by Virginia Governor William H. Mann. This manse is now part of the Woodrow Wilson Presidential Library. Woodrow Wilson Presidential Library.

Governors on deck of the USS *Wyoming*: The Atlantic Fleet battleships pass in review as governors attending the 1915 Governors' Conference in Boston watch from the deck of the USS *Wyoming*. The Boston meeting, August 24–27, was hosted by Massachusetts Governor David Walsh (shown shaking hands with New York Governor Charles Whitman—at right—on board the *Wyoming*). National Archives.

Governors meet in Yellowstone National Park: In July 1926, governors convened in Cheyenne, Wyoming, for their annual meeting. Host Governor Nellie Tayloe Ross (the first woman inaugurated governor) is on the seat of the Yellowstone National Park stagecoach. Wyoming State Archives.

Four presidential hopefuls at 1931 conference: Governors Gifford Pinchot of Pennsylvania, Franklin Roosevelt of New York, Albert Ritchie of Maryland, and George White of Ohio, all presidential hopefuls, gather at the 1931 Governors' Conference meeting in French Lick, Indiana. *Indianapolis Star.*

Huey Long: Former governor of Louisiana and then-Senator Huey Long, gives a speech in 1933. In August 1935, Long announced his candidacy for the presidency. One month later, he was shot by an assassin while at the state capitol in Baton Rouge. Huey P. Long, also known as "the Kingfish," died two days later and was buried on the state capitol grounds. Library of Congress.

Governor Warren addresses ceremony honoring World War II dead: Earl
Warren of California, later Supreme Court chief justice, speaks at a solemn
ceremony held October 10, 1947, on the Marine Green in San Francisco in
honor of the first shipload of World War II dead to be returned to the United
States. National Archives.

Governor Thomas Dewey, 1948: Three-term New York Governor Thomas Dewey meeting with Manhattan GOP leader Thomas J. Curran on Dewey's 1948 presidential campaign tour. Library of Congress.

Governors confer with General Bradley and Secretary Marshall: General Omar
Bradley, chairman of the Joint Chiefs of Staff, briefs the executive committee of
the Governors' Conference, who are conferring with Secretary of Defense
George Marshall in his Pentagon office on February 12, 1951. Left to right:
General Hoyt Vandenberg, Chief of Staff, U.S. Air Force; Governor Frederick
Payne of Maine; Governor Elbert Carvel of Delaware; Governor Frank Lausche
of Ohio; Governor Gordon Browning of Tennessee; General Bradley; Secretary
Marshall; Governor Adlai Stevenson of Illinois; and Governor Sherman Adams
of New Hampshire. National Archives.

Governors tour Korea: Colonel R. Murray (right) briefs governors and their party prior to their tour of the 7th Infantry Division main bunker outpost area on May 26, 1954. Left to right: Major General William Marquat, Mr. E. W. O'Flaherty, Governor John Fine of Pennsylvania, Governor Dan Thornton of Colorado, Governor Allan Shivers of Texas (background), General Maxwell Taylor, and Colonel Murray. National Archives (U.S. Army photo).

President Eisenhower discusses integration with southern governors: In 1957, three years after *Brown v. Board of Education*, Central High School in Little Rock, Arkansas, became the nation's first battleground over the issue of school integration. President Eisenhower requested a meeting on October 1, 1957, with several southern governors to discuss integration. They reached agreement with the president regarding the withdrawal of federal troops from integration-torn Little Rock. But after a statement by Arkansas Governor Orval Faubus the following day, Eisenhower declared the troops would remain. Ultimately, the U.S. Supreme Court ordered integration to continue and Governor Faubus responded by shutting down the city's four high schools. Little Rock's public schools remained closed for almost a year until reopened on August 12, 1959. The above picture from the October 1957 meeting shows governors Frank Clement (Tennessee), Thomas Collins (Florida), Luther Hodges (North Carolina), Theodore McKeldin (Maryland), and the president gathered around Eisenhower's desk in the Oval Office. Library of Congress/*U.S. News & World Report* collection.

President Kennedy meets with the Governors' Conference's Civil Defense
Committee: (From left to right) Governor Ernest Hollings (South Carolina),
Governor John Volpe (Massachusetts), Governor Nelson Rockefeller (New
York), President Kennedy, Governor Stephen McNichols (Colorado), Governor
Edmund Brown (California), and Governor Elmer Andersen (Minnesota) in the
Oval Office on May 9, 1961. John F. Kennedy Presidential Library, White House
photographer Abbie Rowe.

Maryland Governor Tawes opens the final link in the Capital Beltway: In Maryland, the final link of I-495, the Capital Beltway, was opened with a ribbon-cutting ceremony on August 17, 1964. Ribbon cutters (left to right) are Federal Highway Administrator Rex Whitton, Governor J. Millard Tawes, and Chairman John B. Funk of the Maryland State Roads Commission. Federal Highway Administration.

President Johnson meets with governors: In the living room of his Texas ranch, President Lyndon Johnson meets with governors on December 1, 1966. Shown left to right (those facing the camera only) are New Jersey Governor Richard Hughes, President Johnson, White House aide Martin Watson, and Cecil Bryant, a former Florida governor appointed by LBJ to serve as on the National Security Council and in the White House Office of Emergency Planning. Lyndon Baines Johnson Library.

Ronald Reagan with fellow governors: Governor Ronald Reagan of California talks with Massachusetts Governor Francis Sargent (left) and North Dakota Governor William Guy during the 1969 National Governors' Conference annual meeting in Colorado Springs, Colorado. Guy served as NGC chairman in 1966–1967. National Governors Association.

President Nixon addressing governors: Governors listen to President Richard Nixon at the 1970 National Governors' Conference winter meeting held in Washington, D.C. Library of Congress/*U.S. News & World Report* collection.

Governor George Wallace of Alabama: Wallace meets the media at the 1973
National Governors' Conference annual meeting held in Lake Tahoe, Nevada,
on June 3–6. Nevada State Library and Archives.

Governors meet with President Carter: Vermont Governor Richard Snelling
(standing) questions President Jimmy Carter during a meeting in the State
Dining Room at the White House on February 28, 1977. Members of Carter's
cabinet were in attendance. Snelling later served as NGA chair in 1981–1982.
The Jimmy Carter Library & Museum.

Governors Terry Branstad of Iowa, Bill Clinton of Arkansas, and Tom Kean of New Jersey participate in a committee meeting during the 1987 annual meeting of the National Governors' Association in Traverse City, Michigan. National Governors Association.

President Bush and Russian President Yeltsin with NGA Executive Committee: Members of NGA's Executive Committee meeting in the Roosevelt Room of the White House on June 26, 1992 are visited by President George H. W. Bush and special guest, Russian president Boris Yeltsin. That same day, the two presidents signed a joint understanding limiting the number of strategic nuclear warheads for each country. George Bush Presidential Library.

Governor Ann Richards of Texas accepts a special edition Harley-Davidson motorcycle in 1992. Texas State Library and Archives Commission.

Governors George W. Bush of Texas and John Engler of Michigan talk during an NGA meeting in the late 1990s. A two-term governor, Bush was elected president in 2000. Engler served as NGA chair in 2001–2002 and used his Chair's Initiative to focus on State Leadership in the Twenty-first Century. National Governors Association.

Governing the 1960s

In the 1960s, the turbulence of events at home stirred American citizens to action and forced governors to confront controversial issues. Governors could not ignore the grassroots polarization of their constituents, particularly concerning Vietnam and the civil rights movement. Antiwar and civil rights marches attracted hundreds of thousands of Americans across the country. And as the decade neared an end, a new subculture of rebellion flowered among the post–World War II baby boom generation embodied in the hippie movement, experimentation with drugs, and an evolution of rock-and-roll from simple chord progressions and tame lyrics to hard, dissonant sounds bearing words of protest. Literature as well reflected growing disillusionment and distaste for societal conditions, as reflected in such books as *One Flew Over the Cuckoo's Nest* by Ken Kesey and *Catch-22* by Joseph Heller.

The decade began, however, on a note of optimism with the election of the young, handsome, and charismatic John F. Kennedy. This hope remained through several Cold War scares, in particular the 1962 Cuban missile crisis. Then, Kennedy's assassination in November 1963 shocked the nation. Americans supported the new president, Lyndon Johnson, and reelected him in a landslide in 1964. But troubles and discontent plagued the Johnson presidency. Apart from battles over segregation, the nation became more deeply invested in Vietnam with more than 100,000 troops deployed by the end of 1965. Although most Americans initially supported the conflict as another prong in the nation's Communism containment policy, the situation by the late 1960s began to appear unwinnable and, to many, a waste of lives.

Governors, reflecting the sentiments of their constituents, had mixed feelings about the war, and Vietnam frequently resurfaced as a point of debate at meetings of the Governors' Conference, renamed the National Governors' Conference in 1965.[1] Officially, the organization adopted resolutions supporting the president, but these pronouncements did not resolve the discord. Governor Mark Hatfield of Oregon (1959–1967), for example, urged his colleagues to be cautious in their support. Hatfield, who held strong antiwar and anti–nuclear weapons views following his visit to Hiroshima one month after the 1945 bombing, argued, "When we are asked to support the President of the United States, we are concerned with methods and techniques by which he seeks to implement these principles. . . . As Americans I think we not only have the right but the responsibility to differ as long as we differ on a constructive basis, seeking the common goal of peace."[2] Others, including Governor Grant Sawyer of Nevada (1959–1967), disagreed with Hatfield, proclaiming, "It seems to me that the position as stated by the President is supported by the vast majority of the public in this country and by many, if not all, of the Governors here. . . . Any alternative to the position taken by the President of the United States . . . this morning, it seems to me, is unthinkable."[3] Although the actual battles were fought thousands of miles away, constituents expected governors to articulate their position on these foreign affairs.

Vietnam was not the only source of international unease. Governors, like most Americans, were preoccupied with the arms race and the Cold War. Nelson Rockefeller of New York (1959–1973), chair of the Governors' Conference's standing committee on civil defense and once President Eisenhower's special assistant on foreign affairs, used the 1960 meeting to articulate his support for expanding the nation's nuclear weapons stockpile. "The Soviet Union," he argued, "enjoys a position of relative power that no rules could give it. We can—and shall—achieve serious measures of arms control only when our own strength as a nation—joining and serving all our allies leaves Soviet strength no clear advantage. *We do not, as a nation, seek power for the sake of power. We seek power for the sake of peace.*"[4] Rockefeller's colleague Mark Hatfield later, as a member of the U.S. Senate, authored the law ending nuclear testing in the United States.

Apart from these foreign affairs, governors encountered a number of domestic issues in the 1960s that directly affected their ability to govern. Of particular concern for many were the federal implications of President Lyndon Johnson's Great Society programs. These initiatives in education, welfare, and environment, among other areas, further redefined federal-state relations and rejuvenated the ideals of the New Deal. Governors debated the role that states should play in the administration of anti-poverty programs in addition to the other areas of increased governmental responsibility and interest—mass transit, clean water, urban development, higher education, medical care for the elderly, juvenile delinquency, teen drug use, and student unrest. Some feared that the trend of ever-expanding government had gone too far. Daniel Evans of Washington (1965–1977) used the governors' annual meeting in 1966 as a forum to call for a national constitutional convention to try to force the federal government to return a share of federal income taxes to states.[5] In contrast, other leaders, like William Egan (1959–1966, 1970–1974), the first governor of the state of Alaska, demanded more federal assistance. Egan, in response to an earthquake in 1964, declared, "The time has arrived when the government of the United States must seriously consider setting up some kind of a natural disaster funding program."[6] Far from their 1908 counterparts, most governors in the 1960s readily accepted and at times welcomed federal aid. They understood that funding and regulation were twentieth-century necessities. Governors worried, however, that Johnson's Great Society foreshadowed unwarranted growth of government. In the words of Harold Handley of Indiana (1957–1961), "The thing that worries me more than anything else is that I think the image of this great American eagle of ours . . . is turning into the image of a mother hen."[7] In response to concerns like Handley's, governors made the decision to step up their presence and voice at the national level, agreeing to establish an organizational office in the nation's capital and to meet each winter in Washington in addition to holding annual meetings in the states each summer.

The most controversial and divisive issue of the 1960s, however, was civil rights. Again, like the country as a whole, governors held strong opinions on the subject and found themselves divided. The issue first emerged as a major topic of discussion at the July 1–4, 1962 governors' meeting in Hershey, Pennsylvania. After heated debate, filibustering, and enforced breaks to cool tempers, the assembly tabled a resolution expressing support for civil rights, an initiative backed primarily by Republican governors Nelson Rockefeller, Mark Hatfield, and Elmer Andersen of Minnesota. Countering critics who believed that the conference should avoid hotly contested topics, Rockefeller argued that even though the association had "no legislative authority [or] legislative power of action . . . Governors have a responsibility to the people of this country not only to discuss these subjects but also to take positions on them."[8] The debate resumed the following July when governors gathered in Miami Beach, Florida. One attendee, George Wallace of Alabama (1963–1967, 1971–1979, and 1983–1987), had symbolically blocked a door of the University of Alabama just one month earlier trying to prevent integration. He was still reeling from President Kennedy's decision to overrule him and take command of the Alabama National Guard to ensure the safety of the new African American students. Wallace declared that he was "tired of hearing about civil rights" and accused his pro–civil rights colleagues of pushing the issue only to promote their own presidential ambitions.[9] Yet, even governors like Wallace, who in moments of heated debate threatened never to return, typically remained committed to the National Governors' Conference.

In quieter moments, they understood that interstate cooperation was necessary to the success of their own administrations.

The civil rights movement achieved marked success, particularly with the passage of the Civil Rights Act in 1964 and the Voting Rights Act of 1965. Some governors cheered these advancements and even tried to further the case of civil rights in their states. Rockefeller, for example, spearheaded an effort to integrate the building trade unions in New York. In California, Pat Brown (1959–1967) supported the Rumford Act to curtail racial discrimination in housing. In Iowa, Harold Everett Hughes (1963–1969) oversaw the creation of a state civil rights commission. A few governors still protested, but most accepted the change, adhering to the letter of the new federal laws if not always the spirit. These included some southern governors, among them Terry Sanford of North Carolina (1961–1965), who worked to implement antidiscrimination laws and the integration, albeit gradual, of education.

By gathering to air grievances, share concerns, and celebrate successes, governors worked together to weather the storm of the 1960s— not only the trials of Vietnam and integration efforts, but race riots, particularly in Los Angeles and Detroit, and the assassinations of several high-profile leaders: President John F. Kennedy, Martin Luther King, Jr., Malcolm X, and Robert Kennedy. In the midst of these events, however, the country held on to the hope for a better America. In July 1969, national pride swelled with the Apollo moon landing and Neil Armstrong's "giant leap for mankind." In spite of America's troubles, both domestically and internationally, the country was now a leading world power. Camelot was forever gone, but with advances in civil rights and feminism, many believed further progress was inevitable.

Still, the image of George Wallace defiantly blocking the entrance of African American students to his state's university would be etched in the memories of Americans in the 1960s. Although Wallace was not representative of all governors, his influence was widespread and actions well publicized. Delving deeper into George Wallace's governorship sheds light on growing tensions during the 1960s over the role of the states in the federal system and between governors over the scope of their office.

Chapter Five

Governors in the Civil Rights Era

The Wallace Factor

JEFF FREDERICK

In mid-July 1963, Alabama Governor George C. Wallace traveled to Miami Beach, Florida, to attend his first Governors' Conference meeting. Riding a wave of white southern popularity after his infamous inaugural address—"segregation now, segregation tomorrow, segregation forever"—and the staged stand at the schoolhouse door, Wallace could not resist the opportunity to further elevate his profile. "This is the first Conference I have ever attended," Wallace bellowed, "and if it is going to turn out to be a civil rights debating society, it is going to be the last one I ever attend. In my judgment, you are going to destroy the Governors' Conference if you use this Conference for the purpose of protecting certain political elements in the civil rights issue and not others."[1]

Despite his threat, Wallace returned the next year to the Governors' Conference meeting (now the National Governors Association) in Cleveland, Ohio. Less than one month before President Lyndon Johnson signed the landmark Civil Rights Act of 1964 into law, Wallace pressured his colleagues at that meeting to sign a petition denouncing the measure. Nine agreed. A month after the petition was signed and two days after Johnson's stroke of the pen ushered in an era in which discrimination in public accommodations was no longer legal, Wallace responded with more bombast, calling the measure "the most monstrous piece of legislation ever enacted by the United States Congress," claiming, "It is a fraud, a sham, and a hoax. This bill will live in infamy. . . . It dishonors the memory of countless thousands of our dead who offered up their very lives in defense of principles which this bill destroys." The governor later predicted that the new law would lead to the destruction of the free enterprise system, schools, and private property, and that the three branches of the federal government had descended into tyranny, Communism, and heathenism.[2]

During the civil rights era no other governor, northern or southern, represented the nation's reluctance to accept racial change as thoroughly as Wallace. Politically, Wallace was a centrifugal force of American governors, attracting some who mimicked his appeal and causing others to cast themselves as his polar opposite. Within Alabama and throughout the white South, Wallace was wildly popular with voters across class and gender lines. His ideas and actions seemed reasonable to many whites who heard Wallace say the same things their parents, grand-parents, preachers, teachers, coaches, and community leaders had told them all their lives. The only difference was that the governor repeated them with such vigor. Journalist Ralph McGill once asked a fellow white southerner how long freedom riders ought to wait before asking to use all available bus facilities. "Two or three hundred years," the man replied, frustrated by the protestors and convinced they were too impatient. George Wallace understood this sentiment in the South, the people who believed it, and the feeling that the world in which these southern whites lived and loved and died was under attack.[3]

Outside the region and in the minds of southern blacks and progressives, Wallace was chronically underestimated, reviled by members of both major political parties, and castigated as a virtual neanderthal. "Today's bombing was a crime against humanity," Martin Luther King, Jr., charged after a bomb ripped apart the peaceful services of Birmingham's Sixteenth Street Baptist Church and ended the lives of four young girls on a Sunday morning in September 1963. "Governor Wallace is largely responsible for these vicious murders, for his irresponsible words and actions have created the atmosphere for violence and murder." To his many detractors, Wallace was either a racist or an opportunist, though it was not clear which was worse given that at least one was more honest than the other. In short, Wallace was capable of generating either love or hatred, but never apathy.[4]

Wallace was not the first southern politician to exploit race for his own purposes. Antebellum white southerners created an elaborate system of justifications and rationalizations for slavery, many of which were based in abject racism. Post-Reconstruction Democrats regained power for themselves and their party by scapegoating blacks. Southern blacks, historian Eric Foner has concluded, "found themselves enmeshed in a seamless web of oppression, whose interwoven economic, political, and social strands reinforced one another." Alfred Waddell overthrew a duly constituted municipal government in Wilmington, North Carolina, while promising to "never surrender to a ragged raffle of Negroes even if we have to choke the Cape Fear River with carcasses." White Democrats in Virginia, historian J. Douglas Smith noted, accepted Harry Byrd's fiscal conservatism and pro-business philosophy in part because he regularly railed against state blacks. Prior to World War II, southern governors rarely took any meaningful steps to reduce or end lynching. And those that did, like Georgia Governor William J. Northern, found their anti-lynching reforms greeted with a mixture of disdain and disgust.[5]

Another Georgia governor, Eugene Talmadge, expressed a common belief of southern chief executives of the era. "I am a native Georgian," the wild man from Sugar Creek bellowed, "and my ancestors on all sides of my family have been in Georgia for 150 years. I am steeped in southern tradition. . . . Neither I nor my people have ever strayed from the pasture of southern tradition. We have not even leaned against the fence." Southern tradition, it was duly accepted by whites, meant segregation, disfranchisement, and economic and social control of blacks by whites. Talmadge, his biographer noted, characterized blacks as being "childlike, basically stupid, barely removed from a savage ancestry" and in need of direct supervision. As late as 1946, Talmadge, during his last campaign, called his political rivals "nigger lovers" and predicted "four years of chaos, turmoil, and bloodshed" if a good white supremacist like himself were not elected.[6]

After southern states wrote new constitutions around the turn of the twentieth century disfranchising blacks and state lawmakers passed restrictive segregation codes, race was largely a settled issue, at least as a matter of policy, even if candidates continued to evoke white supremacy on the hustings. White governors faced no electoral retribution from black voters, white judges were unlikely to give much credence to black litigants, and white legislators did not enact racial reform. Only at election time did race resurface as candidates jockeyed rhetorically to be the most ardent protector of white womanhood and white southern tradition. Mississippi Governor Theodore Bilbo, South Carolina Governor "Pitchfork" Ben Tillman, and Talmadge were the foremost of many who preached white supremacy and black inferiority. "I was raised among niggers and I understand them," Talmadge boasted during the 1946 gubernatorial campaign. "I want to see them treated fairly and I want to see them have justice in the courts. But I want to deal with the nigger this way; he must come to my backdoor, take off his hat, and say 'Yes Sir.'"[7]

Across the South, race returned to the front burner of gubernatorial policy with the 1954 *Brown v. Board of Education* ruling, which declared separate schools to be inherently unequal. Suddenly, southern governors began to craft new policies in order to protect segregation or at least forestall its demise for as long as possible. Many segregationists believed that integrated schools were the first step on a pathway to "race mixing," a none-too-subtle reference to interracial sexual relationships.

Historian Numan Bartley characterized the furor of antagonism unleashed by whites as a "hysterical reaction." Several southern states responded with a rash of legislation designed to close schools, provide state funds only to segregated public schools, provide funds for all-white segregated private academies, keep classrooms segregated within the walls of an integrated school, and reserve pupil allocation power for governors and their puppet boards of education. White Citizens' Council groups exploded in size and the Klan grew bolder and more violent. Racist mythology about intermarriage and the sexual untrustworthiness of black males proliferated in all quarters of white society. "The Citizens' Council is the South's answer to the mongrelizers," one organization tract announced. "We will not be integrated. We are proud of our white blood and our white heritage."[8]

Ordinary white citizens joined the chorus. "Here in our beloved South," Mrs. Belle Cooke wrote in a letter to the editor of the *Birmingham News*, "we are besieged on all sides by devilish forces going up and down our land." Mrs. Annie White felt similarly oppressed by the black movement for civil rights: "The Negro has been exploited by that power-crazy, vote-groveling gang in Washington. They are hurting their cause irreparably by demonstrating for this and that instead of proving themselves worthy of their demands. Then, and not until then, will the majority of white people consider their demands." Energized by *Brown* as much as the civil rights movement, white southerners evaluated most every action by the federal government over the next decade on the basis of whether it was an attack on their own misguided traditions. Since the end of World War II, white southerners had witnessed the integration of baseball, the integration of the armed forces, and a unanimous 9–0 Supreme Court decision that promised to desegregate neighborhood schools. Segregationists were in no mood for compromise.[9]

For generations, southerners intrinsically linked conceptualizations of honor with liberty. A man without liberty, a term southerners loosely defined as a life free of regulation by outsiders, lacked honor. Any attempt to limit white southern control of the South, therefore, was viewed as a direct assault on individual, local, state, and regional honor. White southerners characterized federal intervention—judicial rulings and later the passage of the Civil Rights Act of 1964 and Voting Rights Act of 1965—as an unauthorized assault on the liberty and honor of the South. Wallace and his ilk, in this contradictory southern world created out of constructed memory, history, and generations of white supremacy, defended their way of life as one as reasonable as spring planting and fall harvest.

Work by political scientist Earl Black suggests a strong correlation between segregationist campaign rhetoric and the Deep South. Both Democrats and later Republicans in the Deep South were likely to advocate staunch anti-integration policies, while those candidates in the Upper South were more likely to champion moderate or even nonsegregationist positions. In his 1976 study, *Southern Governors and Civil Rights*, Black concluded that very few differences existed between Deep South Republicans and Democrats on racial matters in the two decades after *Brown*. Across the region, segregationists were statistically more likely to win gubernatorial elections than nonsegregationists, and segregationists—both moderate and militant—outnumbered nonsegregationist candidates nearly two to one. Southern society changed, though the process was more gradual than immediate, and much of the delay can be attributed to George Wallace and his influence on white southern voters.[10]

Into this poisoned environment of race, constructed memory, and mythology, George Wallace ran for governor of Alabama in 1958, a job he had dreamed of his entire life. As remarkable a pure campaigner as the South ever produced, Wallace relished politics and hoped to be a governor in the way other boys dreamed of becoming quarterbacks, pilots, or business tycoons. He served as an enlisted man rather than an officer during World War II because he believed that such status would render him a more attractive candidate to Alabama voters once the fighting was over. While in the military, he routinely scrawled greetings on Christmas cards to voters back in Barbour County. His persistent campaigning—he borrowed cars and walked to canvass potential voters—and the one-woman correspondence efforts of his wife, Lurleen, herself a future governor, swept him into the state legislature in 1946. Wallace tended to support moderate to progressive economic measures and served as a floor leader for progressive Governor Jim Folsom. By 1952, Wallace had won a judgeship for the Third District Circuit Court, a post that allowed him to extend his political reach further into south Alabama. Four years later he was already planning to enter the 1958 gubernatorial campaign.[11]

The state of Alabama, however, was not ready for him in 1958. Running as a segregationist but one who championed legal strategies rather than forceful defiance, Wallace was trounced by attorney general John Patterson. Wallace's slogan, "Keep Alabama Southern," was too vague to capture the imagination of voters who demanded a more vigorous commitment to fighting integration post *Brown*. Patterson benefited from Klan ties. Though small in number, the Klan could distribute printed material and campaign signs in a hurry, and was more than willing to intimidate prospective voters if necessary. In addition, Wallace was hurt by a National Association for the Advancement of Colored People

(NAACP) endorsement on the eve of the election. "George Wallace was considered soft on the issue in the '58 race," Patterson later recalled, "and that's one of the things that beat him." Disconsolate at his defeat, Wallace quickly surmised the key factor in his defeat and vowed to never let it happen again: "No other son-of-a-bitch will ever out-nigger me again."[12]

That was a promise Wallace kept, crisscrossing the state over the next four years and inventing ways to elevate his profile as a virulent segregationist. Wallace won easily in 1962, outdistancing Ryan deGraffenreid, whose approach to preventing integration was similar to Wallace's 1958 approach. Over the next twenty-five years, George Wallace became the most recognizable southern politician, a foil to civil rights leaders like Martin Luther King, and a linchpin to party realignment and the growing conservative movement. In the process, Wallace's national profile zoomed past other segregationist governors of the South like Patterson, Arkansas's Orval Faubus, Virginia's Thomas Stanley, and Ross Barnett of Mississippi.

Once in office, Wallace governed not through careful attention to Alabama's systemic economic or educational problems but through the politics of perpetual campaigning. As a leadership style, perpetual campaigning—Wallace ran for either governor or president in 1962, 1964, 1966 (for wife, Lurleen), 1968, 1970, 1972, 1974, and 1976—kept him attuned to the pulse of voters. And any chance to call attention to himself was an opportunity to be seized. When Oregon Governor Mark Hatfield called for a suspension of the Governors' Conference rules of procedure so that he might introduce a pro–civil rights resolution, Wallace immediately barked back. "I am going to ask . . . that the rules be suspended," the Alabamian bellowed, "in order that I . . . might introduce a resolution disendorsing the so-called civil rights program now pending in the American Congress." At that same 1963 Governors' Conference meeting, Wallace blasted the federal courts for "telling who can eat with you and who can go to school with you, whom you can swim with and play golf." The governor later announced that citizens in his state could walk the streets of Montgomery or Birmingham without fear—a thinly veiled implication that white supremacy provided safety—while residents of northern and midwestern states were too frightened to venture out at night in their cities. Civil rights, Wallace proclaimed to his colleagues, was a political issue, not a moral one.[13]

Over the course of his first term, Wallace spoke to congressional committees, went on speaking tours of college campuses, campaigned for president in three states in 1964, spoke to Citizens' Council groups all over the South, and ventured far and wide to speak to almost any group that would offer him a podium, a plate of food, and the potential of a camera crew. Over the course of his gubernatorial career, Wallace ran for president four times, captured 13 percent of the vote in 1968 as an independent, and won the electoral votes of five southern states in that campaign. No banquet, barbeque, high school or college graduation, college bowl game, or Civil War centennial event was too small. Wallace was a charismatic speaker, able to gauge the tenor of an audience and punctuate his speeches with snappy applause lines about "sandal-wearing freaks," "pointy-headed intellectuals who can't park their bikes straight," and hecklers who need a "hair cut and a job." And because of Wallace's legendary ability to remember names and hometowns and his willingness to linger in parking lots to chat with folks, his audiences felt a deeper connection to him than to other politicians. Because of his message and political acumen, Wallace emerged as the most recognizable southern governor and perhaps the most famous and infamous of any American governor during that era.[14]

Wallace's ability to capture the imagination of white southerners was noticed by his gubernatorial colleagues across the region. Lester Maddox, who famously brandished an ax handle to prevent the integration of his fried chicken joint, won a closely contested Georgia gubernatorial race in 1966. A year earlier, Maddox had picketed the Federal Building in Atlanta, carrying a sign that captured the essence of his political philosophy: "Down with Johnson, Socialism, Communism; Up with Wallace, Free Enterprise, Capitalism, Liberty, Private Property Rights, America." After his protest, Maddox received a letter of support from Wallace: "Just a note to tell you that many people in the country have been awakened to the dangers of the Civil Rights Bill. . . . Keep up the good fight." Maddox's surprise 1966 victory included a primary victory over a moderate state senator and peanut warehouseman from rural Plains, Georgia—Jimmy Carter. Four years later, Carter turned hard to the right in the 1970 campaign, appearing at segregated private schools, blasting the federal government, championing Wallace, and earning the endorsements of prominent segregationists like Maddox and Roy Harris, an Augusta newspaper editor and prominent Citizens' Council leader. Some members of the Carter campaign distributed racist handbills and doctored photographs that suggested Carter's opponent, moderate Carl Sanders, was too chummy with blacks. "I understand why he ran that kind of ultra-conservative campaign," said black state senator Leroy Johnson. "You have to do that to win. And that's the main thing. I don't believe you can win this state without being a racist." Carter did not govern as he campaigned, stating in his inaugural address, "I say to you quite frankly the time for racial discrimination is over." But the fact remains that to win the office, Carter had to mimic Wallace.[15]

Even though Wallace inspired imitators, his governance in Alabama

was problematic. Alabama was repeatedly sanctioned by the federal government during Wallace's tenure for failing to provide proper support
for dependent children, the mentally ill, and the blind, refusing to integrate facilities as disparate as elementary schools, state parks, and ice
cream parlors, stuffing prisons and mental health facilities until inmates
and patients were sleeping in cots in hallways, and discharging so much
industrial effluent into the state's streams and rivers that millions of fish
floated dead on top of the water. Alabamians made less money, were
educated in classrooms with more students per teacher, had fewer textbooks, paid more regressive taxes, and were more likely to be murdered
than the residents of most any other state in the Union. For all of the
acclaim—positive and negative—that Wallace accumulated due to the
politics of perpetual campaigning, very little changed in Alabama. "I'm
tired of seeing Alabama at the bottom in ratings," Alabamian Foy Batts
wrote his governor in 1974.[16]

All the more troubling about Batts's letter was the fact that it could
have easily been written a decade earlier when Wallace entered office or
a decade later when Wallace served his last term. In 1963, Alabama provided $47.33 per household in aid to dependent children at a time when
the national average was $127.99. In the same year, Alabama was forty-
eighth in the country in per capita income. Federal caseload limits for
social workers suggested that sixty clients was the maximum for efficient
service; Alabama workers averaged twice that many. A report on education written by Truman Pierce, dean of Auburn University, indicated
that the state had yet to make a concerted investment in that field. Alabama prisoners working on road crews—nearly 38 percent of the total
prison population—provided $2.60 per convict in daily revenue at a
time when it cost $9.88 per day to monitor them. All of this inefficiency
and poverty was layered on top of a culture of anti-intellectualism. "Why
is it a law you have to go to school until you are the age of sixteen?"
Talladega native Jimmy Watts wondered. "I think you should be able to
quit after you are 14 years of age because most people in the eighth
grade . . . are big enough to work." As late as 1976, one study indicated
that less than half of Alabamians believed a college education was "very
important" for landing a good job.[17]

During Wallace's last term, which began in 1983, Alabama was still facing many of the same problems. A 1984 report on state industry cited
numerous deficiencies preventing the state economy from approaching
regional or national averages including inadequate tax bases, health
care, education, and environmental regulation, and insufficient numbers of skilled workers and cultural opportunities. "Public education,"
the report noted, "has failed to keep pace at a time when industry is
placing increased emphasis on educational criteria . . . .The real prob-

lem lies in the failure to develop positive alternatives for longstanding negative impressions." According to a survey conducted by the Fantus Company, 71 percent of Alabamians viewed the state education system as substandard. An internal Corrections Department report indicated that the state had 10,031 prisoners at a time when capacity was 7,778 inmates. Despite a series of federal court orders demanding a reduction in overcrowding, the state prison population tripled from 1980 to 1985. And just like in Wallace's first term, an education expert authored a report indicating that the state had yet to make a concerted investment in education: the state was still last in the country in per-pupil expenditures. "The time for talk is over," state education superintendent Wayne Teague concluded. "We must now turn our attention to planning solutions for our identified problems."[18]

Wallace's preferred tactic for positing his state as a leader, despite its clear statistical position as a follower, was to compare Alabama's metrics with itself in previous years, not with peer states in current years. Wallace relished opportunities to tell the citizens of Alabama that they were just as smart and refined as the residents of any northern state. And he pointed to teacher raises, an expanded junior college system, free textbook programs, and educational television programs as proof that Alabama could make tangible progress in education while its governor waged a holy war against civil rights demonstrators, the meddling federal government, and other do-gooders. Many Alabamians heard the reports of 17.64 percent teacher raises, million-dollar capital improvement campaigns, and increased funds for classrooms and assumed Alabama was catching if not passing its neighbors. "I would like to thank you for the consideration shown to educational needs in our state," C. E. Akridge, a school principal, wrote to Lurleen Wallace. "I seriously doubt that any future administrations will be able to match the progress during the last five years."[19]

Ten years later, Alabamians were still convinced that Wallace was responsible for making major progress in education. "Once again," Alabamian Pansy Gewalt wrote her governor, "you have come through for us. You are the only governor we teachers have had in the history of this state." Particularly exemplary, many Alabamians believed, was Wallace's ability to resist the federal government's imperatives mandating busing to achieve racial balance and his opposition to Supreme Court decisions removing prayer and scripture from the schoolhouse. Though such battles put Alabama at odds with the federal government and often resulted in the state becoming subject to federal court decisions, polling revealed that three out of four Alabamians believed an Alabama education was as good as or better than an education from any other southern state. The Wallaces embraced such hagiography from their constituents. "As you know," Lurleen assured Akridge, "George and I have done as much or more for education than any other governor in the history of the state."[20]

The tactic of releasing positive information about growth was effective for increasing confidence in the administration, but belied the fact that Alabama was simply treading water in education as in most other facets of governance. The pay raises failed to move Alabama teachers to regional or national averages—other states were increasing salaries at faster rates—and the state continued to lose teachers to Georgia, Florida, and Tennessee. The junior college system that Wallace expanded was awash in political intrigue as many of the new schools were located, not surprisingly, in areas where Wallace had received significant electoral support. The textbook system was so poorly mismanaged and funded that some students in the state were sharing six-year-old defaced books with their peers instead of having their own new copy. Administration stalwarts were often as likely to complain about suspected Communist authors as they were to bemoan the insufficient number of available textbooks. And although the state provided enough monies for the educational television system to receive matching federal funds, it operated under strict administration pressure to avoid "integrated programs." Despite all of the bluff and bluster of the Wallace administration, one education expert, Truman Pierce, summarized Alabama as stuck at the same proverbial crossroads: "The basic question is not one of whether or not the state is able to afford good education but rather to what extent does the state really wish to do so." A decade later, a separate group—the Alabama Commission on Higher Education—reached similar conclusions: "There remains . . . a long distance to be traveled to reach an acceptable level of meeting the [education] needs of the state."[21]

Administration pronouncements about economic expansion, as with education, seemed encouraging, but belied a larger truth: most of the firms relocating to Alabama offered only low-wage, low-skill employment. "For the second consecutive year," an administration press release announced, "capital investment in new plants and expanded plant facilities has set a new, all-time record in Alabama with more than $623 million in 1965, providing 27,892 job opportunities for Alabamians." The numbers—subsequently revealed to be overstated—suggested that Alabamians were enjoying the greatest expansion of industry in state history. Both the Wallace and Cater Acts, legislation that dated to Wallace's tenure in the state house, provided long-term bond financing to entice corporations with land, buildings, and site development. Road access, airstrip construction, tax breaks, and other sweetheart incentives helped close the deal. In a state advertising campaign, Wallace instructed industrial prospects to call Montgomery: "Ask for George Wallace. When my secretary answers, tell her you're the president of a company. . . . She'll switch you quickly. . . . Down here, profit is a highly respectable word, because when you make money, all of our people benefit."[22]

Despite all of the optimistic numbers emanating out of the governor's press office, Alabama industry—like education—was mostly treading water. The list of new industries lured to Alabama was usually dominated by firms dedicated to lumber and paper products, fertilizer, low-tech manufacturing, and poultry processing. By 1974, broilers and eggs had surpassed cattle, hogs, and cotton production, but paid Alabama workers little more than subsistence wages. As Alabama industry increasingly relocated to third-world nations in the late 1970s, poverty and despair seemed a more realistic portrait of the state economy than the pronouncements of bustling industrial expansion coming from the governor's office. State coffers suffered. "Our inadequate budget," a 1978 Pensions and Security Department press release indicated, "has already made it necessary for us to institute some cuts in assistance and services, and we will be forced to make additional cuts." Although most bureaucrats certainly complain about needing more funds to administer their departments, the situation in Alabama was dire. State welfare commissioner Guy Burns requested a bare-bones budget of $13.5 million for 1979; the state legislature, given the stagnating state economy, appropriated only $5 million.[23]

In addition to failing to make substantive educational or economic progress, the Wallace administration presided over a period of unmatched racial turmoil. Selma, Birmingham, and Tuscaloosa are more than just cities. They stand as defining turf of the civil rights movement, hallmarks of the institutionalized oppression of black southerners at the hands of entrenched political and economic white elites. The Wallace administration, often through the auspices of the State Sovereignty Commission, withheld banking charters, prevented blacks from visiting state parks, and refused federal job funds because they came with provisos mandating integrated participation. Even after the Civil Rights Act of 1964 became law, the administration advocated a "same as before—segregated only" policy for Garrett Coliseum in Montgomery. Legislation was supported by the administration calling for $5,000 fines and five-year jail terms for any government employee participating in a civil rights demonstration. Wallace asked that a bill be drafted to "make it against the law for any person [to] enter the state [for] the purpose of instigating or advocating the violation of State laws or city ordinances." Wallace advanced two seemingly contradictory ideas: the civil rights movement was a Communist front, a supple but broad brush given the heightened intensity of the Cold War; and the civil rights movement was a money-making operation for Martin Luther King and other prominent voices for change. "This so-called civil rights movement," Wallace alleged, "has been very profitable to some Negro leaders and it looks like some other folks are trying to get in on the act." The movement, if one were to believe Wallace's aspersions, was replete with violent, Baptist, money-grubbing, capitalistic Communists.[24]

Wallace stoked the embers of white supremacy in every way imaginable. Long-standing southern sexual mythologies featured a persistent belief among some whites that black men lusted voraciously after white women. These constructed mythologies created out of a flawed memory of the southern past—all the more tragic and ironic given the antebellum history of planter abuses of female slaves—were a common rationalization for lynching. This idea was made manifest by respectable whites in their contention that intermarriage, not integration, was the true goal of the movement. Other whites annunciated their belief in crasser ways. Historian Karen Anderson recounts a story involving Arkansas civil rights leader Daisy Bates. The NAACP activist once received a letter inquiring whether her organization intended "to use bayonets . . . to force those white girls to go to bed with the black boy." Similar letters and public comments were commonplace across the South. Alabama passed laws early in the twentieth century making interracial marriage illegal, codifying two- to seven-year prison sentences for "adultery and fornication between white persons and negroes," and authorizing somewhat lighter sentences for judges and preachers who dared to join the races as man and wife. Wallace made it clear in correspondence that he viewed those laws as essential. "As you know," Wallace assured his constituents, "here in the State of Alabama we have a law banning marriage between the races and in my judgement this law is completely valid and should remain on the books."[25]

A favored tactic of the Wallace administration was to ask legislative floor leaders to pass what were commonly referred to as "nigger resolutions." Such measures were passed frequently by administration allies in the legislature, though they signified little more than a pack of wolves baying at the moon; as non-binding statements, they had no effect on delaying integration. These resolutions were passed any time the governor wanted word circulated throughout the highways and byways that he was fighting integration with every breath of his body. The usual theme of the resolutions was to blame blacks and the federal government for all of Alabama's problems. When the state legislature passed a bill contrary to a direct Wallace campaign promise, state speaker of the house Albert Brewer assumed the governor would veto the measure. "I'll just yell nigger," Wallace told Brewer in his explanation for signing the bill. At a state Democratic Party meeting, Wallace and his Palace Guard fought to keep the phrase "White Supremacy" on the official masthead of the state party. "I consider everyone who voted no [in favor of removing the motto]," a Wallace supporter noted at the meeting, "to be a . . . coward. I never thought that we would substitute white supremacy for black supremacy in Alabama."[26]

Institutionalized white supremacy, systemic racial discrimination, and instances of Wallace inflaming the passions of hatred are legion throughout much of his tenure in office. Simply put, Wallace used race to increase his power over the state legislature and to boost his popularity with white Alabamians. Though he did not champion violence, his words emboldened those who did. Numerous protestors, demonstrators, activists, and racial progressives lost their jobs, their homes, their personal safety, and sometimes their lives at a time when political elites looked the other way. Letters from fringe groups, paramilitary organizations, and racist crackpots poured into the governor's office on a daily basis. Byron de la Beckwith, eventually convicted decades later of murdering Mississippi NAACP leader Medgar Evers, wrote Wallace to inform him, "We haven't had any trouble with that nigger [Evers] since they buried him." Other letter writers advocated bizarre plans such as offering $100 to any black American who would voluntarily agree to sterilization. Klansmen, including Grand Wizard Robert Shelton, had regular access to the administration and often found themselves on the state payroll. When the Lurleen Wallace administration balked at federal guidelines for integration, Alabama Klan members hailed her in writing for "the courageous stand [she had] taken in [resisting] the unlawful and unconstitutional guide lines set pertaining to [the] schools." Many of these same Klansman that saluted the Wallaces swore an oath: "The friends of Negro equality are now and forever shall be my enemies." Every new Citizens' Council member in Alabama received a signed letter of congratulations and a photo of Wallace.[27]

Another result of Wallaceism across the region was the belief among white folks that they were the ones under attack. This backlash, as it has often been called, is exemplified by Wallace's penchant for blaming others for the South's problems. Racial violence was not caused by white southerners, Wallace intimated, but rather by blacks, usually ones who hailed from outside of the South. When the fragile truce of the 1963 Birmingham campaign literally exploded, Wallace blamed "communists . . . outside subversives. . . . This is what Martin Luther King calls nonviolence and passive resistance." A month earlier Wallace had warned the Student Nonviolent Coordinating Committee (SNCC) leader Charles McDew that his organization was responsible for exploiting acts of violence. "Your proposed activities," Wallace railed, "will serve no useful purpose. . . . Your apparent desire to ballyhoo this tragic incident for political and selfish reasons would be an affront to the dignity of the people of Alabama." Every aspect of white southern society honored the sanctity of tradition: sacred family hunting ground where boys took down their first deer and wore stripes of blood across their forehead for the rest of the day; grandma's secret cornbread recipe passed down one granddaughter at a time and never with pencil and paper; Southern Baptist hymnals that dotted the back of pews even as the same songs on the same pages were sung week after week. If the tradition of segregation was under attack, white southerners assumed that all of their other cherished beliefs were soon to be as well. And it was much easier to blame outsiders, as Wallace encouraged every white southerner to do, than to look inward at the tortured racial history of the region.[28]

If Wallace's administrative policies were fashioned around the consistent and sustained use of race for both policy and campaign purposes, other governors in the region found it possible to campaign and govern in a more moderate fashion. In South Carolina, as historian Gordon Harvey has shown, John West made tangible progress in education—expanded technical schools and improvements in medical education—after winning the 1970 campaign as a racial progressive. Political scientist Earl Black called West's inaugural address "liberal even by national standards." West appointed blacks to positions in state government, building on some momentum created by his predecessor Robert McNair, and recruited international corporations such as Korff Industries, Bosch, and Michelin. "The racial thing was a thing of the past," West later reflected, "We had lost, in a sense, in that we no longer were going to have a segregated society. Of course the challenge was to move forward and to minimize the problems, and to take advantage of this tremendous labor pool that was opened up because of our non-discrimination policies." Racial politics in South Carolina did not end with John West, but it ceased to be the defining issue.[29]

Florida Governor Reubin Askew was a similar racial moderate and modernized his state's education system, fostered economic growth based on high-tech manufacturing, and assisted the continued development of the tourism sector. Askew, perhaps more than any other southern governor, sympathized with busing as an "unavoidable" measure for ending segregation. As governor, Askew appointed Florida's first black Supreme Court justice, Joseph Hatchett. Askew's leadership style was based, in his own words, on telling people "what they need to know" as opposed to what they want to hear, a clear difference from Wallace's style of politics by perpetual campaigning. Though he was not a particularly popular governor, Askew's leadership skills and political savvy were substantial. He shepherded a corporate income tax through the state legislature, Florida's first such levy, despite significant opposition from interest groups.[30]

In North Carolina, the acceptance of civil rights and modernization of the state was a slow and conflicted process. Developments at Wake Forest College, a private Baptist school that Governor Terry Sanford—a Methodist—had no direct authority over, exemplified the shifting sands within the state and the slow encroachment of modernity. Wake alumni and faculty alike expressed reservations about integration. "I think it would be a grave mistake," math professor H. A. James wrote, "to admit Negroes now. . . . The older members of the faculty are overwhelmingly against it." H. M. Stroup, a member of the class of 1921, echoed Dr. James: "I want to enter just as strong [a] protest as I know how to make AGAINST admitting Negroes to our Baptist schools and especially Wake Forest." Favoring tradition over modernity, the board of trustees of the college voted, again, to deny student dancing, and affirmed, again, the preference for hiring Baptist faculty and recruiting Baptist students. And nearby Wake Forest Baptist Church agreed to allow black members only because the vote was held when three-quarters of the membership was absent on the Sunday of the Atlantic Coast Conference basketball tournament.[31]

The sentiment among some on the board of trustees was to table the matter as long as possible. Former Lieutenant Governor L. Y. Ballantine, the chair of the committee, said, "I hope the sub-committee on race relations will recommend . . . that further integration at the college be deferred at least until such time as the college community and the Negroes who may be interested in attending will be better prepared for such action." By 1970, Wake Forest was admitting an increasing number of black students, but changes to student demographics were slow. "Sure there are more black students here now," Ed Reynolds, who broke the color barrier at the school in 1962, noted in 1970, "but that doesn't necessarily mean there has been much progress in integration. Most of the black and white students don't have that much to do with each other." The integration at Wake Forest, in short, reflected other trends across the state: moderate whites sought to delay change, activists hoped to foster change, and militant segregationists worked to prevent change. One of the most common sentiments was the idea that black schools should be improved, though maintained as separate institutions. "In our county," North Carolina resident Jacob Pickler declared, "the Negro school buildings are fifty years behind the times. I am in favor of giving them modern buildings and facilities but continuing segregation." Many whites convinced themselves that black children did not want to integrate either. "Most of the Negro people are satisfied and do not want to go to the same schools with the white children. They want better schools and they were justified in that."[32]

In this environment Terry Sanford ran for governor of North Carolina in 1960. Preliminary polling indicated that Sanford was expected to carry the black vote, though pollster Louis Harris suggested, "It is undoubtedly best, in view of past primary history, not to make overt gestures for the Negro vote in this state. . . . At this moment the white electorate is not deeply stirring over racial issues, though some rather ugly overtones can be brought out if one scratches only a bit below the surface." Harris's research indicated that the majority of North Carolinians favored segregation, thought that college student sit-ins should not result in blacks eating with whites, and believed that black civil rights activists had the wrong approach in asking for immediate change. Sanford straddled the racial line, promising to support the Pearsall Plan —the 1956 plan passed by the legislature to circumvent school integration—but also criticizing opponent I. Beverly Lake, a virulent segregationist, as a "Pied Piper of prejudice." Sanford won comfortably, despite the heated tenor of the campaign.[33]

While in office, Sanford enforced the law, allowing integration to proceed, if slowly. He created the Good Neighbor Council, an agency dedicated to employment of all qualified people without regard to race or age. Led by David Coltrane and working through cooperation between white and black churches, recreation facility administrators, local activists, and municipal leaders, the Good Neighbor Council sought to minimize racial conflict. According to Sanford biographers Howard Covington and Marion Ellis, Coltrane convinced community leaders to allow integration for a variety of reasons. "He didn't mind casting any arguments in terms of their self interest," former aide David Gergen remembered, "You don't want violence here. You don't want the national press here. We are all better off if we don't do these things." Progress was measured in small doses: integrated churches, desegregated public libraries, blacks working as sales clerks in stores.[34]

Despite the actions and policies of the Sanford administration, racial progress in North Carolina was slow and painful. Many schools were slow to integrate, and many swimming pools, basketball courts, and employment lines remained contested spaces. Sanford left office an unpopular man in many areas of the state. "Do you want your grand or great-grand children to be black or white?" one frustrated segregationist complained to Sanford. "If a handful of renegade and maverick whites want to swim, dine, and sleep with their black friends," another North Carolinian wrote, "and thus ease their consciences, that is their personal business. We don't want . . . Negro thugs . . . being allowed to enter and revert to their native and natural savagery." And Wallace, not Sanford, was the preferred southern presidential candidate in the state when they clashed in the 1972 Democratic primary.[35]

In the era of the civil rights movement, George Wallace shaped the political landscape for southern governors. Some chose to mimic him, but absent the superb raw political skills of the Alabamian, often found their time in office limited to one or two terms. Others played off of Wallace, positioning themselves as New South governors capable of creating a better image, better schools, and a more balanced economy. In Georgia, New South governors streamlined their budgeting system, watched Atlanta become one of the nation's most important economic hubs, and developed modern economies. "The first thing I tell them," then-Governor Jimmy Carter noted of industrial prospects, "is that if you're looking for cheap labor, we don't want you." Charlotte, North Carolina, became one of the nation's leading banking centers. Miami, Jacksonville, Orlando, Tampa, Charlotte, Atlanta, and New Orleans all received major professional sports franchises by the end of the century, a sure sign that the nation had accepted the South. Edwin Edwards in Louisiana, Dale Bumpers in Arkansas, Jim Holshouser in North Carolina, Winfield Dunn and Ray Blanton in Tennessee, Mills Godwin in Virginia, and several other southern governors had varying degrees of success modernizing state economies, streamlining government, improving education, and reducing racial tension.[36]

By the end of the 1970s, only the last vestiges of overt racism remained. But even then George Wallace was still around. Having apologized, repented, and found a way to win yet another term in 1982, Wallace finally retired in 1987. Nearly blind, deaf, noticeably older, paralyzed, and feeble, George Wallace was still the center of southern gubernatorial politics. Only this time, he represented the possibility and promise of change, not a deep-seated fear of it.

Governing the 1970s

Although Neil Armstrong's walk on the moon in 1969 had left Americans hopeful for the future, a number of pressing issues remained to be resolved and new crises arose in the 1970s that drew governors ever further into national and international concerns. Political scandal made many Americans distrustful of government. As this disaffection grew, governors responded by reviving the ideal of state government as close to its citizens and the protector of American democracy. But the challenges of the decade made this goal difficult. Deindustrialization began as jobs in the manufacturing sector shrank, displacing workers in steel and other industries and triggering a population shift from northern manufacturing centers to cities in the South and Southwest where economic opportunities in other labor sectors were growing.

In addition to this economic unease and displacement, protests over Vietnam reached a fever pitch in the early years of the decade. Much of this antiwar activism centered on college campuses as students rebelled against the policies of the national government and President Richard Nixon's seeming indifference to their concerns. Disagreement escalated to bloodshed on May 4, 1970, when National Guardsmen fired shots into a group of student protestors at Kent State University. Four were left dead, and the country was stunned. Speaking before the 1970 winter meeting of the National Governors' Conference, Spiro Agnew, former governor of Maryland (1967–1969) and Nixon's vice president, called upon the nation's governors to band together and quell the antigovernment discontent. "What is the greatest issue today? It is not the war in Vietnam, nor inflation, nor the environment. . . . Simply stated it is 'Will the Government of this country remain in the hands of its elected officials, or will it descend to the streets?'" He was convinced that governors could control the situation, advising them to "just launch a campaign to exert the force of public opinion to drive these bizarre extremists from the preemptive positions on our television screens, and the front pages of our newspapers."[1] But most governors were hesitant to adopt Agnew's fiery and divisive rhetoric. The United States withdrew from Vietnam in 1973, yet domestic discontent remained.

A series of scandals in the national government contributed to this malaise. Charges of tax evasion forced Agnew to resign. Nixon won reelection by a landslide in 1972 despite his vocal critics, but his victory was soon tainted when *Washington Post* reporters Carl Bernstein and Bob Woodward investigated the Watergate break-in and traced guilt back to the Oval Office. In 1974, Nixon resigned rather than face impeachment. Although his administration made progressive advancements in many areas, including environmental protection and opening relations with China, Nixon became a symbol to the nation's disaffected youth of the potential corruptive power of government.

Living among their electorate, governors were well aware of widespread anger against government. They used the annual meetings of the National Governors' Association (as it was renamed in 1977) to discuss methods for addressing citizens' concerns. Some asserted that governors and state legislatures had the responsibility of making government more responsive to the people. For example, Governor Warren Hearnes of Missouri (1965–1973) argued that a revival of state government could help ameliorate the widespread discontent. "To those who have already written state government out of our federal system," Hearnes explained, "I say they have dangerously misjudged our determination to remain strong and viable in the best interests of our citizens. . . . I say they are badly out of step with the growing wave of citizen sentiment that government close to the people must be strengthened. It is time for the Governors to roll up their sleeves and set about restoring a balance to our federal system."[2] Across the country, governors worked to make their state governments more open, honest, and accountable. Reuben Askew (1971–1979), for example, supported Florida's adoption of the "Sunshine Amendment," setting guidelines for full financial disclosure by public officials and candidates.

In the same vein of revamping the state, governors debated the idea of revenue sharing. This plan—to open up streams of more flexible funding to states and localities and reduce states' dependence on grants-in-aid programs—was part of Nixon's "New Federalism" initiative, but the idea pervaded American politics throughout the last quarter of the twentieth century. In theory, revenue sharing was what the majority of governors had been asking for since the New Deal—more flexible federal funding to the states with, supposedly, fewer strings attached. The reality was more complicated. At times, revenue sharing became an easy out for the federal government to foist increased responsibilities on states without corresponding funds. Despite their complaints about large government, Americans had grown accustomed to its many services. Thus, the question, as it had been for many decades, was: Who should pay for ever-growing public programs?

Most governors enthusiastically supported revenue sharing, believing the federal government needed to return responsibilities and funding to states. At the 1973 annual meeting, Governor Ronald Reagan of California (1967–1975), who later as president tried to extend this policy of devolution, affirmed his support by declaring, "If we really mean what we have been saying at these conferences over the years of wanting more autonomy and more responsibility for programs, plus the means to carry them out, here it is in our hands if every one of us, regardless of affiliation, will begin beating on . . . Congressmen's heads and telling them that this is what we want and that we are fed up with the red tape that we have had over the years."[3] Many governors believed this goal of returning power to the state to be the answer to redeeming citizens' faith in a scandal-plagued and overgrown national government. Governor William Milliken (1969–1983), for example, embraced revenue sharing to help Michigan through the difficult decade. Facing a major depression in his state exacerbated by a troubled automotive industry and an energy crisis, he implemented revenue sharing to aid Detroit. Despite economic hardship, the General Motors strike of 1970, and several Arab oil embargoes, Milliken remained popular because of his effective governance.

In addition to these federalism and morale concerns, governors in the 1970s took a renewed interest in environmental protection, the issue that originally brought governors together in 1908. The founding of the Environmental Protection Agency (EPA) in 1970 by the Nixon administration helped set standards, but many states had already led the way in innovative conservation policy and continued down these paths. The national energy crisis in the mid-to-late 1970s further illustrated the immediacy for cleaner air and water and, in particular, alternative and efficient fuels. Governor Thomas Lee Judge (1973–1981) worked with the state legislature to pass the Montana Environmental Policy Act. Governor Cecil D. Andrus of Idaho (1971–1977, 1987–1995), who later served under President Carter as secretary of the interior, promoted conservation in his state by negotiating a beneficial middle ground between environmentalists and developers. In his later terms, he was a national advocate for the creation of safe nuclear waste disposal sites. In Oregon, Governor Tom McCall (1967–1975) created a state Office of Energy Research and Planning to coordinate research on finding alternative energy sources and more efficient use of existing sources. As governor, he named himself chairman of the State Sanitary Authority and spearheaded an effort to clean the Willamette River. Environmentalism became not only a health and aesthetic issue, but also an international one with the growing violence in the oil-rich Middle East.

Governors increasingly took into account these international concerns when shaping the policies of their administrations. At the 1973 annual meeting, Jimmy Carter, then governor of Georgia (1971–1975), proclaimed his belief that "Governors ought to take every possible advantage to shape major legislation in the national government." Carter had recently returned from a trip to the Middle East and felt "that [governors] can build a tremendous basis for future peace on economic development and mutual investment between foreign governments and our individual States, supportive of, of course, the federal government's responsibility in the field."[4] After his election to the presidency, Carter retained this faith in the positive power of the gubernatorial office. Yet, as the 1970s ended in the midst of an energy crisis and a hostage situation in Iran, Americans' faith in government was again tested.

In the 1970s, governors worked to reenergize states and promote the benefits of their closer ties to the American public. In turn, Americans began a renewed trend of sending governors to the White House, starting with the 1976 election of Jimmy Carter. The success of this transition from governor to president depends on the individual. Ronald Reagan entered California politics as a novice, but quickly learned the importance of bipartisanship and the need to work effectively with the legislature. Nationally, he made headlines by opposing Nixon's proposed federal takeover of welfare through the Family Assistance Plan and eventually passed his own landmark welfare reform bill in California. Reagan's experiences as governor through the turbulent days of Watergate shaped the president he would become.

Chapter Six

Preparing for the Presidency
The Political Education of Ronald Reagan

LOU CANNON

On November 18, 1980, two weeks after he was elected the fortieth president of the United States, Ronald Wilson Reagan sat down with Thomas P. (Tip) O'Neill, Speaker of the House of Representatives. The two men knew one another only by reputation, and O'Neill, whose Democrats held a commanding majority in the House, suspected that Reagan was in over his head. He told the president-elect that Sacramento, where Reagan had spent eight years as governor of California, was the "minor leagues." Now they were in Washington, where O'Neill had been a member of the House since 1952. "This is the big leagues," O'Neill said.[1] Reagan's aides were annoyed at the condescension. Reagan was amused. He understood that O'Neill was testing him and said later that it was advantageous to be underestimated by the Speaker of the House. Weeks later, as the new president's economic programs advanced through the House with Democratic support, O'Neill lamented that he had underrated Reagan. Like others before and after him, the Speaker had failed to detect the formidable politician behind the Reagan smile or understand that eight contentious years in Sacramento had taught Reagan how to hit major-league pitching.

Since the middle of the twentieth century, California has been an eye-catching nation-state with a budget larger than all but a half-dozen countries in the world. For many, California epitomized the American dream, defined by William Faulkner as "sanctuary on earth for individual man."[2] California in the 1960s was also a cockpit of rebellion—in Berkeley, in Watts, and on the industrialized farms of the central valley where farm workers struggled to organize. State government was on the cutting edge of change. During Reagan's governorship Sacramento was a laboratory for controversial policy decisions on abortion, air pollution, tax relief, and welfare reform. The state had a robust permanent government staffed by career bureaucrats who were insulated from partisan politics by civil service. Democrats controlled the legislature. The brightest and most ambitious of them was a sharecropper's son named Jesse Unruh, a larger-than-life politician who as Assembly Speaker had transformed a lobby-ridden house into a modern, well-staffed lawmaking institution. Fourteen years before O'Neill tested him, Reagan battled and bargained with the resourceful Unruh over his spending programs. At the beginning, this seemed an uneven match; Reagan had never spent a day in public office and many of his top aides were similarly inexperienced. As Reagan's rumpled communications director Franklyn Nofziger summed it up retrospectively: "We weren't only amateurs, we were novice amateurs."[3]

Reagan was used to this. Throughout his life he had talked his way into jobs for which he lacked formal qualification and done well in them. He had been a broadcaster, a movie actor, a television host, and a businessman. As president of the Screen Actors Guild he had proved an able negotiator who led his union in a successful strike against the film producers. But when he went into politics Reagan was dismissed as an uninformed amateur in a world of accomplished professionals. To the professionals he seemed too light—and to the Democrats too right—to succeed in politics. Yet succeed he did. How? How was it that this fading movie star, a small-town boy who had graduated from a small-time college in his native Illinois and taught himself to act, was able to reinvent himself at the age of fifty-five and become governor of the nation's most populous state? And how was he able to leap from the governorship of California to the presidency of the United States, win reelection in a forty-nine-state landslide, play a leading role in ending the Cold War, and become a conservative icon and the most revered Republican among twentieth-century presidents? The usual answers to these questions are that Reagan had principles, ideas, determination, exceptional communicative skills, and considerable luck. All this is true, and he was also married to a remarkable woman who helped him make the most of his opportunities. But after observing Reagan as a journalist for three decades and writing five books about him, I am convinced that Reagan might not have made it to the top—and certainly would not have done as well once he got there—without mastering the hard lessons he learned as governor of California. This view is largely shared by key aides who were instrumental in his success in Sacramento and Washington, among them Edwin Meese, William Clark, and the late Michael Deaver.

Interestingly, considering what it ultimately would mean to him, Reagan had no ambition to be governor of California. In the 1960s, as he was nearing the end of his long political odyssey from New Deal Democrat to conservative Republican, Reagan talked almost entirely about international and national issues. On the former, he focused on the threat to the United States posed by the Soviet Union and its surrogates; on the latter, he warned about an expansive federal government. Reagan was in mild demand on the speaking circuit but did not come to broad public attention until October 27, 1964, when he gave a rousing nationally televised speech on behalf of Senator Barry Goldwater of Arizona, the Republican presidential nominee, as usual stressing anti-Soviet and antigovernment themes. Goldwater lost in a landslide a week later, but Reagan became an overnight sensation. David Broder of the *Washington Post* called Reagan's speech "the most successful national political debut since William Jennings Bryan electrified the 1896 Democratic convention with his Cross of Gold speech."[4]

A year later a small band of California entrepreneurs who had been inspired by Reagan's speeches organized "Friends of Ronald Reagan" to raise money for a prospective gubernatorial candidacy. Reagan was flattered but confessed he knew little about state issues. He was more interested, he told the Friends, in challenging President Lyndon B. Johnson, who after defeating Goldwater was expanding his "Great Society" programs and widening U.S. participation in the Vietnam War. The Friends, headed by Los Angeles automobile dealer Holmes Tuttle, told Reagan he was premature. Their idea was that Reagan could establish himself as a national figure by running against Edmund G. (Pat) Brown, the liberal two-term Democratic governor. Reagan thought it over. Then he did something that was an augury of the practicality he would display in office by meeting with Bill Roberts and Stuart Spencer, two rising young political consultants who had managed the near-miss campaign of New York Governor Nelson Rockefeller against Goldwater in the 1964 California primary. Spencer and Roberts had been expected to run the gubernatorial campaign of George Christopher, a centrist former mayor of San Francisco. Instead, they signed on with Reagan—and Reagan with them.

Republican prospects at the time looked dim. Goldwater had carried so many other Republican officeholders down to defeat with him that some analysts were wondering if the party would go the way of the Whigs. The best hope for the GOP was in statehouses; Republicans had held onto all their governorships in 1964 but many of these incumbents had distanced themselves from Goldwater. Having the tag of "Goldwater Republican," as Reagan did, seemed a losing label. The Democrats, after all, had succeeded in demonizing Goldwater as a "right-wing extremist." Many thought Reagan would be similarly tarred. But Goldwater at least was experienced; Reagan's inexperience showed as an issue in every early poll. Small wonder that Reagan looked beatable to

Christopher and to Governor Brown. How was it possible for a novice right-wing extremist to get elected?

Reagan's only evident advantage was name recognition, a by-product of his many movies and years on television, most notably as host of *General Electric Theater*. In celebrity-conscious California, this mattered. Reagan drew crowds and was often besieged by autograph seekers. He had played a good guy in most of his movies, the "heart-warming role of himself," as Garry Wills later wrote, and people liked his directness.[5] Reagan thought the state was spending too much and was badly managed. He didn't pretend to have all the answers. He billed himself as a citizen-politician who would use common sense to solve the arcane problems of state government.

Reagan declared his candidacy on January 4, 1966, and quickly tackled his supposed twin handicaps of inexperience and extremism. "The man who has the job has all the experience, that's why I'm running," Reagan quipped. He said it would be desirable to have an outsider take a fresh look at state government, a contention the political community thought laughable but that voters accepted. Nor did the extremism issue have much resonance. Reagan, with his sunny personality, neither looked nor sounded extreme. Goldwater, it was often said, made the conservative case with a scowl while Reagan did it with a smile. When Reagan's opponents charged that his campaign was permeated by members of the right-wing John Birch Society, Reagan said that any Bircher who supported him was buying his philosophy, not the other way around. Reagan was now doing better in the polls, but Governor Brown continued to underestimate him. Brown had been in politics all of his life and couldn't understand how a movie actor could possibly be governor. This low opinion of Reagan and his profession led Brown into a lapse of political judgment. Since Brown was convinced he would beat Reagan but might lose to Christopher, he authorized a smear of Christopher in the Republican primary campaign. There are, in the old phrase, more tears caused by answered prayers than by those that are not heard. Reagan defeated Christopher handily, and Brown's smear helped unify a hitherto divided Republican Party. (Years later, Christopher told me that he endorsed and worked for Reagan only because he was angry at Brown.)[6] In November, Reagan defeated Brown by nearly a million votes.[7] Paul Laxalt, who later became Reagan's staunchest ally in Washington, was at the same time elected governor of neighboring Nevada.

But what would Reagan do now that he was governor? During the campaign he had spoken mostly in generalities about his programs. Once, when asked in a friendly setting what kind of a governor he would be, he responded, "I don't know. I've never played a governor."[8] Now, he had to match his quips with a successful performance, and he soon realized that this would not be an easy thing to do. Reagan's most pressing problem was a looming budget deficit of immense proportions. California was not supposed to have any deficits at all; the state constitution requires a balanced budget. But Governor Brown's finance director, anxious to avoid an election-year tax increase, had in 1966 changed the state's accounting methods without financing the changeover. As a result, the state had funded a year's spending with fifteen months of revenue. In his inaugural message Reagan accurately described the accounting change as "a gimmick that solved nothing but only postponed the day of reckoning." With the reckoning at hand, however, Reagan lacked the professional expertise to come to grips with it. Reagan's top three choices for the key post of finance director had turned down the job. His fourth choice, who took it, was a management consultant who knew little about state budgeting procedures. As a result, the proposed budget that Reagan submitted to the legislature in January 1967 achieved balance through the arbitrary method of making 10 percent across-the-board reductions in the spending of every state department and agency. Reagan's critics in the legislature called this a cookie-cutter plan, saying it would penalize well-run agencies and reward those with excess staffing. Reagan withdrew the budget. Two months later he submitted a second and more realistic spending plan with an additional $440 million of spending.

Reagan had promised in his inaugural address to "squeeze, cut and trim" the cost of government. He tried, although some of the economies he proposed were trivial. But no amount of cost control would have balanced California's budget in 1967. Reagan recognized this. Two days after he became governor, Reagan told aides he did not want to wait "until everyone forgets that we did not cause the problem—we only inherited it."[9] He proposed a tax increase that as unveiled carried a price tag of $946 million and that when enacted, after protracted negotiations with Unruh and the power brokers in the state senate, reached $1 billion ($6 billion in 2006 dollars). No governor of any state had ever proposed a tax increase of this magnitude; it was four times as large as the previous California record. Democrats and Republicans alike were astounded by the readiness with which Reagan had embraced a tax increase after all his talk about cutting and trimming. Nor was it the amount alone that was stunning. The Reagan tax bill was progressive, increasing income tax rates for the wealthy while providing property tax relief for older and low-income Californians, often synonymous. Low-income seniors received substantial refunds on their property tax bills. At the same time the bill increased tax rates on banks, corporations, and insurance companies. Working together, Unruh and Reagan supporters pried loose the budget bill into which the tax increase had been incorporated from a recalcitrant state senate, which was skeptical of both the Speaker and the governor. Unruh was elated. He favored the bill on its merits but also believed that the tax increase would damage Reagan's standing with the voters. On this occasion the novice governor had better political instincts than the experienced Assembly Speaker. Reagan suspected that by the time he sought reelection in 1970 the tax bill would be ancient history, as indeed it was.[10]

Passage of the budget and the tax increase that supported it—much summarized here, for it took seven months and many twists and turns to accomplish—was a watershed for the Reagan administration. The economy turned upward in the late 1960s, boosting state revenues beyond the level needed to erase the deficit. With the state awash in money, the Reagan administration was able to maintain generous levels of state spending for a myriad of public programs. Reagan was in a protracted struggle with the University of California and to a lesser degree with the state college (now state university) system over tuition and other issues, all this against an emotional background of attempting to crack down on student disorders. He had originally proposed significant cuts in the university budget; solving the budget crisis with a tax increase enabled him to restore most of the reductions. The University of California Board of Regents in turn agreed to impose modest tuitions for incoming students. But the most important consequence of the tax increase was that it stamped Reagan as a skillful politician in the eyes of the public and the legislature. This was not a plus to some conservatives, who worried, not for the last time, about Reagan's pragmatism. Reagan, however, had not abandoned his philosophy. He clung to a broad goal of government economizing and tax reduction, as he would demonstrate in Sacramento and Washington. Indeed, Reagan would in 1973 propose (unsuccessfully) a state constitutional amendment to require lower tax rates at every level of California government. He would as president in 1981 propose personal income tax reductions that were enacted into law. But Reagan was not an abstractionist: he believed in governing successfully even if that at times meant postponing his basic objectives. The circumstances in 1967 required a tax increase, and Reagan did what was necessary, without looking back. This was an elemental lesson in his political education.

Doing what was necessary that first year in Sacramento also required Reagan to make personnel changes in his top circle. That was never Reagan's strong suit—he hated to fire anyone and was always inclined to believe the best about anyone who espoused his agenda. But after a scandal, he replaced his chief of staff with William P. Clark, a soft-spoken lawyer and rancher who had been his cabinet secretary. When Clark left the Reagan administration in Sacramento to become a judge, he was succeeded by Edwin Meese, Reagan's legal affairs secretary, who was chief of staff for the remaining six years of the governorship. The state finance director who had proposed the cookie-cutter budget was also gone within a year, allowed to resign for personal reasons. He was succeeded by Caspar W. Weinberger, later secretary of defense, and Weinberger by Verne Orr, later secretary of the Air Force. All of these successors did well. When Reagan did not appoint the right person at first, he usually kept trying until he did. But there were never wholesale dismissals during the Reagan governorship. Many of Reagan's initial appointees to top and mid-level posts performed capably and stayed for all or most of the governorship. Their quality reflected the high standards of Reagan's first appointments secretary, Thomas C. Reed, later secretary of the Air Force in the Ford administration. Reed, a nuclear physicist turned politician, had been the northern California chairman of Reagan's campaign for governor. He wanted to become Governor Reagan's chief of staff. When this post was not offered, Reed decided to return to private life but agreed to serve for a hundred days as Reagan's appointments secretary. He was ideal for the job: Reed was independently wealthy and immune from the temptation to help persons who might later help him. While a partisan who believed that Republicans should be appointed when possible, Reed was determined not to saddle Reagan with incompetents or party hacks. He winnowed out a number of these, helped by Paul Haerle, a lawyer who focused on judicial selections. Because of their efforts, Reagan wound up with a capable cabinet. Norman (Ike) Livermore, a lumberman and member of the Sierra Club, proved particularly outstanding as state resources director, a sensitive post in environmentally conscious California.

The Sacramento press corps and the legislature, with exceptions in both cases, tended to credit Reagan's accomplishments, especially in his first term, to his appointees. Reagan unwittingly encouraged this. Most governors (and presidents) routinely take credit for everything good that happens on their watch and try to deflect blame on others when things go wrong. Reagan had so little ego that he didn't mind when a Meese or a Weinberger or a Livermore was praised for a policy decision that bore his name nor did he care when a legislator, particularly but not exclusively a Republican legislator, won acclaim for a proposal that had originated with the governor. Reagan's philosophy was expressed by a sign that would adorn his desk in the Oval Office: "There is no limit to what a man can do or where he can go if he doesn't mind who gets the credit."

It was useful for Reagan to credit others in the early months of his governorship because he was unfamiliar with so many state issues. When asked questions of policy, Reagan frequently retreated into platitudes laced with anecdotes that he would repeat as if telling them for the first time. Small wonder that reporters and legislators alike assumed that someone other than Reagan was pulling the strings. A more complex picture emerges from the minutes of Reagan's first-year cabinet meetings, which were secret at the time. (Clark made them available to me for my 2003 book, *Governor Reagan: His Rise to Power.*) The Reagan revealed in these minutes, foreshadowing the Reagan of his later presidential diaries, was often pungent in his comments about various critics: Unruh, environmental groups, and university officials who were sanguine about disruptive student protests. At his worst he seemed out to lunch. During one discussion of proposed budget cuts in the Department of Mental Hygiene, for instance, Reagan's contribution was to say he had a hard time, in the movie *Kings Row*, learning to mispronounce the word "psychiatric," as the role required him to do.[11] But more often, Reagan asked pertinent questions and made good decisions, sometimes against the grain. One example of the latter, incompletely reflected in the minutes, was Reagan's decision on a proposed 730-foot high dam on the middle fork of the Eel River that would have flooded one of California's most scenic valleys. Many expected the project to be routinely approved, all the more so because it would have provided water for thirsty southern California. No California governor had ever rejected such a project; Reagan's business and transportation secretary, his state water resources director, and the powerful California water lobby all favored the Dos Rios Dam. Yet Reagan sided with Livermore and a small Indian tribe in the valley and rejected the project.[12]

Overall, the cabinet minutes and other memos from the period show Reagan to have an executive's temperament. Believing that the best time to make a decision was when it was before him, he rarely temporized. He never asked about the political popularity of a decision but often inquired about its possible economic impact. He changed course on a number of occasions, an attribute that was not always on display in public. And he developed a style of governance that was worthwhile for its own sake but was also valuable training for the presidency.

It is true nonetheless that others sometimes made decisions bearing Reagan's name. Reagan ranked high on the scale of what his subsequent vice president George H. W. Bush would call "the vision thing," but he was rarely a detail person. Reagan was by inclination and sometimes by necessity a delegator. He performed best when he had a chief of staff who understood his modes of behavior and could fill in the details in a manner consistent with Reagan's objectives. Meese fit this bill in Sacramento, as James Baker did when Reagan became president. I know of many occasions where both men negotiated or made agreements in Reagan's name but none in which they exceeded their authority. They made sure that Reagan signed off on everything they did. When Reagan lacked a chief of staff who had these qualities, he did less well. That was not the usual situation. In Clark and Meese he had capable chiefs of staff for seven and a half of his eight years as governor. In James Baker, Howard Baker, and Kenneth Duberstein, he would be similarly well served in six of the eight years of his presidency.

Two other aspects of Reagan's training for the presidency during his first term as governor deserve attention. The first is the process of decision-making in the Reagan cabinet, the second the maturation of his relationships with legislators. On the former, the device that proved most useful to Reagan was a system developed by Clark during his tenure as chief of staff. In an effort to avoid overwhelming Reagan with detail, Clark converted the multipage memoranda prepared for the governor on various issues and reduced them to a single page. Each "mini-memo," as they were called, consisted of four paragraphs. The first stated the issue, the second discussed the facts, the third was a discussion, and the fourth made a recommendation. When this system was revealed in the press, Reagan's critics hooted, seeing it as a sign that he lacked the ability (or interest) to engage issues at any level of complexity. In fact, Clark and Meese after him prepared backup papers for every paragraph, and Reagan sometimes used them. But the critics had a point: Reagan lacked background on many of the issues on which he was required to make decisions. In most cases the mini-memos told him everything he needed to know.[13]

Reagan's relationships with legislators—or more precisely, the lack of such relationships—were problematic early in his governorship. Except for a former actor named Charles Conrad, the 120 California legislators were strangers to Reagan when he became governor, and he did little to make their acquaintance. For all his amiability, Reagan was not much of a mixer. He worked diligently in his corner office of the capitol and did the ceremonies and speeches required of him but preferred at the end of the day to have a quiet dinner at home with Nancy Reagan to socializing with politicians. Nor did the legislators reach out to Reagan. Like state legislators anywhere, most of them were unknown to the general public. Many had spent their lives in politics and resented this movie star whom (as they saw it) had waltzed in to run a government about which he knew so little. It didn't help that Robert Monagan, the able Republican leader in the Assembly, was a moderate, as were most of his lieutenants. Monagan had toyed with a gubernatorial candidacy before endorsing George Christopher against Reagan in the 1966 primary.

Reagan was rescued from detachment by his savvy legislative staff, which arranged for lobbyists to throw a fancy dinner with leading legislators at a well-known Sacramento restaurant. Over the meal the guests took turns telling stories, all of them politically barbed and most of them unprintable. In a day when the legislature was almost entirely male, with a bawdy, locker-room culture, this sort of event was a snap for Reagan. He was a veteran of Hollywood roasts and possessed a solid repertoire of ethnic, off-color, and political anecdotes. The legislators were impressed. Reagan, having shown he could be one of the boys, went back to his early dinners with his wife. The dinner with the legislators, however, began a process that over time improved relationships with lawmakers. In his second term—and in the presidency—Reagan would develop productive relationships with the legislative branch. The first term was slow going, even though Reagan's legislative secretary George Steffes prodded Reagan and Monagan to develop a substantive relationship. They did their best, but were never close.

Reagan ran for the Republican presidential nomination in 1968, encouraged by grassroots conservatives and William Rusher, the publisher of *National Review*. F. Clifton White, who had masterminded the Goldwater nominating drive in 1964, signed on as a consultant. Working with Tom Reed and with seed money raised by Holmes Tuttle, White ran what today would be called an exploratory campaign. Even by this description, it was a half-hearted effort. Reagan was cautious, and his chief of staff Bill Clark believed that a presidential candidacy would reduce his focus on state issues and potentially damage his governorship. The Democrats sensed this, too, and accused Reagan of using the governor's office as a stepping stone to the White House. Reagan was not the only governor with this problem; it was also raised against Michigan Governor George Romney, who for other reasons was soon out of the race. Mindful of the stepping-stone criticism, Reagan remained an undeclared, "favorite son" candidate while Richard Nixon was picking up delegates and commitments across the country. Reagan was more emotionally appealing than Nixon to rank-and-file Republicans and a better speaker who turned out larger crowds. Considering he wasn't an announced candidate, Reagan picked up a surprising number of delegates in the West and South, foreshadowing his future success in these regions in presidential campaigns to come. But in 1968 Nixon had experience, focus, and a far superior organization. By the time Reagan declared his candidacy at the Republican National Convention in Miami Beach, it was all over. Reagan told me that he felt a "sense of relief" when Nixon was nominated.[14] He separately told Nofziger and Deaver that he wasn't ready to be president.[15] Ready or not, the 1968 campaign provided another valuable lesson in the political education of Ronald Reagan. He developed a feel for national campaigning and learned much about whom he could trust (and whom he couldn't) in party politics. When Reagan next ran for president eight years later he was a better candidate because of his 1968 experience.

The Democratic Party unraveled nationally in 1968 in the face of the Vietnam War abroad and civil disorders and student protests at home. Nixon was elected president, and the Republican Party made gains in Congress and statehouses across the nation. In California, Republicans won both houses of the legislature and Monagan replaced Unruh as Speaker of the Assembly. This should have been good news for Reagan. As it turned out, one of the ironies of his governorship was that he accomplished less in the two years the Republicans had a majority in the Assembly than in any of the six years that Democrats were in control. This was not for lack of trying. Reagan put forth a reasonable plan for tax reform in 1969, but Republicans in the Assembly, unaccustomed to being in the majority, had several competing plans of their own and could not agree on any one of them. Reagan tried again in 1970. This time he and the Republican majority in the Assembly were united behind a single plan, contained in two bills authored by Assemblyman Bill Bagley, a friend of Monagan and hitherto a critic of Reagan. The Bagley package, ambitious for an election year, would have given homeowners a property tax exemption of $1,000 plus 20 percent of the evaluation of their homes, decreasing property tax rates by an average of 27 percent. When Democrats in the Assembly held up the bills, Reagan announced he would go into the districts of legislators who voted against the measures and campaign against them. That threat pried the bills loose from the Assembly and sent them to the Senate, in which Republicans had a 20–19 majority with a vacancy. California has a burdensome requirement of a two-thirds majority on tax and budget bills. If every Republican senator voted for the measure, the votes of seven Democrats would also be required for passage. Reagan and the Republican Senate leadership secured the seven Democrats but could not persuade Republican Senator Clark Bradley, an extreme fiscal conservative, to support the package. (Reagan appealed to Bradley to no avail; one aide remembered the discussion as the only time he ever heard the governor swear at a legislator.) The vote in favor was 26–13, one short of the two-thirds majority. Republican legislators were disconsolate. Reagan, with his usual optimism, assumed he would have a second term as governor and could try again.

Reagan's assumption that he would be reelected in 1970 was widely shared. Unruh, the Democratic nominee, was known (to the degree he was known at all) as a bullying wheeler-dealer who had once locked up Republicans in the Assembly chamber in an attempt to force them to vote for the budget. The Unruh image was embodied in his nickname, "Big Daddy," a reference to both his size and his political tactics. Unruh had dieted relentlessly for the campaign, losing a hundred pounds, but was unable to shed his political reputation. Almost no one gave him a chance to win.

Throughout his life Reagan fared well when he was an underdog but tended to become overconfident on the few occasions when he was a front-runner. Unruh added to Reagan's overconfidence in 1970 with a stumbling start. On Labor Day, when campaigns in California traditionally begin, Unruh and his entourage paid a visit to the Bel-Air mansion of oilman Henry Salvatori, one of Reagan's wealthiest supporters. Accompanied by reporters and bearing graphs and charts, Unruh intended to use the Salvatori home as a backdrop to demonstrate his thesis that "the rich" would have benefited inordinately from Reagan's un-enacted tax plan. Salvatori was not supposed to be home. He was, and so was his wife, Grace, who called Unruh a liar and berated him for violating their privacy. Rarely has any campaign had such an unpromising beginning. But Unruh recovered and ran a spirited, populist campaign in which he depicted himself as the representative of the middle class and Reagan as the candidate of the wealthy. Reagan's polls had him twenty points ahead early in September. By mid-October, the margin was only five points. Tom Reed, with help from Stu Spencer, took over the governor's lackluster campaign and rescued it. Reagan won by a margin of half a million votes (nearly eight percentage points) in what was otherwise a good Democratic year.[16] In California, Democrats won control of both houses of the legislature and Reagan's old pal, the song-and-dance man George Murphy, lost his bid for reelection to the U.S. Senate seat to Democrat John Tunney. Nationally, eleven Republican governors were beaten; Reagan and New York Governor Nelson Rockefeller were the only prominent GOP state executives to win.

Despite his less-than-inspiring campaign Reagan approached the 1971 legislative session with confidence. In his command of issues he little resembled the novice governor of 1967 and he now also had a seasoned staff and an experienced finance director. Months before the election Reagan's chief of staff Ed Meese began work on a legislative package that had welfare reform as its centerpiece. Reagan had promised during the campaign to pursue welfare reform, and he named a task force to study the issue. Welfare costs were rising, and California faced a fiscal crisis exacerbated by a national recession. This time Reagan was not in a position to blame the looming budget deficit on his predecessor.

Reagan was already part of a clamorous national conversation on welfare issues. He had joined it in full force after a U.S. Supreme Court decision in 1968 struck down residency requirements for welfare recipients on grounds that it was a violation of their right to travel. California along with many other states had required a year's residency as a condition for receiving benefits. Reagan said that the court's action provided "a bonus for migrating to California to get on our relief rolls."[17] Reagan also took on the Nixon administration. In August 1969 Nixon proposed the Family Assistance Plan, which would have federalized the welfare system and provided a guaranteed income for every American. Reagan opposed it. "I believe that the government is supposed to promote the general welfare," he said. "I don't believe it is supposed to provide it."[18] The Reagan and Nixon administrations were also at odds on other welfare issues. Reagan's welfare director Robert Carleson wanted a waiver from the Department of Health, Education, and Welfare (HEW) so that California could introduce work requirements for recipients of the Aid to Families with Dependent Children (AFDC) program. HEW balked and prodded California to increase payments to AFDC recipients to reflect cost-of-living increases. Negotiations were ongoing when a federal judge ruled on September 10, 1970, in a lawsuit filed by a San Francisco neighborhood group that the state must increase its payments or lose $400 million a year in federal funds. HEW announced that federal AFDC funds for California would be cut off on April 1, 1971, unless the Reagan administration complied with the ruling.

The court decision added a note of urgency to a fiscally volatile situation. AFDC, part of the Social Security Act of 1935, had been designed to strengthen state programs to assist children whose fathers were disabled or had abandoned their families. Federal and state governments shared the costs, with the states determining the level of benefits. For decades it was a minor program. Then as eligibility requirements were relaxed, the program grew rapidly during the 1960s. Late in the decade this growth prompted crackdowns in many states—in New Jersey, for instance, grants to families with unemployed fathers were eliminated while in Kansas benefits for recipients were cut 20 percent across the board. In California the number of AFDC recipients doubled to 769,000 from 1963 to 1967. By December 1969, the number was 1,150,000. A year later, a month after Reagan's reelection, 1,566,000 people were on the AFDC rolls—nearly one in every thirteen Californians—and the caseload was increasing by 40,000 a month. Finance director Verne Orr warned that AFDC would bust the budget. Reagan, in a magazine interview, said that the "welfare monster" would force cutbacks in essential state spending.[19]

Welfare recipients also had reason to be unhappy. Even though AFDC benefits in California were among the most generous in the nation, recipients had not had a cost-of-living raise in twelve years, during eight of which the Democrats controlled state government. If some were fraudulently obtaining benefits, as Reagan charged, they were doing so at the expense of the legitimate recipients. The monthly maximum payment in 1971 for an AFDC family of three in San Francisco was $172, nearly a hundred dollars below the subsistence level.

Reagan's task force addressed both the runaway growth in AFDC rolls and the plight of the recipients. It called for work requirements for those able to work and a "strengthening of family responsibility as the basic element in our society." But the task force report also said that California should "increase assistance to the truly needy who have nowhere else to turn to meet their basic needs." This provided a rationale for a bill that would both tighten eligibility requirements and increase grant level, but the Democrats weren't listening. When Reagan sought to unveil his welfare proposals before a joint session of the legislature, the Democratic leaders turned him down on the flimsy grounds that they had not yet been incorporated into a bill. This tactic backfired. Reagan gave "the speech the Legislature didn't want to hear" to a luncheon group in Los Angeles where it received more television coverage than it would have been given in Sacramento. But when these proposals were put into a bill, it was buried in committee.

While the bill languished, Reagan negotiated with President Nixon to buy time from the court mandate ordering an increase in AFDC payments. Meeting at San Clemente in March, they reached an agreement that was beneficial to Reagan. The governor agreed to bring California into compliance with federal regulations, which he was under court order to do anyway, and to soft-pedal further criticism of the Family Assistance Plan, which Reagan knew was doomed in Congress. In return, Reagan won a three-month delay in raising AFDC payments and approval from HEW to run a pilot welfare program with work requirements. The delay helped Reagan marginally with the budget but it was still out of balance, and his welfare plan remained stymied in committee. Through the spring and into the summer the governor and the legislative leaders warred by press release. The Democrats maintained that the increase in AFDC rolls was solely the result of the recession and accused Reagan of exaggerating the extent of welfare fraud. Reagan urged the public to send letters and telegrams to their legislators demanding a hearing on the bottled-up welfare bill.

The stalemate was broken by the creativity of two aides: William Hauck, the chief of staff for Assembly Speaker Bob Moretti, and George Steffes, the governor's legislative liaison. The two men were friends and unafraid to speak truth to power. Early in the first term Steffes had been appalled at Reagan's public recriminations against Pat Brown, the man he had defeated. He told Reagan this was beneath him. "You're right, and I'm not going to do it anymore," Reagan said.[20] On the welfare bill, Hauck took the first step. He told Moretti that the exchange of charges with Reagan was "debilitating" to both of them. When the Speaker agreed, Hauck, on June 28, 1971, drafted and Moretti signed a letter to Reagan proposing a meeting "in the spirit of reasonable compromise and agreement."[21] Reagan took him up on it the same day ignoring the advice of aides who did not want him to meet with Moretti alone.

Thus began a seminal episode in the political education of Ronald Reagan, a negotiation that would be preparation for the many dialogues he would have with Democratic congressional leaders when he was president and eventually, on issues weightier than welfare, with Soviet leader Mikhail Gorbachev. Reagan had been immersed in negotiations long before he came to Sacramento. The description of him as a political amateur, accurate in other respects, overlooked Reagan's valuable experience as president of the Screen Actors Guild when he negotiated with movie producers during the bitter Hollywood strike of 1960. Reagan valued this memory. At the time of his first meeting with Gorbachev in 1985, I asked Reagan what part of his biography had been most neglected. Negotiating on behalf of the Screen Actors Guild, he replied. What had he learned from that, I asked. "That the purpose of a negotiation is to get an agreement," Reagan replied.[22]

Reagan met Moretti in the governor's corner office the same day he received the letter from the Speaker. Moretti told Reagan that he knew they didn't like each other, but, he said, "We don't have to be in love to work together."[23] Reagan was impressed that Moretti had kept the meeting secret: it told him that the Speaker sought progress rather than publicity. But he knew little about the brash and energetic young man who sat across the table from him. Moretti, of Italian and Armenian descent, talked like a kid off the streets and had in fact grown up in a poor section of Detroit. When he was a teenager, his family moved to Los Angeles, where Moretti and a brother attended the 1960 Democratic National Convention that nominated John F. Kennedy for president. As his sister put it, Moretti was "hooked" on politics from that day. After graduating with honors from Notre Dame with a degree in accounting, Moretti plunged into politics and at twenty-eight became the youngest person ever elected to the California legislature. As a freshman assemblyman he showed a streak of independence, refusing to sign a written pledge of support for Unruh. Moretti told the Unruh aide who brought the pledge to him, "If my word isn't good enough, to hell with you."[24] In 1971 at the age of thirty-four, Moretti became Speaker, succeeding Monagan. Reagan was old enough to be his father. The two men were surprised, they told me in retrospect, to find they liked each other. But they had political reasons for doing so. Moretti wanted to run for governor and needed to establish a legislative record. Reagan harbored presidential ambitions that would be advanced by a successful governorship.

They both knew they would never run against each other; Reagan had foresworn seeking a third term before he won his second.

The Reagan-Moretti meeting, to use a Churchillian phrase, was the end of the beginning. Reagan and Moretti subsequently brought their experts into the negotiations, which at times seemed on the verge of collapse but were rescued by the determination of the principals. It took weeks of hard bargaining. Reagan and Moretti, so unalike in background and philosophy, mirrored one another in their negotiating styles. Both of them made clear from the first that they wanted a genuine reform bill rather than a cosmetic agreement, and they talked bluntly to one another without being insulting. Moretti had distaste for "milquetoast type of people" in leadership roles and was impressed by Reagan's "strong personality" and willingness to express his convictions.[25] Reagan appreciated that Moretti talked in plain English, avoiding what he had come to think of as legislative doubletalk. The truth was that Moretti, as much as Reagan, was easily bored by details, which became laborious in the process of translating complex formulae used to calculate welfare eligibility and benefits into legislation that would accomplish the multiple goals of the negotiators. Fortunately, the surrogates in the negotiations compensated for the principals on this score. On the Speaker's side, the knowledgeable Senator Anthony Beilenson was precise and thorough; on the governor's side, Meese was detail oriented and patient. Steffes meanwhile kept a tight lid on the welfare director, Carleson, whose habit of lecturing about the presumed evils of welfare irritated the Democrats.[26]

These negotiations produced (on August 6) an accord that became the California Welfare Reform Act of 1971, or CWRA, a measure ahead of its time. Eligibility was tightened and a confusing "needs standard" was simplified into a uniform statewide measurement. Counties were given incentives to track absentee fathers, and the state began comparing county welfare payments with employer earnings records. Benefits were raised. The San Francisco welfare family of three that had been getting $172 a month before the act was passed now received $235.

The AFDC rolls began falling soon after passage of the CWRA. Within three years they had declined from a high of 1,608,000 to 1,330,000. Reagan, seeking the Republican presidential nomination in 1976, took the entire credit for the decline. Democrats tried unconvincingly to discredit the law they had helped write (indeed, had mostly written, in Beilenson's view). They attributed the decline in the welfare rolls to the end of the recession despite the fact that the caseload also had risen during periods of prosperity. Frank Levy, a public policy analyst from the Urban League and no fan of Reagan, provided a measured assessment. After studying what happened in California and nationally, Levy determined that the AFDC caseload would have leveled off in the 1970s because most of those who were eligible were already on the rolls. But he also called the CWRA "a one-in-a-thousand policy success" that had saved money and helped more recipients than it hurt. Levy's analysis found that the CWRA and regulations introduced by Carleson to require monthly reporting of income reduced the California AFDC rolls by 6 percent (21,000 people) more than they would have declined in the absence of the law.[27]

The welfare accord produced spillover benefits as well. Reagan, in Moretti's eyes, became "more attentive to the Legislature and individual legislators" and more discerning of "shades of gray" in the resolution of issues.[28] Moretti, a partisan Democrat, thought Reagan had evolved into a good governor. Reagan, for his part, realized that Moretti was trustworthy and could deliver on his promises.[29] The governor and the Speaker attempted to use their newfound comity as a springboard to a major tax reform that might have been enacted in 1971 had not the California Supreme Court declared the state's system of financing education to be unconstitutional. This ruling sent the experts scurrying back to their legislative drawing boards. The result was a landmark bill (SB 90) providing record amounts of property tax relief and school funding. It became law in 1972 with the backing of Reagan and Moretti and much help from the Senate Democratic leader, David Roberti. Moretti considered SB 90 the most significant achievement of his legislative career, but it did not have much of a political payoff for him or Reagan. When Moretti sought the Democratic nomination for governor in 1974, he lost to Jerry Brown. Ten years later, when he was forty-seven, Moretti died of a heart attack while playing tennis. Reagan failed in his bid for the Republican presidential nomination in 1976; he would win both the nomination and the presidency in 1980 for reasons that had little to do with SB 90 or the California Welfare Reform Act.

In terms of his preparation for the presidency, Reagan's negotiations with Moretti were the shaping experience of his second gubernatorial term. After he was elected president but before he was inaugurated, Reagan told me that the experience of the welfare bill and other measures had demonstrated that he would be able to work with Congress. This turned out to be true. The California experience was all the more relevant because Reagan was again confronted with an opposition lower house and needed Democratic votes to win approval of his tax cuts and his increases in military spending, although in 1981 he would obtain them not by negotiating a deal with the Speaker but by outmaneuvering him.

But in my view the preparatory value to Reagan of his negotiations with Moretti went beyond direct application of his Sacramento experiences to Washington. Reagan, as we have seen, brought to the governorship an underappreciated asset from his labor negotiations in Hollywood. But he had never, before his meetings with Moretti, gone it alone in a direct negotiation with a leading political adversary. The fact that several of the governor's aides did not want Reagan to have a solo discussion with Moretti reflected their appreciation of the Speaker's political skills. Moretti was an exceptional leader of a legislature that abounded with future members of Congress, two future governors, and others who would make a name in government or private life. Had he had the chance, Moretti was surely capable of hitting major-league pitching, to paraphrase Tip O'Neill's putdown of Reagan that Sacramento was the "minor leagues." When he made this crack O'Neill knew little about the high quality of politics that had been practiced in Sacramento during Reagan's years as governor of California. Reagan knew. He had held his own with Jesse Unruh and with Bob Moretti, and nothing or no one in Congress held any terror for him.

There is more, of course, to the presidency than dealing with Congress. Nothing in their governorships prepared President Franklin D. Roosevelt for Pearl Harbor or President George W. Bush for the terrorist attacks of September 11, 2001. Nothing that happened in Sacramento readied Reagan for a telephone call at 2:27 A.M. on October 23, 1983, telling him that more than two hundred U.S. Marines had been killed in their bunker by a suicide bomber in Beirut. In such crises presidents draw on their character and the advice of their experts. Reagan had an abundance of both.

Reagan had come to Sacramento as a naïf, distrusting the political profession of which he was now a part. Throughout his life, he maintained an outward disdain for politicians, a pose (and a belief) that enabled him to continue running against Washington even when he was the nation's head of government and its commander-in-chief. But the hurly-burly of Sacramento required Reagan to dirty his hands in the earthy fields of politics, and it was beneficial to him that it did. Although Reagan never formally acknowledged that he had changed his opinion of politics, an exchange he held with a worker at a South Gate plant during the 1970 reelection campaign said more than any announcement. "When are you going to clean up politics?" the worker asked. Replied Reagan: "Politics is more honest than you think."[30]

Reagan was a gifted politician. He had the advantage of becoming a candidate at a time when the nation was ready for his message and the further advantage of running for office when the Republican bench was thin and the Democrats in California had worn out their welcome with the voters. He made the most of these advantages. Becoming a good governor became an end in itself, as it should have been. But it also nurtured Reagan on the possibilities of politics, honed his negotiating skills, and provided him with a core of aides who had also learned the ropes in Sacramento. Reagan knew better than to rely entirely on this cadre when he came to Washington: he wisely expanded it to draw upon a broad spectrum of political experience. But the cadre mostly stayed with him, as did the lessons he had learned in Sacramento. Reagan was a better president because he had been a governor.

Governing the 1980s

As world events improved and discontent was quelled, governors in the 1980s refocused on needed domestic reforms. The first year of the decade, however, witnessed the persistence of many of the same troubles that had plagued the 1970s—an energy crisis, economic downturn, and what President Carter perhaps correctly but unpopularly labeled a "crisis of confidence." The taking of American hostages by Iranian militants in 1979 was among the obstacles to Carter's presidential reelection campaign in 1980 and a factor in his defeat by Ronald Reagan. Then, on January 20, 1981, Iran released their fifty-two remaining American hostages. This event coincided with the presidential inauguration of Reagan, former governor of California and the second consecutive governor to serve in the White House. Americans were relieved that the long ordeal with Iran had ended. The new decade now seemed to offer new hope.

Domestically and internationally the 1980s were ripe with opportunity. In 1981, Sandra Day O'Connor became the first woman appointed to the Supreme Court. The nationwide recession ended in 1982, replaced by a period (although short) of economic prosperity. A revolution in technology made desktop computers available to the general public, improving office production and household management. Culturally, the nation's youth became less interested in political protest and "tuning out" from society. The rebellious post–World War II baby boomers gave way to a new generation that embraced materialism and plugged into MTV consumerism. In international affairs, the Cold War thawed with the Strategic Defense Initiatives and eventually the Berlin Wall fell. Ronald Reagan, drawing on the lessons he had learned as governor, proved a popular president, winning reelection by a landslide in 1984. He remained a favorite among many Americans even after the Iran-Contra investigations in 1986 and 1987.

Even though the Cold War was ending, governors along with the nation continued to worry about the ability of Americans to compete internationally. And as the deindustrialization that had begun in the 1970s persisted, Americans at large faced changing job qualifications, more reliant on higher education than manual labor. These concerns led, in part, to the 1980 creation of the U.S. Department of Education. Governors turned to the challenge of improving the nation's education system with increased urgency. This issue resurfaced as a central topic of discussion at governors' meetings throughout the 1980s, culminating in the 1989 national education summit in Charlottesville, Virginia, at which President George H. W. Bush and governors jointly undertook the development of national education goals. But even six years prior, in 1983, Governor Pierre du Pont IV of Delaware (1977–1985) had called for the establishment of national education standards, arguing that it was "nonsense" for people to suggest that education systems cannot be judged.[1] Many gubernatorial leaders believed that reforms were needed not only to compete internationally, but also to adjust to the ongoing technological revolution. Speaking in 1986, Governor Bob Kerrey of Nebraska (1983–1987) encouraged governors to foresee a future world, telling them to "Begin to imagine that it's possible for an individual to sit in their home in the most remote of locations, at any time of the day or night, and to access sound and to access visual information." It was essential, Kerrey argued, that Americans "not just [be] competitive, but also . . . more understanding of what other people in other parts of the world are doing. It will open up the world to our people in ways that we can't even imagine today."[2] As technology made the world smaller, innovative strategies in education became even more important in preparing the nation's youth and retraining a displaced workforce.

In addition to education and international competition, governors in the 1980s dealt with a number of other domestic problems. Many governors faced rising crime rates and the need for penal reforms, which led some to focus their administrations on crime and law enforcement. Governor John Ashcroft of Missouri (1985–1993), later attorney general under President George W. Bush, pushed for tougher sentences for gun-related crimes, increased the number of state law enforcement officers, and supported Missouri's first hate crimes law. Governors also renewed their focus on welfare. Then-governor Bill Clinton of Arkansas (1979–1981, 1983–1992) made welfare a central issue of his administration, frequently bringing the topic of welfare-to-work before governors' meetings. "Making America Work: Productive People, Productive Policies" became his year-long initiative as chair of NGA in 1986–1987.

In the post–World War II era, internationalism and technological innovation altered the scope of the National Governors' Association. By the 1980s, annual meetings—and now winter meetings in Washington—were opportunities not only for discussion and debate among governors, but also for presentations by the nation's political, economic, scientific, academic, religious, military, and cultural leaders. In addition to presidents Ronald Reagan and George H. W. Bush, a variety of high-profile individuals addressed governors, including Alan Greenspan, Carl Sagan, Andrew Young, Lee Iacocca, David Halberstam, Dan Rather, Ted Turner, Billy Graham, and James Baker, among others. These opportunities furthered the education of modern governors, who were expected to be CEO-oriented administrators, well versed in not only state concerns but also national and international policy. "The old fashioned handshaking . . . baby kissing, back-slapping . . . governor puffing on a big cigar is all but gone," observed author and *USA Today* journalist Phil Pruitt; "That character has been replaced by a more competitive, streamlined, business-type leader."[3] Personality, like that of larger-than-life Huey Long, became less important than experience and professionalism. By the 1980s, the empowerment of governors individually was linked to the growing professionalism of their position, changing public attitudes toward their role, and an increase in their terms of office (the number of states with two-year—as opposed to four-year—terms dropped from fifteen, in 1964, to four, by 1980).[4] By the same token, governors as a group wielded national influence, unified in their concern over federal-state relations.

Throughout the 1980s governors discussed how balance could best be restored to these relations, particularly in the face of growing unfunded federal mandates and regulatory restrictions. Some governors took active roles in achieving balance by accepting appointments to the Advisory Commission on Intergovernmental Relations (ACIR), established in 1959 as an independent, bipartisan agency promoting intergovernmental cooperation. One of the many governors who served on the ACIR was Richard Snelling (1977–1985, 1991), who was elected to an unprecedented five gubernatorial terms in Vermont. Initially appointed by President Carter, Snelling was later reappointed by President Reagan.

Governors also believed that NGA could help restore a federal-state balance by stepping up their promotion of states' interests to Congress and the president. Speaking in a unified voice on national issues became a responsibility rather than just an opportunity. For example, governors were deeply concerned about the growing national debt and the potential consequences of this burden on states. In 1983, Scott Matheson of Utah (1977–1985), then NGA chair, announced proudly, "It is a measure of our ascending influence that the 1984 budget resolution adopted by Congress bears the unmistakable print of the budget resolution we adopted last March." This resolution had marked a historic departure from the past practice of commenting only on portions of the federal budget directly related to states. "As governors," Matheson continued, "we are closer than anyone to the suffering that recession brings to our states. As governors, we know how to balance the budget, even when it means painful budget cuts and unpopular and difficult tax increases."[5] Every governor faced these issues. Govenor Michael Dukakis of Massachusetts (1975–1979, 1983–1991) began his career as a fiscal conservative determined to trim state government, despite his later branding in the 1988 presidential campaign as the quintessential liberal. Economic reality, however, intervened and forced Dukakis to support the largest tax increase in Massachusetts's history in order to balance the budget. Lessons such as these were tough, and governors believed the federal government could learn from their experiences.

In the late twentieth century, the same question remained: How could government best address the concerns of its citizens and which level— local, state, or federal—was better equipped and constitutionally respon- sible for providing specific services? Although a product of the 1970s, the politics of devolution remained central to this debate. Far from the situation facing the men who met in 1908, governors in the 1980s knew that local, state, and federal governments were no longer clearly divided and the delineation of responsibilities was difficult to define. But like their 1908 colleagues, they were concerned about the sovereignty of states. Modern governors accepted that the world in general and govern- ment in particular had changed, but they still believed earnestly in the capability of states to protect and serve their citizens. In 1981, NGA chair Governor George Busbee of Georgia (1975–1983) acknowledged those fears, urging his colleagues to not "simply stand by and watch the states slowly become a political museum piece of interest only to historians, to map makers and sentimental songwriters, and perhaps congressmen once every ten years."[6] Governor David Treen of Louisiana (1980–1984) went one step further, arguing that recent trends held the "seeds of destruction of the federal system."[7] This debate over federalism is cen- tral to understanding the scope and tenets of the modern governorship.

Chapter Seven
Devolution in American Federalism in the Twentieth Century

RICHARD P. NATHAN

The Many Faces of Federalism

Experts have many ways and words to describe American federalism— dual, cooperative, competitive, marble cake, coercive, and picket fence. Actually, there is no one best characterization for all time. *American federalism is not static; it changes over time.* For a century after the Constitution was ratified, the role of American government was relatively much smaller than it is today. The national government generally stayed out of what were considered the appropriate areas of responsibility of state governments and their component local governments. Examples abound of colorful language by presidents warning against the danger of creeping centralization via the adoption by the federal government of responsibilities for what are intrinsically local matters.

In the twentieth century, however, the American federalism bargain changed materially; moreover, the change accelerated over time. As is well known, the federal government's role in domestic affairs expanded under FDR's New Deal, with the civil rights revolution, and as new social programs were created in Washington under Lyndon Johnson's Great Society.

Devolution Emerges

But then the federalism bargain changed again. Devolution came on the scene in the latter third of the twentieth century, and it too has accelerated over time. The genesis of the devolution movement was broad gauged—protests against the Vietnam War, growing frustration with the failures and limitations of the centralizing thrust of the Great Society, and the escalating costs of federal programs.[1] The shift in domestic policy was nonpartisan and not inordinately ideological. An additional and underlying cause of this devolution movement was a growing consensus, with evidence to support it, that state governments were increasing their capacity—modernizing by adding staff, developing better and stronger fiscal and management systems, and generally achieving higher standards of professionalism. A 1985 report by the U.S. Advisory Commission on Intergovernmental Relations (ACIR) stated, "State governments have been transformed in almost every facet of their structure and operations."[2] In particular, governors' offices have become stronger, bigger, and more analytical, allowing for sophisticated policy planning, performance management, and enhanced efforts to influence appointed agency heads to push to have governors' policy goals implemented at the ground level. Likewise, state bureaucracies have become stronger players in policy processes, adding energy and impetus to the move to expand the role of the states.[3] In addition, the civil rights revolution increased the standing of state governments. It did so by creating a changed mood that helped to overcome what Martha Derthick calls "southern exceptionalism" in American federalism. In her words:

Governmental competence and perceptions of it aside, all discussions of American federalism must henceforth be altered by what is arguably the most important new social and political datum of our times: the end to Southern exceptionalism. Until now, arguments favoring the states' side in any dispute over federalism suffered fatally from the burden of the South's deviant social system. Whether or not blacks have been successfully integrated into American society (a separate question), there can be little doubt that the South as a region has been integrated. That change, even if achieved very largely by the instrumentalities of the federal government, holds the possibility that the case for the states can at last begin to be discussed on its merits.[4]

The courts have also helped enhance the state role through decisions that changed the federalism bargain. In the last decade of the twentieth century and continuing into the twenty-first century, the role of William H. Rehnquist on the U.S. Supreme Court (appointed chief justice by President Reagan in 1986) moderated what earlier had been a decidedly nationalizing role of the Court in increasing the legal and programmatic powers of the federal government.

In this setting, both conservative and liberal political leaders were changing their views on the appropriate role of state governments. Revenue sharing (discussed below) was a major symbol of this changed viewpoint. As a new approach in domestic policy making, revenue sharing, in effect, was a method for strengthening the role and enhancing the flexibility of action on the part of state governments. It was advocated in both major party platforms in 1968.

Senator Robert F. Kennedy (D-N.Y.) reflected the shift in opinion of liberals on domestic issues. In his campaign for the 1968 Democratic presidential nomination, Kennedy expressed ideas on domestic programs along lines that bore a striking resemblance to what many Republicans were saying in this period.[5] In March, he told a college audience in Utah, "We must return control to the people themselves," and went so far as to suggest a reversal of his brother's New Frontier policies. "In the last analysis it should be in the cities and towns and villages where the decisions are made, not in Washington. . . . Solutions of the 1930s are not the solutions of today. The solutions of the New Frontier, of the early 1960s, are not necessarily applicable now. We are a new generation with new problems."[6]

Devolution as a twentieth-century theme of domestic policy had its roots in the administrations of presidents Dwight D. Eisenhower and Lyndon B. Johnson. Eisenhower spoke often about reviewing and assessing the "proper roles" of the federal, state, and local governments; he appointed two study groups to do this. Their reports, although widely cited at the time, did not have a sustained impact.[7] At the end of Eisenhower's presidency in 1959, the ACIR was established. It continued in existence for twenty-five years, when, somewhat ironically, it was eliminated in 1996 under the Republican 104th Congress elected in 1994.

After Eisenhower's presidency, some of President Johnson's advisers urged him to take state-favored actions in response to what became an increasingly strong political backlash to the intrusiveness of Johnson's Great Society social policy initiatives. This was when the revenue-sharing idea emerged. Walter Heller, chair of Johnson's Council of Economic Advisors, urged President Johnson to adopt a revenue sharing plan, both as a fiscal stimulus to the lagging economy as well as a method for giving state governments general-purpose fiscal assistance in recognition of the expanded role states wanted in setting their own agendas and priorities and carrying them out in ways that fit the proclivities, values, and needs of different regions of the country. But Johnson would have none of it. The revenue-sharing plan, known in the media at the time as the Heller-Pechman plan, was named for Heller and his co-sponsor, Joseph Pechman, director of economic studies at the Brookings Institution. Heller, a deft phrasemaker, described revenue sharing as a response to "the hardening of the categories," referring to frustrations about the "proliferation" (the word most often used) of narrowly focused and seemingly intrusive federal grants-in-aid. Johnson did create several relatively minor block grants to consolidate categorical programs for public health, but he did not embrace the devolution theme in a strong way. In his 1964 address at the University of Michigan launching the Great Society program, he said, at one point, that what was needed was "not a massive program from Washington." Instead, solutions to urban problems "require us to create new concepts of cooperation, a *creative federal-*

ism, between the National Capital and leaders of local communities."[8] Yet, Johnson's emphasis was not on states but on local governments, particularly those in distressed large cities. In any event, this labeling of a "creative federalism," while it received mention in the press at the time, did not take hold.

Devolution Accelerates

On the other side of the partisan divide, Republicans jumped on the devolution bandwagon with enthusiasm during this period. Richard Nixon, as a candidate for president in 1968, frequently complained about heavy-handed bureaucratic centralization, charging that the federal government did not deliver and that Great Society programs were overly ambitious and expensive. As president, he called for a "New Federalism," a phrase he used often and prominently to characterize his domestic program. Nixon's version of devolution was liberal and big-spending—give states and localities revenue-sharing payments (which he did) and block grants with "sweeteners" added (which he also did).[9] The latter refers to the process of consolidating categorical grants-in-aid to states in major functional areas of domestic policy, along with extra money (that is, the "sweeteners") so that in the final analysis the total amount of aid provided is increased, at least in the short term. These bonuses can be seen as bribes to states, localities, and interest groups supporting the affected public services to give up categorical grant programs and instead accept an enriched and broadened stream of flexible federal funding in the selected functional areas of domestic policy. The recipient state governments could use block grant funds flexibly to set their own priorities.

Nixon was a liberal-decentralist in his first term in these and other ways, although in later years he pulled back from his liberal stance. His New Federalism program, announced in a prime-time address on national television in August 1969, reflected a strategy to preempt the liberal agenda and solve domestic problems the Nixon way. Rockefeller Republicans were still an appreciable force in the Republican Party in this period.[10] Nixon's problem-solving federalism approach was seen by the president and his advisers as necessary to winning a broad political coalition for his domestic program; in effect, his answer to the centralizing domestic programs of his predecessor.

In the latter part of the Nixon presidency, the devolution theme took on a new and more strident shape. The country was turning to the right. Republicans could fly the banner most of them liked the best—a genuinely conservative one. Reduce government's role and intrusiveness. Cut taxes. Deregulate. Strengthen the private sector. To the extent that

Republicans still highlighted federalism and devolution, now it was with tongue-in-cheek. When public service and public advocacy groups called for new programs and new solutions, the Republican mantra was: "Sure, good idea, but the states should do it."

The year 1980, with the election of Ronald Reagan as president, was the turning point. The approach of Reagan's administration was: "We hear you, but that's not our job in Washington"—with fingers crossed behind their backs, in effect using this response as a way to change the subject. "Don't do it with a bold new national program, but at the same time don't blame us for not doing it."

Thirty days after his inauguration, Reagan told a group of governors at the White House, "[It] is a long-time dream of mine, this thing of balancing up the divisions of government." A few months later, he told state legislators that the federal system is like a masonry wall, and that what is needed is "a proper mix" of the bricks (that is, the states) and the mortar (that is, the federal government). "Unfortunately," according to Reagan, "over the years many people have come to believe that Washington is the whole wall—a wall that, incidentally, leans, sags, and bulges under its own weight."[11]

Reagan often defended his theory of federalism by citing the Tenth Amendment to the U.S. Constitution with its so-called reservation clause. It "reserves" to the states and the people "powers not delegated to the United States by the Constitution." Reagan's brand of "new federalism" (he didn't call it that but the press did, hence the lowercase initials used above) could also be called cut-and-run federalism. It returned to the spirit of an earlier time when national officials manifested a strong wariness about the federal government being involved in state programs and local improvements. This wariness was dominant in the nineteenth century, and continued into the twentieth century when the country was keeping "Cool with Coolidge," who was unwilling to go down the progressive road of his time. When the great Mississippi flood inundated 40 percent of America, Coolidge reluctantly agreed to let his commerce secretary Herbert Hoover take charge in the Delta, but Coolidge himself refused to go there or to speak out about the great devastation, much less countenance a federal role of appreciable new spending and bold action to alleviate it. Ironically, the electoral result was Hoover's election in 1928 as president and Huey Long's as governor of Louisiana. Long's special brand of populism included haranguing Coolidge and the federal government for its inaction after the great flood.[12]

The high point of Reagan's federalism-activism as president was his announcement in 1982 of a suggested "swap and turn-back" of federal responsibilities. Reagan proposed that the federal government "assume full responsibility for the cost of the rapidly growing Medicaid program to go along with its existing responsibility for Medicare" (the health-care part of Social Security, which then as now is fully federal). As the state part of this "swap," the president said the states should take "full responsibility for Aid to Families with Dependent Children (AFDC) and food stamps."[13]

But the "swap and turn-back" plan was not to be. Leaders of the National Governors Association (notably Ray Scheppach, NGA's executive director) have since lamented that this was their *golden* opportunity. Scheppach said the governors should have gone all out to support the Reagan proposal. Despite intensive White House bargaining to advance Reagan's plan, it had little traction. It was never even introduced in Congress.

Reagan's vice president and successor, George H. W. Bush, sounded much like Reagan in his public pronouncements on federalism. In a March 1989 speech to the National Conference of State Legislatures, using his own words, Bush unfurled the federalism banner.

The resilience of the State governments in the eighties vindicates, in my view, the wisdom of the Founding Fathers and forever discredits those who would have Washington do it all. And let me assure you, I will preserve and protect a healthy balance, a sharing of power, between the States and Washington, because I fervently believe that federalism works. And I remember meetings that I had with Governors at the time of the campaign, discussing the social issues. And I learned more from the briefings—this happened to be in a partisan context of a campaign—but I learned more from the briefing by the Governors than any of the people here in Washington to whom I had access because I was vice president. And I thought about why it made such a difference and why I learned so much from them. And it was because they're on the cutting edge; they are out there working with you all to solve the problems, to figure out what works, to make the changes. And so, that may sound elementary to some, but I think you must know what I mean. Governors have to deal in what works, and they get that from you all, with the representation you give in your districts.[14]

A subtheme, coming into wide prominence in this period, involved federal mandates, which President Bush sought to roll back. "The national Governors, and I'm talking Democrats and Republicans, tell me that the major problem they have is being saddled with more and more mandates by some of these empowered committee chairmen in Washington that pass legislation after legislation or attempt to pass it that just tells the States how to do everything. And we've got to stand up against that."[15]

Eventually, Congress passed the Unfunded Mandates Relief Act of 1995, setting up a process for costing out mandates and renewing those above a certain threshold. President Clinton, who signed it into law, said, "Today we are making history. . . . We are recognizing that the pendulum had swung too far [toward Washington], and that we have to rely on the initiative, the creativity, the determination, and the decision-making of the people at the state and local level to carry much of the load for America as we move into the 21st century."[16]

In 1994, President Bill Clinton's second year as president, the election of the Republican-controlled 104th Congress reinforced the Reagan/Bush theory of federalism. President Clinton (despite the fact that he was a former governor) did not play up the devolution theme. His health plan was decidedly centrist. His welfare reform, which he often bragged about, in fact, was not really *his* welfare program. It was forced on him by what could be called the "Newt Federalism," named for Newt Gingrich, then speaker of the U.S. House of Representatives.

Republicans, who won control of both houses of Congress, picked up strongly on devolution. In major areas of domestic public affairs (especially health and welfare), Speaker Gingrich and his supporters called for the assignment of greater responsibilities to the states. They kept sending Clinton legislation creating block grants. Block Medicaid, they said. Block welfare. Stop trying to run the country from Washington, reflecting tongue-in-cheek federalism of the Reagan variety.

Clinton deftly vetoed major devolutionary components of the "Newt Federalism." However, he assiduously avoided confronting their block grant plan solution to "the welfare mess." When omnibus block-grant bills were sent to the president's desk by the Congress, Clinton wielded his veto pen in ways that avoided even mentioning the Republicans' proposed welfare block grant. In a famous slogan he used when first elected president in 1992, he had promised "to end welfare as we know it." This slogan turned out to be pure magic on the stump, so Clinton repeated it often. Hence, he was highly committed to welfare reform.

In this setting, Speaker Gingrich and his troops decided to put the president on the spot. They sent him a one-issue welfare block grant on the eve of the presidential election in 1996. Block welfare, they urged (just welfare). Using rhetoric familiar at the time, the Republican plan called for giving the preponderate responsibility for work-focused welfare to the states. Clinton was between a rock and a hard place. Anyway, that was the view of liberals in his administration who hated this "Newt Federalism" welfare reform, which cleverly encompassed a number of Clinton's own welfare reform proposals. These aides urged Clinton to veto the welfare block grant, called the Personal Responsibility Act of 1996.[17] But Clinton didn't veto it, and several prominent members of his administration resigned in protest right after the bill was signed.

Although Speaker Gingrich and colleagues in the Congress pretty much toed the Republican line on devolution, they made exceptions. They particularly made exceptions for laws and regulations that promoted national uniformity in areas involving business interests. Some experts stress these exceptions, calling them "coercive federalism." They assert that these actions, and others like them, should be viewed as a basic qualification to the devolution of policy and administrative responsibilities described in this chapter.[18]

Even after signing the Personal Responsibility Act of 1996, Clinton and Vice President Al Gore did not falter on welfare reform. Indeed, they claimed credit for it. Welfare reform, they said, was a big success. The rolls went down. Human service programs helped welfare family heads (almost entirely women) get and stay in jobs because they could now obtain child care and transportation benefits. As it turned out, because the 1996 Personal Responsibility Act broadly defines what are permissive services and uses a high-level base year for the funding provided to the states, it put in place a set of dynamics that made these advances possible. The "caseload reduction credit" in the law said to the states: You will receive the same amount in federal money for welfare assistance that you received in the base year, 1994. If states were then able to reduce welfare roles by promoting work and enhancing personal responsibility, they could retain the resulting "savings" to use for services to enable welfare families to enter and stay in the labor market.[19] This was an incremental, typically American political deal. There was something in it for both the right and the left. This bipartisan welfare-reform deal lasted for nearly a decade. Eventually, protests on behalf of needy children and families heated up. This was largely the result of the drying up of bonus money from the combined effect of the high base year and the "caseload reduction credit," which in turn was due to state and county strategies to use all the flexible money they could get their hands on to relieve fiscal pressure during the recession of 2000–2001, which hit state and local government especially hard. The juice went out of saving welfare families.[20]

It is difficult to find presidential statements by President George W. Bush that have the same federalism lilt as those of his modern Republican predecessors. As a governor, he took the federalist view, but as president he has had relatively little to say on the subject. His federalism position and record are hard to summarize. Despite the fact that his administration did not use the term "block grants," its proposed caps for major domestic programs—Medicaid, federal aid for low-income housing, child welfare (mostly funding for foster care)—plus its proposal to allow the states to take over and redistribute the funding for the Head Start program are in the tradition and form of what have typically been labeled block grants.[21] These proposals can be seen as having the dual purpose of reining in spending and at the same time giving states greater flexibility. A similar decentralization initiative was the administration's proposal for a "Super Waiver" as part of legislation to reauthorize the 1996 national welfare reform act. The Super Waiver would have permitted states to manipulate and reprogram grant-in-aid money provided for a large number of federally aided social programs.

In contrast, an indication that the conventional Republican federalism theme is not as important to President George W. Bush as it was to his Republican predecessors is shown by his administration's record on the federal role in education. The No Child Left Behind Act of 2001, compelling states to adopt testing systems and related educational reforms, has been advanced in an assertive (sometimes even high-handed) way, despite hotly voiced concerns of state officials that they are not being listened to and properly treated. A similar nationalization strategy has been pursued in the field of homeland security. In both areas, the idea of a federal-state partnership has been put aside in favor of strong leadership for the national government. There is, in short, a decided difference in the tone and rhetoric on the part of the George W. Bush Republican presidency concerning the role of the states.

Rising Role of the States

The flip side of this story of intergovernmental relations in the latter part of the twentieth century and into the twenty-first century is the rising role of the states. Federalism was rediscovered by liberals. This trend has become strongly manifest in many policy areas. An ironic illustration of this is the way Representative Barney Frank (D-Mass.) was compared in 2005 to states' righter and former Senator Strom Thurmond, when Frank argued that the states (with Massachusetts out front) should be the arbiters of gay marriage.[22] Activists in other fields have come to see the states, particularly states with liberal governors, as the best level of government to deal with many domestic programs and issues. And governors have become more visible nationally as global economic issues and foreign policy challenges increasingly dominate policymaking and politics in Washington.

> *Protecting Medicaid*—In spite of national efforts to slow the growth of the Medicaid program, which aids the elderly, the disabled, and poor families, states have been able to stave this off. Because the Medicaid program has such a broad constituency of beneficiary groups (not just the poor) and multiple provider interests, states were able to shield it from retrenchment.
> *Health Reform*—State governments have taken the lead nationally on health policy reforms, particularly in Massachusetts and California. Other states as well have advanced high-visibility proposals and

taken steps to expand health-care coverage and control costs for health-care services.

Cleaning Up the Environment—In this period, many states were ahead of the curve compared to the federal government on environmental issues. This was demonstrated by the nine-state northeastern accord to freeze power plant emissions and similar efforts in California and other states.[23]

Equalizing School Aid—Activists in many states pulled multiple levers—through the courts, the executive, and the legislature—to distribute school aid in ways that gave more aid to poor city and rural communities and provide more aid overall.

Preschool and After-School Programs—In this area, too, states have taken the lead.

Providing Public Infrastructure—Although the federal highway act remains a major source of capital funding, many leaders in the infrastructure field have come to view states as their best avenue for constructing and maintaining streets, roads, and bridges as well as other capital infrastructure—schools, parks, cultural facilities.

The same point applies for regulatory issues:

The Minimum Wage—This is an area where states are out front nationally. According to a survey, seventeen states covering 45 percent of the national population have minimum wages above the federal rate ($5.15 at the time).[24]

Stem Cell Research—Following California's lead with its $3 billion bond issue to support stem cell research, other states have joined the parade, notably Illinois, Connecticut, Maryland, Massachusetts, New Jersey, New York, Iowa, and Missouri.

Sex Education—This, too, is an example of an area where it makes sense for liberals to prefer state action, the expectation being that national action would cater to the more rigid concerns of religious fundamentalists.

End-of-Life Decisions—The intense 2005 debate on the Terri Schiavo case in Florida is another example of an area where liberals are likely to prefer state policies compared to those advanced by national leaders.

This listing is meant to be suggestive, providing a sampling of issues where it makes sense for liberals to look to the states at a time when the conservative mood in Washington is not propitious. The underlying point, to reiterate, is the one made earlier about the changeability of American federalism. Over time and in similar ways, issues move around in American federalism. In an Oregon case before the U.S. Supreme Court, the question at issue was whether the U.S. Attorney General (John Ashcroft) could abrogate a state law permitting the administration of drugs to assist suicides. The *Wall Street Journal* sided with Oregon, referring specifically to the way in which liberals were discovering devolution in an editorial aptly titled "The New New Federalism."[25]

Interpretation

Shifting attitudes and rhetoric about the relative roles of the federal government and the states are endemic in American federalism. Conventionally, federalism has been viewed as an instrument for constraining government. You could call this "tongue-in-check federalism squared." This conventional interpretation says that when there is a liberal mood in the country, the feds can innovate, and when the national mood is conservative the federalism argument can be used to stifle domestic policy activism. In a word, this interpretation is *wrong*.

Alternating cycles of centralization and devolution in American federalism in the twentieth century and beyond are not just rhetoric. They mean business. They change things. State government, with governors in the lead, don't just sit around and twiddle their thumbs when the mood of Washington is conservative and the rhetoric is, "You do it," referring to state governments. Indeed, in the Reagan years, our research on the effect of the president's domestic policies showed that his federalism theory backfired. States picked up in substantial measure on programs that were ended or reduced in Reagan's first budget.[26]

The theoretical linking point for this interpretation is the role of *leading* states. These states develop their own solutions for domestic problems during periods in which a conservative-retrenchment mood dominates in Washington or when the nation is preoccupied with international crises, as is often the case. Innovations are developed, adopted, tested, and incubated in these leading states. Once the kinks are worked out they can spread relatively easily to other states and the federal government, giving governors exciting opportunities for policy diffusion on a range of domestic issues.

It is useful here to look back in history. This process of ratcheting up state initiatives that are pro-government and expand the public sector applies not just to the present period, but also equally to earlier periods in the twentieth century. State governments were innovative before then as well. In an underappreciated book, *The Rise of the States: Evolution of American State Government*, Jon C. Teaford argues that going back to the nineteenth century, predictions of the death of the states "have been exaggerated." His book takes a close look at state finances, their role in transportation and in other policy areas, and the steady process of leading states reforming their structure and operations. Teaford concludes:

Rather than slumbering for the first seven decades of the twentieth century, then suddenly springing to life under the leadership of a new breed of bright and vigorous governors, the states have been vital actors from the 1890s onward. The image of foot-dragging hayseeds in provincial capitals blocking change and thwarting omnipresent dynamos in Washington, D.C., needs to be discarded. Though state governments did change notably in the 1970s and 1980s, they also changed markedly in the 1920s and 1930s. The vitality characteristic of the last quarter of the twentieth century was not a new phenomenon. Instead, the states continually adapted.[27]

Teaford describes governors as gaining stature in the early twentieth century as "powerful initiators of policy," citing Woodrow Wilson in New Jersey, Theodore Roosevelt and Charles Evans Hughes in New York, Hiram Johnson in California, and Robert La Follette in Wisconsin.[28] Hughes in New York, like many governors, emerged nationally as a leader in civil service reform and the creation of executive budget systems.

Again, state governments—not in all the states, but in many states—have been sources of expansion of the public sector in conservative periods in American history. When conservative coalitions controlled national offices in the twentieth century (and in earlier periods), programs first tested and debugged in progressive states later became the basis for national action and reforms. In such periods, client and provider groups for government programs as well as state and local governmental leaders played active roles in protecting existing programs and making retrenchment harder to achieve than otherwise would have been the case.[29]

Historians Allan Nevins and Henry Steele Commager pointed out nearly sixty years ago that "the first great battles of the reform movement were fought out in the states."[30] Compulsory school attendance, vaccination laws, the creation of state boards of education, reforms of political processes, a growing role for state boards of charity, child labor laws, and state regulatory policies in licensing and zoning are examples of state initiatives in domestic policy at the turn of the century that were later expanded and nationalized in the Progressive movement.[31]

This is not to deny that when expansionist views prevail in society, liberals can feast at the federal table or dig in their heels to preempt recalcitrant state actions and activities. But on the whole and over time, it is reasonable for liberals to champion federalism and conservatives to regard it as a Leviathan force (as some now do) that advances governmental growth.[32]

In sum, the American brand of pluralism with multiple points of access and maneuver, both horizontally and vertically, has produced alternating periods of activism on the part of the national government and the states, depending on conditions and values dominant in the society. The overall effect of these shifts over time has been to enhance the roles and responsibilities of government in the society and the economy as a whole.

What is distinctive about this analysis of American federalism is its emphasis on upward momentum. Since the start of the twentieth century, the federalism dynamic has exercised a steady and inexorable expansionist-liberal influence. In periods when expansionist proposals and ideas were on the wane in Washington, the existence of state-level counterforces kept the pressure on. Thus, the picture is one of federalism impelling the growth of governmental power in domestic public affairs, which otherwise would not have occurred in the individualistic political culture of America.

These observations about upward-trending policy activism in American federalism are strengthened by tying them to contemporary writings from both the political left and right that are consistent with this pro-growth theory about the ratcheting-up effect of federalism. There has been a shift among the pundits, with liberals supporting the states more strongly, and conservatives depicting federalism even as a "Leviathan force" for government growth and expansion.[33] This is not to argue about whether this is good or bad, but simply to suggest that this interpretation reflects the point that over time the balancing function of American federalism has become more powerful than its checking function. Textbooks that continue to give emphasis to the latter interpretation may be misleading.

Data on state and local revenue in relation to gross domestic product, for example, shows that the proportion of state and local revenue in the national income and product accounts rose in the Reagan-Bush period (1980–1992) at the same time that national domestic policy and spending became more restrictive. State receipts as a share of the gross domestic product increased from 12.6 percent in 1985 to level out at 13.7 percent in the aftermath of the Reagan-Bush years. There have been laggard states and state anti-spending campaigns in the post-Reagan years. Still, the interest-powered rise in domestic activism buttresses the theory that American federalism is a growth machine for government. In 2001, for the first time, total direct spending of states and localities exceeded that of the federal government.

The lesson—indeed, it is a warning—of this pro-growth interpretation is the challenge it poses for the exercise of fiscal discipline. Promises made at every level in the federal system and from many players in the game of government (executive, legislative, judicial, bureaucratic, and

FIGURE 7.1. GOVERNMENT DIRECT GENERAL EXPENDITURES AS PERCENTAGE OF GDP, FY 1980–2004
(Grants counted in government that finally spends them)

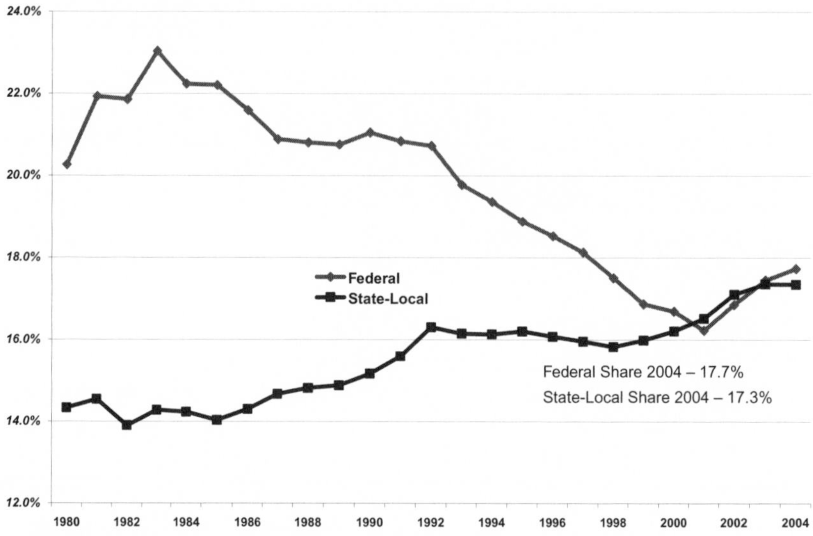

—Federal role has been falling for two decades.
—State-local role has been rising; now the two are roughly equal.
—Crossover points in 2001 and 2003.

Sources: Federal Budget for FY 2007 and U.S. Bureau of the Census, Government Division. This chart was prepared by Donald J. Boyd.

special interest) cumulate. Goals of new policies are often overstated to win a coalition of supporters. New promises have as their legacy hard tasks both for their implementation and for the ability of the public sector to maintain fiscal realism in domestic public affairs.

Ongoing debates question whether altered conditions should be the basis for fundamental changes in the American federalism bargain. The globalization of trade and industry, the information revolution, and global warming are often cited. My view is that the United States is too vast to have all of the affairs of the public sector decided upon and managed centrally. Information technology, with all its bells and whistles, is not up to this challenge. In the mixed economies of the modern age, there are many governmental services and facilities that are not all that grand, but are ubiquitous and critical to the functioning of communities and the lives of citizens. If states did not exist, we would need to invent regional entities to play similar crucial roles—to ensure public safety; care for the most needy; build and maintain roads, streets, parks, sewers, water systems, and waste and water treatment plants; provide public health services; upgrade the labor force; and respond to myriad needs that differ regionally in the nation, but nevertheless come to the fore with constancy and persistence.[34] We could not live five minutes without the services and facilities that state and local governments provide.

The federalism bargain receives constant scrutiny and adjustment. Beyond what some observers may regard as the essentially managerial considerations highlighted so far in this chapter, there is a critical ideological dimension to American federalism that needs consideration when commemorating the centennial anniversary of the National Governors Association and, in the process, reassessing our federal form.

Federalism and Liberty

I recently reread the address by Theodore Roosevelt at the first convocation of the nation's governors, held at the White House in 1908. All but twelve governors attended, along with other dignitaries, both government officials (cabinet members and Supreme Court justices) and private citizens (including TR's sometimes friend and sometimes gadfly opponent, Andrew Carnegie). In a wonderful, caring way, Roosevelt called upon the national government and the states to work together, emphasizing the conservation of the nation's natural and energy resources in terms that resonate with the views of governors today who are leading the way on environmental issues.

Then as now, modern federalism was intrinsic to American government in ways that went beyond the programmatic functioning and management of public programs. Federalism provides a vital sense of community that allows citizens to participate in political affairs in multiple polities (national, state, and local). They do so in ways that shape and signal their basic values and acculturate and train the men and women who become the leaders of their time. As James Madison emphasized long ago, political leaders are no different from the public at large. Their diversity reflects the milieu of values, ideas, and aims whirling around them. Some are more highly dedicated to public service than others, stronger in their commitment to the country and to its governance. As a nation, we benefit from having a number, and diversity, of political leaders and communities. In Madison's words, since people are "not angels," lively, open, active free government protects the rights of free citizens against concentrated power and arbitrary rule.[35] The inspiration of the public policy research institute that I co-direct, Nelson A. Rockefeller, put it this way in the Godkin Lectures, which he delivered at Harvard University in 1962.

Let me first make it clear that I do not speak of the federal idea as merely a mechanical or technical or abstract formula for government operations. I refer to the federal ideal broadly as a concept of government by which a sovereign people, for their greater progress and protection, yield a portion of their sovereignty to a political system that has more than one center of sovereign power, energy, and creativity. No one of these centers or levels has the power to destroy another. Under the Constitution, for example, there are two principal centers of government power—state and federal. As a practical matter, local governments, by delegation of state authority under the principle of "home rule," is a third such key center of power. The federal idea, then, is above all an idea of a shared sovereignty at all times responsive to the needs and will of the people in whom sovereignty ultimately resides.[36]

Indeed, shared sovereignty has its costs. Because there are multiple governmental centers, federalism is expensive. (In this sense, free government is not free.) The preference of Americans for pluralist political forms—both horizontally among the branches and vertically among levels of government (national and state)—reflects a fundamental tradeoff between efficiency and freedom. One can argue that the resulting governmental system has worked in good ways over the course of American history to sustain our political system as the world's longest-serving government under an extant written constitution.

It is not an accident that the countries that have a federal system similar to ours are developed countries that are relatively well off financially. In addition to the United States, the club of modern federalism includes Canada, Switzerland, Germany, Australia, Belgium, and Austria. Less-well-off nations that constitutionally have a written federal form—notably India, Brazil, and Mexico—have been less able to make the federalism bargain vibrant and enduring.

Crucial Role of the Middle Level—The States

In my view, the key to understanding federalism as a political form lies in the strength and character of the *middle level* of regional governments. In the United States and Australia, the middle level is the states. In Switzerland, middle-level governments are called republics; in Germany, *länder*; in Canada, provinces. Modern federalism, according to British political scientist K. C. Wheare, was invented in Philadelphia more than two hundred years ago.[37] Before that, a federal country was simply a league or club of member states. Yet, under the U.S. Constitution, every citizen is a citizen of two governments—national and state. Experts agree that a functioning federal system, composed of a central government and regional governments, must have a democratic political form that provides opportunities for access and participation by citizens at both the national and regional levels. Otherwise, the idea of self-expression by the regional governments would not be meaningful. Most experts also agree that an effective federal form needs to operate under a written constitution that defines not only the role and responsibilities of the central and state governments, but also the role of regional governments in the amendatory process, and the rights of citizenship.

Advocates of federalism believe it is a way to protect against central tyranny, increase citizen participation, encourage innovation (the states as "laboratories"), and strengthen community identity as well as the values of citizenship in a free society. Opponents of the federal form criticize its slowness to respond to new challenges, its difficulty in taking advantage of technological advances, and the cumbersome nature of its governmental decision-making and implementation processes.

Among political scientists, there are debates not only about the character of federalism, but also about its desirability. One school stresses the amorphous nature of federalism and its operational complexity. U.S. political scientist Morton Grodzins likened modern federalism to a marble cake (rather than a layer cake) characterized by constantly shifting, swirling patterns of functions, finances, and administrative arrangements.[38] Some members of the Grodzins school describe federalism as inevitably progressing toward a centralized governmental system. According to this view, federalism is, in effect, a way station to unitary government.

A second school, reflecting the theory I favor, highlights the role of the middle level. A useful way to view the federal bargain is by focusing on the major aspects of the roles of these regional governments. These include: (1) the power of the states to determine, organize, and control their own legal and electoral systems; (2) their fiscal role, referring to the way in which, and the degree to which, the states can set and levy their own taxes; (3) the programmatic dimension of federalism, referring to the functional areas of governmental activity over which the states have sole or predominant responsibility; (4) the role of state governments in the policy-setting process of the central government (for example, in the upper house of the legislature); and (5) the role of the states in determining the form, functions, and finances of local units of government. Although such elements are complex and can immerse readers in legal details, it is in these areas that federalism becomes real and meaningful.

In short and in conclusion, the role of the middle level (in the United States, the states) is to be the heart of the federal form of government—a method for reconciling unity and diversity in society. States advance and protect the rights of citizens. They enhance citizens' opportunities for participation in the governmental process, while at the same time reflecting different regional conditions, needs, and community values.

Governing the 1990s

In the 1990s, America enjoyed an era of relative economic and international ease allowing governors to continue domestic reforms, focus on integrating new technology, and turn greater attention to the demands of economic globalization. Although the decade began with a brief recession in 1991–1992, the 1990s proved prosperous for much of the nation. The "dot-com" industry boomed, and even foreign affairs seemed less dire following the 1989 fall of the Berlin Wall and the successfully short Gulf War in 1991. Political opportunities broadened. For the first time in the nation's history, an African American, Douglas Wilder of Virginia (1990–1994), was elected governor. In 1992, Bill Clinton, governor of Arkansas, became the first former National Governors' Association chairman to be elected to the presidency. As president, Clinton attempted (unsuccessfully) to push through a national health care plan and promoted (successfully) a welfare reform bill, both of which had been frequent topics of discussion at governors' meetings.[1] Clinton also turned his attention to another long-held concern of governors—the growing national deficit. By 1997, he had achieved a balanced budget.

Despite prosperity, the country faced some domestic unrest. Militia groups obsessed with growing governmental power gained considerable press. In 1993, a standoff in Waco, Texas, between the Branch Davidian religious sect and federal law enforcement officials ended in a tragic fire. And in 1995, Timothy McVeigh, although not a formal member of a militia, revealed his strong anti-government feelings by bombing the Murrah Federal Building in Oklahoma City, killing more than 150 people, including a number of children in a day care center. These deadly incidents, however, did not reflect a widespread protest against government. Although many Americans felt more apathetic and distrustful in the post-Watergate era, discontent was typically expressed at the polls, often in support of the party out of power (or simply the party opposite that of the incumbent president). In 1994, Republicans gained control of the House of Representatives for the first time in forty years. Intense partisanship lasted throughout the decade, leading to a temporary government shutdown and later impeachment hearings of President Clinton.

In this the era of rampant party politics, Democratic and Republican governors continued to meet and work together through the National Governors' Association. They discussed shared problems of environmental protection, health care reform, education, and welfare, among assorted other concerns. These gatherings continued to attract an impressive array of guests and experts. President Clinton spoke before the majority of NGA meetings during his tenure, often appealing directly to governors to support his foremost policy initiatives, including health care and welfare reform. In response, governors adopted a number of policy positions, some in support and some in critique of the president and Congress. Governors, as individuals and as a collective, grew ever more confident about their responsibility to speak out on issues of national concern. They also became more confident in the international component of the modern governorship, visiting other countries as representatives of their states' interests. Former professional wrestler Jesse Ventura (1999–2003), born James Janos, traveled to Japan to secure an additional market for pork produced in Minnesota. Ventura made a similar trade mission to Mexico in 2000. Trips like these were now commonplace, emphasizing the importance of economic globalization as the century drew to a close.

As in the previous decade, education remained one of the most important issues facing governors, a domestic concern with an international component of ensuring America's competitiveness. Governors focused increasingly on early childhood development in addition to the National Education Goals developed following the 1989 national education summit. Although the ideal of national standards was generally supported, some governors worried that the national government had become overly involved (as South Carolina Governor Olin Johnston had predicted in 1937 could happen) in dictating what and how schools should teach—a realm of responsibility traditionally reserved for states and localities. At the 1997 NGA annual meeting, Lamar Alexander offered his support of states retaining control of education standards. Alexander, former Tennessee governor, president of the University of Tennessee, secretary of education under President George H. W. Bush, and later U.S. senator, had extensive state and federal experience in education. He stated, "The agenda is this: Number one, rigorous standards, set locally not by Washington." "I think those of us who are Governors [or] who have been Governors," Alexander reflected, "know that math is not necessarily math and English is not necessarily English when Washington gets in the business of defining it."[2] George Voinovich of Ohio (1991–1998), who also later won election to the U.S. Senate, expressed similar concerns in 1993. Discussing the national education standards, the Ohio governor declared, "Now, this is nothing but a special interest group lobbying Congress to mandate on the states what they want the classrooms to look at, and it's the kind of thing that we've been taking too long."[3] This issue of education remained paramount throughout the 1990s as governors across the nation worked to revitalize their states' school systems. Governor George W. Bush (1995–2000) pushed for public school reform in Texas, a policy interest that carried over to his presidency. His gubernatorial predecessor, Ann Richards (1991–1995), also promoted educational innovation during her term, earning her the National Governors' Association Chairman's Award for her State Progress Report in Education in 1992.

As part of these educational concerns, governors strove to keep pace with and adapt to the technological revolution of the late twentieth century. In a short period of time, the world became much smaller as new high-tech products and systems made communication easier and information more widely accessible. The advent of the Internet and the World Wide Web made individual Americans, governors and their electorate, less isolated and more in touch with a national and international perspective. Advances in computer technology also altered the business of state government. The digitization of records made data more readily available to both state bureaucracy and the public. This technology opened new opportunities for governmental efficiency. NGA took an active role in encouraging governors to embrace these advancements, bringing in Bill Gates, chief executive officer of Microsoft, to speak at the 1997 annual meeting in Las Vegas about how computers could revolutionize the business of government and also stimulate American businesses.

Another revolution in the late twentieth century was one of diversity among the ranks of governors. Nellie Tayloe Ross of Wyoming and Miriam "Ma" Ferguson of Texas were both elected governor in 1924 and Lurleen Wallace in 1966, but the first election of a woman in her own right, not by association with her husband, did not take place until 1974 with Ella Grasso's gubernatorial win in Connecticut. Following Grasso's election, five states chose women governors between 1975 and 1990.[4] In the 1990s, six more were elected.[5] From 2000 to 2007, thirteen more women became governors.[6] And in 2006, Janet Napolitano, elected by Arizona in 2002, became the first female chair of NGA. In addition to these advances in terms of gender, racial and ethnic diversity also began in the late twentieth century, albeit more slowly. In 1986, John Waihee of Hawaii (1986–1994) became the first governor of Hawaiian descent. Eleven years later, the state of Washington elected Gary Locke (1997–2005), the son of immigrants and the first Asian American to serve as governor of a "mainland" state. In 2003, Bill Richardson, an experienced public official having served as a member of Congress, secretary of energy, and U.S. ambassador to the United Nations, won the governorship of New Mexico—becoming the sixth Latino governor of a southwestern state in the twentieth century. And in 2006, Deval Patrick of Massachusetts, assistant attorney general for civil rights in the Clinton administration, became the second African American elected governor. These men and women have redefined mindsets about who can be governor. President Clinton, speaking to governors in 1997, remarked, "This country is changing in dramatic ways. Race, ethnicity, and religion . . . [are] convulsing the rest of the world. If we can somehow not only respect but actually celebrate our diversity, and still have people say, 'but the most important thing is that I'm an American and we have one America,' [then] this is an unbelievable opportunity for us in a new century."[7]

Even before the twenty-first century began the 1990 election of Ann Richards brought a new dynamic into the American governorship—a true feminist who challenged the "good old boys" politics of her state. The "silver-haired, silver tongued Richards" became a force to be reckoned with both inside and outside of Texas.[8]

Chapter Eight

The Case of Ann Richards

Women in the Gubernatorial Office

Jan Reid

Hardly anyone who witnessed Ann Richards's inauguration as governor of Texas in January 1991 has any idea what she said in her speech. She was drowned out by her own celebrity.[1]

Three years earlier, she had been a fifty-five-year-old state treasurer who was little known outside Texas liberal and feminist circles. A divorced mother of four, a former schoolteacher, and a recovering alcoholic who first won office as a county commissioner in Austin, Richards had a long record as a civil rights and Democratic Party activist and a reputation as a witty, sharp-tongued orator. One afternoon a travel aide gave her a list of calls to return on a Houston airport pay phone; one was from the national Democratic Party chairman. "Well," Richards babbled when he asked her to deliver the keynote address to the party's national convention, "that is simply incredible. Never, ever, in my wildest dreams, would I have thought that I would be invited to do such a thing."[2]

A top speechwriter in Washington was recommended. She also enlisted her inner circle of close friends and advisers, especially her treasury chief of staff, Mary Beth Rogers, speechwriter Suzanne Coleman, and longtime confidante and big-picture strategist Jane Hickie.[3] They pulled late nights in Richards's tiny political office. Having won the treasurer's office by ousting a Democrat who'd been indicted on felony counts of assigning employees campaign tasks while working on state time, Richards was a stickler for never crossing that line of ethics and legality. Richards thought the speech being faxed back and forth was a mishmash, and when the Washington speechwriter called and said her speech had been consumed in a computer meltdown, the Texas women and press aide Bill Cryer worked into the night one more time; at last Richards's ideas and voice broke through.

"Poor George," she mocked the elder Bush, "he was born with a silver *foot* in his mouth."[4] And on she went, relishing her delivery of lines about pondering the nation's future while rolling a ball on a Baptist pallet with her infant granddaughter Lily and about Ginger Rogers matching Fred Astaire's every move while dancing backward in high heels. Richards believed that she got the Rogers-Astaire line, which she'd been using for years, from journalist Linda Ellerbee, who made no claims of inventing it. Mary Beth Rogers recalled that comediennes Lily Tomlin and Jane Wagner suggested using the line in the speech. The speech was an instant hallmark of American political theater. The life of the woman with the silver hair and resplendent blue dress would never be the same.

Bush routed Massachusetts Governor Michael Dukakis in the November election, but the 1988 keynote vaulted Richards into a harrowing race for governor of her state two years later. In her long-shot campaign she promised supporters that the morning she took office, they were going to march up Congress Avenue in Austin and reclaim the state capitol for the people of Texas. And here indeed they had come, singing and chanting, arm-in-arm.

After all the buildup, her inaugural speech on the steps of the capitol was bound for anticlimax. "Twenty, fifty, one hundred years from now," she began, "school children will open their textbooks—or, perhaps, switch on their video texts—and they will see a picture. They will see us standing proudly on this bright winter noon . . . we'll seem as distant and ancient as portraits of our ancestors seem to us."[5] In the New Texas—an ad man's lame slogan—barriers of race, color, and gender would fall and the doors of government would open. She envisioned a state with clean air and water, good jobs aplenty, compassion and help for those in need, and a public education system that enabled all children to attain the full promise of their lives. The speech contained just one concrete proposal—creation in her office of an ombudsman who would respond to people's complaints about state government.

But Richards's first speech as governor is not forgotten because of the vagueness and clichés. No one could *hear* it. Intent on scooping the image of her ascent to power, a television news crew continually hovered a helicopter over the pink granite dome. The roar and echoed whacking of the rotors was like the opening scene and credits of the sitcom *M*A*S*H**, without the bittersweet score.

Still, anyone who doubted that the state was fundamentally changed might have followed a group of her aides into an executive office building after the speech. Their attire ran to jeans, sneakers, and the campaign's satiny blue and white windbreakers, modeled on those of the Los Angeles Dodgers. The jabbering aides jogged along a corridor to a set of elevators, eager to claim their new desks and cubicles and *get started.* The elevator doors opened, and they lurched one step forward and braked. The representatives of Richards's staff stood face to face with aides of the outgoing GOP governor, Bill Clements.

A gruff Dallas oilman, Clements had in 1978 become the first Republican elected governor of Texas since Reconstruction. In 1982 Clements lost to an attorney general, Mark White, in a Democratic sweep that featured a number of attractive down-ballot newcomers, among them Ann Richards. But the old driller handily won the rematch against White four years later. Riding the elevator for the last time as his staff, Clements's aides were well-groomed men in suits, carrying briefcases. They took in the new crowd in power and blanched. They slipped past without a word, awaiting another election, a new day.

Ann Richards was not the first woman elected governor of Texas. Miriam "Ma" Ferguson won her first term in 1924 and was inaugurated fifteen days after Wyoming's Nellie Ross, who won a special election to succeed her deceased husband and officially became the first woman elected governor in the United States. Ma Ferguson campaigned largely on a mission to unmask the Ku Klux Klan, and she delivered on that promise. Her campaign offered "two governors for the price of one"—she was on the ballot because her husband, James "Pa" Ferguson, had been impeached.[6] Her proxy administration was accused of taking bribes for pardons of convicts and kickbacks on road-building projects; she lost her race for reelection in 1926. But her husband's quasi-populist demagoguery won her another term when the Depression arrived with cruel force in 1932.

For the first 199 years of the United States' existence, only three women, all Democrats, were elected governors. They ran on the strength of their husbands' names and, in the cases of Ferguson and George Wallace's wife, Lurleen, in Alabama, who served in 1967 and 1968, they governed as surrogates of men who could not hold the office. (Wallace and his wife evaded an Alabama limit on consecutive terms.) The revolt and success of women as governors corresponded in the last quarter of the twentieth century with assertions of women's striving throughout American life. Until Ann Richards, it was a mistake to categorize those pioneers as feminists. They had more in common with suffragettes, whose triumph in 1920 was the Nineteenth Amendment, which gave women the right to vote.

In Connecticut in 1974 Ella Grasso was the first American woman elected governor in her own right. The well-educated daughter of Italian immigrants, Grasso had married in 1942 and, while rearing two children, she ascended in Democratic politics as a legislator and member of Congress during the two years of Watergate tumult. At fifty-five Grasso ran for governor. She upset an attorney general by two thousand votes in the Democratic primary and then turned back a Republican congressman in the general election. She drove her staff hard and tried to manage an inherited $70 million state debt without imposing an income tax. In late 1975 she called a special session of the state assembly to deal with the fiscal crisis, proposing a raid on a veterans' fund. The legislators declined, and she laid off more than five hundred state employees just days before Christmas. She was called austere and hard-hearted.

Institution of a lottery helped turn the deficit into a surplus, but her popularity did not rebound until she took the lead providing relief to victims of a terrible blizzard in early 1978. Now called "Mother Ella," she defeated a Republican that fall by 189,000 votes. She poured energy into programs for the poor, but gasoline and heating oil shortages brought on by OPEC's embargo of Western nations put state revenues in freefall. Confronted with a $128 million deficit, Grasso had to preside over a sales tax increase that gave Connecticut one of the highest rates in the country. In 1980 she was diagnosed with cancer, and she announced she would resign the last day of the year. She died just over a month later, on February 5, 1981. Grasso was a New Deal–era progressive who prided herself as a tough-minded keeper of fiscal order. She rode the crest of the times but hardly embraced the modish feminism of Betty Friedan and Germaine Greer. She opposed abortion as a Catholic, she was indifferent about the ill-fated Equal Rights Amendment, but her example buoyed the hopes of women who followed.[7]

The next three women governors were also Democrats—Washington's Dixy Lee Ray, Kentucky's Martha Layne Collins, and Vermont's Madeline Kunin, who won three successive terms starting in 1984. But the uprising was not a one-party affair. Born, reared, and educated in Iowa, Kay Orr married and moved to Lincoln, Nebraska, when she was twenty-four. Republican politics became a passion for Orr in the 1964 presidential race of Barry Goldwater. She worked for Richard Nixon's subsequent campaigns and, in 1976, she co-chaired Nebraska's organization for Ronald Reagan, then trying to wrest the Republican nomination from President Gerald Ford. In 1978 she ran the winning campaign of congressman Charles Thone for Nebraska governor. Thone made Orr his chief of staff, and in 1981 he appointed her to fill a vacancy as treasurer. In 1986, the enigmatic Democratic governor, Bob Kerrey, surprised Nebraskans by saying he wouldn't seek reelection. That fall, Orr, declaring that she opposed abortion under any circumstance, defeated former Lincoln mayor Helen Boosalis in the first gubernatorial election in which both candidates were women.

Orr focused on economic development and pressed the legislature to modify tax laws to benefit expansion of business. But values of agricultural lands plummeted, banks in farm towns collapsed, and the plains were gripped by drought. In the 1990 race a conservative Democrat, Ben Nelson, attacked Orr because her tax reform initiatives had been followed by tax increases for almost everyone, and he seized on Nebraska being party to a five-state compact to dispose of low-level radioactive waste. The bid of a sparsely populated county on the Iowa border had won the contract. Orr said she was unenthusiastic about the nuclear dump but favored granting the license. Nelson ran on the issue and won, though the state's attempt to back out of the contract would later cost taxpayers $145 million in a lawsuit settlement.

Three other women represented their parties in the gubernatorial elections of 1990. Many observers thought that Democratic San Francisco mayor Dianne Feinstein had a good chance in California against Pete Wilson, the GOP U.S. senator who was running for governor. When Wilson edged Feinstein, she ran in a special election for his vacated seat in the Senate, where she remains a force twenty-five years later. Another intriguing race was in bellwether Kansas. Joan Finney, a mother of three, had worked sixteen years on the staff of a Republican U.S. senator, and in 1972 she ran for Congress as a GOP candidate. After her defeat she switched parties and was elected a Democratic state treasurer, an office she held fifteen years. In 1990, at sixty-five, Finney became the first woman to defeat an incumbent governor. She easily turned out Republican Mike Hayden, who had mishandled a statewide property reassessment, and in her term she tried to deliver property tax relief by bringing more goods and services under the sales tax. Governing as a populist, she vetoed a workers' compensation bill that would have limited coverage of injuries and reduced rates paid by employers. She vetoed another measure that she claimed would unfairly benefit hog packers and corporate farmers. The first Catholic governor of her state, Finney strongly opposed abortion. In 1991 she pleaded for calm and respect for the law to angry protestors of the Wichita clinic of a doctor who specialized in late-term abortions. Finney won high praise for her moral leadership, but two summers later, a woman from Oregon shot and wounded the doctor.

In vivid contrast to Orr and Finney, Ann Richards had worked in Austin for the legislator who successfully argued *Roe v. Wade* before the Supreme Court. If she became governor of Texas, a legislature would be poorly advised to send her a bill that tried to constrain a woman's right of choice. But that was a large "if." Republicans in Texas were confident that the Democratic machine personified by Lyndon Johnson was a decrepit wreck—within a decade the GOP would hold every statewide office in Texas. And Richards knew it would be a hard fight in the Democratic primary against the attorney general, Jim Mattox. Richards told a group of key supporters and feminist activists in Austin that her heart might be more in a race for lieutenant governor. Several women argued passionately that it was time for her in Texas, and that it was time for them—they all but begged her to run.

Richards had been a prominent player in Austin's storied revelry of the 1970s. She was now a dedicated member of Alcoholics Anonymous, but in a Democratic debate at a Dallas public television station in the spring of 1990, that element of her past caught up with her. When a panelist asked the candidates if they had ever used illegal drugs, Mattox and Mark White, the former governor who had joined the race, said proudly that they had not. Richards began, "I want to address my answer to all of you out there who have had problems in your life."[8] She went on to say that she wanted to assure them that they could seek help for their problems without fearing the mistakes would be brought up to them again and again. *Texas Monthly*'s Paul Burka, a panelist, later wrote, "I have never been in a place where silence was such a presence, except for her voice. A small audience was in the studio, and not even a cough broke the stillness. I thought we were watching Ann self-destruct on statewide television and that she had lost the race by dodging the question."[9]

Richards defeated Mattox and White but came out of the primary and runoff battered and wounded. One of the co-managers of Richards's Democratic contests was an amiable young Austin politico named Mark McKinnon, who would later resurface as the top media adviser in George W. Bush's presidential races. Members of Richards's inner circle, who were women, were heard to refer in exasperation, if not fairness, to McKinnon and other men involved in the campaign as "the *guys.*"[10] Meanwhile, the millions of campaign dollars and good ol' boy charm of a west Texas oilman and rancher, Clayton Williams, buried the hopes of several able GOP rivals. Williams pranced down main streets on his horse, grinning from ear to ear and waving his Stetson like Roy Rogers. The pairing made for great television—"Claytie and the Lady," the race was slugged.

Richards enlisted her most trusted adviser, Mary Beth Rogers, to take over as campaign manager, but Richards trailed by more than twenty points after Labor Day. Yet the long odds made her a more inspiring campaigner, and she got an unending string of lucky breaks. Williams cracked a joke to reporters in a soggy campout that, like rape victims, they might as well just lie back and enjoy it. He refused to shake Richards's hand at a joint appearance and boasted he was going to "head her and hoof her"—a calf-roping expression.[11] He also remarked that in a recent year he had not been required to pay any income taxes. It hadn't seemed possible Richards could win that race, but she did, by more than 99,000 votes. Richards's victory was widely attributed to the emergence of a force of well-educated, middle-class "soccer moms." Still, she got just 49.6 percent of nearly four million votes cast.

"We were so far behind," Rogers said with a laugh, years later, "that we hadn't given a great deal of thought to what we'd do if she won."[12] Right after the election, Richards and her inner circle gathered in condominiums on South Padre Island and pressed their analysis of the state's urgent needs, issue by issue. Areas of responsibility and management would be assigned in the administration to many of those women. Rogers would be chief of staff, and Suzanne Coleman would continue to be arguably the nation's best and doubtless its most prolific speechwriter. Pat Cole would oversee social services, Jane Hickie the Washington office of federal-state relations, and Cathy Bonner the Department of Commerce. Annette LoVoi, the much-emphasized ombudsman, soon fielded two hundred gripes about state government a week. In high-profile signals of her intent to emphasize women and ethnic minorities in her appointments, Richards picked Reverend Zan Holmes of Dallas for a seat on the powerful University of Texas Board of Regents, and Barbara Jordan, the former congresswoman and voice of conscience and constitutionality in the Watergate crisis, served as her special counsel on ethics. In addition to these women, Bill Cryer came from the treasury as director of public information, and Joe Holley, later a writer and editor with the *Washington Post*, digested and crafted information from the South Padre meetings into the *Blueprint for the New Texas*. The document contained sections on no fewer than eighty-two priorities.

In many ways Texas was a mess. In 1978 a convict named David Ruiz had filed a class-action lawsuit alleging inhumane conditions caused by prison overcrowding, and the inmates' lawyers won. Since then, federal judges had effectively run the Texas prison system. Texas faced an uphill fight in another lawsuit filed over past reductions of payments to hospitals through its $2 billion Medicaid program. And just a week after Richards's inauguration, the state's supreme court held that the method of funding the public schools was unconstitutional.

The liberal feminist grandmother delivered a stinging, ambitious, bravura performance in her January 1991 state of the state address to the legislature. Richards promised an administration that would not wait to act "until prodded by court order."[13] Her appointees and staff would be compelled by public service and ethics, not personal gain, and would be sworn to eliminate inefficiency and waste. She promised that prisons with space for 39,000 new beds would be built within the next biennium and that her administration would innovatively address the social roots of crime. She predicted the proposed NAFTA agreement would make

Texas "the geopolitical center" of trade with Mexico, and said her office would promote clean, homegrown industries such as filmmaking, a particular enthusiasm throughout her term.[14]

She threw down gauntlets in the speech. Of the inequitable and underachieving public school system, she said, "You know, we have perpetrated a hoax about local control. The hoax has been that school districts had control because they could assess and collect taxes. In fact, our state government has usurped their power years ago with mandates that require tax increases and regulations that turn educators into Austin-controlled robots. Local control is a myth when Austin bureaucrats draft ten rules for every action a teacher takes."[15]

On the environment, every major city was dealing with air pollution, which in addition to threatening health, put them in danger of noncompliance with the Clean Air Act, which could lead to a cutoff of federal highway funds. Texas was rivaled only by Louisiana as the nation's worst in the Environmental Protection Agency's inventories of toxic pollution. Richards promoted alternative fuels programs that might help the cities gain control of air pollution caused by vehicle traffic, and she issued a brash challenge to executives of the petrochemical plants and refineries along the Gulf Coast, and their powerful lobbyists, the Chemical Council.

She took on the insurance industry and the state insurance board appointed by her predecessor. "Just last week," she said, "after I pressed the board to hold off on a thirty percent auto rate increase, they announced a delay so they could audit the data the industry had given them. Isn't that what they are supposed to be doing all along?"[16] Richards demanded that insurance board members appointed by Clements resign at once, and said if they did not, she would move to put the regulatory body under direction of a conservator.

Texas legislators were not historically inclined to jump through the hoops of any governor. The state seceded during the Civil War, and it has an unwieldy constitution written in 1876 by people who believed they were abused by the power of governors during Reconstruction. Conventional wisdom holds that this constitution ensures a weak governor. Agencies such as the agriculture commission, comptroller of public accounts, land office, and railroad commission (who spend most of their time and resources regulating oil and gas production) are directed by statewide elected officials who can heed a governor's wishes or ignore them. But strength or weakness depends on the governor. Appointments to boards of other agencies are the nexus of gubernatorial power to enact policy.

Richards sent shock waves through the agencies, legislature, and lobby with her appointments in the spring of 1991. In one that balanced adroit symbolism with policy direction, she named Ellen Halbert, a 1986 victim of a brutal rape and near-murder and a nationally renowned victims' rights advocate, to the board of the Department of Criminal Justice, which had always been the secretive domain of white males. At the swearing-in ceremony of John Hall, a tall, soft-spoken African American who was her new chairman of the lead environmental protection agency, the governor declared: "Beginning today, no new permits will be issued for commercial hazardous waste sites until the Water Commission adopts extensive new regulations to implement this legislation. No hearings will be held on permit applications until all the rules are in place. No permit will be issued that does not fully comply with the new rules and meet the new standards laid out in the law. Business as usual at the Water Commission ends today."[17]

Richards did not want to have to wait until midway through her term until she had a majority of appointees on the boards, and she aspired to streamline and consolidate agencies. Unlike most past governors of her state, Richards took her case for change to open committees of the legislature. Her adversaries fought back, often with help from newspaper editorial boards. A week after her March 1991 testimony on insurance reform, the *Fort Worth Star-Telegram* blasted one provision of the bill as a brazen power grab by plaintiffs' lawyers. But the legislation passed.

Also elected to a first term in 1990, Lieutenant Governor Bob Bullock was both an ally and rival—and many analysts and historians have contended that the Texas constitution endows the lieutenant governor with greater power than the governor. The Democratic former legislator and comptroller had been Richards's mentor and often her drinking partner before they both gained control of their addictions (leaving the state some wild folklore). Unlike Richards, Bullock did not care a whit for national politics. In the 1980s he had announced that he was going to run for governor, but then concluded he could never win the office. He was a powerful comptroller, the state's tax collector. Roughed up by legislators and editorial boards when he said the state could not continue to function without a state income tax, Bullock, as the lieutenant governor, reversed his stance and engineered a bill that made an income tax effectively impossible, for it could be enacted only if voters approved a constitutional amendment. Yet an inequity in school funding resulted from the state's almost total reliance on sales and property taxes.

Much of Richards's time and energy was expended in the imbroglio of the prisons. The new attorney general, Dan Morales, negotiated a settlement of the Ruiz lawsuit early in her term, yet the specter of intervention by federal judges refused to go away. To avoid offending the judiciary with more overcrowding, Clements and his criminal justice boards had regularly accelerated paroles in a much-criticized "backdoor" solution to the problem. Richards ordered her appointees to grant no early releases to felons convicted of serious crimes, which created a logjam of sentenced convicts in county jails, awaiting prison space at great cost to local taxpayers. As a result Richards oversaw an unprecedented surge in prison construction—one official projected a total of 54,300 more beds at forty-seven new facilities by 1994. At the same time, she was convinced that convicts with drug and alcohol abuse problems inside the prisons were guaranteed recidivists when they were released to the streets. In the 1991 and 1993 sessions of the legislature, the governor said she wanted $14,000 reserved for the "substance abuse felony punishment facilities," and the legislature agreed to it, pulling the hierarchy of wardens along, and making believers of many.

Richards pushed fast and hard for the changes she desired, yet she didn't come across as strident. Her personal popularity soared. In June 1991 she attended an annual reunion of Texas Rangers in her girlhood hometown of Waco. "'Can you shoot? Can you ride? Can you cook?'" she rhetorically teased the old cops and troopers. "Those were the three criteria of Texas Rangers a hundred fifty years ago. . . . I'm pleased that retired Senior Ranger Captain Clint Peoples, now living in Waco after a long and distinguished career, is with us. I heard a rumor that this is the very same Clint Peoples who said during the governor's race last year that he would never support a 'petticoat governor.' It's good to see you, Clint."[18]

Four months later, in September 1991, a man named George Hennard rammed his pickup into a Luby's Cafeteria in the central Texas army town of Killeen, using two handguns to kill twenty-three trapped people and wounding twenty more before he killed himself. (It ranked as the worst mass murder in American history until the 2007 slayings of thirty-two students and faculty on the campus of Virginia Tech.) Killeen was in the rural and small-town part of the state where the governor had grown up. From late 1992 through the spring of 1993, a surreal drama compounded her shock over the cafeteria massacre. Amid rolling hills a few miles east of her former hometown of Waco, activities inside a compound of a religious cult called the Branch Davidians first alarmed local caseworkers of the state agency Child Protective Services, and reports of automatic weapons and explosives aroused local law enforcement officials and agents of the federal Bureau of Alcohol, Tobacco, and Firearms (ATF). In December ATF agents approached the Richards administration with requests to "borrow" state aerial reconnaissance equipment. Perhaps motivated by desire to foist some of the operations cost on Texas, the federal request was a formality in any case. The governor was titular commander of the Texas National Guard, but ATF easily got what it wanted through military channels. In January and February 1993 aerial photos and infrared videos conveyed a "hot spot" image that the agents interpreted as an illegal weapons cache. Despite the endorsement of the ATF operation by the military chain of command, Richards and her legal counsel believed the National Guard could participate in arrest missions only if illegal drugs were involved. ATF made allegations, never proven, that methamphetamines were being manufactured in the compound, Mt. Carmel. With support from three National Guard helicopters and crews, ATF agents tried to serve warrants for firearms violations on the last day of February. In a vicious firefight four ATF agents and at least six residents of Mt. Carmel were killed, including the two-year-old daughter of the cult's leader, David Koresh.

On the fourth day of the siege, speaking at a scheduled "Waco Day" at the Capitol, Richards said, "The sad part about a situation like this is that you're trying to make sense out of a senseless event. I'm worried about those children in the compound. I want them to get the kids out. Then if the adults make a choice they want to stay there, then they have to live with the consequences. But kids don't have a choice."[19] The governor said in that press conference that she wanted to take a "serious look" at legislation to ban assault weapons. The standoff grew more tense and bizarre every day. FBI negotiators listened for hours as Koresh ranted; the Branch Davidians hung out a huge banner saying "God Help Us, We Want Press." Richards learned the foray of the National Guard unit had resulted in three shot-up helicopters and state expenditures of $300,000. "The thing that frightens me," she said as the siege wore on, "is that everyone wearies of it. I think eventually we can reach a peaceful solution, but I'm going to respect the decisions that are made by the FBI. I think they're all sort of tired of listening to the evangelizing on the telephone, and I can't say I blame them."[20] She observed in anguish as the madman said that God was giving him this chance to reveal the mystery of the seven seals in Revelations. The FBI blasted the besieged at night with recordings of chanting Tibetan monks, the whine of a dentist's drill, shrieks of rabbits being slaughtered. A tank destroyed Koresh's prized Camaro. At 5:30 A.M. on the fifty-first day, the commanding officer of the National Guard informed Richards's office that the FBI was going in, using tear gas.

The outcome stamped on the nation's consciousness a uniquely Texas image of explosions and inferno. The tragic loss of life to gunfire in Killeen and the Branch Davidian compound deepened Richards's resolve on a matter of principle that she believed cost her a second term.

Despite her personal popularity, Richards's internal polling told her she could never count on more than 47 percent of the vote. Succeeded as chief of staff by John Fainter, Mary Beth Rogers left to teach at the University of Texas and write a biography of Barbara Jordan. Rogers would return as campaign manager, but at one point she said, "Ann, you really don't have to run again."[21] But Richards told her friend that she *did* have to run—too many good people were counting on her.

Karl Rove was then unknown as a strategist outside Texas. George W. Bush was a failed wildcatter and showpiece owner of the Texas Rangers baseball team, in which he actually held a minute share. Bill Clinton turned his father out of the presidency in the 1992 election. But Rove persuaded the younger Bush that he could defeat the popular governor. The strategy was to stick to a well-honed message on a few issues like education, juvenile crime, and tort reform—code words for cutting the legs out from under plaintiffs' lawyers—and to avoid direct personal attacks on Richards. Indirect attacks by surrogates and political allies were encouraged and choreographed by the campaign.

Working closely with Rove and the Bush campaign, in the state party headquarters a former television journalist, Karen Hughes, kept up a constant and effective barrage of accusations of mismanagement by the governor's office. Complying with freedom of information requests became virtually a full-time job for Bill Cryer. Richards often warned that Bush should not be taken lightly. But she was influenced by the belief of campaign aides and Democratic politicos that he was a hothead, and would blow up under pressure. Bush never did.

Richards had some successes after the first burst of achievement in her administration. In early 1992 she used her office as a bully pulpit to persuade General Motors to rescind its announced decision to close a plant in Arlington, between Dallas and Fort Worth. Working with a local alliance of activists called Valley Interfaith and the legislature, she brought water and sewage to unincorporated *colonias* along the Rio Grande. Facilitated by her persuasion of airline executives to provide direct flights between Los Angeles and Austin, the Texas movie industry mushroomed. In 1993 she championed and signed the state's first hate crimes law. On school finance, Richards, Lieutenant Governor Bullock, and their staffs worked together with senators on a formula in which property-rich school districts shared their abundant tax revenue with poor ones. Though the fix appeased the state supreme court, it was unpopular in affluent communities, where it was known by the pejorative "Robin Hood." And Richards's relationship with Bullock deteriorated to the point where they no longer spoke. The lieutenant governor chewed out Richards's appointed heads of agencies with fury well known by his staff; he sent word to the governor and her aides that they could no longer talk to "his senators" without his permission. Bullock was flattered and charmed by Bush. Many Richards aides and allies were convinced Bullock maneuvered behind the scenes to help Bush in his race to unseat the governor.

Richards's agenda of reorganizing state agencies evaporated. Lobbyists for insurance and petrochemical corporations assailed members of her policy council as incompetents. Richards's gubernatorial press office was increasingly paralyzed by the volume of freedom of information demands by reporters, Hughes's state GOP operation, and Republican legislators. Yet on ethics, the closest her administration came to a scandal was when chief of staff Fainter was obliged to write a memo to staff that read: "Prohibited use of state phones include: personal business calls, personal social calls, and political calls of any kind."[22] But political embarrassments hounded Richards in 1992 and 1993. She appointed one of the young stars of her inner circle, Lena Guerrero, to a vacancy as railroad commissioner. Karl Rove tipped a reporter that Guerrero had lied brazenly about having a college diploma; in the 1992 election the GOP candidate trounced her. After winning the presidency, Bill Clinton named Texas's patrician U.S. senator, Lloyd Bentsen, his treasury secretary. Richards learned that her top two choices as Bentsen's successor had espoused anti-abortion views. She at last appointed to the seat Bob Krueger, a former congressman whose best race for the Senate was fourteen years behind him. Richards's GOP successor as state treasurer, Kay Bailey Hutchison, routed Krueger in the special election. The growing weakness of the Democrats in Texas—and Richards's inability to turn that tide—were thoroughly exposed.

In April 1993, a federal judge and officials of the U.S. Fish and Wildlife Service indicated that several aquatic species that lived only in springs of the Edwards Aquifer, in central Texas, qualified for protection under the Endangered Species Act. The species included a blind salamander. Texas's third largest city, San Antonio, several other communities, and large-scale irrigated agriculture in central and west Texas relied on pumping from the aquifer to meet their water needs. A rebellious uproar ensued over the judge's power and these endangered species, especially the symbolic blind lizard-like amphibian—and the federal Endangered Species Act itself. The staffs of Richards, Bullock, and the Democratic house speaker Pete Laney asked Clinton's interior secretary, former Arizona Governor Bruce Babbitt, to state clearly and publicly the consequences of failing to protect the species through some regulation of pumping the groundwater. Richards bracketed that part of the memo and with a characteristic star of emphasis wrote, "Important to get done."[23] Babbitt solemnly wrote that inaction could cause "federal funds (for highways, military bases, crop subsidies, etc.) to be shut off."[24] In August 1994 another official of the U.S. Fish and Wildlife Service stirred more outrage among property rights activists by suggesting that

use of choice Texas ranchland and development acreage might be con-
strained by the habitat of the golden-cheeked warbler.

In a consistent earmark of campaigns directed by Rove, Richards was
deeply wounded when a respected Democratic senator from east Texas
who had worked closely with her on education called a press conference
and volunteered moral objections to her coterie of "lesbians." Richards
was the mother of four children and for decades after her divorce Richards's steady date was an esteemed author, Bud Shrake—no one could
plausibly question her sexual orientation. But apart from the opposition's innuendo-laden tactics, Richards found, like many other women
in American politics, that her private life, choice of friends, and even
her appearance were "issues" in ways that seldom hinder male candidates, unless they are caught up in genuine scandals. Comfortable with
Bush, legions of soccer moms abandoned Richards. And in national politics, 1994 was the year of Clinton's national health care debacle, which
had been directed by his wife, Hillary. Striking electoral gold with an
agenda styled as the "Contract with America," Newt Gingrich and other
GOP conservatives in Congress capitalized on the swooning popularity
of the president and the policy-wonk first lady, and in a stunning sweep
captured the House of Representatives from the Democrats for the first
time in forty years.

Richards was not the only high-profile Democrat whose luck ran out
that fall. Symbols of the sea change in American politics, she and
another newly jobless star Democrat, New York's Mario Cuomo, were left
dolefully munching chips in a Super Bowl commercial. Her personal
approval rating remained well over 50 percent, yet she lost by 334,000
votes, carrying just 45.9 percent to Bush's 53.5. Richards could not deny
that Bush was the far more disciplined and energetic candidate. But the
liberal who tried to govern as a centrist was convinced she lost because
she refused to compromise her principles on guns.

A survivor of the Luby's Cafeteria massacre inspired many Texans by
claiming that if she hadn't left her .38 revolver in the car she could have
shot the maniac and saved both her murdered parents. The National
Rifle Association distributed to members Richards's remark during the
Branch Davidian siege that she would seriously consider a ban on assault
weapons. In April 1993 the legislature signaled it would send her a bill
to allow licensed private citizens to carry concealed handguns. Richards
promised she would veto it: "The people of this state do not need to be
reminded that weapons of violence produce death to innocent children
and adults. I am an avid hunter and believe strongly in the rights of individuals to own guns. That is not the question here. This legislation will
only increase the level of violence on our streets. I have not talked to
one law enforcement officer who supports this bill and I cannot in good

conscience ask them to patrol the streets of this state and face additional hazards that this bill will encourage. Frankly, the only outcome of the passage of this bill will be more people killed by gunfire."[25]

A month later, she heightened her rhetoric. "The move by sponsors to report out a stripped-down version of the concealed gun bill is nothing more than game-playing by a few legislators who appear intent on embarrassing this great state as a place where gun-toting vigilantes roam the streets."[26] The legislature passed the bill, she vetoed it, and in a speech she turned to police chiefs, county sheriffs, and constables who supported her veto; her voice rang with withering contempt for her adversaries. "I especially want to thank you for choosing to stand by me on this day when we say no to the amateur gunslingers who think they will be braver and smarter with gun in hand."[27] Bush didn't have to run on the issue of concealed handguns. He just had to promise he'd sign the bill when he was governor, and he did.

The next American woman governor of comparable stature had also figured prominently in the 1990 elections. Christine Todd Whitman was born in 1946 in New York City, where her father's engineering firm helped build the Rockefeller Center, the RCA Building, and Radio City Music Hall. She grew up in a New Jersey farmhouse that had stood since 1768. Her mother was finance chair of Nelson Rockefeller's presidential campaigns. A Republican of blue-blood pedigree, Whitman worked in the Nixon administration under Donald Rumsfeld in the Office of Economic Opportunity. She served on boards of a New Jersey community college and was elected to two terms on a county commission, then spent two years in the cabinet of Governor Thomas Kean, presiding over the board of public utilities. Whitman was a forty-four-year-old with elegant bearing and a slight résumé when she challenged Senator Bill Bradley in 1990. Bradley had been a legendary basketball player for Princeton and the New York Knicks and was a serious contender for the presidency. He seemed befuddled and condescending when Whitman ran against New Jersey's taxation. They were candidates, he reminded her, for a federal office. Bradley won another term by 53 to 47 percent. But in public and media perception, New Jersey voters had taken the aloof senator to the woodshed, and Whitman was a rising GOP star.[28]

In 1993 Whitman challenged Democratic Governor James Florio, attacking him for pushing a $2.8 billion tax increase through the legislature. Presenting herself as a moderate pro-choice Republican, Whitman promised a 30 percent reduction in income taxes in three years. She overtook the incumbent in the last week of the race, winning with a plurality margin of 26,000 votes. But at once she had to defend her character and ethics when her campaign manager, Ed Rollins, popped off to reporters that she won because they paid African American ministers to discourage voting by members of their churches. The newly elected governor could only be mystified why her campaign manager would cheapen her victory with braggadocio about campaign fraud—especially since federal investigators found no evidence that the egotistical boast was true. (And Rollins quickly indicated he had lied.) During her first term, Whitman led the legislature to roll back income taxes 30 percent in two years, not three. *People* magazine hailed her as "a one-woman political slogan," but in 1997 she defeated a Woodridge mayor by only 47 to 46 percent. Whitman built an admirable record on environmental protection. The number of days New Jersey violated federal standards for ground-level ozone pollution fell from forty-five in 1988 to four in 2000, a new watershed management program allowed the state to take the U.S. lead in opening shellfish beds for harvest, and she won voter approval and funding to preserve one million acres of natural areas and farmland.

Following the 2000 presidential election, she resigned as governor to join the cabinet of George W. Bush and direct the Environmental Protection Agency. Her contribution as a presidential cabinet member was neither as happy nor as hailed as her performance as New Jersey's governor. She immediately found herself in embattled defense of the administration's canceling of stronger limits on arsenic in drinking water (which the Clinton administration had enacted in its last days) and Bush's decision to reject the Kyoto Protocol on global warming. Whitman pointed with pride to requirements for cleaner-burning diesel engines, a plan to remove polychlorinated biphenyls (PCBs) from the Hudson River, and the EPA's handling of anthrax mailed to a Senate office building in Washington, but following the terrorist attacks of September 11, 2001, her remarks concerning environmental damage, especially in New York, subjected her to fierce criticism. An EPA inspector general's report quoted her: "The outdoor or ambient air was fine," and ten days after the attacks, she assured New Yorkers that tests of drinking water had not detected any asbestos, bacterial contaminants, or PCBs.[29] In June 2003 Whitman resigned, saying she wished to spend more time with her family. In February 2006, hearing a class-action suit filed by New York plaintiffs alleging extreme damages to their health, federal judge Deborah Batts described Whitman's actions after September 11 as "conscience-shocking" and denied her request for immunity from the lawsuit.[30] Whitman later wrote a book critical of the Bush administration titled *It's My Party Too: The Battle for the Heart of the GOP and the Future of America*.[31] In 2007 the *Washington Post* quoted her as saying the real reason she departed the administration was because Vice President Dick Cheney dictated an EPA rule that excused refurbished power plants and oil refineries from having to install updated and greatly improved pollution controls: "I just couldn't sign it," she told the *Post* reporters, so she wrote her letter of resignation.[32]

By 2003 women were governors of seven states and Puerto Rico. Sila María Calderón won election in 2001 as governor of the Commonwealth of Puerto Rico, representing the Popular Democratic Party, and served an assertive, at times controversial four-year term. The new wave also included Kansas Democrat Kathleen Sebelius, whose father, John Gilligan, was a former governor of Ohio. The mother of two and wife of a federal magistrate, Sebelius had served eight years as a legislator and eight as insurance commissioner, an office she used to block the acquisition of the state's largest health insurer by an Indiana corporation. She ran for governor in 2002 against a Republican state treasurer who counted on pro-gun and anti-abortion positions and a large GOP majority of registered voters to carry the day. Pro-choice and an opponent of capital punishment, she won that race 53 to 45 percent. When Sebelius came into office the state was in fiscal disarray—about $225 million in budget cuts were required immediately. She responded with top-to-bottom performance audits of the agencies, taking measures like the sale of an unneeded fleet of seven hundred cars. Citing her efforts to trim government waste and her inclusion of Republicans in her cabinet, *Time* magazine lauded her as one of the nation's top five governors in 2005.

Sebelius is Catholic, and her archbishop condemned her for vetoing a measure that would have required abortion clinics to document reasons women gave for seeking late-term abortions. Like Ann Richards, Sebelius has spent much of her tenure trying to solve the complex riddles of public education finance—the state supreme court ordered the legislature to increase funding in 2005. And like Richards, Sebelius vetoed a measure that would have allowed citizens to carry concealed handguns. In 2004, a survey of registered voters in Kansas found that 50 percent identified themselves as Republicans, while 27 percent said they were Democrats. But Sebelius, who served on the executive committee of the National Governors Association, won reelection over a GOP state senator in 2006 with 57.8 percent to her opponent's 40.5.

No less a feminist, the Democrat Janet Napolitano won election in 2002 as Arizona's third woman governor. Born in New York City, Napolitano grew up in Pittsburgh and Albuquerque. After graduating from college in California and the University of Virginia law school, Napolitano joined and became a partner of a Phoenix law firm. In 1991 she was the lead counsel of Anita Hill in her Senate testimony that U.S. Supreme Court nominee Clarence Thomas had subjected her to sexual harassment. In 1993, President Clinton appointed Napolitano as a U.S. attorney in Arizona. As a prosecutor she played a lead role in the investigation of Michael Fortier, an accomplice of Timothy McVeigh in the bombing of a federal building in Oklahoma City. She was elected attorney general of Arizona in 1998. A survivor of breast cancer, Napolitano ran in 2002 to succeed Republican Governor Jane Dee Hull. With strong support from women and Latino voters, she edged a former congressman, Jeff Salmon, with a 46 percent plurality and one-point margin.

In her first term Napolitano brought the legislature a plan to eliminate a $1 billion budget deficit without raising taxes. By 2005 the state had a budget surplus of $300 million. Her administration provided all-day kindergartens for 150 of the state's poorest schools. Along with California's Arnold Schwarzenegger and New Mexico's Bill Richardson, she committed Arizona to a five-state compact to exceed the federal government's efforts to reduce emissions of greenhouse gases. Napolitano has been on the front line and come under intense political attack over the influx of undocumented immigrants from Latin America. Her emphasis has been on pressuring employers to hire legal workers, not building a wall along the border. She has been forceful in challenging her state and nation to rise to the occasion of a global economy. Chair of the National Governors Association for 2006–2007, she presented an *Innovation America* initiative that convened a task force of governors, business leaders, and university presidents. "In today's economy," Napolitano wrote, "competition between nations is less relevant than competition between regions of innovation."[33] Among her points: China has overtaken the United States as the world's leader in exporting information-technology products, in 2005 only four American companies ranked among the top ten recipients of patents granted in the United States, and the same year less than two-fifths of U.S. fourth- and eighth-grade students were proficient in math and science.

However broad the vision, leadership in government is rooted in politics and the verity that all politics is local. Succeeding as a governor requires winning elections and influencing others to compromise or change their minds. In 2006 Janet Napolitano ran against a Republican man who tried to make an issue of her being unmarried. She won reelection with 62.6 percent. But she has to deal with regional political realities personified by her legislature—by mid-2006 she had set a record for Arizona governors with 127 vetoes.

After two centuries of prejudice, since 1975 fourteen Democratic women and twelve Republican women have been elected governors of American states. Though African Americans, Asian Americans, and Native Americans are unrepresented in this group, that is an impressive start and an almost even political split. Ann Richards, who died from cancer in October 2006, never considered running for office again. But her legacy endures. She was a tireless champion of organizations like Emily's List, which encourages and recruits women to seek office. Even Sarah Palin, Alaska's newly elected young Republican governor, who would have agreed on few issues with Richards, had one commonality: they were both brave enough to challenge male leaders of their parties on ethics.

At a conference on women's history a few months before Richards lost her 1994 race to a future two-term president, she reflected on how locality and tradition help shape aspiration. Women in Texas, she drawled, don't mind their place on earth "being thought of as the native habitat of the good ol' boy." She went on,

"You all know what I'm talking about. These are the guys whose preferred method of transportation is a pickup with a bad clutch, a gun rack that's not for show, and a bumper sticker that reads 'I Don't Brake for Liberals.'

"The women in this audience know these guys well. When they are still in the dating stage, they show respect for women by hanging an air freshener on the rear-view mirror. We've all seen the deep blue of a starlit night and the orange glow of the campfire, and around it another group of good ol' boys, doing what real he-men do—drinking beer and staring at nothing in particular.

"Now, you look at that image and the historical and stereotypical concepts that go with it, and you might begin to think that Texas is not the kind of place where change is readily accepted. But here I am as governor—so you know that something is going on.

"In an incredibly short time, we have moved from watching the parade to joining the end of the procession, and now we move, with our brothers, to the head of the procession—to leadership of the procession. We ask only that our perspective as women be valued. Not because it is better, but because it's different—and it has been missing."[34]

Conclusion

The Evolution of the Gubernatorial Office

United States Governors over the Twentieth Century

THAD L. BEYLE

The modern American governorship evolved from a very difficult beginning under a colonial regime. In the seventeenth and eighteenth centuries, the English monarch appointed governors to serve as representatives and enforcers of British rule. Colonists came to resent these men as impediments to their liberty. After the revolutionaries signed the Declaration of Independence in 1776 and led their states into open rebellion, representatives creating new state governments were considerably more inclined to place power in the hands of state legislatures rather than in those of governors. Fearing a return to the oppressive colonial style of governing, these Americans instituted a major shift, creating a new form of federalist government reliant on a system of checks and balances.

The terms of office given to governors by the first state constitutional conventions illustrated this intended lack of power. Of the thirteen original states in 1789, seven had one-year terms, another had a two-year term, and five had three-year terms. There has been a considerable increase in the terms of office given governors over the past two centuries (see Table 9.1). Now, all but two states—New Hampshire and Vermont—provide their governors with four-year terms, and only one state—Virginia—does not allow governors to seek a second consecutive term. Clearly, over time, Americans overcame the legacy of colonial distrust and recognized the need for stronger executive leadership.

In the twentieth century, governorships evolved as considerable additional powers were granted. One of the forces behind this growth was the rise in the number of former governors who were able to win election to the presidency (see Table 9.2). Former governors held the presidency from 1893 to 1909—sixteen years—and one of them, Theodore Roosevelt (1901–1909), a former governor of New York, was the presi-

TABLE 9.1. LENGTH OF GUBERNATORIAL TERMS, 1789–2008

Year	States	1-year	2-year	3-year	4-year
1789	13	7[a]	1[b]	5[c]	—
1808	17	7[d]	3[e]	6[f]	1[g]
1908	46	2[h]	21[i]	1[j]	22[k]
2008	50	—	2[l]	—	48[m]

Source: Gubernatorial Elections, 1787–1997 (Washington, D.C.: Congressional Quarterly, 1998) and www.unc.edu/~beyle, gubernatorial elections.

[a] One-year term states—Connecticut, Maryland, Massachusetts, New Hampshire, New Jersey, North Carolina, Rhode Island.

[b] Two-year term state—South Carolina.

[c] Three-year term states—Delaware, Georgia, New York, Pennsylvania, Virginia.

[d] One-year term states—Connecticut, Georgia, Massachusetts, New Hampshire, North Carolina, Rhode Island, Vermont.

[e] Two-year term states—Ohio, South Carolina, Tennessee.

[f] Three-year term states—Delaware, New Jersey, New York, Pennsylvania, Virginia.

[g] Four-year term state—Kentucky.

[h] One-year term states—Massachusetts, Rhode Island.

[i] Two-year term states—Arkansas, Colorado, Connecticut, Georgia, Idaho, Iowa, Kansas, Maine, Michigan, Minnesota, Nebraska, New York, North Dakota, Ohio, South Carolina, South Dakota, Tennessee, Texas, Wisconsin.

[j] Three-year term state—New Jersey.

[k] Four-year term states—Alabama, California, Delaware, Florida, Illinois, Indiana, Kentucky, Louisiana, Maryland, Mississippi, Missouri, Montana, Nevada, North Carolina, Oklahoma, Oregon, Pennsylvania, Utah, Virginia, Washington, West Virginia, Wyoming.

[l] Two-year term states—New Hampshire, Vermont.

[m] Four-year term states—all but New Hampshire and Vermont.

dent who first called governors together in 1908 to discuss conservation issues. Out of that meeting evolved the National Governors Association. Woodrow Wilson (1913–1921), a former governor of New Jersey, soon followed Teddy Roosevelt into the presidency. Then during the Depression, Franklin Roosevelt (1933–1945), another former governor of New York, joined this list and worked to help the country out of the Depression with his New Deal approach to handling the nation's economy and social services. Roosevelt led the country almost all the way through World War II.

More recently, Americans have witnessed another era in which governors have made their way to the White House, helping the country recover from the scares of the Richard Nixon administration and Nixon's resignation in 1974 following the Watergate scandal. Four of the last five presidents moved up from a gubernatorial chair into the presidency—former Georgia Governor Jimmy Carter in 1976, former California Governor Ronald Reagan in 1980 and 1984, former Arkansas Governor Bill Clinton in 1992 and 1996, and former Texas Governor George W. Bush in 2000 and 2004. The only race that did not promote

TABLE 9.2. GOVERNORS WHO BECAME PRESIDENT

	Years Served	Gubernatorial Experience: State, Election Year, Years Served
Thomas Jefferson	1801–9	Virginia (colony), 1779, served 1779–81
James Monroe	1817–25	Virginia, 1799, served 1799–1802, 1811
Andrew Jackson	1829–37	(Provisional Gov.) Florida, 1821, served four months[a]
Martin Van Buren	1837–41	New York, 1828, served 1829–30
William Henry Harrison	1841	Indiana territory, 1800, served 1800–1812
John Tyler	1841–45	Virginia, 1825, served 1825–27
James K. Polk	1845–49	Tennessee, 1839, served 1840–41
Andrew Johnson	1865–69	Tennessee, 1853, 1855, served 1854–58
Rutherford Hayes	1877–81	Ohio, 1867, 1869, 1875, served 1868–72, 1876–77
Grover Cleveland	1885–89, 93–97	New York, 1882, served 1883–85
William McKinley	1897–1901	Ohio, 1891, 1893, served 1892–96
Theodore Roosevelt	1901–9	New York, 1898, served 1899–1900
Woodrow Wilson	1913–21	New Jersey, 1910, served 1911–13
Calvin Coolidge	1923–29	Massachusetts, 1918, 1919, served 1919–20
Franklin Roosevelt	1933–45	New York, 1928, 1930, served 1929–32
Jimmy Carter	1977–81	Georgia, 1970, served 1971–75
Ronald Reagan	1981–89	California, 1966, 1970, served 1967–75
Bill Clinton	1993–2001	Arkansas—1978, 1982, 1984, 1986, 1988, served 1979–81, 1983–93
George W. Bush	2001–	Texas, 1994, 1998, served 1995–2000

Source: *Gubernatorial Elections, 1787–1997* (Washington, D.C.: Congressional Quarterly, 1998)
[a] Jackson was appointed to this position of provisional governor.

a governor to the presidency since the mid-1970s was in 1988, when George H. W. Bush defeated Massachusetts Governor Michael Dukakis.

Over the twentieth century, several waves of reform have aimed to make state governments more efficient and capable of performing the roles they have gained in America's federal system.[1] These improvements have positively influenced and expanded the gubernatorial office.

The first wave of reform "followed a 1912 report by President Taft's Federal Economy and Efficiency Commission, which recommended adoption of an executive budget system for the federal government."[2] Although that report did not immediately bring changes to the national level, many state leaders were impressed with it, leading twenty-six states to reorganize—many of them comprehensively.[3] Illinois and New York were at the forefront, led by governors Frank Lowden in Illinois and Alfred E. Smith in New York. One result of these reforms was that "administratively and politically the Illinois governor ascended to new eminence and influence" based on the adoption "of the first comprehensive plan of administrative reorganization."[4] New York soon followed, along with other states.

Nine years later, in 1921, the National Municipal League entered into this reformist discussion by publishing "A Model State Constitution." Here, "a centralized plan of State organization, headed by the governor, a single-house legislature, and unified court structure" were the central guidelines for states to follow.[5] The report gave states more innovations to consider, aimed directly at the state governments and their leaders.

President Franklin Roosevelt's 1937 establishment of a federal commission to suggest needed reforms in the nation's government stimulated a second wave of reorganization. As part of this initiative, more than a dozen states reworked their governments. Reformers in eleven states strove "to make the governor in fact, as well as in theory, the responsible chief executive of the state."[6]

The third wave had to wait on the nation's distraction with World War II, and came in response to the Hoover Commission's (active in the Truman and Eisenhower administrations) recommendations of ways to reorganize and restructure the national government's executive branch. Following this example, quite a few states created "'little Hoover Commissions' in states and cities, indicating that keeping state government, or any government, organized for action [was] a never-ending task." The major goal of these "little Hoover Commissions" was to concentrate authority and responsibility, with state governors clearly in focus.

In the 1960s, states entered a fourth wave of reform in response to major alterations in the federal system resulting from the Great Society initiatives launched under President Lyndon Johnson. Governmental grant-in-aid programs expanded into new areas, and the responsibilities placed on state and local governments increased considerably. Building on previous reforms, many states reorganized their governments in light of the increased presence and pushing of the federal government to attack many of the problems that both states and the nation faced. As former North Carolina Governor Terry Sanford (1961–65) argued in his 1967 book, *Storm Over the States*, "I detect a sense of direction and the excitement of action in our American states. Reapportionment, the accumulating activity of the national government, and the developing confidence of the states in their ability to improve have com-bined to move the governors to new ventures, to new hopes, and to new determination."[7]

Sanford's goals for state reform on behalf of the governors were also very clear. He listed these as follows:

- Make the chief executive of the state the chief executive in fact.
- The two-year term for governors should be replaced with a four-year term, and a governor should be allowed to seek to succeed himself at least once. Maybe, if succession is not favored in some states, a six-year single term might be considered.
- The governor should be given the dominant authority in the budget process, preferably as budget director.
- The governor, as chief planner for his state, must conduct his administration to enable his state to look beyond his term of office to the future.
- Like the President of the United States, each governor should have the authority to reorganize and regroup his executive agencies sub-ject to legislative veto within a specified period of time.
- The governor must have adequate staff to represent adequately the public interest.
- The governor's office should be organized to be receptive to new ideas and use the experiences of other states in seeking fresh solu-tions to problems.[8]

Over the next few decades nearly every state reworked its government, stimulated by these waves of reforms, the aftermath of court decisions on legislative redistricting, and other stimuli. As the data presented in the next section will show, governorships prospered under these initia-tives.

Measuring Change in American State Governorships, 1960 to 2008

As already noted, the institution of the governorship has changed con-siderably over the past five decades as part of a fourth reform wave. Polit-ical scientists have been able to analyze this evolution using a line of research and measurement introduced in the 1960s by Joseph A. Schle-singer in his chapter, "The Politics of the Executive," in *Politics in the American States*.[9] In later editions of the book, I was asked to update that chapter and continue Schlesinger's work. The book is updated regularly to stay current.

This important index that Schlesinger started in 1960 and I have updated to 2007 measures the institutional powers of governorships across the fifty states. This index uses six separate measures of the institutional powers of governors: (1) the number of separately elected executive branch officials; (2) the tenure potential that a governor has in terms of length of term and ability to seek another term; (3) a governor's appointment power over executive branch leadership positions; (4) a governor's state budgetary power; (5) the type of veto power a governor has vis-à-vis legislation passed by the state legislature; and (6) how much party control the governor's party has in the state legislature (See Table 9.3).

Each of these measures is judged on a five-point scale, with five being the greatest power and one or zero being the least.[10] The six scores are totaled for each state and then divided by six to give each state a score within the five-point range. The notes to Table 9.3 explain in detail how these scores are determined.

The data in Table 9.3 reveals that, overall, there has not been a considerable increase in the institutional powers of governors from 1960 to 2007. Governors averaged 3.3 on the five-point scale in 1960 and 3.5 in 2007—only a 6 percent increase of 0.2 points over nearly five decades. In 1960, there were seven states with scores of 4.0 or more: New York, New Jersey, Maryland, Virginia, Hawaii, Illinois, and Pennsylvania. In 2007, there were also seven states with scores of 4.0 or more: Massachusetts, Alaska, Maryland, New Jersey, New York, West Virginia, and Utah. Only three of these states were at the top both years—Maryland, New Jersey, and New York. In 1960, there were six states with scores of 2.3 or less: Mississippi, South Carolina, Texas, West Virginia, Arizona, and North Dakota. In 2007, seven states had scores of 2.9 or less: Vermont, Rhode Island, Alabama, Oklahoma, Indiana, Mississippi, and North Carolina. Only Mississippi ranked among the weakest gubernatorial institutional powers for both years.

However, Table 9.3 highlights some very interesting changes from 1960 to 2007. First, states' gubernatorial veto powers have increased dramatically, rising from a score of 2.8 in 1960 to a 4.5 score in 2007—a 60.7 percent increase. The North Carolina governor gaining the veto for the first time in the mid-1990s contributed to this uptick, but more significant was the increase in gubernatorial ability to have and use an item veto when reviewing the passed legislation put before them. This ability was especially important in considering state budgets passed by the legislature. In ten states, the score in this veto category jumped by two, three, or more points between 1960 and 2007: West Virginia, Florida, Iowa, Mississippi, Nebraska, South Carolina, Arizona, Kansas, North Carolina, and Texas.

Second, the tenure potential of governors increased by 24 percent.

TABLE 9.3. COMPARISON OF INSTITUTIONAL GUBERNATORIAL POWERS, 1960 vs. 2007

State	SEP 60/07	TP 60/07	AP 60/07	BP 60/07	VP 60/07	PC 60/07	SCORE[a] 60/07	Point Change
AL	1/1	3/4	3/3	5/3	4/4	5/2	3.5/2.8	− 0.7
AK	4.5/5	4/4	1/3.5	3/3	5/5	5/4	3.8/4.1	+ 0.3
AZ	2/2.5	2/4	3/4	2/3	3/5	2/2	2.3/3.4	+ 1.1
AR	2.5/2.5	2/4	2/3	5/3	2/4	5/5	3.1/3/6	+ 0.5
CA	2/1	5/4	3/4	5/3	4/5	4/2	3.8/3.2	− 0.6
CO	4/4	5/4	1/3.5	4/3	4/5	4/4	3.7/3.9	+ 0.2
CT	4/4	5/5	4/2.5	4/3	2/5	4/2	3.8/3.6	− 0.2
DE	2.5/2.5	4/4	1/3.5	1/3	4/5	2/3	2.4/3.5	+ 1.1
FL	3/3	3/4	2/2.5	1/3	2/5	5/4	2.7/3.6	+ 0.9
GA	1/1	3/4	1/2	5/3	3/5	5/4	3.0/3.2	+ 0.2
HI	5/5	5/4	3.1/2.5	3/3	5/5	3/1	4.0/3.4	− 0.6
ID	2/2	5/4	5/2	1/3	3/5	2/4	3.0/3.3	+ 0.3
IL	3/3	5/5	5/3	5/3	3/5	3/4	4.0/3.8	− 0.2
IN	3/3	3/4	5/2.5	3/3	1/2	3/3	3.0/2.9	− 0.1
IA	3/3	2/5	3/3	5/3	2/5	2/4	2.8/3.8	+ 1.0
KS	3/3	2/4	2/3	4/3	3/5	2/2	2.7/3.3	+ 0.6
KY	3/3	3/4	4/4	5/3	2/4	5/2	3.7/3.3	− 0.4
LA	1/1	3/4	2/3.5	4/3	4/5	5/4	3.2/3.4	+ 0.2
ME	5/5	4/4	1/3.5	4/3	2/2	4/4	3.3/3.6	+ 0.3
MD	4/4	4/4	5/2.5	5/5	2/5	5/4	4.2/4.1	− 0.1
MA	4/4	2/5	1/3.5	5/3	4/5	4/5	3.3/4.3	+ 1.0
MI	3/4	2/4	4/3.5	5/3	3/5	3/2	3.3/3.6	+ 0.3
MN	4/4	2/5	4/2.5	5/3	3/5	3/2	3.5/3.6	+ 0.1
MS	1/1.5	3/4	1/2	1/3	2/5	5/2	2.2/2.9	+ 0.7
MO	2.5/2.5	3/4	4/3	5/3	4/5	4/4	3.8/3.6	− 0.2
MT	3/3	5/4	2/3	5/3	4/5	2/3	3.5/3.5	—
NE	3/4	2/4	3/3	5/4	2/5	3/3	3.0/3.8	+ 0.8
NV	2.5/2.5	5/4	2/3.5	5/3	2/2	3/3	3.3/3.0	− 0.3
NH	5/5	2/2	1/3	5/3	2/2	4/4	3.2/3.2	—
NJ	5/5	4/4	5/3.5	5/3	4/5	3/4	4.3/4.1	− 0.2
NM	3/3	1/4	3/3	4/3	3/5	5/4	3.2/3.7	+ 0.5
NY	4/4	5/5	5/3.5	5/4	4/5	4/3	4.5/4.1	− 0.4
NC	1/1	3/4	2/3.5	4/3	0/2	5/4	2.5/2.9	+ 0.4
ND	3/3	2/5	1/3.5	1/3	3/5	4/4	2.3/3.9	+ 1.6
OH	4/4	4/4	4/3.5	5/3	2/5	4/2	3.8/3.6	− 0.2
OK	1/1	3/4	1/1	5/3	4/5	5/3	3.2/2.8	− 0.4
OR	2/2	4/4	4/3	5/3	3/5	2/4	3.3/3.5	+ 0.2
PA	4/4	3/4	5/4	5/3	4/5	3/3	4.0/3.8	− 0.2
RI	2.5/2.5	2/4	3/3	4/3	1/2	2/1	2.4/2.6	+ 0.2
SC	1/1	3/4	1/2	1/2	2/5	5/4	2.2/3.0	+ 0.8

TABLE 9.3. (CONTINUED)

State	SEP 60/07	TP 60/07	AP 60/07	BP 60/07	VP 60/07	PC 60/07	SCORE[a] 60/07	Point Change
SD	3/1	1/4	2/2	5/2	3/5	3/4	2.8/3.0	+0.2
TN	4/4.5	3/4	5/4	5/3	1/4	5/3	3.8/3.8	—
TX	1/2	2/5	1/1	1/2	3/5	5/3	2.2/3.2	+1.0
UT	4/4	5/5	3/3	5/3	3/5	3/4	3.8/4.0	+0.2
VT	2.5/2.5	2/2	4/3.5	2/3	2/2	4/2	2.8/2.5	−0.3
VA	2.5/2.5	3/3	5/3.5	5/3	4/5	5/2	4.1/3.2	−0.9
WA	1/1	5/5	4/3.5	5/3	3/5	4/4	3.7/3.6	−0.1
WV	3/2.5	3/4	3/4	1/5	1/5	2/4	2.2/4.1	+1.9
WI	3/3	2/5	2/2	5/3	3/5	3/3	3.0/3.5	+0.5
WY	2/2	5/4	3/3.5	5/3	3/5	3/1	3.5/3.1	−0.4
Avg.	2.9/2.9	3.3/4.1	2.9/3.0	4/3.1	2.8/4.5	3.7/3.2	3.3/3.5	+0.2
Change	—	+0.9	+0.1	−0.9	+1.7	−0.5	+0.2	
%chg.	—	+28	+3.5	−22.5	+60.7	−13.5	+6.0	

The Specific Institutional Powers of the Governorships

SEP—Separately elected executive branch officials:
5 = only governor or governor/ lieutenant governor team elected
4.5 = governor or governor/lieutenant governor team elected, with one other official elected
4 = governor/lieutenant governor team with some process officials (attorney general, secretary of state, treasurer, auditor) elected
3 = governor/lieutenant governor team with process officials, and some major and minor policy officials elected
2.5 = governor (no team) with six or fewer officials elected, but none are major policy officials
2 = governor (no team) with six or fewer officials elected, including one major policy official
1.5 = governor (no team) with six or fewer officials elected, but two are major policy officials
1 = governor (no team) with seven or more process and several major policy officials elected

TP—Tenure potential of governors:
5 = four-year term, no restraint on reelection
4.5 = four-year term, only three consecutive terms permitted
4 = four-year term, only two consecutive terms permitted
3 = four-year term, no consecutive election permitted
2 = two-year term, no restraint on reelection
1 = two-year term, only two terms permitted

TABLE 9.3. (CONTINUED)

AP—Governor's appointment powers in six major functional areas: corrections, K-12 education, health, highways/transportation, public utility regulation, and welfare. The six individual office scores are totaled and then averaged and rounded to the nearest .5 for the state score.
5 = governor appoints, no other approval needed
4 = governor appoints, a board, council or legislature approves
3 = someone else appoints, governor approves or shares appointment
2 = someone else appoints, governor and others approve
1 = someone else appoints, no approval or confirmation needed

BP—Governor's budget power:
5 = governor has full responsibility, legislature may not increase executive budget
4 = governor has full responsibility, legislature can increase by special majority vote or subject to item veto
3 = governor has full responsibility, legislature has unlimited power to change executive budget
2 = governor shares responsibility, legislature has unlimited power to change executive budget
1 = governor shares responsibility with other elected official, legislature has unlimited power to change executive budget

VP—Governor's veto power:
5 = has item veto and a special majority vote of the legislature is needed to override a veto (three-fifths of the legislators elected or two-thirds of the legislators present)
4 = has item veto with a majority of the legislators elected needed to override
3 = has item veto with only a majority of the legislators present needed to override
2 = has no item veto, with a special legislative majority needed to override a regular veto
1 = has no item veto, only a simple legislative majority needed to override a regular veto

PC—Gubernatorial party control:
5 = has a substantial majority (75 percent or more) in both houses
4 = has a simple majority in both houses (under 75 percent), or a substantial majority in one house and a simple majority in the other
3 = split party control in the legislature or a nonpartisan legislature
2 = has a simple minority (25 percent or more) in both houses, or a simple minority in one and a substantial minority (under 25 percent) in the other
1 = has a substantial minority in both houses

Sources: Joseph A. Schlesinger, "The Politics of the Executive" in Herbert Jacob and Kenneth N. Vines, eds., *Politics in the American States* (Boston: Little Brown, 1965), and Thad L. Beyle and Margaret R. Ferguson, "The Governors," in Virginia Gray and Russell L. Hanson, eds., *Politics in the American States: A Comparative Analysis,* 9th ed. (Washington, D.C.: CQ Press, 2007).
[a] This is the total of the six separate indices divided by six to keep within the five-point scoring range.

The score moved upward from 3.3 in 1960 to 4.1 in 2007. The number of states with two-year terms dropped considerably. Now only two states—New Hampshire and Vermont—still have those short terms. Also, the push in many of the states to place term limits on state legislators did not extend to the state governors' terms. In ten states, the tenure potential score jumped by two or three points between 1960 and 2007: Iowa, Massachusetts, North Dakota, South Dakota, Texas, Wisconsin, Arizona, Kansas, Nebraska, and Rhode Island.

Third, gubernatorial budget power experienced a considerable decline. The score dropped by 22.5 percent, from 4.0 in 1960 to 3.1 in 2007. The reason for this drop was the aforementioned reform initiatives of state legislatures. One of these major reforms was to increase the legislature's power in terms of developing and working on the budget. Thus, this change was less about governors losing power over their part of the budget process than about state legislatures gaining power in that area.

Fourth, there was a significant decrease in the governor's party strength in their state legislatures. The primary reason for this change has been the rise of the Republican Party in southern states. This shift led to many party splits in those states, resulting in many situations where a governor faced a legislature in which either one or both of the houses were controlled by the opposition party. In 1960, all fourteen southern states had Democratic governors, with both houses in each state substantially Democratic. In 2007, there were seven Democratic and seven Republican governors in these southern states, and while four Democrats and four Republicans saw the legislature controlled by their own party, there were six states in which political power was split between the two branches—Alabama, Kentucky, Mississippi, Oklahoma, Tennessee, and Virginia.

Finally, the 1960–2007 governors' institutional power scores reveal some intriguing regional differences (See Table 9.4). The greatest evolution in these powers occurred in midwestern and southern states. In the Midwest, states increased their gubernatorial veto powers and tenure potential while losing some budgetary control resulting from the rise in legislative power. In the South, state governors gained more veto power vis-à-vis the state legislatures, but, as already noted, lost political party power vis-à-vis the state legislatures. Less overall change occurred in northeastern and western states.

Getting to Be Governor

A comparison of the governors serving in 1908 when President Theodore Roosevelt first called them together in Washington to those serving

TABLE 9.4. GOVERNORS' PARTY AFFILIATIONS, 1908 vs. 2007

Region	States	1908	Governors [a]	States	2007	Governors
Northeast	11	2 D	9 R	11	8 D	3 R
South	14	12 D	2 R	14	7 D	7 R
Midwest	12	3 D	9 R	12	6 D	6 R
West	9	3 D	6 R	13	7 D	6 R
Totals	46	20 D	26 R	50	28 D	22 R

Source: Gubernatorial Elections, 1787–1997 (Washington, D.C.: Congressional Quarterly, 1998).

[a] Four western territories were not in operation as states in 1908—Alaska, Arizona, Hawaii, and New Mexico.

in 2007 uncovers some intriguing partisan differences. In 1908, there were 26 Republican governors to 20 Democratic governors in the 46 states. In 2007, there are 28 Democratic governors to 22 Republican governors in the fifty states. This shift reflects the recent increase in Democratic wins in gubernatorial races in the first decade of the twenty-first century.

Regionally, in 1908 Republican governors dominated all the regions 24 to 8, except in the South, where the Democrats dominated the fourteen southern states 12 to 2. In 2007, the party breaks are virtually even—20 Democrats to 19 Republicans—in all the regions except in the Northeast, where the Democrats hold an 8 to 3 majority.

Another question to consider is, where do those individuals seeking and winning the governorship come from? They are obviously citizens of the state, but what steps did they take before running for office? Analyzing successful candidates' stepping-stone positions from where they launched their campaigns for governor provides insight into who exactly is winning office.

Between 1900 and 2006, states elected 1,005 individuals to the office of governor. These men and women came from a variety of positions in government, politics, and elsewhere. Twenty-two percent of them moved into the governorship after being elected to and holding a statewide elective position. Some of these were "accidental governors" who as the successor in line became governors upon the death, removal, or resignation of the incumbent governor. Nineteen percent came from a position in the state legislature as either a legislative leader or just a legislator able to make a successful run. Another 17 percent came out of law enforcement positions. Eleven percent came from important administrative positions in the state. Another 11 percent were members of the U.S. Congress, and 7 percent moved up from a local elective position. The final 10 percent had held no prior elective position until running for and winning the governorship—this was their starting point in elective politics.

Breaking down these results even further shows that there have been significant shifts in the stepping-stone offices of new governors since 1981. Nearly 30 percent came from statewide elective positions, 17 percent came from congressional positions, and 16 percent held no previous elective position. Now, considerably fewer governors come from the law enforcement ranks (9 percent) or from administrative positions (5 percent).

The politics and process of running for the governorship have changed dramatically over the past few decades. Simply, gubernatorial elections have become much more expensive. Prior to the mid-1970s, the reporting of how much money candidates raised and spent was not a widespread policy. Some states had such requirements, but most did not. The campaign scandals embroiled in the Watergate debacle that engulfed President Nixon in the early 1970s stimulated more states to require the financial reporting of gubernatorial and other campaigns. By the mid-1970s, all states had enacted laws requiring reports on how much money was raised, from whom, and the amount and way those funds were spent for each campaign. In some states, a few categories of candidates could opt out of such reports, but, for the most part, financial records exist for most campaigns from 1977 onward (see Table 9.5).

Fifty-four gubernatorial campaigns were waged between 1977 and 1980. Candidates spent just over $524 million in equivalent 2006 dollars. The average amount spent in these fifty-four campaigns was $9,704,190. Three decades later, reports filed for the fifty-two campaigns for the governorship between 2002 and 2005 indicate that more than $1.267 billion in equivalent 2006 dollars were spent—an increase of 142 percent. The average spent per campaign was $24,370,860. In recent decades, campaigns have moved from a focus on who you know and meet to the quality, distribution, and frequency of television ads. Now candidates hire professional political consultants for many jobs formerly held by political friends and volunteers. The cost of creating those ads and getting them placed and run drives the need to raise a great deal of money—especially in larger states with high-priced media markets. And hiring experienced consultants costs a great deal more than relying on political friends.

The New York race in 2002, reelecting Governor George Pataki to a second term, was the most expensive gubernatorial election up to 2005. It cost more than $164 million in equivalent 2006 dollars. The situation was similar in California. There, the 1998 election cost nearly $154 million, and the state's 2002 election ran over $135 million. Then in 2003, a recall and replacement election saw incumbent Democratic Governor

TABLE   9.5. COST OF GUBERNATORIAL ELECTIONS: 1977–80 TO 2002–5

Years	Number of Races	Expenditures (in 2006 dollars)	Cost Per Race	Percentage Change
1977	2	$ 40,904,927	$ 20,452,464	
2005	2	$ 136,218,852	$ 68,109,426	+233.0
1978	36	$ 305,070,000	$ 8,474,167	
2002	36	$ 934,265,123	$25,951,809	+206.2
1979	3	$ 90,954,653	$30,318,218	
2003[a]	13	$ 76,603,574	$25,534,525	− 15.8
1980	13	$ 87,096,653	$ 6,699,743	
2004[b]	11	$ 120,197,431	$10,927,039	+ 38.0
1977–80	54	$ 524,026,233	$ 9,704,190	
2002–5	52	$1,267,284,710	$24,370,860	+141.8

[a] The California recall and replacement election was held this year but those data are not included here.

[b] Arkansas and Rhode Island changed their gubernatorial terms from two years to four years between these two election years, and chose to have their gubernatorial elections on the even mid-year between presidential elections, hence the change in the number of gubernatorial elections from thirteen in 1980 to eleven in 2004.

Gray Davis (who had won both the 1998 and 2002 elections) lose his job to Republican movie actor and businessman Arnold Schwarzenegger in an election in which 9 of the 135 candidates reported spending just under $20.3 million in equivalent 2006 dollars. Similarly, the 2002 election in Texas resulted in more than $130 million spent to reelect an incumbent governor.

Another startling perspective in understanding campaign costs is to consider the amount spent per vote cast in the general election. For example, the 2002 election in New Hampshire cost only $20,890,119 in 2006 dollars, but that meant the expenditures were $47.16 per voter to win an open seat! Thus, even the smaller states can chalk up what must be considered very expensive campaigns. This reality obviously helps determine who can seek the governorship—typically those who have considerable funds or access to such funds.

One additional observation concerning the new governors elected in recent years is that there have been greater numbers of stronger women candidates, like Ann Richards in Texas. The public has become more accepting of female governors. Thus, nine of the incumbent governors serving in 2007 are women. Prior to the 1970s, the only women elected governor were the wives of male governors. Then, beginning in the

1970s, women began individually moving up state political ladders, running for governor, and winning.[11] Furthermore, for the second time in the past two decades an African American won the governorship—in 1989 it was Douglas Wilder in Virginia and, in 2006, Deval Patrick in Massachusetts. In New Mexico, Bill Richardson, a Hispanic, was elected governor in 2002 and then reelected in 2006. And in 2007, Louisiana elected Bobby Jindal, an Indian American. Governors are becoming increasingly diverse.

Governors in Association

Governors have taken significant steps to revitalize and redirect multistate organizations during the past few decades.[12] Foremost among these organizations is the National Governors Association. The organization's precursor, the Governors' Conference, emerged in 1908 following President Theodore Roosevelt's historic first meeting with the nation's governors.

Getting Organized

After this 1908 meeting, the Governors' Conference met annually to discuss a broad agenda, with the Council of State Governments (CSG) serving as its secretary (a relationship that lasted until 1975). During the mid-1960s, as federal grant-in-aid programs proliferated and the federal presence intruded further into the states in the form of President Lyndon Johnson's Great Society programs, the governors felt the need for a more permanent organization, so they set up an office in Washington, D.C., to press their views, interests, and needs upon the federal government. During these years, state legislative and local government leaders took similar steps.

In the new Washington office, the original staff of four increased in size, capability, and versatility. The Governors' Conference began working with the National Conference of State Legislatures (NCSL) and the five other members of the "Big Seven"—the Council of State Governments (CSG), the National Association of Counties, the National League of Cities, the U.S. Conference of Mayors, and the International City Managers Association—in serving as lobbyists for state and local governments.

This development of a strong showing of governors' and legislators' organizations, individual governors, and state offices in Washington, D.C., was significant. Distrusting the efficacy of the U.S. Congress, state leaders felt that a strong and independent state presence in Washington was one of several steps necessary for adequate representation in the national policy process.[13]

Growth of the National Governors Association

Under the leadership of a series of strong governors, the Governors' Conference began to broaden its agenda and approach.[14] In 1965, it changed its name to the National Governors' Conference (NGC) "to distinguish it clearly from the regional conferences which had sprung up."[15] During the 1960s, NGC switched from an ad hoc committee structure to a system of eleven standing committees and began meeting twice annually. They shifted from adopting short-lived resolutions to developing a body of policy positions that were agreed upon at annual meetings.[16] In 1977, NGC was renamed the National Governors' Association (NGA) "to signify the broad scope and on going nature of the organization."[17] In 2003, the name was simplified to the National Governors Association.

During the 1970s, NGA instituted a series of activities to improve the performance and preparation of individual governors. In addition to the Center for Best Practices and the Office of Management Consulting and Training, the organization formalized its "The New Governors' Seminar," which was held within two weeks after the general election in even-numbered years. Incumbent governors served as the faculty. The subjects addressed were of direct concern to the newly elected governors: organizing the governor's office; press and public relations; management of the executive branch; executive-legislative relations; intergovernmental relations; the governorship as a partnership involving one's spouse; and the transition period.[18] In addition, NGA printed materials and prepared guidebooks for the newly elected governors to take back to their home states. If requested, the association gave additional transition assistance.[19]

In these years, scholars began to place a greater emphasis on states and governors as innovators through a series of surveys, reports, and articles.[20] These publications helped disseminate ideas across states on how to solve problems through innovative programs. What had formerly been known as a governor's "show and tell" became more systematic and analytical. Two national organizations of gubernatorial staff—the Council of State Planning Agencies (CSPA) and the National Association of State Budget Officers (NASBO)—became NGA affiliates, thereby providing NGA with needed policy and budget-planning capabilities.[21]

In 1976, NGA moved its Washington headquarters to Capitol Hill and into the Hall of the States, "a long held-dream of Washington Governor Daniel Evans."[22] Joining the association were many of the other state organizations, including the NCSL, CSG, CSPA, and NASBO, and, as of 2007, thirty-three state governors' Washington offices.[23]

Political scientist Carol Weissert concluded that NGA "has gone from serving primarily as a social event to providing information, technical assistance and research needed for responsible state leadership; from shying away from taking issue stands to assuming leadership in charting a national policy course; and from having no Washington presence to spearheading a strong Washington lobbying effort."[24] Another renowned scholar, Larry Sabato, argued that governors have used NGA as a vehicle to assert themselves at the "national level in an unprecedented and surprisingly effective manner . . . revolutionized from the hollow shell of yore to a bustling, professional lobby that can achieve results (and overcome the serious handicaps to effectiveness inherent in a high-powered constituency such as the governors)."[25]

In addition, regional governors' associations—the Midwestern, Northeastern, Southern, and Western—have become more active in policy concerns. Some policy interests flowed naturally from the region itself—energy and natural resources in the West, agriculture in the Midwest, and race and economic development in the South. Some stemmed from the allocation of federal grant-in-aid funds or other federal decisions. The most notable example was the conflict that arose over the formula for distributing federal funds, which was to the advantage of the Sun Belt states and to the disadvantage of the Snow Belt states.[26] Other examples were those instances in which states of a region banded together to provide better services, as in higher education with the Southern Regional Educational Board, or to seek a particular federal "pork barrel" project.

Although the results of these activities vary, the governors of the fifty states, by joining together, have become part of the national policymaking process. By taking new and innovative steps, they have given their states enhanced representation at the national level.

NGA opens the door for incumbent governors to broaden their contacts across the nation and reach out to other serving governors. This opportunity helps to overcome some of the problems that can occur when a governor becomes overly immersed in regional issues and spends too much time working only with the governors of neighboring states and regional governors' associations. NGA encourages governors to think nationally and internationally. For example, take the case of North Carolina Governor Terry Sanford. Elected in 1960, he was what some called a new type of southern governor, one who tried to overcome some of the negatives of those working hard to preserve southern white cultural traditions. In fact, while Sanford served, several of his nearby colleagues, including George Wallace in Alabama, fought hard to maintain segregation.

The National Governors Association offered Sanford, like so many others, the experience and venue to look beyond his region and think about the broader implications of the governorship. Through this association, he developed some very close gubernatorial colleagues and these positive relationships continued well beyond their terms as governors. In Sanford's case, the two governors whom he met with, sat near, and discussed a range of ideas and concerns with were Republican Governor John Chafee of Rhode Island (1963–1969) and Democratic Governor Phil Hoff of Vermont (1963–1969). Their friendship stemmed from the organization's rule that governors sit in the order in which their states entered the Union. Hence governors Sanford, Chafee, and Hoff were nearby companions at NGA meetings, and their respect for each other and their interactions grew over their tenures in office. There have been many similar situations among those who have served as governor over the past one hundred years. As the organization enters its next century, NGA will continue to offer opportunities for the nation's governors to consider broadly the meaning of the governorship and how the evolution of time has shaped the office of today.

Afterword

Governing the Twenty-First Century

CLAYTON McCLURE BROOKS

From the Great Depression to the Great Society, World War I to the Iraq war, U.S. governors have answered the call of history. Their experiences have shaped the modern governorship with its increased responsibilities, broader perspectives, and heightened expectations. Over the past one hundred years, governors moved into national and international political circles. But their primary responsibilities still lie at home. Within the constraints of a federal system, governors have a unique opportunity for creativity working in the middle space of American government—the states. A freedom when wielded by the right hands to redefine government, blaze trails down paths of progress, and lead the nation in innovation; a freedom not replicated in the national government. Speaking before the annual NGA meeting in 2006, Tommy Thompson, former governor of Wisconsin (1987–2001) and later secretary of health and human services under President George W. Bush, reflected on the benefits of being governor. "You don't realize how wonderful it is to be a Governor until you leave and go to Washington and become a Secretary," Thompson mused. "When you're a Governor, you can wake up in the morning and you can have an idea and you can have somebody working on it by 11 o'clock in the morning. When you go to Washington . . . I get up, get the same idea, go in. Then you have to vet it with 67,000 people who all believe sincerely they're smarter than you."[1]

Modern governors continue to be sources of creativity and innovation, although the blurred lines of federalism, particularly from the New Deal onward, have at times obscured the centrality of the state. The policies of governors shape the daily lives of citizens, from the roads they drive on to the schools where they send their children. Rather than withering in the shadow of an overpowering national government, states and their governors are stronger than ever. States, over the course of the past one hundred years, indeed lost control over some of their realms of responsibility. But this was never a story of states receiving a smaller portion of the governmental pie. Instead, government on all levels—local, state, and national—grew. The increased services and functions of this new era of activist state governments have multiplied the duties of governors. Gubernatorial powers have expanded, but gubernatorial responsibilities have mushroomed. New programs, new services, and new demands revolutionized the scope and aim of government.

These changes in the federalism bargain coincided with the advent of large-scale, organized interstate cooperation. Governors no longer had the choice to work primarily confined within their state borders, but needed to branch out, cooperate, and compete with not only other states but also the national government and foreign countries. Modernity forced governors to rethink the old federalism model stressing state self-reliance that had been in place since the founding of the country. Technological innovation, a national and global marketplace, and the emergence of the nation as a world superpower, among other factors, have redefined the gubernatorial office. States remain powerful entities, and state borders still signify unique historical and cultural differences. But states can no longer act in isolation. Modern technological developments, like the building of a national interstate system, could not have been accomplished without states and state governors working together. If a state refuses to cooperate and compete, then its citizens are left behind politically, technologically, and economically.

The more than one thousand governors who have served since 1908 irrevocably shaped the gubernatorial office and made it an institution that thrives today. Their individualistic and regional diversity is the essence of what makes American democracy work. In the late 1920s, Huey Long gained near-complete control of Louisiana through his indomitable will, but sheer strength of personality is no longer enough. Now more than public appeal and charisma is needed. With the expansion of state government and bureaucracy, increased professionalism is expected across the board, particularly in governors. To be successful, governors must be effective administrators, boosters, businessmen, negotiators, and executives. The goodwill of citizens is no longer sustained only through perpetual campaigning, as was the style of George Wallace, but by concrete results. Demagogues have less appeal as the country becomes materially and economically better off and more culturally unified. With the end of the Great Depression and later the end of Jim Crow laws in the South, credentials rather than passion became more important in choosing candidates. Performance weighs on the minds of voters, particularly during reelection, as much as or more than personality. Celebrity continues to help win elections, as in the case of the actor Arnold Schwarzenegger in 2003. But he would not have won reelection in 2006 in California without developing as an effective governor who learned to work across party lines. The same was true of Ronald Reagan's administration, and even that of Thomas Dewey. Show without substance is often found lacking. The transition from Long to Schwarzenegger is less about how people get elected than how they govern and how effectively they lead their legislatures. Although efficient and effective state governments are sometimes underappreciated, inefficient or corrupt administrations are seldom forgotten.

Trials of the twenty-first century are testing this ability to govern. Already, governors have faced unprecedented challenges forcing administrations to further extend the responsibilities and duties of the modern governorship. Homeland security had always been a concern. But this threat became tragically real with the terrorist attacks on New York City and Washington, D.C., on September 11, 2001. Addressing the nation's governors at the 2003 annual NGA meeting, former defense secretary William Cohen reflected, "Up until about two years ago Governors were generally involved in foreign policy only to the extent that you were concerned about promoting state goods in overseas markets. . . . But today, after September 11th . . . your interests in foreign policy . . . pertain . . . to not only our economic security but our physical security."[2] Governors have accepted this challenge, working together and with the national government to find strategies for countering terrorism. A former governor of Texas, President George W. Bush, led the country through this tense period that witnessed the terrorist attacks of Al Qaeda as well as wars in Afghanistan and Iraq.

But terrorism and war were not the only emergencies governors confronted in the early twenty-first century. Further tragedy in the form of natural disasters struck in late summer 2005 with the deadly hurricanes Katrina and Rita. Parts of the Gulf Coast were decimated, and floodwaters devastated the city of New Orleans when the levees were breached. Americans watched their televisions in horror for the second time in less than five years as a major American city appeared more like a distant war zone. Violence in the nation's schools also became a concern. In April 2007, the massacre of thirty-two students and professors on the campus of Virginia Tech in Blacksburg, Virginia, shocked the country. Although George Pataki of New York, Jim Gilmore and Tim Kaine of Virginia, Kathleen Blanco of Louisiana, and Haley Barbour of Mississippi dealt most directly with these tragedies, governors across the nation labored to ensure the safety and well-being of their citizens.

In the midst of these events, governors continue to convene. They discuss the policy concerns of the twenty-first century, not only homeland security but also globalization, technology, environmental regulation, health care, and education. Over the past hundred years, the National Governors Association (as the name was simplified in 2003) has grown from an informal annual gathering into an effectively organized, multifaceted institution with a large full-time staff and permanent office in the Hall of States in Washington, D.C., led since 1983 by executive director Raymond C. Scheppach. At this D.C. office, the association's Center for Best Practices functions as a consulting firm for governors, a resource of innovative solutions for state governments, as well as a factgathering and dispersion agency. By adhering to a bipartisan policy, the organization has created a neutral forum for diverse governors to meet and learn from one another.

The modern governorship, gradually unfolding over the past one hundred years, has necessitated greater communication and organization among governors. In 1908, after President Theodore Roosevelt called the nation's governors together for their first historic meeting, these men realized that a new day had dawned and determined a national governors' conference was needed. Over time, the National Governors Association established itself as an agency of modernity dedicated to preparing governors for the ever-evolving demands of their office. The organization has strengthened governorships by creating a sense of unity and encouraging these men and women to expand their horizons, regionally, nationally, and internationally.

Timeline of Governors and States in the Twentieth Century

1900   Hawaii acquires territorial status.

      Hurricane devastates Galveston, Tex.

1901   Former New York governor/current vice president Theodore Roosevelt becomes president upon assassination of William McKinley.

      Connecticut becomes first state to pass an automobile law, setting speed limit at twelve miles per hour.

1905   U.S. Forest Service created. Gifford Pinchot, later governor of Pennsylvania, is first director.

      Colorado has three governors in one day due to a political squabble.

      California becomes model in separating state and local revenue sources, leaving property taxes within the purview of local governments.

      Former Idaho Governor Frank Steunenberg killed by bomb. Famed union organizer "Big Bill" Haywood of the Western Federation of Miners is among accused perpetrators.

1906   Earthquake and related fires destroy much of San Francisco.

      People of New Mexico and Arizona vote on joint statehood. New Mexico votes in favor and Arizona against.

1907   Roosevelt administration establishes the Inland Waterways Commission. This commission recommends holding a conference of governors to discuss conservation.

      New York and Wisconsin become first states to establish public utility commissions.

      Oklahoma becomes a state.

1908   Washington, D.C., May 13–15. Governors meet for the first time at request of President Roosevelt to discuss conservation.

      Oregon's Corrupt Practices Act (regulating campaign expenditures and practices) adopted.

1910   NGA meetings: Washington, D.C., May 13–15, and Frankfort and Louisville, Ky., Nov. 29–Dec. 1. Governors begin meeting independently. They discuss women's suffrage and state automobile laws.

Governor Charles Evans Hughes of New York appointed to U.S. Supreme Court.

1911   NGA meeting: Spring Lake, N.J. Governors take their first official action as a group, appointing three governors to represent the organization in pending Supreme Court case. Governors discuss gubernatorial powers.

Illinois becomes first state to provide mothers' pensions statewide.

California and Wisconsin establish boards to prepare state budgets.

Wisconsin becomes first state to adopt workers' compensation program.

Kansas becomes first state to pass a "blue sky" law (regulating sale of securities).

Wisconsin adopts income tax law that becomes a model for other states, using nonpolitical state officials in collection and relying on individual taxpayer self-reporting.

1912   NGA meeting: Richmond, Va. Governors adopt Articles of Organization for Governors' Conference. Organization's purposes are to exchange views on subjects of importance to states, promote greater uniformity in state legislation, and attain greater efficiency in state administration. Governors discuss divorce laws.

Arizona and New Mexico join the Union. After admission, Arizona restores provision for recall of judges by popular vote—the basis for its statehood being vetoed by President Taft in 1911.

Alaska acquires territorial status.

Massachusetts legislature enacts first minimum wage law for women and children.

1913   NGA meeting: Colorado Springs, Colo. Governors discuss state initiatives and referendums, campaign finance, and candidates' use of private money and contributions.

Former New Jersey Governor Woodrow Wilson inaugurated president. Former Indiana Governor Thomas Marshall inaugurated vice president.

Sixteenth and Seventeenth Amendments to Constitution (federal income tax and direct election of U.S. senators) ratified.

Minnesota rate cases—U.S. Supreme Court rules that Interstate Commerce Commission has authority to regulate intrastate rail rates discriminating against interstate commerce.

Illinois implements first comprehensive administrative reorganization program.

Ford introduces moving assembly line process, reducing automobile prices.

1914   NGA meeting: Madison, Wis. Western governors express concern over federal control of lands and its potential threat to tax revenue.

Federal Trade Commission Act (prevents unfair competition in interstate trade) passed.

Smith-Lever Act (provides grants for agricultural extension programs) passed.

American Association of Labor Legislation begins national campaign for compulsory health insurance.

Moses Alexander of Idaho elected first Jewish governor.

1915   NGA meeting: Boston, Mass. Governors discuss capital punishment.

Nevada legislation simplifies divorce process.

First official Western Governors' Conference takes place.

Alaska adopts old-age pension law—first among states and territories.

Great Migration begins. Ku Klux Klan revived with the release of the movie *Birth of a Nation.*

1916   NGA meeting: Washington, D.C. Governors discuss relatively new concept of an "executive budget" and problem of legislative appropriations exceeding revenue. War Department official thanks governors of Arizona, New Mexico, and Texas for providing troops to assist in fighting Mexican guerrilla forces.

Federal Road Act passed.

U.S. Supreme Court justice and former New York Governor Charles Evans Hughes is Republican nominee for president, loses to incumbent Wilson.

1917   Smith-Hughes Act provides federal funds to states for vocational education teachers.

Residents of Puerto Rico become U.S. citizens.

U.S. enters World War I. Only year since the adoption of bylaws that governors do not meet.

1918   NGA meeting: Annapolis, Md. The secretary of war addresses governors. Governors discuss whether demobilization and reconversion following the war will lead to labor unrest.

Mississippi becomes last existing state to enact a compulsory education law.

1919   NGA meeting: Salt Lake City, Utah. Governors discuss high cost of living and recent conference of the seven governors most affected by nationwide coal strike.

Eighteenth Amendment to Constitution (prohibition) ratified.

Oregon becomes first state to levy a gasoline tax.

1920   NGA meeting: Harrisburg, Pa. Governors discuss affordable housing shortage, farmers' financial crisis, and fears that population shift from rural to urban will lead to starvation in cities.

U.S. Census reports urban residents now outnumber rural residents.

Nineteenth Amendment to Constitution (women's suffrage) ratified.

1921   NGA meeting: Charleston, S.C. Governors discuss recommendations of the Committee on Inter-State Compacts.

Former Governor Calvin Coolidge of Massachusetts becomes vice president.

North Dakota first state in which a governor (Lynn Frazier) is recalled.

Federal Aid Highway Act (ensures that federal aid is expended on major roads) passed.

Sheppard-Towner Act (provides funding to states for maternal and child health care) is passed.

1922   NGA meeting: White Sulphur Springs, W.Va. Governors hear an address on the uniformity of marriage and divorce laws and discuss Ku Klux Klan.

Seven states—Arizona, California, Colorado, Nevada, New Mexico, Utah, and Wyoming—sign an interstate compact governing the allocation of water from the Colorado River.

Georgia Governor Thomas Hardwick appoints first female member of U.S. Senate—Rebecca Felton—following her husband's death.

1923   NGA meeting: West Baden, Ind. Governors discuss uniformity of state laws and the plight of farmers.

Upon Harding's death, Calvin Coolidge inaugurated president.

Oklahoma Governor J. C. Walton declares martial law because of widespread violence perpetrated by the Ku Klux Klan.

1924   NGA meeting: Jacksonville, Fla. Executive Committee enlarged from three to five members. Governors discuss state use of prison labor.

American Indians accorded U.S. citizenship.

1925   NGA meeting: Poland Springs, Maine. Director of federal Budget Bureau urges states to follow federal suit and reduce spending. Governors discuss federal aid and their concerns that accepting matching grants gives too much control to the federal government.

Nellie Tayloe Ross (Wyoming) and Ma Ferguson (Texas) become the first women governors.

Great Tri-State Tornado—Missouri, Illinois, and Indiana—kills nearly 700 people.

1926   NGA meeting: Cheyenne, Wyo. Governors adopt resolution urging Congress to pass legislation aiding agriculture in attaining equal footing with other industries in the world market.

States adopt plan for first interstate highway system, the U.S. Routes.

1927   NGA meeting: Mackinac Island, Mich. Governors discuss federal government's encroachment on state authority with Water Power Act of 1920 and National Defense Act of 1926, and recent flooding of the Mississippi River.

1928   NGA meeting: New Orleans, La. Governors discuss severance tax and wisdom of governmental intervention with the failing economy.

1929   NGA meeting: New London, Conn. Governors discuss crime and gun control, and aviation.

Stock market crash triggers Great Depression.

1930   NGA meeting: Salt Lake City, Utah. Governors hold first "governors-only session." New York Governor Franklin Roosevelt speaks in favor of unemployment insurance.

Former New York Governor Charles Evan Hughes becomes chief justice of U.S. Supreme Court.

1931   NGA meeting: French Lick, Ind. Governors reject recommendation to establish a research arm for the association. They discuss what power states should have over local expenditures.

1932   NGA meeting: Richmond, Va. President Hoover addresses governors regarding nation's economic problems.

Al Capone imprisoned for tax evasion. Dwight Green, future governor of Illinois, served as a prosecutor in the trial.

Emergency Relief and Construction Act (makes funds available to states for relief efforts) passed.

Wisconsin becomes first state to enact an unemployment insurance plan.

Mississippi becomes first state to adopt a general sales tax.

Federal government adopts its first gasoline tax.

1933   NGA meeting: Sacramento and San Francisco, Calif. Former Governor George Dern of Utah, now secretary of war, speaks to governors about the National Industrial Recovery Act. Governors adopt resolution supporting federal efforts to fight organized crime.

New York Governor Franklin D. Roosevelt inaugurated president.

Twentieth and Twenty-first Amendments to Constitution (presidential terms of succession and repealing prohibition) ratified.

Roosevelt's New Deal begins: Federal Deposit Insurance Corporation; Civilian Conservation Corps; Public Works Administration; and the Tennessee Valley Authority.

Federal Emergency Relief Act passed (disburses $500 million in assistance to states).

Dust storms sweep the Midwest.

1934   NGA meeting: Mackinac Island, Mich. Attendance low due to transportation interruptions associated with nationwide labor strikes. Governors discuss gangsterism and state response to repeal of prohibition. Federal officials speak to governors regarding relief programs.

Hayden-Cartwright Act penalizes states that divert state gasoline tax revenue to non-highway purposes.

Unicameral legislature adopted in Nebraska.

Southern Governors' Association founded.

Dust storms sweep the Plains states.

1935   NGA meeting: Biloxi, Miss. Governors discuss federal plans to use relief funds for road construction. They are briefed on federal legislation providing old-age assistance and aid for dependent children.

Social Security Act passed.

Rural Electrification Administration established.

Interstate Crime Conference held to discuss state and federal cooperation in combating crime and developing interstate parole compacts.

U.S. Senator Huey Long—former governor of Louisiana—assassinated.

1936   NGA meeting: St. Louis, Mo. Governors discuss Social Security Act and new requirements for state unemployment programs. Puerto Rico approved for membership in the association.

Former Kansas Governor Harry Woodring becomes secretary of war.

1937   NGA meeting: Atlantic City, N.J. Governors discuss pending legislation that would for the first time provide federal education aid to the states. They call for a conference on conflicting taxation between levels of government. After meeting, governors travel to Washington to meet with Roosevelt.

New England Governors' Conference founded.

Missouri establishes first-of-its-kind conservation commission.

1938   NGA meeting: Oklahoma City, Okla. Great New England Hurricane results in low attendance. Governors discuss how state laws and regulations (e.g., trucking rules and taxes) create interstate trade barriers.

New York becomes first state to pass law requiring a medical test as a prerequisite for marriage license.

Construction begins on the nation's first superhighway, the Pennsylvania Turnpike.

1939   NGA meeting: Albany and New York, N.Y. Governors discuss history of federal involvement in state public health matters and the extent to which state budgets are burdened by provisions of the Social Security Act.

Former Michigan Governor Frank Murphy becomes U.S. attorney general.

1940   NGA meeting: Duluth, Minn. Governors discuss state-federal relations in administration of public relief programs. Adopt resolution expressing consensus that all necessary steps should be taken to provide for the defense of the United States and pledging each state's resources.

1941   NGA meeting: Boston and Cambridge, Mass. Fiorello LaGuardia, director of civilian defense, addresses governors regarding role of states in event of enemy attack. Resolution urges that matters of civilian defense go through states, not localities.

States agree to "loan" employment service to federal government for war production emergency.

James Byrnes, later governor of South Carolina, appointed to U.S. Supreme Court.

Governor Eugene Talmadge fires University of Georgia education dean for promoting racial equality, leading to revocation of university's accreditation.

Attack on Pearl Harbor leads to U.S. entry into World War II.

1942   NGA meeting: Asheville, N.C. Governors discuss federal emergency wartime authority and returning of state authority after the war. Adopt resolution objecting to federal interference with respect to inherent taxation powers of state and local governments.

Roosevelt authorizes internment of Japanese Americans.

Gasoline rationing initiated in seventeen eastern states and expands to all states by year's end.

1943   NGA meeting: Columbus, Ohio. General George Marshall addresses governors regarding strategy for military victory.

Executive Committee enlarged to nine members to ensure quorum.

Roosevelt freezes wages and prices in effort to curb inflation.

1944   NGA meeting: Hershey, Pa. Governors meet at Gettysburg battlefield. One northern and one southern governor speak. Federal officials urge support of legislation facilitating the conversion of wartime to peacetime industry for sake of maintaining stable employment levels. Resolution requests returning control of employment services to states.

White House conference on rural education assesses prospects for federal educational assistance to states.

1945   NGA meeting: Mackinac Island, Mich. Governors discuss United Nations Charter, returning veterans, postwar industrial recovery, aviation, and prepaid health care coverage.

New York passes first state anti-discrimination law, establishes State Division of Human Rights.

Roosevelt dies and Vice President Harry Truman becomes president.

World War II ends.

1946   NGA meeting: Oklahoma City, Okla. Generals Dwight Eisenhower and Omar Bradley address governors. Governors discuss veterans and lagging educational system.

Federal Airport Act passed (provides federal aid for airport development).

Federal government officially returns Employment Service system to states.

1947   NGA meeting: Salt Lake City, Utah. Governors discuss the responsibility of states and the organization of state government, housing for veterans, agricultural subsidies, water resources, and tourism.

Conference of members of Congress and governors discusses coordination of national and state taxation.

President Truman advocates compulsory national health insurance.

1948   NGA meeting: Portsmouth, N.H. Edward R. Murrow speaks on end of U.S. isolationism and espouses position that U.S. influence around the world will come not from spending but from setting a positive example.

Ohio River Valley Water Sanitation Compact (Illinois, Indiana, Kentucky, New York, Ohio, Pennsylvania, Virginia, and West Virginia) established.

Former Massachusetts Governor Maurice Tobin appointed secretary of labor.

Fourteen southern governors establish Board of Control for Regional Education.

1949   NGA meeting: Colorado Springs, Colo. Subjects of discussion include social security, welfare, highways, education, and intergovernmental relations.

Following Ku Klux Klan raids, Governor James Folsom of Alabama signs legislation forbidding the wearing of masks.

Soviets detonate their first atomic bomb.

1950   NGA meeting: White Sulphur Springs, W.Va. Governors discuss water resources.

Federal Civil Defense Act and Disaster Relief Act (first federal emergency response programs)

Social Security Act amended to provide Medical Vendor Program allowing states to use federal matching funds to pay medical providers directly for services to public assistance recipients.

America enters Korean conflict.

1951   NGA meeting: Gatlinburg, Tenn. Governors addressed by federal officials regarding Korean conflict and defense readiness. Administrator of Civil Defense argues modern warfare will be won or lost on the home front, requiring preparations.

Twenty-second Amendment to U.S. Constitution (limits presidency to two terms) ratified.

1952   NGA meeting: Houston, Tex. Resolution asks for revenue from federal gasoline tax and freedom to build highways and bridges without federal interference.

Governors' Interstate Indian Conference held, attended by governors of sixteen states with large Native American populations.

Oregon Governor James McKay appointed secretary of interior.

Puerto Rico becomes a commonwealth.

Illinois Governor Adlai Stevenson is Democratic candidate for president, loses to Eisenhower.

1953   NGA meeting: Seattle, Wash. Governors discuss baby boom and its anticipated effect on education system.

Korean War armistice signed.

Governor Earl Warren of California appointed chief justice of the U.S. Supreme Court.

1954   NGA meeting: Lake George, N.Y. Vice President Nixon asks for governors' support of Eisenhower's plan for new interstate highway program. Committee formed to examine proposal.

Governors hold national conference on mental health.

Brown v. Board of Education outlaws racial segregation in public education.

1955   NGA meeting: Chicago, Ill. Governors discuss recent defeat of
       federal highway aid legislation and financing methods, juvenile
       delinquency, and mental illness.
       Air Pollution Control Act passed. First White House Conference
       on Education held.

1956   NGA meeting: Atlantic City, N.J. Governors discuss White House
       Conference on Education.
       Federal Aid Highway Act passed.
       Great Lakes Commission represents eight states on environmen-
       tal and economic issues.

1957   NGA meeting: Williamsburg, Va. Governors request appointment
       of a committee to study problem of air pollution. Eisenhower
       warns that failure of states to assume traditional state responsi-
       bilities is likely to result in further federal incursion.
       Eisenhower sends federal troops to enforce integration of Cen-
       tral High School in Little Rock, Arkansas, after resistance by
       Governor Orval Faubus.
       Soviet Union launches Sputnik.

1958   NGA meeting: Bal Harbour, Fla. Dag Hammarskjold, secretary-
       general of United Nations, addresses governors about Cold
       War and peaceful uses of atomic energy. Governors adopt reso-
       lutions urging federal funding for construction of fallout shel-
       ters.
       Association's 50th Anniversary.
       National Defense Education Act passed.

1959   NGA meeting: San Juan, P.R. Executive Committee members
       report on their trip to Soviet Union. Office of Chairman estab-
       lished, to alternate annually between two parties. Standing
       Committee on Roads and Highway Safety established. Gover-
       nors addressed on likely effects of nuclear fallout.
       Alaska and Hawaii become states.
       Former Massachusetts Governor Christian Herter appointed sec-
       retary of state.
       Permanent Advisory Commission on Intergovernmental Rela-
       tions established.

1960   NGA meeting: Glacier National Park, Mont. Governors discuss
       pending legislation to provide medical care for the elderly and
       Soviet superiority in the arms race and education.
       Kerr-Mills Act passed (provides funding to states to aid medical
       coverage of elderly).
       Congress passes the first general aid-to-education bill.

1961   NGA meeting: Honolulu, Hawaii. Federal officials ask governors
       to support federal education assistance to states. Resolution

urges Congress to enact program providing federal grants-in-aid to assist construction of classroom facilities, loans for the construction and improvement of facilities for higher education, and funds to expand adult education programs.

Former North Carolina Governor Luther Hodges appointed secretary of commerce.

Delaware River Basin Compact includes Delaware, New Jersey, New York, and Pennsylvania.

1962   NGA meeting: Hershey, Pa. Heated debate over civil rights. Resolution defeated to endorse program of medical care for the aged. Resolution adopted urging constitutional amendment for voluntary participation in prayer in public schools.

Baker v. Carr establishes that the issue of reapportionment is justiciable, enabling courts to intervene in cases of legislative reapportionment.

Governor Ross Barnett tries to block African American James Meredith's admission to University of Mississippi. Found guilty of contempt.

Midwestern Governors Association founded.

1963   NGA meeting: Miami Beach, Fla. Vice President Lyndon Johnson relates that civil rights is top priority for Kennedy administration.

University of Alabama desegregated after Governor George Wallace is confronted by federally deployed National Guard troops.

President John F. Kennedy assassinated.

Republican Governors Association founded.

1964   NGA meeting: Cleveland, Ohio. Governors discuss civil rights, Cold War education, extending civil defense to natural disasters, support for medical assistance to elderly, Economic Opportunity Act of 1964, and pending legislation to involve the federal government in child support enforcement.

President Johnson declares War on Poverty.

Twenty-fourth Amendment to U.S. Constitution (prohibiting poll tax) ratified.

Reynolds v. Sims establishes that both houses of a state legislature must be apportioned on the basis of population.

Civil Rights Act passed.

Wilderness Act and Land and Water Conservation Fund Bill passed.

1965   NGA meeting: Minneapolis, Minn. Via video message, Johnson asks governors to support his goals in Vietnam and sends plane to bring governors to White House. Resolution to study problem of water pollution. Name of organization changed to National Governors' Conference.

First U.S. combat troops arrive in Vietnam.

Massachusetts becomes first state to pass "Racial Imbalance" legislation, leading to busing protests.

New York Governor Nelson Rockefeller launches Pure Waters Program.

Congress creates Medicaid.

Elementary and Secondary Education Act passed and Project Head Start initiated.

Voting Rights Act passed.

1966   NGA annual meeting: Los Angeles, Calif. Governors resolve to hold conference on juvenile delinquency and urge states to establish commissions on crime and delinquency. First "interim meeting" held, leading to regular winter meetings. Office of Federal-State Relations established. Resolution reaffirms support for president's Vietnam policies.

Kentucky becomes first southern state to enact comprehensive civil rights legislation.

Medicare begins.

1967   Governors hold their annual meeting in part aboard the *S.S. Independence* en route to the Virgin Islands. Governors discuss principles of tax sharing and consolidating more than 200 existing federal grants. Resolution affirms law enforcement to be responsibility of state and local governments.

Twenty-fifth Amendment to U.S. Constitution (terms for succession to presidency) ratified.

National Bellas-Hess, Inc. v. Illinois Department of Revenue rules that states cannot levy sales tax on mail-order products purchased from out-of-state companies.

Loving v. Virginia declares interracial marriage laws unconstitutional, affecting sixteen states.

Illinois Governor Otto Kerner named head of National Advisory Commission on Civil Disorders.

1968   NGA annual meeting: Cincinnati, Ohio. Governors discuss poverty and urban America. Astronaut Neil Armstrong talks about upcoming launch of first Apollo space mission and how every state contributed resources. Committee on Transportation established, chaired by Governor Ronald Reagan. Resolutions urge federal shift from categorical to block grants and support revenue sharing. Association holds first official winter meeting and first seminar for new governors.

Martin Luther King, Jr., and Robert Kennedy assassinated.

1969   NGA annual meeting: Colorado Springs, Colo. President Nixon
       speaks on revenue sharing, welfare, and universal health insur-
       ance program. Governors express support for shift from fed-
       eral-state program of assistance to the aged, blind, disabled,
       and dependent children to a federally financed, state-adminis-
       tered program. At winter meeting, Vice President Agnew
       announces establishment of Office of Intergovernmental Rela-
       tions.
       Maryland Governor Spiro Agnew becomes vice president.
       Michigan Governor George Romney appointed secretary of hous-
       ing and urban development.
       Massachusetts Governor John Volpe appointed secretary of trans-
       portation.
       In *Shapiro v. Thompson*, rules that residency requirements for wel-
       fare eligibility violate fundamental right to travel.
       President Nixon proposes Family Assistance Plan.
       Alexander v. Holmes County mandates immediate school integra-
       tion in fourteen states.

1970   NGA annual meeting: Lake of the Ozarks, Mo. Director of the
       Office of Management and Budget discusses proposal for Envi-
       ronmental Protection Agency. Governors endorse continua-
       tion of Highway Trust Fund and for establishment of Airport/
       Airways Development and Urban Mass Transportation Trust
       Funds. Resolution declares third week in April "Earth Week."
       At winter meeting, President Nixon addresses governors
       regarding his welfare reform plan (Family Assistance Plan).
       Four students killed at Kent State University by Ohio National
       Guardsmen. Former Pennsylvania Governor William Scranton
       heads Commission on Campus Unrest in the wake of these
       deaths and those of two students at Jackson State University in
       Mississippi.
       Federal Airport Act passed (reflects NGA endorsement of Airport
       and Airway Trust Fund).
       California passes nation's first no-fault divorce law.
       Despite strong anti-busing sentiment in Virginia, Governor Lin-
       wood Holton enrolls daughters in predominantly African
       American schools in Richmond.
       Clean Air Act passed.

1971   NGA annual meeting: San Juan, P.R. Agnew reports positive
       response to administration's wage-price freeze sparked by ris-
       ing inflation. Governors discuss national health insurance, no-
       fault auto insurance, and, after Attica prison riot, prisons. At

winter meeting, President Nixon briefs governors on revenue sharing program.

Melvin Evans elected first black governor of Virgin Islands.

Swann v. Charlotte-Mecklenburg County says busing appropriate remedy for racial segregation in schools.

Twenty-sixth Amendment to U.S. Constitution (voting age eighteen) ratified.

1972   NGA annual meeting: Houston, Tex. Governors discuss rising crime rates, drug abuse, and court rulings against the use of property taxes as the primary source of school financing. Astronaut Alan Shepard presents states with flags carried to moon on Apollo 14 mission. Representatives of the National Welfare Rights Organization disrupt winter meeting discussion of welfare reform.

Alabama Governor George Wallace shot while campaigning for presidency in Maryland.

Watergate scandal begins.

Furman v. Georgia suspends state capital punishment laws.

General Revenue Sharing begins.

1973   NGA annual meeting: Lake Tahoe, Nev. Governors discuss energy crisis and revenue sharing proposals pending in Congress. Resolution supports federal assumption of welfare payments for aged, blind, and disabled. At winter meeting, governors discuss federal initiatives in domestic policy and details of revenue sharing.

Roe v. Wade decision issued.

U.S. soldiers leave Vietnam.

Vice President Agnew resigns and pleads no contest to income tax evasion charges.

OPEC begins oil embargo against United States and other Western nations.

To conserve fuel and heighten safety, federal government orders states to reduce interstates' speed limit to fifty-five miles per hour.

1974   NGA annual meeting: Seattle, Wash. Governors discuss government reform in aftermath of Watergate scandal. At winter meeting, governors discuss the energy crisis. Responsibilities are assigned to an executive director. Center for Policy Research and Analysis established.

Emergency Highway Energy Conservation Act prohibits approval of federal highway projects in states with speed limits over fifty-five miles per hour.

Rather than face impeachment, President Nixon resigns. Gerald

Ford becomes president and former New York Governor Nelson Rockefeller is confirmed as vice president.

Community Development Block Grant program authorized.

James Longley of Maine becomes first popularly elected Independent governor.

1975   NGA annual meeting: New Orleans, La. Governors discuss state-local relations, oil research and development, and gas taxes. At winter meeting, governors discuss the nation's energy needs. Association disaffiliates from Council of State Governments.

Ella Grasso of Connecticut takes office as the first female governor elected in own right.

Individuals with Disabilities Education Act (IDEA) passed.

1976   NGA annual meeting: Hershey, Pa. Governors endorse welfare reform, to include elimination of work disincentives. At winter meeting, revenue sharing is discussed.

Gregg v. Georgia leads to resumption of the use of capital punishment suspended in 1972.

Federal Resource Conservation and Recovery Act passed.

Coalition of Northeastern Governors founded.

1977   NGA annual meeting: Detroit, Mich. Governors discuss President Carter's proposals for welfare reform. At winter meeting, governors discuss energy shortage and need for overhaul of Medicaid administration. Name changed to National Governors' Association (NGA).

Former Georgia Governor Jimmy Carter inaugurated president.

Former Idaho Governor Cecil Andrus becomes secretary of interior.

North Dakota becomes first state to finish assigned mileage in Federal Controlled Access Highway System.

Clean Water Act passed.

1978   NGA annual meeting: Boston, Mass. Governors debate whether to continue supporting the goal of a balanced federal budget. At winter meeting, governors discuss Supreme Court's pending decision on affirmative action in education. Association membership approved for Northern Mariana Islands.

California's Proposition 13, a tax limit initiative, ushers in new era of direct democracy.

President Jimmy Carter declares a federal emergency at Love Canal (buried chemical waste creating serious health hazard).

UC-Davis v. Bakke establishes affirmative action in education constitutional under specific conditions.

Western Governors' Policy Office founded.

Camp David Accords signed.

1979   NGA annual meeting: Louisville, Ky. Carter cancels scheduled speech to preside over energy crisis summit. Governors discuss Carter's strategy for dealing with rising oil prices. Resolutions support deregulation of domestic oil prices and extending revenue sharing. At winter meeting, governors discuss recent establishment of Committee on International Trade and Foreign Relations.

Federal Emergency Management Agency created (in response to NGA request).

Partial core meltdown occurs at the nuclear generating plant at Three Mile Island in Pennsylvania.

Carter holds ten-day energy summit at Camp David to discuss plan to reduce dependence on foreign oil. Governors participate.

Neil Goldschmidt, later governor of Oregon, appointed secretary of transportation.

Sagebrush Rebellion: legislatures of five western states call for state control of lands managed by the federal Bureau of Land Management.

Iranian militants storm U.S. Embassy in Tehran, seizing ninety hostages.

1980   NGA annual meeting: Denver, Colo. Governors launch multiyear discussion and strategy for restoring balance to the federal system. During winter meeting, conference held with representatives of federal government, state governments, private sector, and academia to discuss national hazardous waste management program.

Boatlift from Port of Mariel brings 125,000 Cuban refugees.

U.S. Department of Education established.

Former Maine Governor Edmund Muskie appointed secretary of state.

Mount St. Helens erupts in Washington, killing sixty-one people.

Superfund and Low-Level Radioactive Waste Policy Act passed.

Revenue-sharing program ends.

1981   NGA annual meeting: Atlantic City, N.J. Vice President George H. W. Bush assures governors of congressional support for President Reagan's budget and tax recommendations and also for regulatory relief. At winter meeting, governors are addressed regarding president's economic recovery program.

Former California Governor Ronald Reagan inaugurated president.

Former South Carolina Governor James Edwards becomes secretary of energy.

Assassination attempt injures Reagan and his press secretary, James Brady.

AIDS first detected.

IBM introduces personal computer.

Omnibus Budget Reconciliation Act passed (tightens welfare eligibility).

Sandra Day O'Connor appointed as first woman Supreme Court justice.

Social Services Block Grant created.

1982   NGA annual meeting: Afton, Okla. At winter meeting, a compromise federalism policy statement is approved unanimously by governors. At both meetings, proposal for support of a constitutional amendment to balance the federal budget defeated.

1983   NGA annual meeting: Portland, Maine. Governors begin long-term discussions of education reform. At winter meeting, governors call on Congress to adopt a budget resolution for fiscal 1984 that would reduce federal deficit to about 2 percent of GNP by 1988. Position of Vice Chairman/Chairman-elect established.

National Commission on Excellence in Education issues report *A Nation at Risk.*

Democratic Governors Association founded.

Two terrorist attacks in Lebanon—U.S. Embassy and Marine base—kill more than 150 people.

1984   NGA annual meeting: Nashville, Tenn. Governors discuss employment issues. At winter meeting, they talk about health care. They adopt a proposal targeted at raising federal revenue by 5 percent over two years, reducing defense and entitlement program spending, and giving the president line-item veto authority.

Congress passes legislation to cut federal highway funds to states that do not raise the legal drinking age to twenty-one.

Western Governors' Association formed through merger of Western Governors' Conference and Western Governors' Policy Office.

1985   NGA annual meeting: Boise, Idaho. Governors discuss the trade deficit. Recommend that the federal government should define standards for solid waste disposal and leave enforcement to state and local authorities. At winter meeting, Alan Greenspan addresses governors regarding economic conditions.

Former Indiana Governor Otis Ray Bowen becomes secretary of health and human services.

1986   NGA annual meeting: Hilton Head, S.C. Governors hear reports
of seven task forces created the previous year to study school
leadership and management, teaching, school choice, readiness, school facilities, technology, and whether college students are learning. At winter meeting, U.S. Supreme Court
Chief Justice Warren Burger emphasizes the role of the states
in nation's establishment and system of government. NGA
issues *Time for Results: The Governors' 1991 Report on Education.*

Nebraska: Kay Orr defeats Helen Boosalis in the first gubernatorial race between two women.

1987   NGA annual meeting: Traverse City, Mich. Bill Clinton serves as
chair. Governors discuss Barriers Project, composed of five
NGA task forces on welfare dependency, school dropouts, teen
pregnancy, adult illiteracy, and alcohol and drug abuse. At winter meeting, governors adopt policy position seeking welfare
reform.

Federal-Aid Highway Act allows states to increase speed limits to
sixty-five miles per hour on rural interstate highways without
incurring federal highway project penalties.

Dow Jones Industrial Average drops 22.6 percent, on Black Mon-
day (October 19).

Iran-Contra scandal develops.

1988   NGA annual meeting: Cincinnati, Ohio. Governors discuss
aspects of federalism (unfunded and underfunded mandates,
preemption of traditional state authority, and Supreme Court
decisions removing Tenth Amendment protections). At winter
meeting, federalism experts make presentations on the history
and current status of state-federal relations. Former Governor
Busbee of Georgia proposes a constitutional convention to sort
out local, state, and federal responsibilities.

Evan Mecham of Arizona becomes first governor in more than
fifty years to be impeached.

Former Pennsylvania Governor Richard Thornburgh becomes
U.S. attorney general.

Family Support Act expands Aid to Families with Dependent
Children (AFDC) and creates Jobs Opportunities and Basic
Skills Training Program (JOBS).

Indian Gaming Regulatory Act passed.

Massachusetts Governor Michael Dukakis defeated in presidential election by George H. W. Bush.

Disaster Relief and Emergency Assistance Act (Stafford Act)
passed.

1989   NGA annual meeting: Chicago, Ill., President Bush speaks about welfare reform via the Family Support Act of 1988. At winter meeting, governors discuss health care, education, and foreign relations. Henry Kissinger tells governors not to place trust in a single Soviet leader like Mikhail Gorbachev. Governors call for stronger auto emission control measures.

First National Summit on Education held in Charlottesville, Virginia.

1990   NGA annual meeting: Mobile, Ala. At both the annual and winter meetings, governors discuss global climate change and goals from 1989 National Education Summit.

Reunification of Germany and breakup of Soviet Union occur.

California new car emissions and clean fuel requirements become a model for other states.

Joan Finney of Kansas becomes first woman to defeat an incumbent governor.

1991   NGA annual meeting: Seattle, Wash. Governors discuss achieving affordable and comprehensive national health care system within next decade. At winter meeting, governors addressed concerning high cost of health care and President Bush's block grant proposal.

Douglas Wilder of Virginia takes office as the first elected African American governor.

Operation Desert Storm forces Iraqi withdrawal from Kuwait.

Former Tennessee Governor Lamar Alexander appointed secretary of education.

Minnesota becomes first state to enact a Charter School law.

Intermodal Surface Transportation Efficiency Act (ISTEA) passed.

1992   NGA annual meeting: Princeton, N.J. Annual and winter meetings focus on need for improvement in educational system.

Twenty-seventh Amendment to U.S. Constitution (compensation restrictions for congressmen) ratified.

Quill v. North Dakota establishes that with a company's insufficient presence in a state, its mail-order products can not be subject to state's sales tax.

Federal Facilities Compliance Act compels federal government to comply with federal, state, and local solid and hazardous waste regulations.

1993   NGA annual meeting: Tulsa, Okla. President Clinton addresses governors about his proposal for health care reform. Governors adopt a "permanent policy" on federalism, calling for a new partnership based on federal forbearance and the avoidance of federal preemption of traditional state roles, and for program flexibility for states in administering federal initiatives. At winter meeting, Clinton addresses governors concerning welfare reform.

Arkansas Governor Bill Clinton inaugurated president.

Former South Carolina Governor Richard Riley becomes secretary of education.

Former Arizona Governor Bruce Babbitt appointed secretary of interior.

Branch Davidians standoff takes place in Waco, Texas.

Mississippi River flooding occurs in Illinois, Iowa, Kansas, Minnesota, Missouri, Nebraska, North Dakota, South Dakota, and Wisconsin.

North Carolina's Smart Start program establishes a national model.

1994   NGA annual meeting: Boston, Mass. Steven Spielberg, director of *Schindler's List,* speaks about using film as a tool to teach tolerance. At winter meeting, governors discuss Goals 2000 Educate America Act pending in Congress as well as Medicaid.

North American Free Trade Agreement (NAFTA).

School-to-Work Opportunities Act passed.

Republican Party wins control of U.S. House of Representatives for first time in forty years.

1995   NGA annual meeting: Burlington, Vt. Governors focus on importance of early childhood development. At winter meeting, governors also discuss childhood development and legislation pending in Congress for relief from unfunded federal mandates.

Unfunded Mandates Reform Act passed.

Bombing of Alfred P. Murrah Federal Building in Oklahoma City kills 168 people.

Congress lifts speed limits as a condition of receiving approval for federal highway projects.

1996   NGA annual meeting held in Fajardo, P.R. Governors discuss welfare reform, the changing role of the media in elections, and interstate sharing of ideas on a wide variety of issues. At winter meeting, governors reach bipartisan agreement on federal welfare reform that influences federal legislation giving states primary responsibility for welfare to work. Center for Policy Research renamed as Center for Best Practices.

Personal Responsibility and Work Opportunity Act passed (returns control of most welfare to the states).

Advisory Commission on Intergovernmental Relations disbanded.

1997   NGA annual meeting: Las Vegas, Nev. Bill Gates speaks on impor-
        tance of technology to American education. Governors discuss
        early childhood development at both annual and winter meet-
        ings.

        Gary Locke of Washington becomes first Asian American gover-
        nor in forty-eight continental states.

        State Children's Health Insurance Program (S-CHIP) begins
        (coverage for low-income children).

1998   NGA annual meeting: Milwaukee, Wis. At winter and annual
        meetings, governors discuss effect on states of policies regard-
        ing taxation of electronic commerce.

        Transportation Equity Act for the 21st Century (TEA-21) passed.

        Workforce Investment Act passed.

        Bill Richardson, later governor of New Mexico, appointed secre-
        tary of energy.

        Internet Tax Freedom Act passed.

        Forty-six states, two commonwealths, three territories, and D.C.
        sign agreement with tobacco industry for reimbursement over
        twenty-five years of $206 billion in health care costs linked to
        tobacco usage.

        President Bill Clinton impeached for perjury and obstruction of
        justice.

1999   NGA annual meeting: St. Louis, Mo: President Clinton updates
        governors on progress with welfare reform. Governors discuss
        environmental management. At winter meeting, they discuss
        educational and technological improvements to make states
        more competitive. Governors outline challenges for states in
        developing a national domestic terrorism strategy and clarify-
        ing the role of National Guard.

        President Clinton acquitted by U.S. Senate.

        Education Flexibility Partnership Act (Ed-Flex) passed.

        Shootings occur at Columbine High School in Littleton, Colo-
        rado.

2000   NGA annual meeting: State College, Pa. At annual and winter
        meetings, governors discuss competitiveness in the new global
        economy.

        Governor George Ryan of Illinois declares moratorium on death
        penalty.

        Streamlined Sales Tax Project is established to seek uniformity
        among states of definitions for exempt and nonexempt items.

        Aviation investment and Reform Act for the Twenty-first Century
        passed.

        Vermont becomes first state to legalize same-sex unions.

2001   NGA annual meeting: Providence, R.I. Theodore Roosevelt IV, great-grandson of Teddy Roosevelt, addresses governors on conservation. At winter meeting, governors hear reports on the federal budget surplus and need to rebuild traditional communities. Governors urge Congress to reform Medicaid.

Texas Governor George W. Bush inaugurated president.

Former Missouri Governor John Ashcroft becomes U.S. attorney general.

New Jersey Governor Christine Todd Whitman appointed head of Environmental Protection Agency (EPA).

Governor Tommy Thompson of Wisconsin appointed secretary of health and human services.

Terrorist attacks occur on September 11 at World Trade Center and Pentagon.

2002   NGA annual meeting: Boise, Idaho: Governors discuss state leadership in new global economy. At winter meeting, governors discuss state and regional economic competitiveness.

No Child Left Behind Act passed.

2003   NGA annual meeting: Indianapolis, Ind. Governors discuss school accountability and student performance as well as role of National Guard in homeland security. At winter meeting, governors continue discussions of childhood development. Name of organization simplified to National Governors Association.

Pennsylvania Governor Tom Ridge becomes the first secretary of homeland security.

U.S. invades Iraq.

Georgia adopts a new flag, eliminating depiction of Confederate battle flag in design.

Federal government provides fiscal relief to the states for Medicaid.

2004   NGA annual meeting: Seattle, Wash. Governors call for enhanced prevention of juvenile delinquency. At winter meeting, governors discuss the subject of aging with dignity and health care for older Americans.

Congress passes Goals 2000 (enhances role of states in education reform).

Internet Tax Nondiscrimination Act passed.

EPA informs thirty-one states that new pollution controls must be developed to meet federal standards.

Improving America's School Act passed (targets needs of disadvantaged students).

2005   NGA annual meeting: Des Moines, Iowa. For the first time, states reach a common definition for their high school graduation rate. At winter meeting, governors hold National Education Summit on High Schools.

Nebraska Governor Mike Johanns appointed secretary of agriculture.

Former Utah Governor Mike Leavitt appointed secretary of health and human services.

Safe, Accountable, Flexible, Efficient Transportation Equity Act (SAFETEA) passed.

Hurricane Katrina devastates New Orleans and much of the Gulf Coast.

Federal Deficit Reduction Act passed (provides more flexibility for governors in Medicaid administration).

2006   NGA annual meeting held in Charleston, S.C. In aftermath of Katrina, governors call for greater coordination between the federal government and state governments in economic recovery from disasters. Janet Napolitano (Arizona) becomes first woman to chair NGA. At winter meeting, governors discuss health and wellness.

Idaho Governor Dirk Kempthorne appointed secretary of interior.

2007   NGA annual meeting: Traverse City, Mich. At annual and winter meetings, governors urge increased federal funding for State Children's Health Insurance Program (S-CHIP) and discuss improving the nation's economic competitiveness through innovation.

Massacre on campus of Virginia Tech occurs.

Collapse of Minneapolis interstate highway bridge triggers Federal Highway Administration to instruct states to inspect similarly designed bridges.

2008   NGA celebrates its centennial in Philadelphia.

Sources

Baughman, Judith S., Victor Bondi, Richard Layman, Tandy McConnell, and Vincent Tompkins, eds. *American Decades*, 9 vols. Detroit: Gale Research, 1996.

Carter, Susan et al. *Historical Statistics of the United States.* New York: Cambridge University Press, 2006.

SHG Resources, www.shgresources.com/resources/facts.

State Government (monthly publication of American Legislators' Association/ Council of State Governments)

Teaford, Jon. *The Rise of the States: Evolution of American State Government.* Baltimore: Johns Hopkins University Press, 2002.

"Timeline of Twentieth Century," http://history1900s.about.com/library/ weekly/aa110900a.htm

"Year by year, 1900–2007," www.infoplease.com/yearbyyear.html.
Thanks to the following individuals for their assistance: Bob Cullen, American Association of State Highway and Transportation Officials; Harley Duncan, Federation of Tax Administrators; Liz Purdy, Southern Governors' Association; Chris McKinnon, Western Governors' Association; and Bert Waisanen, National Conference of State Legislatures.

Notes

Introduction

1. For more information on the National Governors Association's history, see Glenn E. Brooks, *When Governors Convene: The Governors' Conference and National Politics* (Baltimore: John Hopkins University Press, 1961). In addition to governors' biographies, extensive summaries of annual meetings can be found at NGA's Web site at www.nga.org. Unless page numbers are noted, the quotes in the introduction, decade histories, and epilogue can be found on this Web site; Joseph W. Folk quoted in W. J. McGee, Newton C. Blanchard, chairman, John Franklin Fort, James O. Davidson, John C. Cutler, and Martin F. Ansel, *Proceedings of a Conference of Governors in the White House, Washington, D.C., May 13–15, 1908* (Washington, D.C.: Government Printing Office, 1909).

2. Twelve governors did not attend. These were from California, Florida, Georgia, Iowa, Maine, Maryland, Massachusetts, Nevada, Oklahoma, Oregon, Tennessee, and Texas.

3. Elihu Root quoted in McGee et al., *Proceedings of a Conference of Governors in the White House,* 55–56.

4. James Garfield quoted in ibid., 180.

5. Newton C. Blanchard quoted in ibid., 195.

6. Dan Rather, "Proceedings of the National Governors' Association 1989," unpublished.

Governing the 1910s

1. Charles Hughes, *Proceedings of the Meeting of the Governors of the States of the Union 18–20 January 1910* (Lakewood, N.J.: Lakewood Press, 1910).

2. Adam Pothier, *Proceedings of the Meeting of the Governors of the States of the Union November 1910* (Lakewood, N.J.: Lakewood Press, 1910).

3. Augustus Willson, ibid.

4. Tasker L. Oddie, *Proceedings of the Fifth Meeting of the Governors of the States of the Union 1912* (Lakewood, N.J.: Lakewood Press, 1912).

5. James Hawley, ibid.

6. Woodrow Wilson, *Proceedings of the Meeting of the Governors of the States of the Union November 1910.*

Chapter 1. Challenges of a New Century

1. On Smith and his role in New Jersey politics, see Arthur S. Link, *Wilson: The Road to the White House* (Princeton, N.J.: Princeton University Press, 1947), 140–141.

2. Harvey and Wilson quoted in "Editorial Note: Colonel Harvey's Plan for Wilson's Entry into Politics," in Arthur S. Link, ed., *The Papers of Woodrow Wilson* (Princeton, N.J.: Princeton University Press, 1975; hereafter *Wilson Papers*), 20:147; Wilson to Ellen Axson Wilson, February 25, 1910, ibid., 20:177. The first quotations come from an article written by one of Harvey's assistants in *Collier's Weekly* in 1916.

3. Wilson statement, *Newark Evening News,* July 15, 1910, *Wilson Papers,* 20:581. On the meeting with the party bosses, see "Editorial Note: The Lawyers' Club Conference," ibid., 565–566. On the meeting between Smith and Hurley, see John Maynard Harlan to Wilson, June 11, 1910, ibid., 519–520; Hurley to Harland, July 2, 1910, ibid., 556–557; Harland to Hurley, July 4, 1910, ibid., 557; Edward N. Hurley, *The Bridge to France* (Philadelphia: J. B. Lippincott Company, 1927), 3–4. Harlan was the son and father of justices of the U.S. Supreme Court, both named John Marshall Harlan.

4. Nugent quoted in James Kerney, *The Political Education of Woodrow Wilson* (New York: Century Company, 1926), 38; Wilson to Edgar Williamson, August 25, 1910, *Wilson Papers,* 21:60; Wilson speech to American Bar Association, August 31, 1910, *Wilson Papers,* 21:65, 71. For Wilson's platform suggestions, see *Wilson Papers,* 21:43–46.

5. Wilson to Edwin F. Goltra, July 21, 1910, *Wilson Papers,* 21:17; Wilson to Harvey, August 8, 1910, *Wilson Papers,* 21:42; Wilson to Mary Allen Hulbert Peck, August 12, 1910, *Wilson Papers,* 21:51.

6. Kerney, *The Political Education of Woodrow Wilson,* 51; remark quoted in Stockton Axson notes on manuscript of Baker biography, Ray Stannard Baker Papers, Library of Congress (hereafter RSB Papers). For accounts of the convention by people who were there, see Kerney, *The Political Education of Woodrow Wilson,* 51–54, and Joseph P. Tumulty, *Woodrow Wilson as I Know Him* (Garden City, N.Y.: Doubleday, Page, & Co., 1921), 16–22.

7. Wilson speech at Trenton, September 15, 1910, *Wilson Papers,* 21:91–94.

8. *Trenton True American,* September 17, 1910, *Wilson Papers,* 21:118–120.

9. Tumulty, *Wilson as I Know Him,* 22; Platt to Wilson, September 19, 1910, *Wilson Papers,* 21:141–142. For a similar assessment of the delegates' reaction, see William Hughes to Wilson, September 20, 1920, *Wilson Papers,* 21:145.

10. Kerney, *The Political Education of Woodrow Wilson,* 62–64; Eleanor Wilson McAdoo, *The Woodrow Wilsons* (New York: Macmillan, 1937), 110; Eleanor Wilson McAdoo, ed., *The Priceless Gift: The Love Letters of Woodrow Wilson and Ellen Axson Wilson* (New York: McGraw-Hill, 1962), 263.

11. *Trenton Evening Times,* September 16, 1910, *Wilson Papers,* 21:98; *Newark Evening News,* September 17, 1910, *Wilson Papers,* 21:126; Wilson to Edwin A. Van Valkenburg, September 25, 1910, *Wilson Papers,* 21:165; Wilson speech at Jersey City, September 28, 1910, *Wilson Papers,* 21:191. Wilson did tack the other way a bit in an earlier speech in Jersey City by taking a slap at Theodore Roosevelt's recent advocacy of recall of judicial decisions. He maintained that judges and courts might be "imperfect," but "the moment you flout at the instrumentalities of the law you flout at the instrumentalities of order and therefore of progress." *New York World,* September 21, 1910, *Wilson Papers,* 21:147.

12. Wilson to David B. Jones, September 25, 1910, *Wilson Papers,* 21:163. For the estimate of campaign spending, see Link, *Wilson: Road to White House,* 187–188.

13. *Philadelphia Record,* October 2, 1910, *Wilson Papers,* 21:223; Speech at Long Branch, October 3, 1910, *Wilson Papers,* 21:227.

14. Lewis speech, September 20, 1910, quoted in *Wilson Papers*, 21:219, n. 1. On Record and the New Idea Republicans, see Ransom E. Noble, Jr., *New Jersey Progressivism Before Wilson* (Princeton, N.J.: Princeton University Press, 1946), 65–99.

15. Wilson speech at Trenton, October 3, 1910, *Wilson Papers*, 21:229–230; speech at Woodbury, October 5, 1910, *Wilson Papers*, 2:250–251. For the editor's suggestions, see H. E. Alexander to Wilson [ca. October 1, 1910], [October] 2, 1910, *Wilson Papers*, 21:219, 225–226.

16. Wilson to Garfield, October 25, 1910, *Wilson Papers*, 21:421; speech at Atlantic City, October 13, 1910, *Wilson Papers*, 21:318; speech at Flemington, October 20, 1910, *Wilson Papers*, 21:375; speech at Newton, October 22, 1910, *Wilson Papers*, 21:400.

17. Baker interview with Record, April 6, 1928, Box 120, RSB Papers; Record to Wilson, October 17, 1910, *Wilson Papers*, 21:338–347.

18. Wilson to Record, October 24, 1911, *Wilson Papers*, 21:406–411. Wilson originally wrote some of his answers in shorthand on Record's letter and later produced several drafts on his own typewriter. See *Wilson Papers*, 21:411, n. 1.

19. Record quoted in Link, *Wilson: Road to White House*, 195; Record interview with Baker, April 6, 1928, Box 120, RSB Papers; Richard V. Linabury to Wilson, October 27, 1910, *Wilson Papers*, 21:450. For other reactions, see Tumulty and Mark Sullivan to Wilson, October 25, 1910, *Wilson Papers*, 21:433; Otto Wittpenn to Wilson, October 25, 1910, *Wilson Papers*, 21:434; James F. Fielder to Wilson, October 26, 1910, *Wilson Papers*, 21:442–443.

20. Record interview with Baker, April 6, 1928, Box 120, RSB Papers; Wilson speech at Rutherford, October 27, 1910, *Wilson Papers*, 21:447–448; speech at Perth Amboy, November 4, 1910, *Wilson Papers*, 21:551; speech at Newark, November 5, 1910, *Wilson Papers*, 21:556–576. Record also told Baker, "I was disappointed with it at the time but as I look back I can see that it was good politics for him. He could catch the uneasy conservatives of the northern part of the state who were nominally Republicans by taking a strong stand on general progressive principles, whereas he might have alienated many of them by too detailed discussions of specific measures." Record interview with Baker, April 6, 1928, Box 120, RSB Papers.

21. Cleveland Dodge to Wilson, October 21, 1910, *Wilson Papers*, 21:385; Wilson to Lawrence C. Woods, October 27, 1910, *Wilson Papers*, 21: 444; Wilson speech at Flemington, October 20, 1910, *Wilson Papers*, 21:369. On the trustees' action, see Minutes, October 20, 1910, *Wilson Papers*, 21:364–366; editorial comment, *Wilson Papers*, 21:362, n. 1.

22. Wilson, quoted in Link, *Wilson: Road to White House*, 201; Wilson statement, November 8, 1910, *Wilson Papers*, 21:589–590. For an analysis of the returns, see *Wilson Papers*, 21:584, n. 1. At that time, New Jersey elected governors to three-year terms, so the two previous elections had taken place in 1904 and 1907.

23. See *Wilson Papers*, 22:73, n. 3, for both the quotations and the judgment of the editors of the *Wilson Papers*.

24. Wilson to Harvey, November 15, 1910, *Wilson Papers*, 21:46–48.

25. Wilson quoted in *Wilson Papers*, 21:142, n. 1; Wilson statement, December 8, 1910, *Wilson Papers*, 21:154. On the meetings with the Jersey City boss and legislators, see Tumulty to Wilson, November 30, 1910, *Wilson Papers*, 21:118–120, 81, n. 1.

26. Wilson to Mary Allen Hulbert Peck, December 9, December 17, 1910, *Wil-*

son Papers, 21:141, 210; Wilson to Thomas D. Jones, December 8, 1910, *Wilson Papers,* 21:154; Wilson statement, December 23, 1910, *Wilson Papers,* 21:250; Wilson to Villard, January 2, 1911, *Wilson Papers,* 21:288.

27. Wilson speech at Jersey City, January 5, 1917, *Wilson Papers,* 21:296, 299; speech at Newark, January 16, 1917, *Wilson Papers,* 21:337.

28. Wilson to Mary Allen Hulbert Peck, January 29, 1911, *Wilson Papers,* 21:392. For an account of the caucus and legislative actions, see Link, *Wilson: Road to White House,* 233–235.

29. *New York World,* January 28, 1911; Henry Watterson to Harvey, January 29, 1911, quoted in *Wilson Papers,* 22:435, n. 1; Wilson to Mary Allen Hulbert Peck, January 3, 1911, *Wilson Papers,* 22:293. For the newspaper coverage of the controversy, see Link, *Wilson: Road to White House,* 236, n. 112.

30. *Trenton Evening Times,* November 10, 1910, *Wilson Papers,* 22:5; Wilson speech at Frankfort, Kentucky, November 29, 1910, *Wilson Papers,* 22: 108–109; Address to American Political Science Association, December 27, 1910, *Wilson Papers,* 22:269–271.

31. On the family affairs, see Frances Wright Saunders, *Ellen Axson Wilson: First Lady Between Two Worlds* (Chapel Hill: University of North Carolina Press, 1985), 212–214. Much later, there would be two governors' mansions in Princeton: first, Morven, the home of Richard Stockton, a signer of the Declaration of Independence; then Drumthwacket, which had been the home of "Momo" Pyne, Wilson's nemesis on the board of trustees.

32. On Tumulty, see John M. Blum, *Joe Tumulty and the Wilson Era* (Boston: Houghton Mifflin, 1951). Tumulty's memoir, *Woodrow Wilson as I Know Him,* tends toward sentimental exaggeration, although it does have useful parts.

33. *Trenton Evening Times,* January 19, 1911, *Wilson Papers,* 22:357–358. For an eyewitness account of the meeting, see Kerney, *The Political Education of Wilson,* 103–104.

34. Wilson speech, January 17, 1911, *Wilson Papers,* 22:344–354.

35. Ida B. Taylor to Baker, November 11, 1927, Box 122, RSB Papers; Wilson to Mary Allen Hulbert Peck, February 12, 1911, *Wilson Papers,* 22:424.

36. Wilson speech at Atlantic City, January 28, 1913, *Wilson Papers,* 27:85; Wilson to Mary Allen Hulbert Peck, April 2, 1911, *Wilson Papers,* 27:532.

37. On the Geran bill, see Link, *Wilson: Road to White House,* 245–248.

38. Wilson speech at Harrison, February 28, 1911, *Wilson Papers,* 22:461, 464; Wilson to Mary Allen Hulbert Peck, February 12, 1911, *Wilson Papers,* 22:426.

39. Wilson to Mary Allen Hulbert Peck, March 5, 1911, *Wilson Papers,* 22:477; Wilson speech at Hoboken, March 3, 1911, quoted in Link, *Wilson: Road to White House,* 249; Wilson quoted in *Wilson Papers,* 22:505, n. 1.

40. *Trenton Evening Times,* March 1911, *Wilson Papers,* 22:504; unnamed legislator, quoted in *Wilson Papers,* 22:505, n. 1.

41. *Trenton True American,* March 14, 1911, *Wilson Papers,* 22:505, n. 1; legislator and description quoted in ibid.

42. Wilson statement, March 20, 1910, *Wilson Papers,* 22:512–513; Wilson to Mary Allen Hulbert Peck, March 26, 1911, *Wilson Papers,* 22:518. On Tumulty's activities, see Blum, *Tumulty and Wilson Era,* 27–28.

43. Wilson quoted in Link, *Wilson: Road to White House,* 258; on the passage of the bill see ibid., 256–258.

44. On these bills, see ibid., 259–264; *Wilson Papers,* 22:546 n. 5, 579 n. 3, 580 n. 4.

45. On these measures, see Link, *Wilson: Road to White House,* 264–267; *Wilson Papers,* 22:550 n. 2.

46. Wilson message, March 1911, *Wilson Papers*, 22:512.

47. Wilson to Mary Allen Hulbert Peck, April 23, 1911, *Wilson Papers*, 22:581–582.

Governing the 1920s and 1930s

1. Nellie Tayloe Ross, *Proceedings of the Governors' Conference 1925* (Governors' Conference, 1925).

2. Gifford Pinchot, *Proceedings of the Governors' Conference 1927* (Tallahassee, Fla.: Governors' Conference, 1927).

3. George Shafer, *Proceedings of the Governors' Conference 1929* (Tallahassee, Fla.: Governors' Conference, 1929).

4. Franklin D. Roosevelt, *Proceedings of the Governors' Conference 1931* (Chicago: Governors' Conference, 1931).

5. John Winant, ibid.

6. Olin Johnston, *Proceedings of the Governors' Conference 1937* (Chicago: Governors' Conference, 1937).

Chapter 2. Huey Long and the Great Depression

1. Robert E. Snyder, "Huey Long and the Presidential Election of 1936," *Louisiana History* 16 (Spring 1975): 121.

2. *St. Louis Post-Dispatch*, March 3, 1935.

3. Louis D. Rubin, "Versions of the Kingfish," *Sewanee Review* 101 (Fall 1993): 5. Attributed to T. Harry Williams.

4. Peter J. King, "Huey Long: The Louisiana Kingfish," *History Today* 14 (March 1964): 158.

5. Walter Davenport, "Yes, Your Excellency!" *Collier's*, December 13, 1930, 23.

6. Raymond Moley, *After Seven Years* (New York: Harper & Bros., 1939).

7. Carleton Beals, *The Story of Huey P. Long* (Westport, Conn.: Greenwood, 1971), 15. Originally published in 1935.

8. Hodding Carter, "Huey Long: American Dictator," in Isabel Leighton, ed., *The Aspirin Age: 1919–1941* (New York: Simon and Schuster, 1949), 343–344.

9. Allan A. Michie, "Huey Long's Heritage," *Nation*, July 29, 1939, 108.

10. T. O. Harris, *The Kingfish* (New Orleans, La.: Pelican, 1938), 181–182.

11. Ibid., 208.

12. Thomas Martin, *Dynasty: The Longs of Louisiana* (New York: Putnam, 1960), 24–25.

13. Glen Jeansonne, *Messiah of the Masses: Huey P. Long and the Great Depression* (New York: Harper Collins, 1993), 8.

14. Huey Pierce Long, *Every Man a King: The Autobiography of Huey P. Long* (New Orleans, La.: National Book Company, 1933), 8; Harnett Thomas Kane, *Louisiana Hayride: The American Rehearsal for Dictatorship* (New York: W. Morrow, 1941), 42; William Ivy Hair, *The Kingfish and His Realm: The Life and Times of Huey P. Long* (Baton Rouge: Louisiana State University Press, 1991), 42.

15. Rose McConnell Long, interview, March 17, 1960, T. Harry Williams Papers MSS 2489, Louisiana and Lower Mississippi Valley Collection, Louisiana State University (hereafter THW Papers); Hair, *The Kingfish and His Realm*, 44.

16. Forrest Davis, *Huey Long: A Candid Biography* (New York: Dodge Publishing Company, 1935), 86.

17. Rupert Peyton, interview, January 28, 1958, THW Papers.

18. Wayne Parent, *Inside the Carnival: Unmasking Louisiana Politics* (Baton Rouge: Louisiana State University Press, 2004), 25.

19. *New Orleans States*, January 15, 1928, Huey P. Long Papers MSS 2005, Louisiana and Lower Mississippi Valley Collection, Louisiana State University (hereafter HPL Papers); Jeansonne, *Messiah of the Masses*, 50.

20. Martin, *Dynasty*, 38.

21. Harold Mixon, "Huey P. Long's 1927–1928 Gubernatorial Primary Campaign: A Case Study in the Rhetoric of Agitation," in Cal M. Logue and Howard Dorgan, eds., *The Oratory of Southern Demagogues* (Baton Rouge: Louisiana State University Press, 1981), 184.

22. Richard D. White, Jr., *Kingfish: The Reign of Huey P. Long* (New York: Random House, 2006), 306.

23. Parent, *Inside the Carnival*, 69.

24. Davis, *Huey Long: A Candid Biography*, 97.

25. Mildred Adams, "Huey the Great," *Forum* 89 (February 1933): 73.

26. Harris, *The Kingfish*, 77; Beals, *The Story of Huey Long*, 168.

27. Davis, *Huey Long: A Candid Biography*, 97

28. Suzanne LeVert, *Huey Long: The Kingfish of Louisiana* (New York: Facts on File, 1995), 77.

29. Stan Opotowsky, *The Longs of Louisiana* (New York: Dutton, 1960), 45.

30. George N. Coad, "I'm the Constitution in Louisiana," *Nation*, April 10, 1929, 419; Webster Smith, *The Kingfish: A Biography of Huey P. Long* (New York: G. P. Putnam's Sons, 1933), ii.

31. *Louisiana Acts*, Regular Session, 1928, No. 99.

32. Long, *Every Man a King*, 260.

33. Smith, *The Kingfish*, 183.

34. "Democrats: Incredible Kingfish," *Time*, October 3, 1932, 11; Jeansonne, *Messiah of the Masses*, 66.

35. *New Orleans States*, March 16, 1929; Jeansonne, *Messiah of the Masses*, 72.

36. Long, *Every Man a King*, 123.

37. J. Y. Sanders, Jr., interview, THW Papers; *New Orleans States*, March 26, 1929.

38. *Louisiana House Journal*, Fifth Extra Session, 1929, 12–54.

39. Ibid., 186–187.

40. Ibid., I:291–292.

41. Long, *Every Man a King*, 169–171.

42. Mrs. W. M. Knott, interview, April 18, 1960, THW Papers.

43. Hermann Deutsch, "Hattie and Huey," *Saturday Evening Post*, October 15, 1932, 6–7, 88–90, 92; David Malone, *Hattie and Huey: An Arkansas Tour* (Fayetteville: University of Arkansas Press, 1989), 25, 50, 63; Snyder, "Huey Long and the Presidential Election of 1936," 128–129; Martin, *Dynasty*, 108–109.

44. Bennett, *Demagogues in the Depression: American Radicals and the Union Party, 1932–1936* (New Brunswick, N.J.: Rutgers University Press, 1969), 125; Snyder, "Huey Long and the Presidential Election of 1936," 121.

45. Snyder, "Huey Long and the Presidential Election of 1936," 120.

46. Robert E. Snyder, "The Concept of Demagoguery: Huey Long and His Literary Critics," *Louisiana Studies*, 15 (Spring 1976): 81.

47. Hair, *The Kingfish and His Realm*, 289; Glen Jeansonne, *Huey at 100: Centen-*

nial Essays on Huey P. Long (Ruston, La.: McGinty Publications: Department of History, Louisiana Tech University, 1995), 39.

48. Martin, *Dynasty*, 104.

49. Harris, *The Kingfish*, 275.

50. W. A. Cooper, interview, THW Papers.

51. Glen Jeansonne, "Challenge to the New Deal: Huey P. Long and the Redistribution of National Wealth," *Louisiana History*, Fall 1980, 336–337. In 1929, per capita wealth in Louisiana was $1,449; in 1934 it had fallen to $1,127.

52. Beals, *The Story of Huey Long*, 21; Perry H. Howard, *Political Tendencies in Louisiana* (Baton Rouge: Louisiana State University, 1971), 130.

53. W. J. Cash, *The Mind of the South* (New York: Knopf, 1941), 284; Jeansonne, *Messiah of the Masses*, 137; T. Harry Williams, *Huey Long* (New York: Knopf, 1969), 552, n. 5.

54. Glen Jeansonne, "Huey P. Long, Robin Hood or Tyrant? A Critique of Huey Long," *Regional Dimensions: Studies of Southeast Louisiana* (Lafayette: University of Southeast Louisiana, 1986), 29; Frances Parkinson Keyes, *All This Is Louisiana* (New York: Harper, 1950), 21.

55. J. Paul Leslie, Jr., "Louisiana Hayride Revisited," *Louisiana Studies* (Winter 1972): 282.

56. Sender Garlin, *The Real Huey P. Long* (New York: Workers Library, 1935), 15.

57. Beals, *The Story of Huey Long*, 372.

58. H. C. Campbell, "Huey Long Chokes New Orleans," *Nation*, July 24, 1935, 93; Harris, *The Kingfish*, 107.

59. Martin, *Dynasty*, 126–128.

60. Williams, *Huey Long*, 855.

61. Beals, *The Story of Huey Long*, 358–360; Jeansonne, *Huey at 100*, 9.

62. Kane, *Louisiana Hayride*, 129.

63. F. Raymond Daniell, "The Gentleman from Louisiana," *Current History* (November 1934), 174.

64. Basso, "The Huey Long Legend," *Life*, December 9, 1946, 121.

65. Alan Brinkley, "Robert Penn Warren, T. Harry Williams, and Huey Long: Mass Politics in the Literary and Historical Imaginations," in Jeansonne, *Huey at 100*, 25.

66. Raymond Gram Swing, "The Menace of Huey Long," *Nation*, January 9, 1935, 100.

Governing the 1940s

1. Herbert O'Conor, *Proceedings of the Governors' Conference 1940* (Chicago: Governors' Conference, 1940).

2. Earl Warren, *Proceedings of the Governors' Conference 1944* (Chicago: Governors' Conference, 1944).

3. Roy Turner, *Proceedings of the Governors' Conference 1947* (Chicago: Governors' Conference, 1947).

4. Dwight Green, *Proceedings of the Governors' Conference 1945* (Chicago: Governors' Conference, 1945).

5. Adlai Stevenson, *Proceedings of the Governors' Conference 1949* (Chicago: Governors' Conference, 1949).

6. J. Bracken Lee, *Proceedings of the Governors' Conference 1949*.

7. Thomas E. Dewey, *Proceedings of the Governors' Conference 1944*.

Chapter 3. The Gangbuster as Governor

1. Robert H. Connery and Gerald Benjamin, *Rockefeller of New York: Executive Power in the Statehouse* (Ithaca, N.Y.: Cornell University Press, 1979), 23–26. Much of what follows, as is embarrassingly evident from these notes, is grounded in my 1982 biography *Thomas E. Dewey and His Times*. Fortunately, the editors suggested grounding Dewey, and his governorship, in the rich, dense, and colorful history of the Empire State. It seems only fitting that the origins of New York's governorship should be addressed by the most astute students of Nelson Rockefeller's Albany career, for only one other governor of the state, George Clinton, held as much power or exercised it longer than his twentieth-century counterpart.

Theodore Roosevelt's governorship receives surprisingly little attention in the biographies by Henry Pringle and William Harbaugh. More generous, in every sense, is Edmund Morris, *The Rise of Theodore Roosevelt* (New York: Coward, McCann, & Geoghegan, 1979). A more recent work is Paul Grondahl, *I Rose Like a Rocket: The Political Education of Theodore Roosevelt* (New York: Free Press, 2004).

The standard work on Hughes is Merlo J. Pusey, *Charles Evans Hughes* (New York: Macmillan, 1951). Al Smith has generated far more notice, with biographical treatments by scholars like Oscar Hardlin, the aforementioned Henry Pringle, and Smith's own daughter, Emily Smith Warner. A recent revival of interest has produced two fine portraits of Smith and his times: Robert A. Slayton, *Empire Statesman: The Rise and Redemption of Al Smith* (New York: Free Press, 2001); and, just one year later, Christopher M. Finan's *Alfred Smith: the Happy Warrior* (New York: Hill and Wang, 2002).

As with his distinguished, if distant, cousin, Franklin D. Roosevelt has been the subject of innumerable books; unlike the earlier Roosevelt, however, no serious FDR biographer can neglect his governorship, in so many respects a dress rehearsal for the New Deal to come. The most comprehensive treatment is in Kenneth S. Davis, *FDR: The New York Years, 1928–1933* (New York: Random House, 1994). More concise, yet still valuable, is Ted Morgan, *FDR* (New York: Simon and Schuster, 1985).

Languishing, to some extent, in his predecessor's historical shadow, Herbert Lehman nevertheless is the subject of an impressive "life and times" by the dean of modern American historians, no less: Allan Nevins, *Herbert H. Lehman and His Era* (New York: Scribner, 1963).

2. Richard Norton Smith, *Thomas E. Dewey and His Times* (New York: Simon and Schuster, 1982), 352.

3. Milton M. Klein, ed., *The Empire State: A History of New York* (Ithaca, N.Y.: Cornell University Press, 2001).

4. Robert Caro, *The Power Broker: Robert Moses and the Fall of New York* (New York: Knopf, 1974), 187–188.

5. Klein, *The Empire State*, 580–589.

6. Smith, *Dewey*, 141.

7. Ibid., 115–116.

8. Ibid., 643.

9. Ibid.,18.

10. Ibid., 299, 376.

11. Ibid., 25.

12. Ibid., 263–264.

13. Ibid., 267.

14. Ibid., 349.

15. H. W. Brands, *TR: The Last Romantic* (New York: Basic Books, 1997), 383; Smith, *Dewey*, 359.

16. Smith, *Dewey*, 352, 363.

17. Ibid., 363.

18. Ibid., 271.

19. Ibid., 453.

20. Ibid., 38.

21. Ibid., 624.

22. Ibid., 374.

23. Ibid., 355.

24. To ensure that his law granting equal pay for equal work was more than an admirable, futile gesture, Dewey in 1948 created a state Women's Council.

25. Smith, *Dewey*, 448.

26. Ibid., 32.

27. Ibid., 535–536.

28. Ibid., 545.

29. Ibid., 549.

30. Ibid., 559–560.

31. Ibid., 574.

32. Ibid., 611.

Governing the 1950s

1. Cecil Underwood, *Proceedings of the Governors' Conference 1959* (Chicago: Governors' Conference, 1959).

2. G. Mennen Williams, *Proceedings of the Governors' Conference 1957* (Chicago: Governors' Conference, 1957).

3. Val Peterson, *Proceedings of the Governors' Conference 1952* (Chicago: Governors' Conference, 1952).

4. G. Mennen Williams, *Proceedings of the Governors' Conference 1954* (Chicago: Governors' Conference, 1954).

Chapter 4. Connecting the United States

I greatly appreciate the steady guidance of this book's editor, Clayton Brooks, who oversaw each rendition of my work. My researcher, Heather Kennaway, dug deep into the archives to give the governors their collective voice. Finally, Richard Wiengroff of the Federal Highway Administration has become a colleague that I depend on for nearly every piece I write about highways.

1. Findings compiled from the National Governors Association's database found on its Web site (www.nga.org) and individual state Web sites.

2. "New England Interstate Highways of the 1920s," http://www.roadgeek .org/nehwys/.

3. James R. Powell, "Birthplace of Route 66," *Show Me, Route 66* 12, no. 4 (Fall 2001): 29.

4. Federal Highway Administration, *America's Highways, 1776–1976: A History of the Federal-Aid Program* (Washington, D.C.: Government Printing Office, 1977), 128.

5. Federal Highway Administration, *America's Highways*, 135.

6. Pennsylvania Historical and Museum Commission, www.phmc.state.pa.us/bah/dam/governors/earle.asp?secid = 31.

7. Dan Cupper, *The Pennsylvania Turnpike: A History* (Lebanon, Pa.: 1990).

8. Federal Highway Administration, *America's Highways*, 166.

9. Phil Patton, *Open Road: A Celebration of the American Highway* (New York: Simon and Schuster, 1986), 74.

10. Federal Highway Administration, *America's Highways*.

11. Susan Croce Kelly and Quinta Scott, *Route 66: The Highway and Its People* (Norman: University of Oklahoma Press, 1988), 148.

12. David McCullough, *Truman* (New York: Simon and Schuster, 1992), 621.

13. New Jersey Turnpike, 1949 Annual Report.

14. Armand Schwab Jr., "City Linked To Superhighway," *New York Times*, January 20, 1952, x17.

15. "America's Finest Highway: The New Jersey Turnpike," *Road International*, Spring 1952. Herbert Spencer, "The New Jersey Turnpike: One of America's Heavy-Duty Highways," *Asphalt Quarterly* (October 1951): 6.

16. George F. Will, "The Decade of Buying Happily," *Washington Post*, November 26, 2006, B07.

17. The Presidential Papers of Dwight David Eisenhower, www.eisenhower-memorial.org/presidential-papers/first-term/documents/1.cfm.

18. Richard Weingroff, "Firing Thomas H. MacDonald—Twice," July 14, 2006, U.S. Department of Transportation, Federal Highway Administration, www.fhwa.dot.gov/infrastructure/firing.htm.

19. Dwight D. Eisenhower, *At Ease: Stories I Tell to Friends* (Garden City, N.Y.: Doubleday, 1967), 186

20. Stephen E. Ambrose, *Citizen Soldiers: The U.S. Army from the Normandy Beaches to the Bulge to the Surrender of Germany, June 7, 1944–May 7, 1945* (New York: Simon and Schuster, 1997), 201; Eisenhower, *At Ease*, 166–167.

21. Tom Lewis, *Divided Highways: Building the Interstate Highways, Transforming American Life* (New York: Viking, 1997), 92.

22. Richard F. Weingroff, "A Partnership That Makes a Difference: An Anniversary Look at 1916 and 1956" (Federal Highway Administration, 1996), 185.

23. Weingroff, "A Partnership That Makes a Difference," 211.

24. Richard Weingroff, "President Eisenhower Takes Charge, Part IV," *Clearly Vicious as a Matter of Policy: The Fight Against Federal-Aid* (Washington, D.C.: Federal Highway Administration, August 2005), 176.

25. Richard Nixon, July 12, 1954, *Proceedings of the Governors' Conference 1954* (Chicago: Governors' Conference, 1954), 90.

26. Ibid., 91.

27. Richard Weingroff, "The Man Who Changed America, Part 1," *Public Roads*, (March–April 2003), 29.

28. Richard Nixon, July 12, 1954, *Proceedings of the Governors' Conference 1954*, 88.

29. Ibid., 92.

30. Weingroff, "The Man Who Changed America, Part I," 29.

31. Federal Highway Administration, *America's Highways*, 166; *Proceedings of the Governors' Conference 1953* (Chicago: Governors' Conference, 1953).

32. Weingroff, "A Partnership That Makes a Difference," 232.

33. Richard Nixon, July 12, 1954, *Proceedings of the Governors' Conference 1954*, 92.

34. Richard Nixon, July 12, 1954, ibid., 96.

35. Lawrence Wetherby, July 13, 1954, ibid., 98.

36. Thomas Dewey, July 13, 1954, ibid., 133.

37. *Proceedings of the Governors' Conference 1954*, 115.

38. Thomas Stanley, July 13, 1954, ibid., 117.

39. Sigurd Anderson, July 13, 1954, ibid., 124–125.

40. Charles Russell, July 13, 1954, ibid., 125.

41. Thomas Dewey, July 13, 1954, ibid., 130.

42. Goodwin Knight, July 13, 1954, ibid., 103–104.

43. John Fine, July 13, 1954, ibid., 100–101.

44. Ibid., 102.

45. G. Mennen Williams, John Fine, July 13, 1954, ibid., 128.

46. Paul Patterson, July 13, 1954, ibid., 107.

47. Federal Highway Administration, *America's Highways*, 114.

48. Paul Patterson, July 13, 1954, *Proceedings of the Governors' Conference 1954*, 108.

49. Richard Weingroff, e-mail message to author, August 6, 2007.

50. Walter Kohler, June 25, 1955, *Proceedings of the Governors' Conference 1955*, 9.

51. Ibid., 9–10.

52. Ibid., 10.

53. Raymond Gary, June 25, 1955, ibid., 14.

54. Ibid., 15.

55. Joseph Blaine Johnson, June 25, 1955, ibid., 34.

56. Theodore McKeldin, June 25, 1955, ibid., 17.

57. Orval Faubus, June 25, 1955, ibid., 29.

58. Robert Meyner, June 25, 1955, ibid., 32.

59. Walter Kohler, June 25, 1955, ibid., 10.

60. Ibid., 10.

61. Dwight D. Eisenhower, *Mandate for Change, 1953–1956: The White House Years* (Garden City, N.Y.: Doubleday, 1963), 502.

62. Richard Weingroff, e-mail message to author, August 6, 2007.

63. Eisenhower, *Mandate for Change*, 548.

Governing the 1960s

1. The organization's name changed from the Governors' Conference to the National Governors' Conference in 1965.

2. Mark Hatfield, *Proceedings of the National Governors' Conference 1965* (Chicago: Governors' Conference, 1965).

3. Grant Sawyer, *Proceedings of the National Governors' Conference 1965*.

4. Nelson Rockefeller, *Proceedings of the Governors' Conference 1960* (Chicago: Governors' Conference, 1960). Italics are author's emphasis.

5. Daniel Evans, *Proceedings of the National Governors' Conference 1966* (Chicago: Governors' Conference, 1966).

6. William Egan, *Proceedings of the Governors' Conference 1964* (Chicago: Governors' Conference, 1964).

7. Harold Handley, *Proceedings of the Governors' Conference 1960*.

8. Nelson Rockefeller, *Proceedings of the Governors' Conference 1962* (Chicago: Governors' Conference, 1962).

9. George Wallace, *Proceedings of the Governors' Conference 1963* (Chicago: Governors' Conference, 1963).

Chapter 5. Governors in the Civil Rights Era

1. National Governors Association, "Meeting Summary of the 1963 National Governors Association Annual Meeting," July 21–24, 1963, www.nga.org; "1963 Inaugural Address of Governor George C. Wallace," Montgomery, Alabama, January 14, 1963, copy in author's possession.

2. *Montgomery Advertiser,* June 10, 1964; "The Civil Rights Movement: A Fraud, Sham and Hoax," speech given by Governor George C. Wallace in Atlanta, Georgia, July 4, 1964, copy in author's possession.

3. Ralph McGill, *The South and the Southerner* (Boston: Little, Brown, 1959), 222.

4. *Montgomery Advertiser,* September 16, 1963; *Birmingham News,* September 16, 1963.

5. Eric Foner, *Reconstruction: America's Unfinished Revolution, 1863–1877* (New York: Harper and Row, 1988), 598; H. Leon Prather, Sr., "We Have Taken a City: A Centennial Essay," in David S. Cecelski and Timothy B. Tyson, eds., *Democracy Betrayed: The Wilmington Race Riot of 1898 and Its Legacy* (Chapel Hill: University of North Carolina Press, 1998), 26; J. Douglas Smith, *Managing White Supremacy: Race, Politics, and Citizenship in Jim Crow Virginia* (Chapel Hill: University of North Carolina Press, 2002), 130–132; David F. Godshalk, "William J. Northen's Public and Personal Struggles Against Lynching," in Jane Dailey, Glenda Elizabeth Gilmore, and Bryant Simon, eds., *Jumpin' Jim Crow: Southern Politics from Civil War to Civil Rights* (Princeton, N.J.: Princeton University Press, 2000), 140–152.

6. William Anderson, *The Wild Man from Sugar Creek* (Baton Rouge: Louisiana State University Press, 1975), 16–31; Laura Wexler, *Fire in a Canebrake: The Last Mass Lynching in America* (New York: Scribner, 2003), 34–44.

7. Anderson, *Wild Man from Sugar Creek,* 230.

8. Numan V. Bartley, *The Rise of Massive Resistance* (Baton Rouge: Louisiana State University Press, 1969), 81; Kari Frederickson, *The Dixiecrat Revolt and the End of the Solid South, 1932–1968* (Chapel Hill: University of North Carolina Press, 2001), 232–235; "The Citizens' Council," undated pamphlet, Bruce J. Henderson Papers, Alabama Department of Archives and History (hereafter cited as ADAH).

9. Jeff Frederick, "'Stand By Your Man': Race, Alabama Women, and George Wallace in 1963," *Gulf South Historical Review* 18, no. 1 (2002): 47–75; *Birmingham News,* September 27–28, 1963.

10. Earl Black, *Southern Governors and Civil Rights: Racial Segregation as a Campaign Issue in the Second Reconstruction* (Cambridge, Mass.: Harvard University Press, 1976), 252–259, 283–287.

11. Jeff Frederick, "Command and Control: George Wallace, Governor of Alabama, 1963–1972," Ph.D. diss., Auburn University, 2003, 22–30. For more on George Wallace, see Jeff Frederick, *Stand Up for Alabama: Governor George C. Wallace* (Tuscaloosa: University of Alabama Press, 2007).

12. Howell Raines, *My Soul Is Rested* (New York: Penguin Books, 1983), 304–311; John Patterson, interview by author, 2001; Frederick, "Command and Control," 33.

13. *Proceedings of the Governors' Conference 1963* (Chicago: The Conference, 1963), 129–130.

14. Albert Brewer, interview by author, 2001; Bill Jones, interview by author, 1999; George Wallace, Jr., interview by author, 2002.

15. Lester Maddox, *Speaking Out: The Autobiography of Lester Garfield Maddox*

(New York: Doubleday, 1975), 69–82; letter from George Wallace to Lester Maddox, August 24, 1964, Administrative Files of Governor George C. Wallace, SG22381, ADAH; Peter Bourne, *Jimmy Carter: A Comprehensive Biography from Plains to Post-Presidency* (New York: Scribner, 1997), 199; Randy Sanders, "The Sad Duty of Politics," *Georgia Historical Quarterly* 76, no. 3 (1992): 612–638; Jeff Frederick, "The Gubernatorial Campaigns of Jimmy Carter," master's thesis, University of Central Florida, 1998, 50–108.

16. Copy of speech of Truman Pierce, Dean of Auburn School of Education, undated in 1964 or 1965, Administrative Files of Governor George C. Wallace, SG22363, ADAH; Foy Batts to George Wallace, December 30, 1974, Administrative Files of Governor George C. Wallace, SG23370, ADAH.

17. Alabama Social Welfare Annual Report, 1962–1963, Administrative Files of Governor George C. Wallace, SG22378, ADAH; memo from Ruben King to the State Board of Pensions and Security about the 1963–1964 Fiscal Year, undated, Administrative Files of Governor George C. Wallace, SG22378, ADAH; copy of speech of Truman Pierce, Dean of Auburn School of Education, undated in 1964 or 1965, Administrative Files of Governor George C. Wallace, SG22363, ADAH; "Final Report of Study Commission Investigating Use of Convict Labor on State Highways," October 7, 1964, Administrative Files of Governor George C. Wallace, SG22384, ADAH; Jimmy Watts to Governor Lurleen Wallace, undated in 1967 or 1968, Administrative Files of Governor Lurleen Wallace, SG22442, ADAH; "Preliminary Results of a Survey on Opinions and Attitudes of Alabama Citizens on Post-Secondary Education," conducted by the University of Alabama, June 29, 1976, Administrative Files of Governor George C. Wallace, SG23406, ADAH.

18. Fantus Company, "State of Alabama Comparative Business Climate Analysis," June 29, 1984, Administrative Files of Governor George C. Wallace, SG4757, ADAH; Department of Corrections Annual Report, September 30, 1982, Administrative Files of Governor George C. Wallace, SG4719, ADAH; Wayne Teague, "A Plan for Excellence, Alabama's Public Schools: A Report to the Alabama State Board of Education, Governor George C. Wallace, and to the Legislature and People of Alabama," January 12, 1984, Administrative Files of Governor George C. Wallace, SG4741, ADAH.

19. Southern Regional Education Board Press Release, February 10, 1963, Administrative Files of Governor George C. Wallace, SG22364, ADAH; Report of the Southern Regional Education Board, March 28, 1963, Administrative Files of Governor George C. Wallace, SG22364, ADAH; press release of A. R. Meadows, State Superintendent of Education, December 19, 1963, Administrative Files of Governor George C. Wallace, SG22373, ADAH; letter from C. E. Akridge to Lurleeen Wallace, November 9, 1967, Administrative Files of Governor Lurleen Wallace, SG22442, ADAH.

20. Pansy Gewalt to George Wallace, October 11, 1975, Administrative Files of Governor George C. Wallace, SG22371, ADAH; "Preliminary Results of a Survey on Opinions and Attitudes of Alabama Citizens on Post-Secondary Education," conducted by the University of Alabama, Administrative Files of Governor George C. Wallace, SG23406, ADAH; Lurleen Wallace to C. E. Akridge, November 15, 1967, Administrative Files of Governor Lurleen Wallace, SG22442, ADAH.

21. Free Textbook Act, Section Eight, Administrative Files of Governor George C. Wallace, SG22387, ADAH; Mrs. George F. Comer to George Wallace, September 23, 1966, Administrative Files of Governor George C. Wallace,

SG22387, ADAH; "Alabama Schools in 1965," Remarks of Truman M. Pierce, Dean of Education of Auburn University, Administrative Files of Governor George C. Wallace, SG22386, ADAH; memo from Raymond Hurlburt to Cecil Jackson, includes marginalia written by Jackson, undated in 1963, Administrative Files of Governor George C. Wallace, SG22364, ADAH; "Alabama Commission on Higher Education 1976–1977 Budget Requests and Staff Recommendations for Appropriations," Administrative Files of Governor George C. Wallace, SG23406, ADAH.

22. "News Release of the State of Alabama Planning and Industrial Board," January 4, 1966, Administrative Files of Governor George C. Wallace, SG22393, ADAH; "Alabama: An Ideal Location for Industry, a publication of the State of Alabama Planning and Industrial Development Board," Administrative Files of Governor George C. Wallace, SG22379, ADAH; *Wall Street Journal*, January 19, 1966; *Business Week*, January 22, February 12, 1966; Bob Ingram, interview by author, 2001.

23. "News Release of the State of Alabama Planning and Industrial Board," January 4, 1966, Administrative Files of Governor George C. Wallace, SG22393, ADAH; "Alabama Agriculture Top Ten Producers for 1974," Administrative Files of Governor George C. Wallace, SG23366, ADAH; "Press Release of the Department of Pensions and Security," undated in 1978, Administrative Files of Governor George C. Wallace, SG23434, ADAH; memorandum from Guy Burns to George Wallace, June 12, 1978, Administrative Files of Governor George C. Wallace, SG23434, ADAH.

24. C. Carroll Pierce to Bob Cleckler, undated in 1963, Administrative Files of Governor George C. Wallace, SG22362, ADAH; telegram from Willard Wirtz to George Wallace and marginalia written by Cecil Jackson, March 13, 1963, Administrative Files of Governor George C. Wallace, SG22362, ADAH; memorandum from Bill Jones to Cecil Jackson, August 17, 1964, Administrative Files of Governor George C. Wallace, SG22370, ADAH; Bill Jones to Carter Hardwick, August 20, 1964, Administrative Files of Governor George C. Wallace, SG22370, ADAH; telegram from George Wallace to Carl Elliot, April 24, 1963, Administrative Files of Governor George C. Wallace, SG22368, ADAH; telegram from Sam Gibbons to George Wallace, March 15, 1963, Administrative Files of Governor George C. Wallace, SG22363, ADAH; George Wallace to Charles Cooper, May 13, 1963, Administrative Files of Governor George C. Wallace, SG22365, ADAH; *Montgomery Advertiser*, April 8, July 16–17, October 16, 1963.

25. Karen Anderson, "Massive Resistance, Violence, and Southern Social Relations: The Little Rock, Arkansas, School Integration Crisis, 1954–1960," in Clive Webb, ed., *Massive Resistance: Southern Opposition to the Second Reconstruction* (New York: Oxford University Press, 2005), 209–210; Memorandum from Legislative Reference Service Department of the State of Alabama to Roberta Hahn, February 18, 1966, Administrative Files of Governor George C. Wallace, SG22410, ADAH; George Wallace to Dede Smith, June 10, 1966, Administrative Files of Governor George C. Wallace, SG22416, ADAH.

26. Albert Brewer, interview by author, 2001.

27. Byron de la Beckwith to George Wallace, July 2, 1967, Administrative Files of Governor George C. Wallace, SG22422, ADAH; Cecil Jackson to Byron de la Beckwith, July 19, 1967, Administrative Files of Governor George C. Wallace, SG22422, ADAH; letter from the Members of Klavern 59 to Lurleen B. Wallace, April 13, 1967, Administrative Files of Governor Lurleen B. Wallace, SG22423, ADAH; various letters to George Wallace, Administrative Files of Governor

George C. Wallace, SG22387-SG22417, ADAH; letter from WASP to George Wallace, March 25, 1966, Administrative Files of Governor George C. Wallace, SG22416, ADAH; Dan T. Carter, *The Politics of Rage* (Baton Rouge: Louisiana State University Press, 1995), 300; *Montgomery Advertiser,* February 9, 1966. "Legendary Oath of the North Carolina Ku Klux," Thaddeus S. Ferree Papers, Series 1523, North Carolina State Archives (hereafter NCSA), Raleigh, North Carolina.

28. Glenn T. Eskew, *But for Birmingham: The Local and National Movements in the Civil Rights Struggle* (Chapel Hill: University of North Carolina Press, 1997), 299–311; Telegram from George Wallace to Charles McDew, April 26, 1963, Administrative Files of Governor George C. Wallace, SG22368, ADAH; James C. Cobb, *Away Down South: A History of Southern Identity* (New York: Oxford University Press, 2005).

29. Gordon E. Harvey, *A Question of Justice: New South Governors and Education, 1968–1976* (Tuscaloosa: University of Alabama Press, 2002); Black, *Southern Governors and Civil Rights,* 84–85; University of South Carolina, College of Arts and Sciences, John C. West Forum on Politics and Policy, Governor West quotes, http://www.westforum.sc.edu/GovWestInterviews/030716/InterviewGovWest 030716 Tex t01.htm#racial.

30. Black, *Southern Governors and Civil Rights,* 97–98; David Colburn and Richard Sher, *Florida's Gubernatorial Politics in the Twentieth Century* (Gainesville: University Press of Florida, 1981); *Lakewood (Fla.) Ledger Online,* Lakewood, Florida, "Top 50 Most Important Floridians of the Twentieth Century," http://www.theledger.com/static/top50/pages/askew.html.

31. Gerald Johnson to Chairman of the Board of Trustees of Wake Forest College, April 4, 1961, L. Y. Ballentine Papers, Series 1464, NCSA; H. A. James to L. Y. Ballentine, 25 April 1961, L. Y. Ballentine Papers, Series 1464, NCSA; H. M. Stroup to L. Y. Ballentine, January 19, 1962, L. Y. Ballentine Papers, Series 1464, NCSA; Minutes of the Meetings of the Board of Trustees of Wake Forest College, April 28, 1961, January 11, 1963, L. Y. Ballentine Papers, Series 1464, NCSA.

32. L. Y. Ballentine to L. E. Dailey, April 24, 1962, L. Y. Ballentine Papers, Series 1464, NCSA; Minutes of the Meeting of the Board of Trustees of Wake Forest College, April 27, 1962, L. Y. Ballentine Papers, Series 1464, NCSA; Jacob Pickler to Clarence Poe, May 21, 1954, Clarence H. Poe Papers, Series 256, NCSA; I. M. and Myrna Smith to Clarence Poe, May 22, 1954, Clarence H. Poe Papers, Series 256, NCSA; Linda Lee, "Just Being There," *Wake Forest Magazine,* July 1970, http://www.wfu.edu/history/HST_WFU/beingthere.htm.

33. Louis Harris and Associates, "A Study of the Democratic Primary for Governor in North Carolina," January 1960, Roy Wilder Papers, Series 1513, NCSA; Louis Harris and Associates, "Second Survey of the Democratic Primary for Governor in North Carolina," April 1, 1960, Roy Wilder Papers, Series 1513, NCSA; Louis Harris and Associates, "Key Statistical Tables on the Race for Governor in North Carolina," October 1, 1960, Roy Wilder Papers, Series 1513, NCSA; Howard E. Covington, Jr., and Marion A. Ellis, *Terry Sanford: Politics, Progress, and Outrageous Ambitions* (Durham, N.C.: Duke University Press, 1999), 201–237.

34. Minutes of the Good Neighbor Council Meeting, January 21, 1964, Administrative Files of Governor Terry Sanford, Box 386, NCSA; speech of Terry Sanford on the Progress of Equal Employment Opportunity in Raleigh, undated, Administrative Files of Governor Terry Sanford, Box 386, NCSA; Survey of Employment in State Government by Good Neighbor Council, undated, Administrative Files of Governor Terry Sanford, Box 386, NCSA; Covington and Ellis, *Terry Sanford,* 322–325.

35. Letter from "An Enraged White Protestant Presbyterian Citizen" to Terry Sanford, November 17, 1962, Administrative Files of Governor Terry Sanford, Box 232, NCSA; Postcard from "A White American Citizen" to Terry Sanford, July 28, 1963, Administrative Files of Governor Terry Sanford, Box 346, NCSA.

36. *Charlotte (N.C.) Observer*, August 19, 1974.

Governing the 1970s

1. Spiro Agnew, *Proceedings of the National Governors' Conference Winter Meeting 1970* (Lexington, Ky.: National Governors' Conference, 1970).

2. Warren Hearnes, *Proceedings of the National Governors' Conference Annual Meeting1971* (Lexington, Ky.: National Governors' Conference, 1971).

3. Ronald Reagan, *Proceedings of the National Governors' Conference Annual Meeting 1973* (Lexington, Ky.: National Governors' Conference, 1973).

4. Jimmy Carter, *Proceedings of the National Governors' Conference Annual Meeting 1973*.

Chapter 6. Preparing for the Presidency

1. This chapter draws upon my five books about Ronald Reagan, especially *Governor Reagan: His Rise to Power* (New York: Public Affairs, 2003), but also *Ronnie and Jesse: A Political Odyssey* (Garden City, N.Y.: Doubleday, 1969); *Reagan* (New York: G. P. Putnam's and Sons, 1982); *Ronald Reagan: The Presidential Portfolio* (New York: Public Affairs, 2001); and *President Reagan: The Role of a Lifetime* (New York: Simon and Schuster, 1991; New York: Public Affairs, 2000). Page references for the latter book are to the updated 2000 edition. It also draws upon my coverage of Reagan as a reporter for the *San Jose Mercury-News* during his 1966 and 1970 gubernatorial campaigns and the early years of his governorship and my later coverage for the *Washington Post* of Reagan's presidency. The exchange between Reagan and O'Neill was described to me, with slightly different emphasis, by aides for both men; *Reagan*, 71; *President Reagan: The Role of a Lifetime*, 752–753.

2. William Faulkner, "On Privacy," *Harper's*, July 1955.

3. Lyn Nofziger, interview by author, 1968, April 19, 2002.

4. Stephen Hess and David S. Broder, *The Republican Establishment* (New York: Harper and Row, 1967), 253–254.

5. Garry Wills, *Reagan's America: Innocents at Home* (Garden City, N.Y.: Doubleday, 1987), 179.

6. George Christopher, conversation with author, May 12, 2000.

7. For a detailed account of the 1966 campaign, see *Governor Reagan: His Rise to Power*, 129–161. In addition to observations drawn from my own coverage, my account here is based on 1968 interviews with Lyn Nofziger, Bill Roberts, and Holmes Tuttle, all since deceased and a June 7, 2002, interview with Stuart Spencer.

8. Ronald Reagan, *The Reagan Wit*, ed. Bill Adler and Bill Adler, Jr. (Aurora, Ill.: Caroline House Publishers, 1981), 30. Reagan campaign consultant Bill Roberts told me in 1968 that Reagan often used this one-liner when speaking to Republican groups in late 1965 and early 1966 in a characteristic attempt to defuse criticism, in this case about his inexperience, with self-deprecating humor.

9. Many of the Republican legislators who favored tax increases had expected Reagan to be resistant to them and were surprised by his pragmatism. State senator (and future governor) George Deukmejian carried the Reagan tax bill. In a July 27, 2002, interview, he told me: "A lot of people, including me, thought [Reagan] would be ideological. We learned quickly that he was very practical."

10. In *Governor Reagan: His Rise to Power*, 200–201, I recount a conversation with Reagan during a 1968 airplane trip in which I pressed the governor to discuss the politics of the tax bill. As always, Reagan denied political motives for his actions, but he did point out that he had raised taxes in 1967 and that the next gubernatorial election was in 1970. I concluded, in *Governor Reagan*: "Reagan was not a plotter, but he knew what he had done."

11. Minutes of Governor Reagan's cabinet meeting, March 15, 1967. Minutes of the first eight months of the Reagan governorship are in the custody of William Clark, the cabinet secretary at the time, who made them available to me. These are the most substantial internal records of the Reagan governorship. Records of subsequent cabinet meetings, many of them brief summaries, are in the gubernatorial collection at the Ronald Reagan Presidential Library in Simi Valley, California, and were made available by the Ronald Reagan Foundation.

12. I wrote extensively about the Dos Rios Dam and the effort to save the wild rivers of California's north coast, beginning with a story in the summer 1968 issue of the now-defunct *Cry California*, "High Dam in the Valley of the Tall Grass." An account of Reagan's decision to halt construction of the dam appears in *Governor Reagan*, 309–321. For an extended examination of the controversy, focusing on the rancher (Richard Wilson) who launched the battle to stop the dam, see Ted Simon, *The River Stops Here: How One Man's Battle to Save His Valley Changed the Fate of California* (New York: Random House, 1994).

13. For an account of the birth of the mini-memos, see *Ronnie and Jesse*, 137–139. Although many Democrats ridiculed the mini-memos after I wrote about them in the *San Jose Mercury*, they won praise from James Alexander, the respected cabinet secretary for Reagan's Democratic predecessor, Governor Pat Brown. Alexander said the flow of information into and out of the governor's office was so great that "you absolutely needed something like that."

14. *Governor Reagan*, 270.

15. Ibid., pp. 269–270.

16. For an account of the campaign, see ibid., 332–347.

17. *U.S. News and World Report*, May 5, 1969, p. 32.

18. *The Advocates*, PBS television, December 1, 1970, p. 11 of transcript.

19. Interview with Ronald Reagan, *California Journal* (December 1970).

20. George Steffes, interview with author, 1980. Quoted in *Governor Reagan*, 20.

21. *Governor Reagan*, 355.

22. Ronald Reagan, interview with author, undated. Quoted in *Ronald Reagan: The Presidential Portfolio*, 27.

23. Bob Moretti, interview with author, August 5, 1981.

24. Bob Moretti, interview by Sherry Bebitch Jeffe, February 2, 1983, *Oral History of the Modern Speakership of the California State Assembly*, Institute of Politics and Government, University of Southern California, 10–11.

25. Bob Moretti, interview with author, August 5, 1981.

26. For an account of the negotiations that produced the welfare compromise legislation, see *Governor Reagan*, 348–367.

27. Frank Levy, *What Ronald Reagan Can Teach the U.S. About Welfare Reform* (Washington, D.C.: Urban Institute, 1977).

28. Bob Moretti, interview with author, August 5, 1981.

29. Lou Cannon, "The Reagan Years," *California Journal* (November 1974). When an aide questioned if Moretti would do something he had promised, Reagan replied trustingly, "He gave me his word."

30. *Governor Reagan,* 343; attributed to an undated story in the *Los Angeles Times* by Bill Boyarsky, who covered both of Reagan's gubernatorial campaigns. Boyarsky found Reagan shy and remote in the 1966 campaign. In contrast, in 1970, Reagan shook hands freely, and in Modesto when a group of pickets heckled him Reagan "heckled them back."

Governing the 1980s

1. Pierre du Pont, *Proceedings of the National Governors' Association Annual Meeting 1983* (Washington, D.C.: National Governors' Association, 1983).

2. Bob Kerrey, "Proceedings of the National Governors' Association Annual Meeting 1986," unpublished.

3. Phil Pruitt, "Proceedings of the National Governors' Association Annual Meeting 1988," unpublished.

4. Jon Teaford, *Rise of the States: Evolution of American State Government* (Baltimore: Johns Hopkins University Press, 2002), 203.

5. Scott Matheson, Minutes, *Proceedings of the National Governors' Association Annual Meeting 1983.*

6. George Busbee, *Proceedings of the National Governors' Association Annual Meeting 1981* (Washington, D.C.: National Governors' Association, 1981).

7. David Treen, *Proceedings of the National Governors' Association Annual Meeting 1980* (Washington, D.C.: National Governors' Association, 1980).

Chapter 7. Devolution in American Federalism in the Twentieth Century

Heather Trela provided valuable assistance in the preparation of this chapter.

1. I have always found the lectures given by economist Albert O. Hirschman in 1979 to be insightful about how attitudes toward government action change over time. His Eliot Janeway Lectures on Historical Economics were delivered at Princeton. See Albert O. Hirschman, *Shifting Involvements, Private Interest and Public Action* (Princeton, N.J.: Princeton University Press, 1982).

2. U.S. Advisory Commission on Intergovernmental Relations, *The Question of State Government Capacity* A-98 (Washington, D.C.: ACIR, 1985), 2.

3. Thomas L. Gais and James W. Fossett, "Federalism and the Executive Branch," in Joel D. Aberbach and Mark A. Peterson, eds., *The Executive Branch* (New York: Oxford University Press, Institutions of American Democracy Series, 2005), 486–522.

4. Martha Derthick, "American Federalism: Madison's Middle Ground in the 1980s," *Public Administration Review* 47, no. 1 (January–February 1987): 72.

5. Richard P. Nathan, *The Administrative Presidency* (New York: John Wiley and Sons, 1983), 16–17; Robert Kennedy was shot by an assassin on June 5, 1968, and died the following day.

6. John Herbers, "Kennedy to Enter Indiana's Primary," *New York Times,* March 28, 1968, 1.

7. Report of the Commission on Intergovernmental Relations, *A Report to the President for Transmittal to the Congress* (Washington D.C.: Government Printing

Office, 1955); Dwight D. Eisenhower, "Letter Appointing Federal Members of the Joint Federal-State Action Committee," July 20, 1957, The American Presidency Project, http://www.presidency.ucsb.edu/ws/index.php?pid = 10843.

8. Lyndon Baines Johnson, "Remarks at the University of Michigan," May 22, 1964, Lyndon Baines Johnson Library and Museum, National Archives and Records Administration, http://www.lbjlib.utexas.edu/johnson/archives.hom/speeches.hom/640522.asp. Italics added.

9. Tom Wicker, *One of Us: Richard Nixon and the American Dream* (New York: Random House, 1991), 523–541. See also Richard P. Nathan, *The Plot That Failed: Nixon and the Administrative Presidency* (New York: John Wiley and Sons, 1975), ch. 12 and 163–169.

10. Richard Nixon, "324—Address to the Nation on Domestic Programs," August 8, 1969, The American Presidency Project, http://www.presidency.ucsb.edu/ws/index.php?pid = 2191.

11. This section draws on Richard P. Nathan, Fred C. Doolittle, and Associates, *Reagan and the States* (Princeton, N.J.: Princeton University Press, 1987), 5–6.

12. John M. Barry, *Rising Tide: The Great Mississippi Flood of 1927 and How It Changed America* (New York: Touchstone, 1997).

13. Ronald Reagan, "Address Before a Joint Session of the Congress Reporting on the State of the Union," January 26, 1982, The American Presidency Project, http://www.presidency.ucsb.edu/ws/index.php?pid = 42687.

14. George H. W. Bush, "Remarks to Members of the National Conference of State Legislators," March 10, 1989, The American Presidency Project, http://www.presidency.ucsb.edu/ws/index.php?pid = 16760.

15. George H. W. Bush, "Remarks at the Fundraising Dinner for Senator Christopher S. Bond in St. Louis Missouri," November 13, 1991, The Museum at the George Bush Presidential Library, http://bushlibrary.tamu.edu/research/papers/1991/91111310.html.

16. William J. Clinton, "Remarks on Signing the Unfunded Mandates Reform Act of 1995, March 22, 1995, The American Presidency Project, http://www.presidency.ucsb.edu/ws/index.php?pid = 51131. This discussion of George H. W. Bush's federalism policies is taken from Richard P. Nathan, Thomas L. Gais, and James W. Fossett, "Bush Federalism: Is There One, What Is It, and How Does It Differ?" presented at the Association for Public Policy Analysis and Management Annual Research Conference, November 7, 2003.

17. Richard P. Nathan and Thomas L. Gais, *Implementing the Personal Responsibility Act of 1996: A First Look* (Albany, N.Y.: Rockefeller Institute of Government, 1999).

18. John Kincaid, "From Cooperative to Coercive Federalism," *Annals of the American Academy of Political and Social Science* 509 (May 1990): 139–152: Joseph F. Zimmerman, *Congressional Preemption: Regulatory Federalism* (Albany: State University of New York Press, 2005).

19. Thomas L. Gais, Richard P. Nathan, Irene Lurie, and Thomas Kaplan, "Implementation of the Personal Responsibility Act of 1996," in Rebecca Blank and Ron Haskins, eds., *The New World of Welfare* (Washington, D.C.: Brookings Institution Press, 2001), 35–69.

20. Courtney Burke, James Fossett, and Thomas Gais, *Funding Faith-Based Services in a Time of Fiscal Pressures* (Albany, N.Y.: Rockefeller Institute of Government, October 2004), 17–22.

21. The administration's initial proposal for Medicaid reform, which the gov-

ernors nixed, would have provided increased aid in the short term in exchange for placing a cap on future allocations over a ten-year phase-in period for states that chose this option. Mimicking TANF, the Bush administration at one point sought to convert the Section 8 housing-voucher program to HANF, Housing Assistance for Needy Families, and barriers would regularly be reduced. Flexible grants would be provided with a "strong emphasis on prevention," according to the administration. Under this plan, governors would be offered the opportunity to integrate preschool programs with Head Start for the state or a region within the state under the administration's proposed "state-option" approach.

22. Franklin Foer, "The Joy of Federalism," *New York Times Book Review*, March 6, 2005. This article contains a useful scan of liberal views on state activism.

23. Anthony DePalma, "Nine States in Plan to Cut Emissions by Power Plants," *New York Times*, August 24, 2005, A1.

24. Dennis Cauchan, "States Say $5.15 an Hour Too Little," *USA Today*, May 30, 2005, A1.

25. "The New New Federalism," *Wall Street Journal*, October 5, 2005, A20. See also Linda Greenhouse, "Justices Explore U.S. Authority over States on Assisted Suicide," *New York Times*, October 6, 2005, A1.

26. Richard P. Nathan and Fred C. Doolittle, "The Untold Story of Reagan's New Federalism," *Public Interest* 77 (1984): 96–106. See also Nathan et al., *Reagan and the States*, and Richard P. Nathan and Martha Derthick, "Reagan's Legacy: A New Liberalism Among the States," *New York Times*, December 18, 1987, A39.

27. Jon C. Teaford, *The Rise of the States: Evolution of American State Government* (Baltimore: Johns Hopkins University Press, 2002), 5.

28. Ibid., 16–18.

29. In recent times, the history of the Medicaid program offers a good example of how this happens. Richard P. Nathan, "Federalism and Health Policy," *Health Affairs* 24, no. 6 (November–December 2005): 1458–1466.

30. Allan Nevins and Henry Steele Commager, *A Pocket History of the United States* (New York: Washington Square Press, 1981), 346.

31. See James T. Patterson, *The New Deal and the States: Federalism in Transition* (Princeton, N.J.: Princeton University Press, 1969), 4. Also see Richard P. Nathan, "Federalism: The Great 'Composition,'" in A. King, ed., *The New American Political System* (Washington, D.C.: AEI Press, 1990), 241–242.

32. See especially Michael S. Greve, "Madison with a Minus Sign," American Enterprise Institute. Available at http://federalismproject.org/depository/Madisonminussign.pdf, pp. 1–2.

33. Ibid.

34. See as a contemporary example of this point Gar Alperovitz, "California Split," *New York Times*, February 10, 2007, A15.

35. James Madison, Federalist Paper No. 51, in Alexander Hamilton, James Madison, and John Jay, *The Federalist Papers* (New York: Signet Classics, 1961).

36. Nelson A. Rockefeller, *The Future of Federalism* (Cambridge, Mass.: Harvard University Press, 1962), 6.

37. This section draws on the definition of federalism by the author in Joel Krieger, ed., *The Oxford Companion to Politics of the World*, 2nd ed. (New York: Oxford University Press, 2001), 276–277.

38. Morton Grodzins, "The Federal System," in *Goals for Americans: The Report of the President's Commission on National Goals* (New York: Columbia University Press, 1960), 265.

Governing the 1990s

1. National health care was a frequent topic of debate at NGA meetings. For example, in 1991, when Clinton attended as governor of Arkansas, health care was one of the main points of discussion. See 1991 NGA annual meeting minutes, August 18–24, Seattle, Washington; "Proceedings of the National Governors' Association Annual Meeting 1991," unpublished.

2. Lamar Alexander, "Proceedings of the National Governors' Association Annual Meeting 1997," unpublished.

3. George Voinovich, "Proceedings of the National Governors' Association Annual Meeting 1993," unpublished.

4. These were Dixy Lee Ray (D-Wash.) 1977–1981, Martha Layne Collins (D-Ky.) 1984–1987, Madeleine Kunin (D-Vt.) 1985–1991, Kay Orr (R-Neb.) 1987–1991, and Rose Mofford (D-Ariz.) 1988–1991. A sixth, Vesta Roy (R-N.H.), served as acting governor in 1982–1983 for seven days.

5. These were Joan Finney (D-Kan.) 1991–1995, Ann Richards (D-Tex.) 1991–1995, Barbara Roberts (D-Ore.) 1991–1995, Christine Todd Whitman (R-N.J.) 1994–2001, Jeanne Shaheen (D-N.H.) 1997–2003, and Jane Dee Hull (R-Ariz.) 1997–2003. A seventh, Nancy Hollister (R-Ohio) served as acting governor for eleven days in 1998–1999.

6. These include Jane Swift (R-Mass.) 2001–2003, Judy Martz (R-Mont.) 2001–2005, Sila Calderon (Puerto Rico) 2001–1005, Olene Walker (R-Utah) 2003–2005, Ruth Ann Minner (D-Del.) 2001–present, Jennifer M. Granholm (D-Mich.) 2003–present, Linda Lingle (R-Hawaii) 2003–present, Janet Napolitano (D-Ariz.) 2003–present, Kathleen Sebelius (D-Kan.) 2003–present, Kathleen Blanco (D-La.) 2004–present, M. Jodi Rell (R-Conn.) 2004–present, Christine Gregoire (D-Wash.) 2004–present, and Sarah Palin (R-Ak.) 2007–present.

7. Bill Clinton, "Proceedings of the National Governors' Association Annual Meeting 1997."

8. Kelley Shannon, "Former Texas Gov. Ann Richards Dies: Known for Wit, Commitment to Opening Government," September 14, 2006, Associated Press.

Chapter 8. The Case of Ann Richards

1. Unlike many elected officials today, Ann Richards ensured that a documentary record of her public service would be readily available to scholars and interested members of the public. Only a few files dealing with personnel and legal matters are withheld from the Ann W. Richards Papers, 1933–1999, at the Center for American History, University of Texas at Austin. The archive largely focuses on her terms as a Travis County commissioner in Austin, the state treasurer (an office that no longer exists in Texas), and her term as governor of Texas. In addition to documents, the archive also contains a photo and video record of her years in office. In planning this retrospective of the emergence of women as governors in the United States, the editor and I agreed that the focus should be more on governance, less on politics, and, less still, personality and private life. The Ann Richards archive is such a rich and accessible resource that the decision was easy to draw this narrative from these documentary sources.

2. Ann Richards with Peter Knobler, *Straight from the Heart: My Life in Politics and Other Places* (New York: Simon and Schuster, 1989), 15.

3. Mary Beth Rogers, Richards's chief of staff at both the treasury and governor's office, and the manager of her gubernatorial campaigns, was immensely

helpful in an interview. Richards's speechwriter, Suzanne Coleman, her director of public information at both agencies, Bill Cryer, and many others who worked in those endeavors have contributed and added to my knowledge over many years. Many members of the Richards administration have also contributed their files to archive. The day-by-day account of the Branch Davidian crisis from the viewpoint of Ann Richards and her colleagues, which was shared by her second chief of staff, John Fainter, is a remarkable document of American history.

4. Richards's Keynote Address to the Democratic National Convention, July 18, 1988, Ann W. Richards Papers, 1933–1999, Center for American History, University of Texas at Austin (hereafter cited as AWR Papers).

5. Richards's Inaugural Address as Governor of Texas, January 15, 1991, AWR Papers.

6. John D. Huddleston, "Ferguson, Miriam Amanda Wallace," Texas State Historical Association, The Handbook of Texas Online, http://www.tsha .utexas.edu/handbook/online/articles/FF/ffe6.html.

7. The administrations and policies of governors Ella Grasso (Connecticut), Kay Orr (Nebraska), Janet Napolitano (Arizona), and Joan Finney and Kathleen Sebelius (both of Kansas) are well documented and pointed the way to the narrative arc I sought in this study. Many other women governors, past and present, have stories and records of public service that are just as fascinating. Books, articles, and speeches that are well worth the search and reading: Richards and Knobler, *Straight from the Heart*; Christine Todd Whitman, *It's My Party Too: The Battle for the Heart of the GOP and the Future of America* (New York: Penguin, 2005); Joseph I. Lieberman, *The Legacy: Connecticut Politics, 1930–1980* (Hartford: Spoonwood Press, 1981); John Barrette, "Ella Grasso: As She Saw Herself," *Connecticut Review* (Spring 1995): 23–29; George H. W. Bush, "Remarks at a Fundraising Breakfast for Governor Kay Orr in Omaha, Nebraska," February 8, 1990, The American Presidency Project, http://www.presidency.ucsb.edu/ws/index .php?pid = 18131; Joan Finney, Warren B. Armstrong, and Dee A Harris, *Populism Revived: The Selected Records of Governor Joan Finney, 1991–1995* (Wichita, Ks.: Hugo Wall School of Urban and Public Affairs, Wichita State University, 1998); Janet Napolitano, *Securing Arizona: A Roadmap for Arizona Homeland Security* (Phoenix: State of Arizona, 2003); Kathleen Sebelius, *The Power of Women's Voices: Past, Present, and Future* (Pittsburgh, Ks.: Pittsburgh State University, PSU Foundation, 2001).

8. Paul Burka, executive editor and political analyst for *Texas Monthly*, reminisced about the debate in his Web log following Richards's death September 4, 2006. http://www.texasmonthly.com/blogs.

9. Ibid.

10. Recollection of author.

11. Williams's remark and series of gaffes were widely reported by the *Dallas Morning News, Fort Worth Star-Telegram, Texas Observer*, and other news organizations.

12. Mary Beth Rogers, interview with author, 2007.

13. Governor's State of the State Address to the Texas Legislature, February 6, 1991, AWR Papers.

14. Ibid.

15. Ibid.

16. Ibid.

17. Governor's remarks at swearing-in of Texas Water Commission, May 28, 1991, AWR Papers.

18. Governor's remarks at Texas Rangers Annual Reunion, June 7, 1991, AWR Papers.

19. Governor's remarks on the Branch Davidian Siege, March 3, 1993, AWR Papers.

20. Governor's remarks on the Branch Davidian Siege, March 11, 1993, AWR Papers.

21. Mary Beth Rogers, interview with author, 2007.

22. Memo to Governor's Office staff from John Fainter, chief of staff, April 11, 1994, AWR Papers.

23. Richards's handwritten response to letter from Susan Rieff to John Fainter, April 13, 1993, AWR Papers.

24. Bruce Babbitt, U.S. Secretary of the Interior, to Governor Ann Richards, Lieutenant Governor Bob Bullock, and Speaker of the House Pete Laney, April 16, 1993, AWR Papers.

25. Governor's remarks on a proposed conceal-and-carry bill in the Texas House of Representatives, April 27, 1993, AWR Papers.

26. Governor's remarks on a revised conceal-and-carry bill, May 30, 1993, AWR Papers.

27. Governor's remarks to guest law enforcement officials at press conference regarding her veto the conceal-and-carry H.B. 1776, June 3, 1993, AWR Papers.

28. Sara J. Weir, an associate professor of political science at Western Washington University, provided a valuable overview of this subject in her essay "The Feminist Face of State Executive Leadership: Women as Governors" (Western Washington University, http://www.ac.wwu.edu/~sweir/womengovs98.htm). The Center for American Women and Politics at Rutgers University provides general information that was useful in our deciding which governors would be highlighted in this short space. The political and governmental career of New Jersey's Christine Todd Whitman resembles that of Richards in the wealth of books and articles that have been added to the public record. (Like Richards, Whitman is an able author in her own right.) An inspector general's report of the Environmental Protection Agency sheds valuable light on the emergency that jolted the nation and all levels of government after the September 11, 2001, terrorist attacks on the World Trade Center and the Pentagon. Terry Gross's interview with Christine Todd Whitman on National Public Radio illumines the career and philosophy of this important American governor (*Fresh Air,* January 27, 2005).

29. Office of the Inspector General, Office of Investigations, Environmental Protection Agency, *Report of Investigation Concerning Christine Todd Whitman,* case number: 2002–2003, undated, 9, www.epa.gov/oig/reports/2002/ROIUNRED ACTED.pdf.

30. For a summary of the eighty-three-page ruling by U.S. District Court Judge Deborah H. Batts, see Jeff McKay, "Judge Says Government Mislead Public on 9/11 Air Quality," February 6, 2006, Cyber Cast News Service, http://www.cnsnews.com.

31. See Whitman, *It's My Party Too.*

32. Hendrik Hertzberg, "Comment: The Darksider," *New Yorker,* July 9 and July 16, 2007, 36. The article analyzes the Whitman-Cheney disagreement revealed in a four-part *Washington Post* series on the vice president.

33. Janet Napolitano, "Innovation America," 2006–2007 National Governors Association Chair's Initiative, www.nga.org.

34. Governor Ann Richards's speech to Conference on Women's History, June 3, 1994, AWR Papers.

Conclusion. The Evolution of the Gubernatorial Office

1. This section on the waves of reform is adapted from former North Carolina Governor Terry Sanford's book *Storm over the States* (New York: McGraw Hill, 1967), 42–45. I worked with Governor Sanford on this book and helped write portions of it while with him in the Study of American States at Duke University, 1965–1967.

2. Ibid., 42.

3. A. E. Buck, *The Reorganization of State Governments in the United States* (New York: Columbia University Press, 1938), 7–8.

4. Herbert Kaufman, "Emerging Conflicts in the Doctrines of Public Administration," *American Political Science Review* 50 (December 1956): 1065.

5. Buck, *Reorganization of State Governments*, 12.

6. Ibid., 14.

7. Sanford, *Storm over the States*, 44.

8. Ibid., 188–206, passim.

9. Joseph A. Schlesinger, "The Politics of the Executive," in Herbert Jacob and Kenneth N. Vines, eds., *Politics in the American States* (Boston: Little, Brown, 1965), 207–237.

10. There was only one zero applied in these 600 separate measures across the fifty states, and that was for the North Carolina governor's lack of any veto power in 1960, a power that was finally provided by a constitutional amendment approved by the North Carolina state legislature and North Carolina voters in the mid-1990s.

11. For a listing of these women governors, see "Table D: Women Governors," in *The Book of the States: 2007* (Lexington, Ky.: Council of State Governments, 2007), 160.

12. Much of what is in the next section is taken from Thad L. Beyle, "From Governor to Governors," in Carl E. Van Horn, ed., *The State of the States* (Washington, D.C.: CQ Press, 1989), 56–61, and Beyle, "Being Governor," in Van Horn, ed., *The State of the States*, 3rd ed. (Washington, D.C.: CQ Press, 1996), 96–97.

13. Jacqueline Calmes, "444 North Capitol Street: Where State Lobbyists Are Learning Coalition Politics," *Governing* (February 1988): 17–18, 20–21.

14. Among these governors were: John Volpe (R-Massachusetts, 1965–1969); Marvin Mandell (D-Maryland, 1969–1977); Daniel Evans (R-Washington, 1965–1977); Calvin Rampton (D-Utah, 1965–1977); Robert Ray (R-Iowa, 1969–1983); Scott Matheson (D-Utah, 1977–1985); and Lamar Alexander (R-Tennessee, 1979–1987).

15. Carol Weissert, "The National Governors' Association: 1908–1983," *State Government* 56 (1983): 49.

16. Ibid., 50.

17. Ibid., 49.

18. Thad L. Beyle, "Gubernatorial Transitions: Lessons from the 1982–1983 Experience," *Publius* 14 (Summer 1984): 13.

19. National Governors' Association, *The Critical Hundred Days: A Handbook for New Governors* (Washington, D.C.: National Governors' Association, 1975); National Governors' Association, *The Governor's Office* (Washington, D.C.:

National Governors' Association, 1976); National Governors' Association, *Governing the American States: A Handbook for New Governors* (Washington, D.C.: National Governors' Association, 1978); National Governors' Association, *Transition and the New Governors: A Critical Overview* (Washington, D.C.: National Governors' Association, 1982); and National Governors' Association, Office of State Services, *The Transition: A View from Academia* (Washington, D.C.: National Governors' Association, 1986).

20. National Governors' Conference, *Innovations in State Government* (Washington, D.C.: National Governors' Conference, 1974); National Governors' Association, Center for Policy Research, *Governors' Policy Initiatives: Meeting the Challenges of the 1980s* (Washington, D.C.: National Governors' Association, 1980). The 1982 survey was conducted by the National Governors' Association, the Council of State Planning Agencies, and the Governors' Center at Duke University. The 1983 survey was conducted by the Council of State Planning Agencies. CSPA no longer exists.

21. Scott Matheson, *Out of Balance* (Salt Lake City: Peregrine Smith Books, 1986), 240.

22. Weissert, "The National Governors' Association: 1908–1983," 50; Calmes, "444 North Capitol Street," 20.

23. See the National Governors Association's Web site, www.nga.org.

24. Weissert, "The National Governors' Association: 1908–1983," 52.

25. Larry Sabato, *Goodbye to Goodtime Charlie: The American Governorship Transformed*, 2nd ed. (Washington, D.C.: CQ Press, 1983), 180.

26. For a discussion of this conflict, see Deil S. Wright, *Understanding Intergovernmental Relations*, 2nd ed. (Monterey, Calif.: Brooks/Cole, 1982), 171–175.

Afterword

1. Tommy G. Thompson, "Proceedings of the National Governors Association Annual Meeting 2006," unpublished.

2. William Cohen, "Proceedings of the National Governors Association Annual Meeting 2003," unpublished.

Further Resources

For more information on governors, states, and the National Governors Association, see NGA's Web site at www.nga.org. In addition to current news on the organization's centers and initiatives, there is an extensive database of current and past governors, a comprehensive timeline, detailed summaries of the organization's annual meetings, and numerous resources in celebration of their 2008 centennial.

The Woodrow Wilson Presidential Library, which helped in this project by hosting postdoctoral fellows, has an expansive e-library on President Wilson and the Wilsonian era. To access this library and find out more information about visiting the presidential library and birthplace museum, see its Web site at www.woodrowwilson.org.

Contributors

Thad L. Beyle is a professor emeritus from the University of North Carolina Chapel Hill, appointed the Thomas C. Pearsall Professor of Political Science in 1993. A political scientist, writer, and consultant, Beyle has written extensively on gubernatorial politics and also has worked with a number of public and private agencies. In the 1960s, Beyle worked at Duke University with Governor Terry Sanford on "A Study of American States" through which they set up the Education Commission of the States and wrote *Storm Over the States*. He served as the director of the Center for Policy Research and Analysis for the National Governors' Conference during the 1970s. His publications include: *State and Local Government* (originally titled *State Government*; published annually from 1985 to 2004), *Governors and Hard Times, Re-Electing the Governor, The American Governor in Behavioral Perspective, State Government Reorganization: A Bibliography*, and *New Governor in North Carolina*.

Clayton McClure Brooks received her Ph.D. from the University of Virginia. Apart from government and politics, her research focuses on the twentieth century American South. She is currently at work on a book about segregation and interracial cooperation in Jim Crow Virginia, entitled *Conversations Across the Color Line*.

Lou Cannon, considered the foremost biographer of Ronald Reagan, covered him as a reporter throughout his political career for the *San Jose Mercury-News* and *The Washington Post*. His six books about Reagan include the acclaimed *President Reagan: The Role of a Lifetime*, originally published in 1991 and updated in 2000. *Governor Reagan: His Rise to Power*, which focuses on the Reagan governorship, was published in 2003.

John Milton Cooper, Jr., is the E. Gordon Fox Professor of American Institutions in the department of history at the University of Wisconsin–Madison. He is the author of many books, including *Warrior and the Priest: Woodrow Wilson and Theodore Roosevelt; Breaking the Heart of the World; Walter Hines Page: The Southerner as American, 1855–1918; The Vanity of*

Power: America Isolationism and the First World War, 1914–1917; Causes and Consequences of World War I; and *The Pivotal Decades: The United States, 1900–1920.* Cooper is currently writing a biography of Woodrow Wilson.

Jeff Frederick is an assistant professor of history at the University of North Carolina at Pembroke. His work broadly considers the effect of politics on southern society at large during the twentieth century. His recent work, *Stand Up for Alabama: Governor George Wallace,* was published by the University of Alabama Press in 2007. His current project examines the effect of sports—local, collegiate, and professional—and recreation on white responses to integration.

Dan McNichol is a best-selling author, journalist, and nationally recognized expert on the United States Interstate System. He has published several books, including *The Roads That Built America, Paving the Way,* and *The Big Dig.* McNichol has also written for *The New York Times,* as well as other newspapers.

Richard P. Nathan is the co-director of the Nelson A. Rockefeller Institute of Government, the public policy research arm of the State University of New York. The views expressed in his chapter are his own. Sections of the chapter draw on recent papers he has written, including "There Will Always Be a New Federalism" in the *Journal of Public Administration Research and Theory,* "Rethinking the Politics of Federalism" in *Governing Magazine,* and "Updating Theories of American Federalism," a paper presented at the 2006 Annual Meeting of the American Political Science Association. Nathan served as an official in the U.S. Office of Management and Budget from 1969 to 1972 as one of the architects of Richard Nixon's "New Federalism" program.

Jan Reid is an Austin-based writer whose articles and essays have appeared in *Esquire, Slate, Men's Journal, GQ,* the *New York Times, Mother Jones,* and *Texas Monthly.* His ten books include an award-winning novel, *Deerinwater,* and a memoir of experiences in Mexico, *The Bullet Meant for Me.* Reid's wife, Dorothy Browne, served as a senior policy administrator for Texas Governor Ann Richards.

Richard Norton Smith, past director of the Hoover, Eisenhower, Reagan, Ford, and Lincoln Presidential Libraries, as well as the Robert J. Dole Institute of Politics at the University of Kansas, is currently scholar in residence at George Mason University. He has authored biographies of Thomas E. Dewey, George Washington, Herbert Hoover, and Colonel

Robert R. McCormick, and is currently at work on a biography of Governor Nelson A. Rockefeller.

Richard D. White, Jr., is the Marjory Ourso Excellence in Teaching Professor at Louisiana State University, where he teaches in the Public Administration Institute. He is the author of *Kingfish: The Reign of Huey P. Long* and *Roosevelt the Reformer: Theodore Roosevelt as Civil Service Commissioner, 1889–1895.*

Index

Acknowledgments

This book could not have been completed without the help of many individuals. The editor wishes to thank the National Governors Association, which has provided extensive and invaluable support, particularly Jay Hyde, Jodi Omear, Nelle Sandridge, Ray Scheppach, Laura Shiflett, and Barry Van Lare. She is also very grateful for all the assistance and support she received from everyone at the Woodrow Wilson Presidential Library, the organization that hosted her postdoctoral fellowship. The number of people to thank there are numerous, including Ethan Sribnick and Eric Vettel. Also, the editor thanks the nine contributors of this volume for their hard work and patience with deadlines under a tight schedule: Thad L. Beyle, Lou Cannon, John Milton Cooper, Jr., Jeff Frederick, Dan McNichol, Richard P. Nathan, Jan Reid, Richard Norton Smith, and Richard D. White, Jr. Finally, she wishes to thank Thomas Brooks and Lois McClure for their endless support.